Praise for *Fraud of the Century*

"A rollicking portrait of electoral chicanery past. Political junkies bored by the present GOP monopoly or just seeking escape from unsettling current events are advised to join Morris in 1876, when 'his Fraudulency, Ruther-fraud' B. Hayes, triumphed over 'Centennial Sam' Tilden to extend post-bellum Republican rule."

—*The Baltimore Sun*

"[A] historical account given in gorgeous detail that is hard to stop read-ing. Morris is a splendid historian and writer and regales the reader with stories of the scheming and plotting that surround any presidential cam-paign and election."

—*San Francisco Chronicle*

"A riveting political history."

—*The Atlanta Journal-Constitution*

"*Fraud of the Century* is an excellent book—thoughtful and well researched. It may be the last word on America's most embarrassing election."

—*The Washington Times*

"Reading Roy Morris's *Fraud of the Century* convinced me that history re-peats itself. His spirited account of the disputed Hayes-Tilden election of 1876 is as gripping as the newspaper stories we all read after the Bush-Gore contest. This lively history is a warning of the fragility of our politi-cal system, as well as a commentary on the basic strength of our democratic institutions. *Fraud of the Century* is first-rate narrative history."

—David Herbert Donald, author of *Lincoln*

"The similarities between the 2000 and 1876 elections are striking—right down to the temperament of the candidates. . . . Morris' fine, objective ac-count of the 1876 election debacle . . . is an informative, insightful and, yes, entertaining act of memory."

—*The Denver Post*

"Authoritative. . . . *Fraud of the Century* . . . has the immediacy of the last election."

—*The Boston Globe*

"A fascinating narrative. . . . No contest, not even the Gore-Bush entanglement in 2000, matches the drama of the one that pitted Hayes and Tilden against each other. The details of the serpentine path of intrigue and infighting that the encounter took are entrancing. . . . No one has told the story better than Roy Morris. . . . A first-rate account."

—*The New Leader*

"A revealing, dramatic, and timely account of a presidential election that proved to be a crossroads event in American history."

—Michael Beschloss, author of *The Conquerors: Roosevelt, Truman and the Destruction of Hitler's Germany, 1941–1945*

"*Fraud of the Century* is riveting and timely. . . . Roy Morris reminds us of history's long reach and of how contemporary events rarely are novel and unprecedented. . . . A fine read and a compelling story."

—Jeffry D. Wert, author of *Gettysburg, Day Three*

"Respected biographer Morris reconstructs in amazing detail a presidential election that profaned the rule of law and nearly rekindled the Civil War. . . . One of the nation's darkest chapters, brilliantly exhumed and analyzed with due attention to its obvious contemporary relevance."

—*Kirkus Reviews* (starred)

"Morris has an eye for detail and a lively writing style that make this highly detailed, first-rate work of history read more like a whodunnit than a historical examination."

—*Library Journal* (starred)

"For those who think the election of George W. Bush over Al Gore in 2000 represented the nadir of American electoral politics, Morris provides some much-needed historical perspective. . . . Well researched and written in clear prose. . . . Morris's account of the 1876 election reminds us that character can triumph over politics."

—*Publishers Weekly*

"Dense with well-documented historical color and insights into a very different age. . . . If former Vice President Al Gore had learned from Mr. Tilden's missteps, history might not have repeated itself."

—*New York Law Journal*

OTHER BOOKS BY ROY MORRIS, JR.

The Better Angel: Walt Whitman in the Civil War
Ambrose Bierce: Alone in Bad Company
Sheridan: The Life and Wars of General Phil Sheridan

FRAUD

OF THE

CENTURY

Rutherford B. Hayes,
Samuel Tilden, and the
Stolen Election of 1876

ROY MORRIS, JR.

SIMON & SCHUSTER

NEW YORK   LONDON   TORONTO   SYDNEY

This book is dedicated to my father,
Roy Morris, and to the memory of my mother,
Margaret Brew Coode Morris (1922–1999),
two more members of the Greatest Generation.

SIMON & SCHUSTER
Rockefeller Center
1230 Avenue of the Americas
New York, NY 10020

First Simon & Schuster trade paperback edition 2004

SIMON & SCHUSTER and colophon are registered trademarks
of Simon & Schuster, Inc.

For information about special discounts for bulk purchases,
please contact Simon & Schuster Special Sales:
1-800-456-6798 or business@simonandschuster.com

Manufactured in the United States of America

3   5   7   9   10   8   6   4   2

The Library of Congress has cataloged the hardcover edition as follows:
Morris, Roy.
Fraud of the century : Rutherford B. Hayes, Samuel Tilden,
and the stolen election of 1876 / Roy Morris, Jr.
Includes bibliographical references and index.
p. cm.
1. Presidents—United States—Election—1876. 2. Contested elections—
United States—History—19th century. 3. Elections—Corrupt practices—
United States—History—19th century. 4. Political corruption—United States—
History—19th century. 5. Hayes, Rutherford Birchard, 1822–1893.
6. Tilden, Samuel J. (Samuel Jones), 1814–1886. 7. Presidential
candidates—United States—Biography. I. Title.
E680 .M85 2003
324.973082—dc21   2002036507

ISBN 0-7432-2386-1
0-7432-5552-6 (Pbk)

Credits and permissions appear on page 311.

CONTENTS

INTRODUCTION

History, said Karl Marx, repeats itself, first as tragedy, then as farce. The American presidential election of 2000, with its hanging chads, butterfly ballots, flummoxed oldsters, and pop-eyed Florida election officials, certainly qualifies as farcical, in its procedures if not necessarily its outcome. But its historical parallels to another disputed presidential election, one that took place on the same date 124 years earlier, call to mind the first part of Marx's aphorism as well. The 1876 contest between Republican nominee Rutherford B. Hayes and Democratic nominee Samuel J. Tilden also involved the state of Florida, and it, too, ultimately was decided by the vote of a single Republican member of the U.S. Supreme Court. As with the 2000 election, there were charges of fraud, intimidation, lost ballots, and racism. Hordes of political operatives descended hungrily on the state, while the nation waited, anxiously if not breathlessly, for the winning candidate to be determined. When it was over, four months after election day, the candidate who probably had lost the election in Florida and definitely had lost the popular vote nationwide nevertheless was declared the winner, not just of Florida's electoral votes but of the presidency itself.

But if the 2000 election was something of a farce, the 1876 election was nothing less than a tragedy. Ironically, in a year that saw the United States celebrating the centennial of its birth, the American political system nearly broke apart under the powerful oppositional pull of party politics, personal ambitions, and lingering sectional animosities. The result was a singularly sordid presidential election, perhaps the most bitterly contested in the nation's history, and one whose eventual winner was decided not in the nation's multitudinous polling booths but in a single meeting room inside the Capitol, not by the American people en masse but by a fifteen-man Electoral Commission that was every bit as partisan and petty as the shadiest ward heeler in New York City or the most unreconstructed Rebel in South Carolina. It was an election that did little credit to anyone, except perhaps its ultimate loser.

In a larger sense, there were no real winners in 1876. Rutherford B. Hayes did eventually take the presidential oath of office—not once but twice, in the space of three days, as events transpired—but in both personal and political terms he was as much a loser as the man he defeated. The shameless ways in which Samuel Tilden's electoral triumph eventually was overturned so compromised Hayes that, had he not already declared that he would serve only one term as president, he still would have been virtually a lame duck from the day he took office. As it was, his legal and moral title to the presidency was never accepted as legitimate by at least half the country, and he has been tarred ever since with such unflattering nicknames as "His Fraudulency," "the Great Usurper," and "Rutherfraud B. Hayes."

As for Tilden, no one, not even fellow Democrat Al Gore in 2000, came so close to becoming president without actually being declared the winner. Gore received 540,000 more popular votes than George W. Bush, while Tilden got, proportionally, the modern equivalent of 1.3 million more popular votes than Hayes. Some of those votes, however, came from three southern states—Florida, Louisiana, and South Carolina—where Tilden's apparent victory margins were immediately contested by the Republicans, who still controlled the statehouses there and, more importantly, the returning boards that would formally certify the election results in each state. Although Tilden, like Gore, officially lost the state of Florida, he almost certainly won the state of Louisiana, only to have it stripped from his electoral column in one of the most brazen political thefts in American history. If Gore was stopped figuratively at the gates of the White House, then Tilden, needing only one more electoral vote to win the election, was stopped at the very door to the Executive Mansion. Each man had a plausible claim to victory, but Tilden's was much more plausible. Indeed, both he and Hayes went to bed on election night believing that Tilden had won. The Republican National Committee chairman believed it, too; he went to bed with a bottle of whiskey. Had it not been for the dramatic, late-night intervention of two canny Republican politicos and a bitterly partisan newspaper editor, the election would never have been contested in the first place, and the nation would not have been subjected to four long months of bold-faced political chicanery masquerading as statesmanship.

Tilden and Hayes were not the only losers in 1876. By formally acquiescing to what modern historian Paul Johnson has aptly termed "a legalized fraud," leaders of both parties in Congress heedlessly fostered an atmosphere of mutual suspicion, antagonism, and hatred that lingered over the political landscape for the better part of a century. The election and its aftermath gave rise in the South to the infamous Jim Crow laws that officially sanctioned the social and political disenfranchisement of millions of southern blacks. The Republican party there was overthrown, and the unprecedented experiment in social engineering known as Reconstruction came to an abrupt, if largely predetermined, end. It would be another ninety years before southern blacks stepped free from the shackles of legalized segregation and a radically different Republican party reemerged as a viable political force in the South. At the same time, more than four million Democratic voters, in the North as well as the South, saw their ballots effectively rendered meaningless; and the shining cause of political reform, which Tilden long had championed and for which the American people openly hungered, guttered out in the shadows of a cynical political compromise that few people wanted and fewer still respected.

The election itself, in many ways, was the last battle of the Civil War. When Judson Kilpatrick, Hayes's old Union army comrade, advised him to wage "a bloody shirt campaign, with money," in Kilpatrick's home state of Indiana, he might just as well have been speaking of the country as a whole. The Republican party, embattled and embarrassed by the myriad scandals of President Ulysses S. Grant's administration, fell back on the tried-and-true method of sectional division known evocatively as "waving the bloody shirt." With the Civil War less than a dozen years in the past, and a resurgent Democratic party in the South threatening to retake control of the region, the Republicans insistently urged their supporters to "vote as you shot." Behind this nakedly emotional appeal lay the pervasive worry on the part of northern veterans that the benefits they had won on the battlefield—not least of which was the right of 700,000 former slaves to vote freely and openly in political elections—were about to be lost at the polling booth.

On the other side of the coin was the palpable desire of Democrats everywhere to "throw the rascals out," as *New York Sun* editor Charles A. Dana memorably demanded, to exact some revenge, however belated, for the numerous indignities inflicted on them by Republicans. Such indignities ranged from unsubstantiated charges of disloyalty in the North to military defeat and occupation in the South. Both northern and southern Democrats were united in their hatred of the corrupt Grant administration and in their belief that Tilden would usher in a new era of honest government and personal accountability. The battle lines were clearly drawn and intensely defended. If it is true, as Karl von Clausewitz said, that war is merely politics by other means, then the reverse is also true. More than any other election in American history, the election of 1876 was war by other means.

Like many close and bitterly fought presidential elections, the Hayes-Tilden contest of 1876 was a riveting personal struggle between two unique, humanly flawed individuals with very different strengths and weaknesses. Tilden, nine years older and a good deal more experienced in national politics than Hayes, was a highly organized if somewhat cerebral politician with long-standing credentials as a proven reformer. His appeal was intellectual, not personal, and his tendency to aloof self-containment would cause him to be strangely passive at the most inopportune time—when the presidency itself was hanging in the balance. Hayes, conversely, was a placid, outgoing individual with an unshakable belief in his own essential rectitude. This characteristic would serve him well when he confronted—and carefully overlooked—evidence of electoral misbehavior by some of his closest friends and supporters. Unhindered by doubt and buoyed by an inner strength he had discovered as a volunteer soldier in the Civil War, Hayes ironically proved to be a better practical politician than Tilden, who had spent virtually his entire life preparing for the presidency. It would prove to be a crucial difference.

In the century and a quarter since the election of 1876 took place, the Hayes-Tilden contest has receded in the national memory. Partly this is due to the peculiarly American habit of historical indifference, of always looking ahead rather than looking back, where, as Satchel Paige once warned, "something might be gaining on you." Partly, too, it is due to the equivocal way in which modern historians have generally treated the election. Recognizing that partisans on both sides were guilty of engaging in ethically questionable and sometimes illegal activities to suppress or reduce the votes of their opponents, historians have carefully straddled the line between corrupt Republican election practices and violent Democratic campaign abuses. The tendency of historians in recent years, influenced to a degree by heightened sensitivity to the racial implications of the election, has been to excuse Republican fraud as a necessary antidote to Democratic intimidation. Even if Hayes (so the thinking goes) stole the election from Tilden, he was only stealing back what the Democrats already had stolen from him. This book, as its subtitle makes clear, does not subscribe to such moral relativism: many wrongs do not make one right.

Primarily, however, the relative obscurity of the 1876 election is due to its peaceful resolution, an outcome which at the time seemed far from inevitable. Indeed, one ill-chosen word from Tilden might well have ignited another Civil War, this time between rival political parties rather than discrete geographical regions. Both Hayes and Grant made it clear that they were prepared to go to any lengths to prevent the Democrats from returning to power. Tilden was not. "We have just emerged from one Civil War," he said. "It will never do to engage in another; it would end in the destruction of free government." That Tilden had the good grace and inherent patriotism to avert such a social catastrophe was the one inspiring element in a distinctly uninspiring election.

How Hayes and Tilden, two essentially decent men, came to play reluctant leading roles in the most corrupt presidential election in American history is a story that still deserves to be remembered today, both for its inherent dramatic interest and for its cautionary relevance to recent events. History, after all, is memory, whether its lineaments be tragedy or farce. This book is an act of remembering.

ELECTION NIGHT, 1876

THE NEXT PRESIDENT of the United States went to bed late on election night, November 7, 1876.

For New York governor Samuel J. Tilden, the Democratic party's standard-bearer, it had been a particularly tiring day. Tilden's physical stamina, never very great to begin with, had been sorely taxed by a brutal political campaign that, for all its public obeisance to the new civic god of reform, had quickly descended into a vicious personal attack on the governor's honesty, patriotism, morals—even his sanity. Now, thankfully, the campaign was over. After one last day of pressing the flesh, of seeing and being seen, Tilden shared a quiet dinner with friends in New York City and then made a quick visit to Democratic headquarters at the Everett House on Union Square. There, the sixty-two-year-old candidate heard the electrifying news that he had carried the toss-up states of Indiana, New Jersey, and Connecticut. With his own state safely in hand and a blizzard of electoral votes expected momentarily from the newly unreconstructed states down south, it now seemed increasingly likely that "Centennial Sam" Tilden, boasting a jaunty new nickname and an equally sportive red carnation in the buttonhole of his somber black suit, was about to exchange one executive mansion for another.

Certainly it seemed that way to Tilden's Republican rival, fellow governor Rutherford B. Hayes of Ohio. The politically astute if physically unprepossessing Hayes, a two-term United States congressman and three-term governor, had been sensing defeat for several days. Although publicly maintaining a confident front, in private Hayes had been acting very much like a beaten candidate. "The contest is close and yet doubtful with the chances, as I see them, rather against us," he confided to his diary on November 1. Fraud and violence, particularly in the South, were highly probable, Hayes believed, and "the chances are that we shall lose the election." A few days earlier he had given campaign workhorse Carl Schurz the meager assurance, "I shall find many things to console me if defeated." On the morning of the election, Hayes was still predicting that "Democratic chances [are] the best."

He had ample reason to be concerned. Gubernatorial elections a month earlier in Indiana and West Virginia had resulted in bellwether Democratic victories, and the victory of Hoosier populist James D. "Blue Jeans" Williams, in particular, seemed to presage an inevitable Tilden triumph. "Tilden is really going to be elected," Pennsylvania congressman Samuel Randall observed, a little wonderingly, after the Indiana vote. "I can see it all around me." Illinois state Democratic committeeman J. A. Mallory could scarcely contain his sense of joy. "After sixteen long years of *darkness*, daylight is at last breaking," he wrote. In the face of such discouraging portents, the one note of hopeful qualification that Hayes had allowed himself was the unlikely possibility that a close election might lead to a "contested result," which in turn could provoke "a conflict of arms." The former Union general had no doubt that he would meet such a challenge with courage and firmness, but "bloodshed and civil war must be averted if possible."

The possibility of bloodshed was no idle worry. For many, if not most, of the partisans on both sides of the political spectrum, the presidential election of 1876 represented the final act in a bitter conflict dating back to the election of Abraham Lincoln sixteen years earlier. The triumph of the fledgling Republican party and the almost immediate commencement of the Civil War had left the Republicans in complete control of the national government, and not even Lincoln's assassination four years later and the accidental interregnum of the much-despised Andrew Johnson had loosened the Republicans' hold on power. Congressional Reconstruction, the process by which the war-ravaged states of the former Confederacy were readmitted grudgingly into the Union, had extended the party's hold on the previously Democratic South, where newly empowered blacks had joined hands with white Republicans to take control of state governments from Virginia to Louisiana. Determined southern whites had fought back grimly, violently, and unremittingly to "redeem" their states from Republican rule; by 1876 all but three southern states had been redeemed.

To northern Republicans, the return to power of thousands of former Confederates represented an intolerable political affront and a rank betrayal of patriotic values. Equally bad, in their eyes, was the possibility of a Democratic president, particularly one who had stayed on the sidelines during the Civil War and given the Union war effort—so they believed—only scant and grudging support. A Tilden victory threatened to arrest, if not indeed reverse, the social, financial, and political advances the Republican party had made in the past two decades. Such an outcome was anathema to loyal Republicans, even as it was the fondest dream of Democrats on both sides of the Mason-Dixon line. The apparent closeness of the presidential race served, if anything, to heighten emotions in the days leading up to the election. Whoever won the White House would inevitably confront a phalanx of angry and disappointed losers.

Hayes, for his part, had some experience with close elections. While serving in the Union army in 1864, he had been elected to Congress by a less than overwhelming margin of 2,400 votes, in a wartime election that was tailor-made for Republicans. His first campaign for governor had gone down to the wire as well, with Hayes eventually winning by six tenths of one percent of the vote. His following two terms had been won by slightly larger, but scarcely landslide, margins. About the best that could be said for his vote-getting prowess was that he had never lost a statewide election, however close. Now even that modest distinction seemed to be coming to an abrupt, decisive end.

The small group of family and friends who gathered at Hayes's home in Columbus, Ohio, on that raw and windy election night found little to cheer about. The candidate was not doing as well as he had hoped in Ohio, and the news that Tilden had carried several doubtful northern states added another layer of gloom to an already sodden evening. Hayes's ordinarily witty and vivacious wife, Lucy, kept mostly to the kitchen, busying herself with refreshments, before disappearing upstairs with a headache. When word came that Tilden had carried

New York City by fifty thousand votes, Hayes resigned himself manfully to defeat. "From that time I never supposed there was a chance for Republican success," he confided to his diary. Shortly after midnight he joined his wife in bed, consoling her with the thought that now, at least, their lives would be easier without the added burden of having to move into the White House. The couple, wrote Hayes, "soon fell into a refreshing sleep and the affair seemed over."

IT WAS NOT. While Tilden, a bachelor, slept alone in New York and Hayes and his disappointed wife of twenty-three years cuddled together in far-off Columbus, others in the country had not yet gone to bed. One such night owl was former Union general Daniel E. Sickles. By election night 1876, "Devil Dan" Sickles was a man with a long and controversial career already behind him. Once a rising star in the Democratic party, the personal protégé of President James Buchanan, the thirty-nine-year-old New York congressman had effectively ruined his political career in 1859 by shooting down an unarmed man (Philip Barton Key, son of "Star-Spangled Banner" composer Francis Scott Key) who was having an affair with his wife. With the help of Abraham Lincoln's future secretary of war, Edwin Stanton, Sickles was acquitted of his crime by reason of temporary insanity, the first time such a legal defense had been used successfully in an American court of law. After a brief but comfortable exile in New York City, the disgraced politico successfully rehabilitated himself, raising and leading a Union brigade during the Civil War, losing a leg at Gettysburg but winning a Medal of Honor for his pains.

Having begun his political life as a Democrat, Sickles smoothly switched sides after the Civil War, becoming one of the leaders in the unsuccessful efforts by Radical Republicans to remove President Andrew Johnson from office. His sinuous political machinations, prompted more by self-preservation than by ideals—Johnson had already removed him from military command of the Reconstruction district of North and South Carolina—were suitably rewarded when Johnson's bitter rival Ulysses S. Grant became president in 1869. Ignoring Sickles's less than stellar reputation, Grant appointed him the American minister to Spain, where his notorious dalliance with that country's deposed queen, Isabella II, subsequently earned him the not entirely undeserved or un-welcomed nickname "the Yankee King of Spain."

By the time of the 1876 presidential campaign, Sickles had resigned his ministerial post to embark on an extended tour of Europe. He was in Paris that September visiting the American ambassador to Versailles when word came (erroneously, as it turned out) that Vermont, a state that was predictably Republican in its leanings, had nearly elected a Dem-ocratic governor. "That looks like the election of Tilden," Ambassador Elihu B. Washburne observed. "Yes," said Sickles, "I quite agree with you and as I don't want to see that 'copperhead' elected president, I shall take the steamer tomorrow for home and take part in the canvas[s]."

Not one to hesitate during times of crisis, Sickles rushed back to America and offered his services to the Republican party. Former New York governor Edwin D. Morgan, the party's national chairman, po-litely declined Sickles's help, but the general did make a brief campaign visit to Hayes's home state of Ohio, where he urged his former Union brother in arms to "rouse the old Republican war enthusiasm" by wav-ing once more the bloody shirt. Hayes, locked in a tight race with a bril-liant and resourceful opponent, did not need much convincing. Ever since the day in 1868 when Massachusetts congressman Benjamin F. Butler had flourished on the floor of Congress the torn and blood-stained shirt of a federal tax collector whipped by the Ku Klux Klan in Mississippi, the bloody shirt had become the Republican party's most effective propaganda weapon. One month before Sickles's visit, another Union general turned politician, Judson Kilpatrick, had written to Hayes advising him to run "a bloody shirt campaign, with money." Sick-les reiterated the point, warning Hayes that he was in danger of losing his home state if he did not step up his attacks. Sickles then returned to New York, convinced that he had done his duty. Thereafter, he "pro-ceeded to take only a languid interest in the canvas[s], as I regarded the election of Mr. Tilden as inevitable."

On election night, still sensing a Democratic victory, Sickles sought to lose his political cares in the fleeting diversions of a Broadway play. Returning to his home at 23 Fifth Avenue around midnight, he made a spur-of-the-moment decision to drop by Republican party headquarters at the nearby Fifth Avenue Hotel, a six-story marble edifice overlooking

Madison Square at the corner of 23rd Street and Fifth Avenue, four blocks west of Gramercy Park, where Samuel Tilden was then in the process of drifting off to sleep. Sickles entered the headquarters expecting to find it a beehive of activity. What he found instead was more like a drafty funeral home after the mourners have left the wake and the corpse has been wheeled into cold storage for the night. A single diligent if disheartened clerk, M. C. Clancy, was still on duty, packing up the remnants of a lost campaign. Tilden, he said gloomily, had been elected. Undeterred, Sickles asked to see the latest returns. "You will find them on the desk of Mr. Chandler," Clancy said, referring to national party chairman Zachariah Chandler. "He retired an hour ago, saying he didn't want to see anybody." The clerk added, perhaps unnecessarily, that Chandler had taken a bottle of whiskey upstairs with him.

Sickles sat down at Chandler's desk and riffled through a stack of telegrams from Republican state headquarters across the country. What he saw on paper gave him hope. "After a careful scrutiny," Sickles recalled, "[I] reached the conclusions that the contest was really very close and doubtful, but by no means hopeless. According to my figures, based on fair probabilities, Hayes was elected by at least one majority in the Electoral College." Sickles's estimate assumed that Hayes would win the electoral votes of South Carolina, Louisiana, Florida, and Oregon, giving him the 185 electoral votes he needed for victory. As subsequent events would demonstrate, that was a very large assumption to make, but Sickles followed up his intuition by drafting telegrams to leading Republican functionaries in the four questionable states, each containing the same urgent message: "With your state sure for Hayes, he is elected. Hold your state."

Sickles called Clancy to his side, showed him the telegrams, and asked the clerk to sign Chandler's name to the dispatches. Before Clancy could respond, Sickles heard the familiar voice of Chester A. Arthur, the longtime collector of the port of New York, outside in the hall. Sickles went to the door and asked Arthur to come into the room, where he showed him a copy of the election returns and the various telegrams. "If you advise it," said Sickles, "I have no doubt the chief clerk will feel authorized to send off these telegrams with the signature of the chairman." Arthur agreed, the telegrams were sent, and Sickles prepared to take his leave, having functioned for the better part of an hour as a one-legged, one-man Republican National Committee. Assuming wrongly that Arthur would want to stay behind and wait for an answer from the states in question, Sickles headed for the door. But Arthur, who owed his lucrative sinecure to the very sort of machine politics that Hayes had sworn to root out when he came into office, begged off the night watch. His own date with presidential destiny still five years in the future, Arthur went home to be with his conveniently sick wife, and Sickles sat back down at Chandler's desk to wait.

WHILE THE GENERAL conducted his lonely vigil at Republican headquarters in New York, morning newspapers across the country were coming to their own conclusions about the race. The vast majority followed the lead of the *Chicago Tribune,* a pro-Republican paper that despaired: "Lost. The Country Given Over to Democratic Greed and Plunder." The Democratic-leaning *New York Tribune* was terser, if no less convinced of the result. "Tilden Elected," it reported. The Democratic nominee's lead now topped 250,000 votes. Still, the slightest air of uncertainty lingered in the minds of some high-ranking Democrats. The party, after all, had been out of power for the better part of sixteen years, and had not won a presidential election in two decades. And even with a decidedly uninspiring candidate at the head of the Republican ticket and a sorry eight-year record of venality, corruption, and economic depression to defend, the party of Lincoln nevertheless had managed to carry, however closely, most of the northern and midwestern states. Despite Tilden's widening lead in the popular vote, his margin in the all-important Electoral College seemed to be shrinking. At 3:45 that morning, two jittery Democratic officials sought to allay their growing doubts. Unfortunately for them and their now sleeping champion, those doubts would prove to be both well founded and contagious.

The Democrats in question were Daniel A. Magone, an Ogdensburg, New York, lawyer who was Tilden's handpicked choice to succeed him as the state party chairman, and Connecticut senator William Barnum, a wealthy financier with a long-standing reputation for political chicanery. The two men, independent of each other, had taken it upon themselves to send telegrams to the *New York Times*, then a distinctly unfriendly Republican party organ, to inquire after the latest returns. "Please give your estimate of electoral votes for Tilden," Magone wired. "Answer at once." Barnum's telegram was more specific, asking about the returns from Florida, Louisiana, and South Carolina, the last three southern states where Republican-led Reconstruction governments still remained in power.

Unfortunately for the Democrats, the *Times* editor who received the requests was John C. Reid, a dyed-in-the-wool Republican partisan whose wartime exposure to southern Democrats, in the person of the Confederate cavalrymen who had captured him outside Atlanta, Georgia, in the summer of 1864 and carried him off to Andersonville Prison, had left him with a permanent hatred for all things Democratic. Reid, the *Times*'s managing editor, was a difficult man to get along with in the best of times. A fellow journalist described him as "not a pleasant or popular person . . . [his] red, bloated features warned of his hot temper, his angry little eyes of a disposition to tyrannize." When Tilden's campaign manager, Abram S. Hewitt, had asked him cheekily, a bit earlier in the evening, how many states the *Times* was willing to concede to Tilden, Reid snapped, "None." He did not even bother to answer Magone's or Barnum's telegrams, but he did give their inquiries his personal attention. Why, he wondered, were the damned Democrats so worried?

Reid was engaged just then in an editorial discussion with his fellow Timesmen over how best to report the demoralizing election results. Of the five men involved—Reid, editor-in-chief John Foord, political writers Edward Cary and George Shepard, and assistant editor Charles R. Miller—only Miller was a Tilden supporter. There was never any question of following the *Tribune*'s lead and conceding the election to the Democrats: not only was the *Times* too partisan for that, but Republican sources in Louisiana and South Carolina now were claiming those states for Hayes (perhaps in response to Sickles's earlier telegrams), and the Associated Press was reporting that both sides were declaring victory in Florida. Cary—not Reid, as is usually claimed—persuaded the others to hold off making a definitive call of the race, and instead prepared a lead editorial for the newspaper's first edition under the heading "A Doubtful Election."

Depending on one's political views, Cary's editorial was either a masterpiece of predictive powers or a ridiculous exercise in wishful thinking. "At the time of going to press with our first edition the result of the presidential election is still in doubt," he began. "Enough has been learned to show that the vote has been unprecedentedly heavy; that both parties have exhausted their full legitimate strength . . . and that in some of the states where the shotgun and rifle clubs were relied upon to secure a Democratic victory, there is only too much reason to fear that it has been successful." Cary conceded New York to Tilden—no great stretch—but Louisiana and South Carolina, the two southern states most notorious for their "rifle clubs," were listed arbitrarily in Hayes's column. New Jersey, already conceded to Tilden in most accounts, was still "in doubt." This left Tilden, by Cary's count, with 175 certain electoral votes, Hayes with 178. Oregon, whose initial returns indicated a slight lead for the Republican candidate, was too close to call. Florida, said Cary in a careful understatement, "is claimed by the Democrats."

The *Times*'s second edition, which hit the streets at 6:30 A.M., was even more sanguine about Hayes's chances. In it, Cary removed the pessimistic sentence about shotgun and rifle clubs, returned New Jersey to Tilden's column, and credited Oregon definitely to Hayes. "This leaves Florida alone still in doubt," he wrote. "If the Republicans have carried that state, as they claim, they will have 185 votes—a majority of one." As Cary well knew, a one-vote majority was all that was needed for Rutherford B. Hayes, once the darkest of political dark horses, to ascend the flag-draped reviewing stand outside the Capitol the following March and take the oath of office as the nation's nineteenth president. Stranger things had been known to happen.

WITH THE *TIMES*'S more optimistic estimates in hand, Reid hurried off to Republican headquarters to inform party officials of the news and stave off any premature concession statement. Gaslights across the city were flickering out as Reid made his way uptown from Printing House Square in the financial district to the Fifth Avenue Hotel on Madison Square. The red glow from dozens of Democratic bonfires flared against the inky sky. Early risers, or those who had not yet gone to bed, dodged horse-drawn delivery wagons and private carriages clattering down the rain-slick streets. Newsboys hawked conflicting results—Tilden was elected, the Republicans were ruined, the race was still too close to call. Reid, for his part, paid them little mind. He was a man on a holy mission.

Pushing his way into the hotel through an immense throng of people milling about the 23rd Street entrance, Reid went immediately to party headquarters. No one was there but the cleaning staff; Reid had missed Sickles by half an hour. The indefatigable old lion had retired to his lair after receiving encouraging answers to his earlier telegrams from South Carolina governor Daniel H. Chamberlain and the chairman of the Oregon Republican party state committee. Chamberlain, who was seeking reelection and was in the political fight of his life with former Confederate general Wade Hampton, understood the stakes better than anyone. "All right. South Carolina is for Hayes," he had informed Sickles. "Need more troops." Sickles had duly forwarded the message under his own name to President Grant, who was staying overnight at his friend George W. Childs's Philadelphia estate prior to the formal closing ceremonies of the Centennial Exhibition. After sending followup telegrams to the four undecided states, Sickles had gone home at last for some well-deserved rest.

Reid headed toward the front desk to obtain Chandler's room number. Opening the door to the reading room, he ran—literally—into William E. Chandler (no relation to Zachariah), a battle-scarred Republican operative who was just returning to headquarters after an overnight train ride from his home in New Hampshire. Chandler, who suffered from weak eyesight, was wearing an immense pair of goggles, a hat pulled down over his ears, and a heavy military cloak. Recognizing Reid, who unsurprisingly did not recognize him, Chandler brandished the rolled-up copy of the *New York Tribune* he had been reading on the train. "Damn the men who brought this disaster upon the Republican party!" he cried.

When it came to party politics, William Chandler could speak with some authority. By the age of forty, he had already spent half his life in service to the Republican party, beginning as secretary of the first New Hampshire chapter of the Frémont for President club in 1856. Six years later he had been elected to the state legislature—at twenty-seven he became the youngest speaker of the house in New Hampshire history—before going on to serve as assistant secretary of the treasury under Andrew Johnson. Resigning his post in 1867, Chandler had become a well-paid lobbyist for the railroad interests. His time at the Treasury Department had brought him the friendship of a number of the nation's most powerful financiers, including Jay Cooke, the failure of whose banking empire, Jay Cooke & Company, had singlehandedly brought about the Panic of 1873 and crushed the fortunes of countless investors. Chandler himself had narrowly escaped ruin. He and his son were traveling in Europe when the crash occurred, and it was Daniel Sickles, ironically enough, who had provided him with an emergency letter of credit on which to get home.

While working as a lobbyist, Chandler had kept his hand in politics. As secretary of the Republican National Committee he had functioned as the de facto campaign manager for Ulysses S. Grant's two successful runs for the White House, a role he pointedly declined to play in Hayes's campaign, considering it, at best, a long shot to succeed. Nothing he had seen in the previous night's returns had led him to question that decision. His face as shrouded as his traveling clothes, Chandler unrolled the battered newspaper. "Look at this," he said to Reid, pointing to the headline announcing Tilden's election.

The fact that so experienced a hand as Chandler considered the election lost did not dissuade the implacable Reid. "The Republican Party has sustained no disaster," he insisted. "If you will only keep your heads up there is no question of the election of President Hayes. He has been fairly and honestly elected." Still skeptical, Chandler invited the newsman up to his room, where Reid, with mathematical logic and evangelical certitude, painstakingly explained the Times's position. Chandler permitted himself the slightest glimmer of hope. "We must go and see Zach," he said when Reid had finished.

After a brief, confused search that included knocking twice on the wrong door and "frighten[ing] two lone women nearly out of their wits," the pair succeeded in finding the chairman's room. They began pounding and kicking on the door. "It's me, Chandler. Open the door, quick," said William Chandler. After a brief pause the door swung open and Zachariah Chandler, wearing only a nightshirt and a befuddled expression, greeted his unexpected visitors. "Here is a gentleman who has more news than you have," William said, indicating Reid. "He has some suggestions to make." For the second time in ten minutes, Reid found himself explaining the election returns to a man named Chandler in the Fifth Avenue Hotel. "Very well," said Zachariah, after hearing Reid's analysis, "go ahead and do what you think necessary." He, on the other hand, was going back to bed.

Reid and Chandler hurried downstairs to the telegraph office. It was not quite seven o'clock; it would be another hour, at least, before the office reopened. "I'll have to take these messages to the main office of the Western Union," said Reid. Chandler ordered a carriage brought around to the 23rd Street entrance. While they were waiting, the pair dashed off another spate of messages to Chamberlain, Florida senator Simon B. Conover, Oregon senator John H. Mitchell, and Louisiana governor William P. Kellogg. The wording was identical—hold on to your state.

Messages in hand, Reid jumped into the carriage and hurried off to the telegraph office. "Probably the quickest time ever made by a carriage from the Fifth Avenue Hotel to the Western Union was made that morning," he recalled. Upon arrival, Reid handed the telegrams to the overnight clerk and told him to charge them to the Republican National Committee. "The National Committee has no account here and we can't do it," said the clerk, who fortunately recognized the newsman by sight. "Why not charge them to the New York Times account?" "All right," said Reid. The telegrams went out.

As dawn broke westward over the troubled republic, the next president of the United States was still asleep.

CHAPTER ONE

AMERICAN MECCA

THE PRESIDENTIAL ELECTION of 1876 was the climax—or anti-climax—of a year-long orgy of self-congratulation that inevitably surrounded the nation's one hundredth birthday. "Centennial mania," as it was known, gripped Americans of all social and political persuasions. Its epicenter was Fairmount Park, four miles west of Philadelphia, where the great Centennial Exhibition, the first world's fair held within the United States, sprawled across 450 acres of newly cleared and asphalted grounds dedicated to the physical embodiment of American virtue and American progress, which in most people's minds were one and the same. Five years in the making, the exhibition quickly proved to be the greatest tourist attraction in the nation's history. In its six-month-long existence, the fair hosted a total of 8,804,631 visitors—roughly one fifth the entire population of the United States. Taking into account repeat visitors, it was estimated conservatively that one in fifteen Americans paid fifty cents apiece to pass through the fair's self-counting turnstiles.

Once inside the grounds visitors could behold all the wonders of an "American Mecca." These wonders were primarily mechanical. The Centennial Exhibition, while paying homage to such quaint historical objects as George Washington's false teeth and Benjamin Franklin's hand press, had been carefully designed to display the country's industrial vigor, at a time when such industry was still considered an unalloyed national blessing. The most popular sight at the fair was the giant Corliss engine, named for its inventor, George P. Corliss. Powered by a concealed steam boiler, the engine deftly animated thirteen acres of pullied, shafted, wheeled, and belted machinery, which in turn activated a wide variety of complex job-performing devices. *Atlantic Monthly* editor William Dean Howells, who spent an entire week touring the fair, called the Corliss engine "an athlete of steel and iron." It was, said the writer, the literal voice of the country. "It is in these things of iron and steel that the national genius most freely speaks," Howells wrote, "for the present America is voluble in the strong metals and their infinite uses."

Other exhibits were less inspiring. There was an animated wax sculpture of Cleopatra with a wing-flapping parrot on her arm, advertising a local anatomy museum; a bewildering collection of Victorian-era bric-a-brac, described hopefully in fair literature as an "unstudied harmony of dissimilarity produced by the kaleidoscopic mingling of our composite American life"; a leg-wearying array of overpriced restaurants, beer gardens, ice cream parlors, popcorn vendors, cigar stores, and shoeshine stands; the ominously named Burial Casket Building; and a bronze statue of a freed slave that struck the aesthetically discriminating Howells as "a most offensively Frenchy negro, who has broken his chain, and spreading both his arms and legs abroad is rioting in a declamation of something from Victor Hugo; one longs to clap him back into hopeless bondage."

Across the street from the exhibition was a sort of adjunct fair called variously Dinkytown, Shantyville, or Centennial City, a rough-and-tumble conglomeration of flimsy wood and canvas buildings that boasted its own collection of saloons, beer gardens, oyster bars, and sausage carts. There was even a catch-all "museum" where credulous patrons could view wild men from Borneo, wild children from Australia, "pure and unadulterated man-eaters" from the Fiji Islands, and a 602-pound fat woman whose remarkable avoirdupois was judged "heavy enough to entitle her to a place in Machinery Hall." Exhibition founders were less than thrilled by the unelevating sights and sounds drifting up from Dinkytown, and after a suspicious fire in September came close to reaching the Main Building of the fair, authorities moved in and swiftly demolished the ramshackle tribute to American entrepreneurialism.

The sights and sounds of the Centennial Exhibition were literally overwhelming. Many visitors echoed the sentiments, if not the emotionalism, of a young woman from Wisconsin who wrote, in full, to the folks back home: "Dear Mother, Oh! Oh!! O-o-o-o-o-o-o-o!!!!!" Ironically, the one American who might have made the best sense of the exhibition, Walt Whitman, despite living right across the Delaware River from Philadelphia in Camden, New Jersey, was not invited to participate in the festivities. The poet of the common man apparently was considered a little too common for the national stage. It did not help his cause that a decade earlier, during the Civil War, Whitman had run afoul of exhibition chairman Joseph Hawley's straitlaced wife, Harriet, then serving as a member of the United States Sanitary Commission, while visiting wounded Union soldiers in the hospitals in Washington. Pointedly excluded from the formal proceedings, Whitman paid his own way into the fair and was pushed about the grounds in a rented wheelchair (he was still recovering from a near fatal stroke suffered three years earlier). Characteristically, Whitman was thrilled by both the giant Corliss engine and the quiet simplicities of the Japanese gardens—the opposite ends of the spectrum, as it were, of the fair's wide-ranging sensibilities.

FOR ALL ITS WIDESPREAD popularity, the Centennial Exhibition concealed a fundamental and dismaying truth: the United States was not nearly as united as the name implied. Less than a dozen years removed from a ruinous civil war, the nation was still recovering from its fiery trial. Beneath the surface, sectional tensions continued to boil, and the exhibition nearly failed to get off the ground because of them. A bill releasing $1.5 million in matching funds from the federal government to complete the fair's construction squeaked through Congress at almost the last minute—late January and February 1876—after an acrimonious debate fueled by a grandstanding and frankly divisive speech by Republican congressman James G. Blaine of Maine.

Hoping to shore up his standing with the radical wing of his party, Blaine, the putative front-runner for the 1876 Republican presidential nomination, rose to his feet on January 6 to oppose a bill seeking amnesty for the 750 individuals still barred from holding public office by the Fourteenth Amendment, which had rescinded such rights for anyone who had served the Confederate cause. As a member of the House Rules Commitee, Blaine had voted in favor of an identical measure three years earlier, but now he introduced a new bill specifically excluding former Confederate president Jefferson Davis from the blanket amnesty on the grounds that Davis "was the author, knowingly, deliberately, guiltily and wilfully, of the gigantic murders and crimes at Andersonville," the infamous Confederate prison camp in central Georgia where thousands of Union soldiers had died during the war of disease, starvation, and neglect.

Even for Blaine, an inveterate political gamesman and unapologetic Republican partisan, this was hitting below the belt. Four days earlier the House had adopted a resolution calling for national harmony at the "most auspicious inception of the centennial year" and urging members to "do no act which would unnecessarily disturb the patriotic concord now existing nor wantonly revive bitter memories of the past." But Blaine, who had safely sat out the Civil War in the marbled halls of Congress, blithely ignored the resolution. In a voice throbbing with worked-up emotion, he said of Andersonville, "Some of us had kinsmen there, most of us had friends there, all of us had countrymen there, and in the name of these kinsmen, friends, and countrymen, I here protest . . . against calling back and crowning with the honors of full American citizenship the man that organized that murder. The score of victims would demand his death."

Democrats reacted angrily—and predictably—to Blaine's accusations. Georgia congressman Benjamin Hill, who had served in the Confederate Senate during the war, noted that a mere two hours before his execution prison commandant Henry Wirz had refused an offer of clemency if he would implicate Davis in the horrors of Andersonville. "What Wirz would not say for his life," Hill observed, "the gentleman from Maine says to the country for the sake of keeping his party in power." That was indisputably true, but Hill went too far, maintaining that if President Davis was accountable for the abuses at Andersonville, then President Grant was no less accountable for the various frauds committed during his administration. Grant, he said, "deserved not a third term but twenty years in prison." Even worse for the cause of intersectional amity, Hill charged that the Union prison camp at Elmira,

New York, had been every bit as bad as Andersonville. That was not quite the case. The mortality rate for prisoners at Andersonville was 29 percent, while Elmira's was 24 percent—a negligible difference, perhaps, unless you were one of the extra 5 percent.

As Blaine no doubt anticipated, northern Democrats leaped immediately to their region's defense. Congressmen Thomas Platt, who lived thirty-six miles from Elmira, and Charles Walker, who resided within the hallowed precincts of the city, strongly defended Elmira's honor, denying categorically that there had been any abuse of southern prisoners. Only one New York representative, Samuel Sullivan "Sunset" Cox, took exception to Blaine's speech, denouncing the former speaker for "tear[ing] away the plasters from the green and bleeding wounds of the late civil conflict and raking up all the embers of dead hate." In the ongoing parliamentary debate, he took to addressing Blaine formally as "the honorable hyena from Maine."

The funding bill eventually passed through Congress by the narrow margins of 146–130 in the House and 37–20 in the Senate, but only after Davis's home state of Kentucky had adopted a resolution refusing to take part in the Centennial Exhibition unless universal amnesty was granted (it was not). Several other southern states also declined to participate in the great national celebration, a decision that Hawley, a former Union general, characterized publicly as "very discouraging." Tennessee representative John De Witt Clinton Atkins, himself a former Confederate, spoke for many southerners when he told the House, "I am ready to strike hands across the bloody chasm, but I am not going to vote for this bill." Sectional amity still had its limits.

DESPITE THE EMBARRASSING controversy over its funding, the Centennial Exhibition opened as planned on May 10, 1876, before a surging crowd of 186,672 sun-dazed spectators. The keynote speaker for opening day was, inevitably, the president of the United States. It was a role that Ulysses S. Grant, for many reasons, would have liked to decline, but in the end he was forced to appear. As it was, his bone-dry, four-hundred-word speech pleased no one, including himself, and few in the crowd could even hear the softly delivered address over the din of rustling parasols and shuffling feet. Grant did not help matters by choosing to read his speech while standing sideways on the podium. "He read sulkily and in an undertone," noted a reporter for the *New York Sun*. *Atlantic Monthly*'s Philadelphia correspondent was even less impressed. "There were more groans and hisses than huzzas, as he finished his brief address," the journalist wrote. "Ten years ago earth and sky would have shaken with the thunder of his welcome. What a sublime possession to have thrown away, the confidence and gratitude of a nation!"

If Grant was sulky—and given his general phlegmatic demeanor it was not always easy to distinguish one presidential mood from another—he had good reason to feel that way. The first half of 1876 had been a nightmare, personally and professionally, for the Union war-hero-turned-president. On the personal side, Grant was still recovering from a puzzling and debilitating illness which had come upon him suddenly at the end of March. Diagnosed in the vague way of mid-nineteenth-century medicine as "neuralgia of the brain," the possibly psychosomatic illness left Grant pale and listless for several weeks, and it was widely rumored that he had suffered a stroke. He was still taking quinine for his pernicious condition when he arrived at the Centennial Exhibition on the morning of the grand opening. "How old the president looks!" a woman in the crowd said in a loud stage whisper when Grant's carriage pulled into view. Adding to the president's cup of woe was the failing health of his grandchild and namesake, Grant Greville Sartoris, who would die before the month was out, two months shy of his first birthday.

Along with his personal problems, Grant confronted a steadily worsening political climate. The punishing effects of an economic depression still lingered, three years after the Panic of 1873 had instigated the sharpest financial downturn in American history, leaving three million people out of work and causing the failure of eighteen thousand businesses, at a cost to the economy of over $500 million. The political fallout from the depression had resulted in a Democratic tidal wave in the 1874 congressional elections, and for the first time in nearly two decades the Democrats now held a majority in the House of Representatives. Their first act of business after being sworn in the previous December had been to pass a resolution discouraging Grant from seeking a third term in office, calling such a move "unwise, unpatriotic, and fraught with peril to our free institutions." Publicly, Grant had already gone on record as being uninterested in reelection, but his formidable wife, Julia, among others, was still lobbying hard for him to reconsider. It did not escape the president's attention that an overwhelming number of his fellow Republicans had also voted for the resolution.

Grant's abysmal standing among members of both parties was due largely to a steady stream of scandals that had climaxed, by unfortunate coincidence, exactly one year earlier, on May 10, 1875. On that date, agents from the U.S. Treasury Department had raided the offices of tax collectors and whiskey distillers in St. Louis, Chicago, and Milwaukee, seeking corroborative evidence that a so-called Whiskey Ring had defrauded the country of millions of dollars in unpaid taxes. Heading the investigation was Treasury Secretary Benjamin H. Bristow of Kentucky, an experienced federal prosecutor and the longtime legal partner of future Supreme Court justice John M. Harlan, the "Great Dissenter." Bristow, who would quickly earn Grant's undying enmity, tenaciously traced the conspiracy all the way to the outer office of the White House, where the president's personal secretary, Colonel Orville Babcock, sat at the center of a far-flung web of bribery, coercion, and intimidation stretching back all the way to the Lincoln administration.

When Bristow presented evidence of the conspiracy to Grant, the president at first maintained a solid front. "Let no guilty man escape," he wrote, but added the curious qualifying clause, "if it can be avoided." Subsequent investigation placed presidential crony John A. McDonald, the government revenue agent in St. Louis, at the heart of the scandal. Even worse, it revealed that Babcock, from his vantage point inside the White House, had alerted McDonald to the upcoming raids by means of a series of coded telegrams signed with the mysterious pseudonym "Sylph." It soon developed that the real-life Sylph was a woman of easy virtue named Louise Hawkins, whose cyprian charms had been made available to Babcock whenever he visited St. Louis, usually in conjunction with the transfer of a cigar box full of thousand-dollar bills. McDonald, sounding less like he was describing a lady than a liqueur, called Hawkins "the essence of grace, distilled from the buds of perfection, and with a tongue on which the oil of vivacity and seduction never ceased running; she was, indeed, a sylph and siren, whose presence was like the flavor of the poppy mingled with the perfumes of Araby." Grant, loyal to a fault, refused to believe badly of Babcock, who as his most trusted military aide had personally conducted General Robert E. Lee to the McLean House at Appomattox on the occasion of Lee's surrender in April 1865. Babcock, in return, repaid the president's confidence by hinting privately that Sylph was actually a blackmailer with whom Grant had enjoyed an extramarital affair—a claim that was as bogus as it was absurd.

The more Bristow investigated—and in the process acquired the patina of a true reformer—the more Grant resisted hearing the truth. Convinced, not without reason, that Bristow was seeking to ride his sudden popularity all the way to the White House, Grant dug in his famously stubborn heels. He insisted on testifying in person at Babcock's trial, and only the last-minute intercession of the entire cabinet persuaded him to settle instead for a written deposition. As it was, Grant's personal reputation for honesty, and the residual prestige of the presidency itself, enabled Babcock to escape conviction on all charges save those in the court of public opinion. Nevertheless, for the sake of injured propriety, Grant was forced to rid himself of his controversial aide, and Babcock was quietly transferred to an out-of-the-way post inspecting federal lighthouses. In the pursuance of those sadly diminished duties he later drowned, at the age of forty-eight, in the pounding surf off Mosquito Inlet, Florida.

No sooner had Babcock been acquitted, in February 1876, than a second scandal involving a high-ranking government official and a shadowy woman rocked the Grant administration. In this case the entangling female was the official's own wife. The official involved, Secretary of War William Worth Belknap, was the epitome of a young man in a hurry. Named to his post seven years earlier after the untimely death of his predecessor, John A. Rawlins, the forty-six-year-old Belknap had come from nowhere to the very center of governmental power. The son of a much-admired career army officer, he had served under William Tecumseh Sherman during the Civil War. After the war, it was Sherman's personal recommendation that boosted the obscure young Iowa revenue collector to the first chair at the War Department. Once there,

Belknap and his vivacious southern-belle wife, Carrie, had charmed all of Washington with their good looks, good taste, and bottomless hospitality. More than one experienced politician considered the dashing young war secretary a likely bet to sit one day in Grant's own seat at the White House.

Belknap's problems began when his wife died of tuberculosis in 1870. Four years later he married his dead wife's widowed sister, Amanda "Puss" Tomlinson Bowers. Puss Belknap, if anything, was more charming and attractive than her late sister—and also more expensive. She and her husband continued to entertain lavishly at their G Street residence. How Belknap could maintain such a high-profile lifestyle on his $8,000-a-year salary was an open question. The answer, when it came, was a political bombshell: he and his wife had been regularly receiving kickbacks from the operator of an Indian reservation supply post. Such posts were highly lucrative and much sought after; Grant's own brother and brother-in-law held four between them, and Puss's brother operated another—the only southerner to receive such a plum appointment. It was not her brother, however, who was paying off Mrs. Belknap, but rather the husband of her late sister's friend, Mrs. Caleb P. Marsh. Through the first Mrs. Belknap's timely intercession, Marsh had managed to secure the post concession at Fort Sill, the principal supply point for the Cheyenne, Comanche, and Kiowa tribes in Indian Territory. The cosy arrangement between Marsh and the Belknaps had begun in 1870 and continued without interruption into 1876. As was the usual custom of the time, the payments had gone through Belknap himself, the women being considered too dainty and feminine to handle such messy financial transactions on their own.

Exactly how much Belknap knew of his wives' creative wheeling and dealing is debatable; it is possible that he believed the payments were simple returns on honest investments. Whatever the case, he certainly acted the part of a guilty man after his former college roommate, Pennsylvania congressman Heister Clymer, tipped him to the fact that Clymer's committee was about to recommend that Belknap be impeached for fraud. The shaken secretary hurried to the White House, where he tearfully persuaded Grant to accept his resignation. The resignation, which caught the guileless Grant by surprise, was a legal and tactical masterstroke. Five months later, after reams of damaging and unre-butted testimony, the Senate voted narrowly against convicting Bel-knap, on the grounds that he was now a private citizen and therefore beyond its official reach. His once promising career ruined, Belknap quietly returned to the practice of law. Politically, however, the damage had been done, and any hopes that Grant may have entertained of being nominated for a third term of office were lost forever.

THE MYRIAD SINS of the Grant administration, however limited their effect on the public at large, prevented it from focusing on a more pressing problem, one that affected everyone. That problem was race.

From the moment of its inception, the shadow of slavery hung over the nation like a pall, shrouding every aspect of American life. Six hun-dred thousand soldiers had died in the Civil War contesting, among other things, the continued viability of slavery as a social and financial institution. The North had won, the slaves had been freed, and the Fourteenth and Fifteenth amendments to the Constitution had ren-dered to black men—if not black women—all the privileges of Ameri-can citizenship, including most importantly the right to vote. Given blacks' plenteous numbers in the South and their expected fidelity to the Republican party, this abrupt political empowerment had resulted in a momentous shift in the balance of power between the two parties. As long as federal troops propped up friendly Republican governments in the South, blacks held that balance in their wondering hands. "Bot-tom rail on top now, Massa," one former slave had said to his former owner, and in that simple homily was encapsulated any number of com-plex truths.

For more than a decade after the Civil War, the struggle to define, expand, codify, and protect the political rights of the 700,000 newly freed slaves in the South had dominated the national agenda. It was a struggle linked inextricably, if uneasily, to the larger question of how to bring the rebellious southern states back into the Union, while at the same time vouchsafing the gains—social, racial, financial, and politi-cal—that 360,000 northern soldiers had died to achieve. Taken to-gether, the ongoing efforts came to be known as Reconstruction, and they brought out the worst—and less frequently the best—in the American character.

Even before the war was over, the political reconstruction of the South had begun. As part of his plan to reintegrate the southern states into the Union, Abraham Lincoln in December 1863 had offered to grant full pardons and restore all rights "except as to slaves" to any southerner willing to take a loyalty oath. When the number of loyal men in any state equalled 10 percent of the total number of voters who had participated in the last prewar election in 1860, that state could then establish a new government and send a fresh slate of senators and representatives to Washington, subject to the approval of Congress. The only stipulation was that the state officially abolish slavery in its constitution; no provision had to be made regarding the future voting rights of the "laboring, landless, and homeless class" of former slaves living precariously within its borders.

Lincoln's plan, which was swiftly embraced by pro-Union voters in the occupied portions of Arkansas and Louisiana, infuriated northern radicals in Congress. By failing to make black suffrage a primary requirement for a state's reentry into the Union, the plan "freed the slave and ignored the negro," said abolitionist Wendell Phillips. Without the power of the vote, the radicals warned, freedmen and their families would have no protection from the "unrepentant rebels" who were poised to control the southern governments. Two leading radicals, Ohio senator Benjamin Wade and Maryland congressman Henry W. Davis, introduced a counterproposal to Lincoln's plan in July 1864. The Wade-Davis bill required a much stronger "ironclad oath" of loyalty by southerners; anyone who had served in the Confederate army was disqualified from taking the oath and receiving a pardon. The bill also required that 50 percent of all qualified voters—not the 10 percent mandated in Lincoln's amnesty proclamation—ratify any newly proposed state government.

Although both houses of Congress passed the Wade-Davis bill, Lincoln angrily refused to sign it, noting that in general "there is too much disposition, in certain quarters, to hector and dictate to the people of the South, to refuse to recognize them as fellow-citizens. Such persons have too little respect for Southerners' rights. I do not share feelings of

that kind." In retaliation for Lincoln's pocket veto, Massachusetts senator Charles Sumner organized a filibuster to block the seating of
Louisiana's new senators in February 1865. "The pretended state government in Louisiana," he charged, "is a mere seven-months' abortion,
begotten by the bayonet in criminal conjunction with the spirit of caste,
and born before its time, rickety, unformed, unfinished—whose continued existence will be a burden, a reproach, and a wrong." The filibuster
succeeded and the new senators remained unseated.

After Lincoln's assassination in April 1865, his successor, Andrew
Johnson, a native-born North Carolinian who had grown up in Tennessee, attempted to follow Lincoln's lead by giving political power back
to the same southern whites who had lost it, at least temporarily, on the
crimsoned battlefields of the Civil War. Under Johnson's plan, called
Presidential Reconstruction, the eleven states of the late Confederacy
were empowered to organize new governments, hold constitutional conventions, and elect their own legislators. The only southerners prohibited from voting were former Confederate government officials and the
wealthiest one percent of the planter class, and even they could petition
Johnson individually for a pardon. Despite having threatened earlier to
"punish and impoverish" the leaders of the rebellion, Johnson soon began granting pardons to thousands of southern aristocrats who, one
critic charged, "like the Bourbons have learned nothing and forgotten
nothing." Once a sworn foe of the "plantocracy" that dominated prewar
southern politics, Johnson proved even more magnanimous in victory
than Lincoln had been. By August 1866, despite horrifying race riots in
Memphis and New Orleans, the president felt justified in announcing
that "peace, order, tranquility, and civil authority now exist in and
throughout the whole of the United States."

Congressional radicals in the North—to say nothing of their black
and white supporters in the South—begged to disagree. The newly empowered southern legislatures, with the tacit approval of the president,
had begun enacting a number of repressive new laws, called Black
Codes, aimed at controlling the vast labor pool of former slaves. The
Black Codes varied from state to state, but their intent was the same—
to force black workers back onto the plantations by limiting their freedom of movement and requiring them to work cheaply for their old

masters or else face legal prosecution as vagrants. There were, to be sure, some provisions in the codes granting freedmen minimal civil liberties, including the right to marry, own property, and serve on strictly segregated juries. But the chief aim of the codes, as South Carolina politician Edmund Rhett explained all too frankly, was to insure that the newly freed blacks "be kept as near to the condition of slavery as possible, and as far from the condition of the white man as is practicable." Florida governor William Marvin condescendingly advised the freedmen to forget about the vote, return to the plantations, and "call your old Master—'Master.'"

By passing the Black Codes, revanchist southern legislatures gave added weight to the Radicals' call for stricter federal supervision, and inadvertently dealt a death knell to Presidential Reconstruction. At the same time, they lent added urgency to Republican efforts to reorganize the South as a truly biracial, two-party society. The Reconstruction Act of 1867 was designed to do just that. Passed over Johnson's fruitless veto, the act dissolved the new provisional legislatures, disqualified thousands of former Confederates from voting or holding office, and divided ten of the eleven former Confederate states into military districts governed by U.S. Army generals. States could petition for readmittance to the Union only after they had held new constitutional conventions ratifying the recently enacted Fourteenth Amendment, which prohibited states from discriminating legally against any citizens on the basis of their race. (Tennessee, which had already ratified the amendment, was exempted from the act.) The states were also required to officially repudiate the Confederate war debt and grant universal suffrage to all eligible male voters, black and white. Twenty thousand soldiers were sent back into the South to enforce the law and preserve the peace. Their primary mission, said Charles Sumner, was to ensure "the application of morals to the administration of public affairs."

With the passage of the Reconstruction Act, Congress began vigorously applying those morals to the prostrate South. From the start, Congressional Reconstruction was as much about hard-core partisan politics as it was about racial equality. The widespread disenfranchisement of former Confederates, together with the mandated enrollment of all southern black men on the voting rolls, had the practical effect of driving the Democratic party underground. Its ranks already thinned by war, the party became for a time as much a ghost as the restless shadows that flitted over the battlefields at Shiloh, Chickamauga, and Fredericksburg. In some southern states, Democrats resorted to what was known as the "possum policy"—holding no public meetings, nominating no candidates for office, and masking their former political affiliation in such new, vaguely conciliatory-sounding identities as the Conservative, the Conservative Union, and the Constitutional Union parties. Meanwhile, in the North, the lingering charge that the Democrats had undercut the Union war effort burdened the party with an enormous political handicap. Despite representing, on paper, between 44 and 49.5 percent of all American voters in the four years immediately following the Civil War, the Democratic party found itself, in the words of historian Charles H. Coleman, "in a position of political impotence greater than at any time in its history."

With the Democrats thus in disarray, the Republicans sought to consolidate their hold on power. Paramount to their efforts was the nurturing of friendly new governments in the South. In dozens of quasi-patriotic Union Leagues, private social clubs open to loyal men of both races, Republican party operatives began instructing black voters in the judicious use of their newfound political strength. With most white voters in the South either disqualified from voting or else refusing to participate in what they considered sham elections, Republican governments quickly assumed control in the affected states. Led by an uneasy amalgam of northern-born carpetbaggers, politicians and businessmen who had immigrated to the South after the Civil War, and homegrown scalawags, southern Unionists who had chosen to assist the Reconstruction process for a variety of selfless or not so selfless reasons, the new governments were viewed by most white southerners as nothing more than arrant frauds. Nevertheless, by the fall of 1868 all but three of the former Confederate states had been readmitted to the Union (Georgia, Alabama, and Texas had chosen to remain under army control rather than ratify the Fourteenth Amendment). The national impact was felt immediately when Republican nominee Ulysses S. Grant was elected president by a comfortable majority in the Electoral College, including fifty-two votes from the now reconstructed

South, despite receiving a notable minority of the overall white vote in the country at large.

With Grant's election, the Republican party seemed unassailable. But southern whites soon began a violent and determined struggle to regain political power within their own states. Led by such shadowy organizations as the Knights of the White Camellia, the Black Cavalry, the Red Shirts, the Men of Justice, the White Brotherhood, the Knights of the Rising Sun, the White Line, the Constitutional Union Guard, and most notorious of all, the Ku Klux Klan, disgruntled southerners commenced a largely ad hoc but nevertheless brutally effective campaign of physical force and psychological intimidation aimed at reversing the process of Reconstruction. Carpetbaggers, scalawags, politically active blacks—anyone showing the least Republican leanings—were subjected to all manner of violent abuse, including death. No one knows how many victims, black and white, were assaulted during the peak years of Klan activity between 1868 and 1871, but the numbers certainly totaled in the thousands. A careful count by the Freedmen's Bureau in Georgia in 1868, for example, reported 142 attacks between August and October of that year, including thirty-one killings, forty-three shootings, five stabbings, fifty-five beatings, and eight whippings of between three hundred and five hundred lashes apiece.

Klan violence was never systematic—in some parts of the South there was none at all—nor was it officially condoned by the Democratic party. Nevertheless, if only by default, the Democrats were the political beneficiaries of a ruthless and well-thought-out campaign that was carefully designed to expose and exploit the most glaring weakness of the Reconstruction governments, their inability to protect the lives of their citizens. One former Confederate officer admitted as much, testifying later that the Klan's primary objective had been "to defy the reconstructed State Governments, to treat them with contempt, and show that they have no real existence." South Carolina planter John Winsmith, who was shot seven times in a raging gun battle with forty Klansmen one night in 1870, ruefully conceded that the Klan had proved its point. "I consider a government which does not protect its citizens an utter failure," he said.

Eventually the federal government stepped in to put a stop to the most notorious abuses, passing the Ku Klux Klan Act of 1871, which made politically motivated violence a federal offense. Prosecutors armed with sweeping new powers fanned out across the South, arresting thousands of suspected Klan members—sometimes on the flimsiest of grounds. Democrats in Congress denounced the act as an unwarranted infringement on the legal authority of the individual states, and even some Republicans questioned the constitutionality of the act (Missouri senator Carl Schurz, for one, privately considered the new act "insane"). Despite the resistance, Attorney General Amos T. Akerman, himself a former carpetbagger, managed to convict hundreds of the Klan's alleged ringleaders, sending some to prisons as far away as Albany, New York. But by then great damage had been done to the social comity—and Republican political aspirations—of the region. In state after state southern "redeemers," usually Democrats, recaptured control of their local governments. Once back in power, they did not intend to give it up again without a fight.

IN THE MIDST of the Ku Klux Klan investigations, Grant was reelected president in 1872, defeating a quixotic bid by former abolitionist newspaper editor Horace Greeley to get reform-minded Republicans and southern Democrats to "clasp hands across the bloody chasm" and unite in an effort to unseat the general. Greeley, in his mild-mannered, slightly absentminded way, promised to rid the nation of creeping Grantism, a combination of inept misgovernment, political cronyism, and outright fraud that soon gave the nation such disturbing events as Black Friday, an attempt by Wall Street financiers Jay Gould and James Fisk to corner the gold market (with the help of Grant's brother-in-law Abel R. Corbin); the Emma Mine affair, in which the American ambassador to Great Britain helped peddle shares in a worthless Nevada silver mine to his credulous hosts; and the Crédit Mobilier scandal, in which officers in the frenchified holding company skimmed off huge profits from the federally subsidized Union Pacific Railroad and allegedly bribed selected government officials, including Grant's own vice president, Schuyler Colfax, Speaker of the House James G. Blaine, and future president James A. Garfield, then a young congressman from Ohio.

Outraged and disgusted by the seemingly endless succession of scandals both within and without the Grant administration, a loose coalition of rebellious Republicans had come together in early 1872 in a concerted effort to deny Grant a second term in office. The group, calling themselves Liberal Republicans, was led by Carl Schurz, a former Union general who had learned his first lessons in political morality on the broken barricades of revolutionary Germany. Also enlisting in the fight were Supreme Court Chief Justice Salmon P. Chase, a holdover from the more elevated days of Abraham Lincoln; former secretary of the interior Jacob D. Cox, who had resigned his post in protest of the rampant fraud surrounding the chronically ill-run Indian Bureau; and a virtual Who's Who of East Coast intellectuals, including Harvard historian Henry Adams and his father, elder statesman Charles Francis Adams, Sr.; William Cullen Bryant, James Russell Lowell, Edwin L. Godkin of *The Nation,* and David A. Wells, editor of the *North American Review.* Iowa senator James Grimes, who had first broken party ranks to vote against the impeachment of Andrew Johnson, summarized the Liberal Republican view that the party was "going to the dogs. Like all parties that have an undisturbed power for a long time," said Grimes, "it has become corrupt, and I believe that it is today the most corrupt and debauched political party that has ever existed."

Despite receiving the nominations of both the breakaway Liberal Republican and Democratic parties, Greeley's campaign was a hopeless cause from the start, led by perhaps the most bizarre candidate ever to be nominated by a major party. In his time as editor of the *New York Tribune,* Greeley had championed such outré ideas as vegetarianism, spiritualism, socialism, prohibitionism, and the gastronomical virtues of plain brown bread. To his Republican opponents, particularly in the South, his call for southern home rule and universal amnesty for former Confederates sounded no less bizarre; and his choice of such surrogate spokesmen as Georgia Democrat John B. Gordon, a prominent Confederate general and widely suspected Ku Klux Klan grand dragon, was misguided, to say the least.

Republicans, predictably, struck back hard. "Go vote to burn school houses, desecrate churches and violate women," Massachusetts congressman Benjamin Butler thundered, "or go vote for Horace Greeley, which means the same thing." *Harper's Weekly* cartoonist Thomas Nast, a razor-sharp Republican partisan, lampooned Greeley mercilessly, depicting the candidate shaking hands with a Confederate who has just shot a Union soldier, stretching out his hand to John Wilkes Booth across the grave of Abraham Lincoln, and turning over a defenseless black man to the Ku Klux Klan. "I have been assailed so bitterly," said Greeley in a rare understatement, "that I hardly knew whether I was running for the presidency or the penitentiary." Less than a month after the election, he died in a New York state insane asylum, mentally and physically shattered by his trials.

Grant's reelection, although a personal triumph for the president, marked the beginning of the end of Congressional Reconstruction. Charles Sumner, one of its leading proponents in the Senate, had broken party ranks to support Greeley's candidacy as a way of protesting Grant's planned annexation of the Caribbean nation of Santo Domingo. The temporary marriage of convenience between Liberal Republicans and southern Democrats gave the Democrats an unexpected measure of respectability in northern eyes. At the same time, the utter failure of the fusion ticket confirmed southern hard-liners in their belief that only a "straight-out" campaign of racially divisive politics could drive sufficient numbers of white voters to the polls to overturn the remaining Reconstruction governments. Henceforth, southern Democrats would look to themselves for their deliverance, counting on white pride and white firepower to reverse the tenuous gains that blacks had made. A Mississippi newspaper masthead neatly summed up the growing consensus: "A white man's government, by white men, for the benefit of white men." Political leaders in the state vowed ominously to carry the next election "peaceably if we can, forcibly if we must."

The increased southern militancy was met—as some far-seeing southerners had anticipated—by a growing weariness on the part of northerners to continue concerning themselves with southern affairs. For the better part of two decades, the people of the North had seen their lives dominated, personally and politically, by the implacable and inexhaustible firebrands of the South. Now, nearly a decade after the Civil War had been brought to a successful conclusion, the vacant chairs of dead Union patriots still held their melancholy pride of place at Sunday dinners throughout the North, and defiant southerners, like ungracious dinner guests, were still arguing, resisting, defying, and demanding. It was time, many northerners felt, to get on with their own lives, particularly now that the economy had turned sour and their own pocketbooks were beginning to feel the pinch. "The truth is, our people are tired out with this worn out cry of 'Southern outrages,'" Michigan Republican Thomas Wilson wrote. "Hard times and heavy taxes make them wish the 'nigger,' 'everlasting nigger,' were in ____ or Africa." As any black man living in the South could have told them, he and his fellows were a long way from Africa.

THE FIRST TEST of the new "White Line" system of southern resistance came in Louisiana in 1873. A contested gubernatorial election the previous fall had resulted in two governors, two legislatures, and no effective leadership. The Republican governor, William P. Kellogg, held court in the statehouse, protected by a praetorian guard of United States Army troops dispatched to New Orleans by President Grant at the behest of his brother-in-law James F. Casey, the collector of customs at the city port. Meanwhile, the Democratic gubernatorial claimant, John F. McEnery, set up office in the nearby Odd Fellows Hall. Each "governor" proceeded to issue decrees, confer with his legislature, and appoint his own slate of handpicked loyalists. Kellogg prevailed in New Orleans proper, but in the isolated Louisiana countryside McEnery's supporters conducted a determined campaign of civil disobedience, refusing to pay taxes, obey Kellogg's orders, or turn over the keys to their government buildings. A newly organized paramilitary force, the White League, fought pitched battles with black Republicans in several rural Louisiana towns and wantonly murdered white officials in their homes. One prominent carpetbagger, Marshall H. Twitchell of Vermont, lost three members of his immediate family, as well as both his arms, in separate assassination attempts.

Kept apprised of the depredations, Grant vacillated between sending more federal troops to Louisiana and letting Kellogg and his fellow Republicans go it alone. The president did not like Kellogg—"a first-class cuss," he called him—and wondered privately about the wisdom of continuing to prop up a regime whose power did not extend much farther than the shadows cast by the soldiers' bayonets on the steps of the capitol. "The muddle down there is almost beyond my fathoming," Grant complained to the *New York Herald*. Events came to a head in September 1874, two months before the next legislative election, after Kellogg had signed a law giving him the power to appoint all state voting registrars. Fearing, not illogically, that the Republicans planned to steal the election, a force of several thousand White Leaguers confronted an equal number of metropolitan police and black militia at the Battle of Liberty Place, in downtown New Orleans, on September 14. After routing the Republican forces, the White Leaguers seized the statehouse, city hall, and various police stations and arsenals. Kellogg and his supporters took refuge in the customhouse, where a skeleton force of three hundred U.S. soldiers provided a measure of largely symbolic protection.

Faced with a dearth of palatable choices, from sending in more troops to formally recognizing McEnery to simply doing nothing, Grant left it up to his cabinet to decide. Ultimately, it was felt that the least bad—if not necessarily the best—choice was to restore Kellogg to power, if for no other reason than to dissuade other unredeemed southern states from staging similar coups in the future. Accordingly, Grant dispatched five thousand troops and three gunboats to New Orleans under the command of Major General Phil Sheridan, Grant's fiery old cavalry commander during the war. Sheridan's well-earned reputation for ruthlessness preceded him, and the White Leaguers hastily withdrew from the captured government buildings. Sheridan confidently advised the White House that he did not expect any more trouble.

But the ever-truculent general, who had spent several months in New Orleans the previous decade grappling with the Gordian knot of Louisiana politics, should have known better. As it was, he badly underestimated the brazen resourcefulness of Pelican State Democrats. Following another disputed election in which the Democrats seemed to have carried the day, the state returning board threw out enough votes to reduce the total of Democratic legislators from eighty to fifty-three— by unremarkable coincidence the exact number of Republican members remaining in the body. When the new legislature convened at the be-

ginning of January 1875, the Democrats mounted a lightning-fast parliamentary maneuver, installing their own speaker of the house, appointing a cadre of pistol-packing sergeants-at-arms, and awarding all
the contested seats to their fellow Democrats. When Republican lawmakers resisted the strong-arm tactics by rushing out of the room to
prevent a quorum, the Democrats manhandled five recalcitrant legislators back into the chamber to give them the necessary number of warm
bodies, then persuaded Colonel Phillipe Regis de Trobriand, the commander of federal troops at the statehouse, to forcibly remove the other
Republican "idlers" from the premises.

Sheridan, getting wind of de Trobriand's actions, immediately ordered him to return to the statehouse, readmit the Republican officials,
and expel the newly seated Democrats from the building. The next day,
he made a bad situation worse by recommending to the White House
that anyone resisting his orders be summarily declared "banditti" and
arrested on sight. He proposed to try the offenders before a military tribunal, and urged visiting Massachusetts congressman George F. Hoar
to return to Washington and convince his fellow lawmakers "to suspend the what-do-you-call-it"—meaning the right of habeas corpus—
and leave any further adjudicating to Sheridan himself.

Sheridan's heavy-handed tactics and intemperate language provoked
a firestorm of criticism. Democratic senator Thomas F. Bayard of
Delaware, a likely presidential candidate in 1876, led the way, accusing
Sheridan of "riding rough-shod" over the Bill of Rights. The general, said
Bayard, with a pointed choice of words, was "not even fit to breathe the
air of a republican government." On the other side of the aisle, Missouri
senator Carl Schurz, a leader of the Liberal Republican movement in
1872, found Sheridan's actions "so appalling that every American citizen
who loves his liberty stands aghast. How long before a soldier may stalk
into the national House of Representatives, and pointing to the
Speaker's mace, say 'Take away that bauble!'" Public protests were held
in Boston and New York, and venerable old poet William Cullen Bryant
told the New York gathering that Sheridan should "tear off his epaulets
and break his sword and fling the fragments into the Potomac." Even the
New York Times, a dependable Republican mouthpiece, fretted fastidi-
ously "that a very able graduate of West Point, and a soldier who has so

gallantly and faithfully fought for the supremacy of the Constitution, should know so little of its requirements."

The nation's leading Democratic newspapers were less subdued. Grant, warned the *New York Tribune,* was likely to "decide who shall belong to the next Congress and enforce his decisions by five or six regiments of United States troops." The *Cincinnati Enquirer* termed Sheridan's actions "the crowning iniquity of a Federal administration not wanting in iniquities." And in New Orleans, the *Daily Picayune* noted that "for the first time in the history of the United States, armed soldiers have invaded a legislative hall, and bayonets have been used to expel the representatives of the people from their seats." It was, said the newspaper, "the most violent, the most illegal, the most shameless act yet permitted by an administration whose history is one of violence, illegality and shamelessness unparalleled in the history of any free government."

Shocked and dismayed by the avalanche of criticism, Grant quickly disavowed support of Sheridan's actions. In an extraordinary message to the Senate on January 13, the president maintained—a little weakly, given the circumstances—that he had "no desire to have United States troops interfere in the domestic concerns of Louisiana or any other state." Sheridan, he said, had merely gone to New Orleans "to observe and report." Somewhat plaintively, Grant asked Congress to send a committee to New Orleans to investigate matters and make recommendations. Led by New York representative William A. Wheeler, a moderate Republican, the committee found that the returning board had acted in a way that was "unjust, illegal, and arbitrary," in reducing the apparent Democratic triumph to a legislative dead heat. The committee expressed its "emphatic disapprobation" of the board's high-handed actions, which it described as "attempting to cure one wrong by another."

Following Wheeler's lead, the committee hammered out a compromise that pleased neither party particularly, but that managed to preserve—at least for the time being—what passed for peace in Louisiana. Under the Wheeler compromise, the state House of Representatives was conceded to the Democrats, in return for a promise by White Leaguers not to forcibly eject Kellogg from the governor's chair. It was a transparently face-saving plan, but one that enjoyed widespread popular support in the North. Lost in all the public acclaim was a prescient warning from Andrew Johnson's former attorney general, William M. Evarts, that such "high-handed acts of military subversion of civil government" might encourage similar tampering in future presidential elections.

MISSISSIPPI DEMOCRATS, watching events play out across the border in Louisiana, were quick to test Grant's newfound reluctance to intervene in southern affairs. In the state capital of Jackson, Republican governor Adelbert Ames, Massachusetts congressman Benjamin Butler's son-in-law, maintained a tenuous hold on power, surrounded by a variegated lot of corrupt officials, including a black lieutenant governor who took advantage of Ames's frequent absences from the state (Mrs. Ames could not abide the Mississippi weather) to pardon cronies, levy taxes, and appoint his friends to political positions. State attorney general George E. Harris, himself a scalawag, complained personally to Grant that Ames and his associates "were a close corporation of mercenary men."

Ames did not share Harris's bleak assessment. A West Point graduate, Union general, and certified war hero—he was awarded the Medal of Honor for his gallant conduct at the First Battle of Bull Run—Ames was typical of the many racially idealistic and politically ambitious northerners who had come south following the war to help create a new Republican majority. He had been, at one time or another, provisional governor, military commander, United States senator, and now governor of Mississippi. In each position he saw himself not as an intruder, but as a moral exemplar from a more elevated region of the country. "The carpetbagger represents northern civilization, northern liberty and has a hold on the hearts of the colored people that nothing can destroy," Ames declared. "He is the positive element of the party, and if the South is to be redeemed from the way of slavery it must be done by him."

Despite such lofty ideals, by the autumn of 1874 Ames had managed to fritter away his political advantages in one of the two southern states where blacks constituted a majority (South Carolina was the other). When violence flared in Vicksburg in December 1874, following the election of a black sheriff, Grant acceded to Ames's request and sent a force of several hundred soldiers into the Mississippi River town where eleven years earlier he had won a decisive Civil War victory. The federal soldiers restored the peace, but nine months later, following a full-scale race riot at Clinton after a black policeman had shot two unruly white men at a Republican political rally, the president shied away from renewed intervention. On vacation at the New Jersey seashore, Grant left it up to Attorney General Edwards Pierrepont to decide what—if anything—to do, admitting rather lamely that he was "somewhat perplexed to know what directions to give in the matter." Grant added, in a postscript that Pierrepont immediately quoted back to Ames, "The whole public are tired out with these annual, autumnal outbreaks in the South, and there is so much unwholesome lying done by the press and people in regard to the cause and extent of these breaches of the peace that the great majority are ready now to condemn any interference on the part of the government."

Abandoned to his own devices, with no additional federal troops to back his play, Ames worked out the best deal he could make under the circumstances. Meeting with leading Democrats, he agreed to demobilize the state militia in return for an unenforceable pledge that the Democrats would end the bloodshed and guarantee a fair election that November. The ensuing election, in November 1875, was indeed peaceful, if not exactly fair. There was no need for violence now: an unprecedented turnout of white voters—more than 90 percent, the largest in state history—went to the polls and, in the course of one day, wiped out a decade's worth of Reconstruction in the state. The Democrats won the treasurer's office, the only statewide election, by nearly 32,000 votes, captured four of six congressional seats, and took control of both chambers of the legislature. Ames, who made a show of playing croquet on election day on the front lawn of the executive mansion, shrugged off the results with a weariness that belied his forced insouciance. "No matter if they are going to carry the state," he said, "let them carry it, and let us be at peace and have no more killing." Privately, however, he lamented to his wife that "a revolution has taken place—by force of arms—and a race are disfranchised—they are to be returned to a condition of serfdom—an era of second slavery."

Ames was under no illusions about the ultimate cause of his down-fall. "I am fighting for the Negro," he told his wife, "and to the whole country a white man is better than a 'Nigger.'" He admitted that his call for renewed federal intervention after the Clinton incident may have been an "exploding shell in the political canvass at the North," but he was bitter nonetheless at the lack of interest his fellow northerners had displayed toward blacks in the South. "When the liberties of the people were in jeopardy," Ames said, "the nation abandoned us for political reasons." The Grant administration, he maintained, "should have acted, but it was 'tired of the annual autumnal outbreaks in the South.' The political death of the Negro will forever release the nation from the weariness from such 'political outbreaks.'" And Ames had some pointed words for his fellow Republicans. "The Republican candidate for [the] presidency next year may want this state," he observed, "but he as well might want the moon for a toy."

Ames's political intuitions were sharper than he may have realized at the time. Mississippi congressman John R. Lynch, one of the few black politicians in the state to hold on to their seats in the 1875 land-slide, visited Grant at the White House a few weeks after the election. According to Lynch, the president told him that he had been pressured before the election by a delegation of Ohio Republicans not to intervene in Mississippi. Former Ohio governor Rutherford B. Hayes—not one of the delegation—had been brought out of retirement to reclaim the state from its incumbent Democratic governor. Any federal intervention in Mississippi, Grant's visitors had warned, might redound against Republican chances in Ohio—a state that was considered far more important in the overall scheme of national politics than Louisiana. Lynch did not reveal his meeting with Grant until many years later, but word of the meeting apparently got back to Ames, perhaps through his well-placed father-in-law, Congressman Butler. "I was sacrificed," Ames told his wife a few months later, "that Mr. Hayes might be made Gov[ernor] of Ohio."

Although his own term of office was not up for another three years, Ames resigned the governorship in March 1876, a few weeks after the new Democratic legislature began impeachment proceedings against him for alleged misconduct in office. "Nothing is charged beyond political sins," Ames explained to a northern friend. "Their object is to restore the Confederacy and reduce the colored people to a state of serfdom. I am in their way, consequently they impeach me." Following his resignation, Ames left Mississippi for good. He returned to Massachusetts, bought into a textile mill, and made a fortune. During the remainder of his long and varied life—he lived until the age of ninety-seven, the last surviving Civil War general on either side—Ames hobnobbed with fellow millionaires John D. Rockefeller and Henry M. Flagler, wintered on the French Riviera, and even took part in the Spanish-American War, where he made friends with fellow general Joseph Wheeler, the onetime Confederate cavalry commander. He also patented a number of inventions, from complex flour mill machinery to simple pencil sharpeners. But for all his subsequent financial success, Ames never forgot his days in Mississippi, nor did he apologize for his actions there. Asked why he got into politics in the first place, the old carpetbagger replied: "My explanation may seem ludicrous now, but then, it seemed to me that I had a Mission with a large M."

BY THE SPRING of 1876, that mission was largely finished—not just for Ames but for other like-minded Republicans in the South. With the Democrats' recapture of Mississippi, only South Carolina, Florida, and Louisiana were still unredeemed. Congressional Reconstruction in the South was as good as over, and so it seemed was Republican control of the White House. While most Americans were busy making plans to visit the Centennial Exposition or stockpiling fireworks for the nation's gala birthday celebration, sharp-eyed professionals in both parties were preparing no less intently to choose their presidential nominees. Faced with the prospect of a truly competitive election for the first time since before the Civil War, party elders had no shortage of potential candidates. But eventually, perhaps inevitably, their eyes began to focus on two men who, except for being governors of large northern states, differed from each other in virtually every way possible: governors Rutherford B. Hayes of Ohio and Samuel J. Tilden of New York. On them rested the hopes, the fears, and the unresolved desires of forty million of their fellow Americans, who looked to them for a way out of the social and political morass that sixteen years of war, hatred, greed, and corruption had wrought on the body politic. Nearly eight years after Ulysses S. Grant had been elected president on the vague campaign platform "Let us have peace," the nation was still waiting for that peace to descend, like Noah's dove, out of the dark and lowering sky.

CHAPTER TWO

A THIRD-RATE NONENTITY

F OR ALL THE SEEMING inevitability—after the fact—of Rutherford
B. Hayes's march to the Republican presidential nomination in 1876,
the truth of the matter was that the party entered the centennial year
more perplexed and divided than at any other time during its brief but
eventful twenty-year history. Nowhere was this division more obvious
than in the unhealed split between the current administration of President Ulysses S. Grant and the loose coalition of Liberal Republicans
that had tried, with notable unsuccess, to drive him from office four
years earlier.

A few days after the opening of the Centennial Exhibition in
Philadelphia, a self-described "meeting of notables" convened in New
York City to discuss what role, if any, reform-minded liberals should play
in the upcoming presidential campaign. The prestigious gathering, an
invitation-only affair, reunited two hundred of the leading figures from
the Liberal Republican convention of 1872, which had ill-advisedly nominated the gallant but unelectable Horace Greeley for president, thereby
insuring the landslide reelection of Grant. This time around, the liberals
did not intend to make the same mistake; they would examine potential
candidates carefully before deciding which one to favor with the coveted
if unofficial imprimatur of reformer-in-chief.

The meeting was the brainchild of Henry Adams, an idealistic young
history professor at Harvard. Not yet the apolitical isolate he would become later in life, the Massachusetts-based Adams was an early and enthusiastic booster of Republican treasury secretary Benjamin Bristow of
Kentucky. Bristow's reputation for personal honesty and professional

integrity, as evidenced by his successful prosecution of the Whiskey Ring a few months earlier, had made him the idol of thousands of law-abiding Americans everywhere who were disgusted by the seemingly endless procession of scandals emanating from the nation's capital. At the same time his stand, however principled, had alienated him from Republican party regulars—starting with President Grant—and Bristow had no chance of receiving the party's presidential nomination in 1876. "Nothing is more certain than that Mr. Bristow cannot be nominated," Adams wrote to Liberal Republican leader Carl Schurz on February 14, 1876. "The chances are a thousand to one against the nomination of any man who has made so many enemies as he." Adams hoped, instead, to use Bristow's growing renown and reputation for honesty to found a new, independent "party of the center," with the embattled treasury secretary as its cornerstone. He encouraged Schurz and a half-dozen other leading reformers to send out a circular to other like-minded in-dividuals, inviting them to come to New York and discuss launching such a movement with Bristow as their candidate.

Schurz, who had recently lost his Missouri Senate seat to an old-line southern Democrat, agreed in principle with Adams—he had been considering just such a meeting himself—but he changed the proposed time of the gathering from one week after the Republican National Convention to one month prior to it, in the slender hope that the con-vocation might have some impact, however slight, on the party's choice of standard-bearer. Schurz did not share Adams's enthusiasm for Bristow—or any other candidate, for that matter. The primary aim of the reform movement, he felt, was not to select a particular candi-date, but "to consider what could be done to prevent the national elec-tion of the centennial year from becoming a mere choice of evils." Despite his reservations, Schurz agreed to spearhead the conference, joining William Cullen Bryant of the *New York Evening Post*, President Theodore Dwight Woolsey of Yale, former Massachusetts governor Alexander H. Bullock, and Horace White, editor of the *Chicago Tribune*, in undersigning the invitation.

Still mourning the death that winter of his forty-four-year-old wife, Margarethe, from complications following childbirth, Schurz threw himself headlong into planning the conference. The first order of business, as suggested by Adams, was to sound out Bristow on his willingness to serve as the reformers' candidate. Schurz personally assured Bristow that "your name will not be trifled or made free with, and that you will in no manner be compromised or embarrassed by me and those under my influences." At the same time, he warned Bristow that "the party men would surely prevent the nomination of a true reformer for the presidency, unless they were made very clearly to understand that they cannot do so with impunity. That class of politicians will control the Republican Convention, and they will do the worst they dare. Nothing but the alternative of the nomination of a true reformer, or defeat, will induce them to permit the former."

Schurz sent Henry Cabot Lodge, then a young doctoral student of Adams, to Washington to meet with Bristow and his supporters. Schurz wanted Lodge to ascertain whether Bristow would "give us any sort of assurance that he will if necessary accept an independent nomination." Accordingly, Lodge had several private audiences with the embattled cabinet member, who complained of being "distracted, disavowed and thwarted in every underhand treacherous way possible" by the political spoilsmen around the White House. But Bristow made it clear that he still hoped to win the Republican nomination, and Lodge was reluctant to ask him directly if he would accept an independent bid. Somewhat misleadingly, Lodge assured Schurz that "the approach has been fairly made and his mind prepared," but neglected to add that, like a nervous suitor, he had failed to pop the crucial question.

Given Bristow's continuing reluctance to leave the Republican party, Schurz felt the reformers might have to return to their "first love" and endorse Charles Francis Adams, Sr., the former American minister to Great Britain, who had lost the Liberal Republican nomination to Horace Greeley four years earlier. The unsentimental Henry Adams did not see the wisdom in that; he reluctantly recognized both his father's increasing senility and his glaring lack of a political base, even in his home state of Massachusetts, where within the past year he had lost separate bids for the U.S. Senate and the governorship. Critics described the elder Adams, with some reason, as "that lonely political Selkirk whose cold family lies around him like seals on the Island of

Juan Fernandez." Secretary of State Hamilton Fish, himself a long shot for the Republican presidential nomination, joked that the country had just enjoyed the "annually returning periodical demand for a pure, an exemplary statement in the person of Charles Francis Adams—Governor, President—Town Clerk or something."

Fish may have been amused by the hunger of millions of his fellow citizens for a purer and more exemplary leader than his own superior in the White House had proven to be, but the hunger was still there—if anything, it was growing. The steady accretion of scandals—none of which, to be fair, touched Grant himself—had made the term "Grantism" a much reviled political epithet and imposed on any would-be Republican presidential nominee a formidable, if not fatal, handicap. The task of reform-minded Republicans in 1876 was to find, if possible, a candidate who could somehow embody the bedrock values of the party—high tariffs, sound money, a strong federal government, universal suffrage—while at the same time managing to avoid the widening stain of corruption that, like the mark of Cain, had scarred the face of politics. It was a daunting challenge to both sides of a Liberal Republican's self-identity.

For that matter, not all liberals invited to the conference were Republicans. Some, in fact, favored New York governor Samuel Tilden, a proven reformer and friend of Wall Street who seemed likely to win the Democratic presidential nomination. But Schurz, despite his 1872 apostasy, remained a committed party man, and under no circumstances would he permit the conference to formally endorse Tilden, whom he considered "too much a wire puller and machine politician." If he could not convince the liberals to embrace Charles Francis Adams as a symbol of their high ideals, then Schurz was perfectly willing to wait for the Republican convention before deciding whom to support. He did, however, take the liberty of speaking for everyone in the reform movement when he declared flatly that they would support no candidate, "however conspicuous his position or brilliant his ability [who] is not publicly known to possess those qualities of mind and character which the stern task of genuine reform requires." How, exactly, this disqualified Tilden, Schurz did not say.

The conference got under way on the afternoon of May 15 at the Fifth Avenue Hotel. In attendance was a glittering array of eastern intellectuals drawn primarily from the fields of journalism and education. A few wealthy businessmen, including Theodore Roosevelt, Sr., father of the future president, also made an appearance. One could not move through the potted palms in the lobby, noted a reporter from the *Boston Evening Transcript*, without bumping into "men whose names ring through the country and round the world[,] and upon every face was the plain stamp of intelligence and character." But the delegates, for all their undoubted intelligence, could not agree on whom to support, and the meeting soon foundered amid a welter of mixed motives and vague intentions. Schurz, in a lengthy "Address to the American People," called on the nation to "reestablish the moral character of the government," adding that "the worn-out clap-traps of fair promises in party platforms will not satisfy." An eleventh-hour motion to nominate Adams was so coolly received that it was withdrawn immediately, and Bristow's name was never raised. The meeting adjourned, an embarrassing bust, without deciding on either a candidate or a plan. Henry Adams, who pointedly did not attend the proceedings in protest of Schurz's overly partisan leadership, complained afterward that Bristow, by holding out hope for his nomination by the Republican party, had "cut his and our throats."

Critics scoffed at the Fifth Avenue meeting, calling it a convention of "soreheads and college professors[,] men who had failed in literature and in life." Said one ward heeler from Tammany Hall, the notoriously corrupt patronage machine that controlled New York City politics: "Oh, they have reenacted the moral law and the Ten Commandments for a platform, and have demanded an angel of light for president." The liberals, gibed the *New York Herald*, were the "ancient mariners on the sea of politics," and the meeting's organizers nothing more than "showmen who exhibited the distinguished actors performing a short engagement at the Fifth Avenue." The *New York Commercial Advertiser* punctured the liberals' pretensions to practicing a better form of politics. "Business yesterday at the Fifth Avenue Conference was 'cut and dried,' just as at any other political gathering," it said. Only the *New York Tribune*, a Democratic newspaper, had anything good to say about the meeting; it characterized the participants as "the saving element in American politics" and charged that "it is the parties that failed; not these men." Whether or not American politics could still be saved remained very much an open question.

THE LIBERALS MAY NOT have known who they wanted for president, but they definitely knew who they did not want: Maine congressman James G. Blaine. In this, as in many things, they were in the minority. By the spring of 1876, the charismatic Blaine was clearly the front-runner for the Republican nomination. In an era of determinedly gray, self-consciously respectable politicians, Blaine was a swatch of vivid color. To his many supporters—Blainiacs, they styled themselves—he was practically a force of nature. They called him "the magnetic man" and marveled at his remarkable memory for names and faces, the seemingly irresistible way he had of drawing people into his orbit. A lover of opera and the theater, blessed with a deep voice and an expressive way with words, Blaine was a naturally gifted performer—his stage was the floor of Congress. "Had he been a woman," said an acquaintance after one of Blaine's mellifluous speeches, "people would have rushed off to send expensive flowers."

For the past fourteen years, including six as speaker of the house, Blaine had carefully honed his political skills, always with an eye toward the bigger prize. Throughout the eight years of the Grant administration, he had walked a fine line between supporting the president personally and criticizing the scandalous doings of those around him—men with whom, said Blaine, only "a thief by instinct" had any influence. Even the Democrats were forced to admit that he had been the most effective speaker of the house since Henry Clay. That, in itself, did not stop them from deposing Blaine as soon as they had the chance and replacing him with a fellow Democrat. But, as his notorious attack on Jefferson Davis demonstrated, the loss of the speakership had, if anything, freed Blaine from bipartisan constraints and consensus-building—now he could spend all his time seeking the White House and bashing the Democrats. And despite being, at age forty-six, a little young for the presidency, by May 1876 Blaine already had won the support of a number of Republican state conventions, from his adopted home in Maine to Washington Territory. (At that time, there were no open or contested primary elections.) Momentum was building for a first-ballot nomination when the national convention met in Cincinnati in mid-June. The only thing he feared, said Blaine with airy self-confidence, was "the Great Unknown."

He had good reason to be afraid. Whispers about shady financial transactions, worthless bonds, and sweetheart loans involving Blaine and various high-rolling railroad developers had been swirling through Washington for several months. Curious journalists had parts of the story, and a high-stakes political game was being played behind the scenes to determine where, and when, to break the scoop. Reporters and editors supporting other Republican presidential hopefuls did not want to be the first ones to go public with the damaging charges, in case Blaine survived the initial blast of negative publicity and struck back hard at his tormenters. Ohio governor Rutherford B. Hayes, treasury secretary Benjamin Bristow, and Indiana senator Oliver Morton all learned of the rumors surrounding Blaine from their friends in the press, and all sat on the explosive information for several weeks. The first account of Blaine's questionable business transactions appeared on April 11 in the *Indianapolis Sentinel,* a Democratic newspaper that had no such qualms about bashing the enemy front-runner. After the first story came the deluge.

The story of Blaine's alleged misdoings was a complicated tale of influence-peddling dating back to 1869, his first year as House speaker. As detailed by the *Indianapolis Sentinel,* the *New York Sun,* and other Democratic newspapers, Blaine had overruled a motion to revoke a land grant for the Little Rock and Fort Smith Railroad. In gratitude, one of the railroad's contractors, Warren Fisher, offered him a deal selling railroad bonds on commission. That was not, strictly speaking, illegal, however unseemly it might look to modern eyes. Improving on the opportunity, Blaine told Fisher that he saw "various channels in which I can be useful," and reminded the developer that he had "unwittingly" done the railroad "a great favor" with his earlier ruling. Subsequently, Blaine sold $130,000 worth of railroad bonds to his old friends in Maine, receiving for his trouble an equal amount of stock in commission. Problems arose when the bonds declined rapidly in value. Not wanting to look like a chiseler to his friends, Blaine bought back the devalued bonds with the help of a $64,000 "loan" from Tom Scott, president of the Union Pacific Railroad. The loan was never called in by Scott, a man who knew the value of a good investment. Blaine, who had not really profited from the transaction, put the affair down to painful experience and tried very hard to forget all about it.

Following the first newspaper accounts, Blaine engaged in political damage control, declaring from the floor of the House that his railroad transactions had been "open as the day," and maintaining that "instead of making a large fortune out of that company, I have incurred a severe pecuniary loss from my investment in its securities, which I still retain." He read letters from Scott and various officials in the New York brokerage house which had handled the transactions denying that the speaker had ever received money or stocks in compensation. "This closes the testimony I have wished to offer," Blaine told his colleagues with an air of injured dignity. Friends assured him that he had put the matter to rest.

The House Judiciary Committee, which for some time had been looking into the octopus-like reach of the Union Pacific Railroad, was not persuaded. Committee chairman Proctor Knott, a Kentucky Democrat, appointed a three-man subcommittee to follow up the allegations. Two of the three were southern Democrats, Eppa Hunton of Virginia and Thomas Ashe of North Carolina. Blaine was convinced that the investigation was political payback for his attack on Davis. Knott, he said, had passed over seven northern Democrats on the Judiciary Committee to appoint the only two "who were from the South and had been in the rebel army." He was half right: Hunton had indeed served in the Confederate army, leading a Virginia regiment during the war and taking part in Pickett's Charge at Gettysburg, where he suffered a severe wound and won a promotion to brigadier general. But Ashe, a prewar attorney and former Whig, had not actively served the southern cause (he was close to fifty when the war began), and since the war he had played a lead role in helping his fellow North Carolinians accept the painful verdict of arms.

Blaine's biggest problem with the subcommittee was not its members, but the surprise witness it called to appear on May 31. His name was James Mulligan, and he had kept the books for Warren Fisher, the erstwhile developer of the Little Rock and Fort Smith Railroad. Blaine knew Mulligan through his brother-in-law, Jacob Stanwood, who had fired the clerk on an unrelated matter some years earlier. What he did not know, although he quickly learned, was that Mulligan had in his possession a number of letters that Blaine had written to Fisher detailing the full extent of his personal involvement in the sale and repurchase of the worthless railroad bonds. As soon as Mulligan began his testimony, an ashen-faced Blaine leaned over to the only Republican member of the subcommittee, William Lawrence of Ohio, and whispered urgently, "Move an adjournment." Hunton, who overheard the request, noticed that "the mention of [Mulligan's] letters seemed to have a remarkable effect on Mr. Blaine."

Blaine hurried over to Mulligan's hotel, where, if Mulligan is to be believed, the distraught politician begged him prayerfully to return the letters, asked him to think of Blaine's wife and six children, and even hinted that he was contemplating suicide. As an added inducement, said Mulligan, Blaine "asked me if I would not like a consulship." Using all his vaunted powers of persuasion, Blaine somehow got Mulligan to let him "hold" the letters; he immediately stuffed them into his coat pocket and dashed out of the hotel, leaving the astonished bookkeeper goggling helplessly in his wake.

For the better part of a week, Blaine refused repeated demands from the Judiciary Committee to turn over the letters, saying they had "no more connection with the examination now going on than the man in the moon." Morever, he said, they were "strictly private letters" which Mulligan had been wrong to take from company files in the first place. There was nothing in the letters, Blaine assured the committee, that he would have the slightest occasion to "blush over."

Blaine was in an untenable position, politically if not legally. On the morning of June 5 he rose from his desk in the House of Representatives on a point of personal privilege. Flourishing the bundle of letters above his head, he abruptly slammed it down, declaring forcefully: "I am not afraid to show the letters. Thank God Almighty! I am not afraid to show them. There they are . . . the very original package. And with some sense of humiliation, with a mortification which I do not pretent to conceal, with a sense of outrage which I trust any man in my position would feel, I invite the confidence of forty-four million of my fellow countrymen while I read those letters from this desk."

What followed, said Knott, was "one of the most extraordinary exhibitions of histrionic skill, one of the most consummate pieces of acting that ever occurred upon any stage on earth." For over an hour Blaine read the letters aloud. Or, more accurately, he read portions of the letters. It was the performance of a lifetime, and it almost worked. By shuffling the letters artfully and reading only those parts that showed him in a favorable light, Blaine managed to convey an impression of total candor. House members and an overflow crowd of spectators in the gallery listened transfixed. "I have never witnessed so dramatic a scene since I have been in the House," said Ohio congressman James Garfield. "It may give Blaine the nomination." Knott was unconvinced. "Your friend Blaine," he responded, "is the Goddamnedest scoundrel in America."

Once again Blaine's supporters rushed to congratulate him for weathering the storm. "How splendidly Mr. Blaine held himself in his fight with the ex-Confederates of the committee," wrote New England poet John Greenleaf Whittier. "He has cleared himself of all charges against him." Even Blaine's chief rival for the Republican presidential nomination, Benjamin Bristow, got in on the act. "You have macerated these scamps," he wrote from Philadelphia, where he was attending the Centennial Exposition. "With head erect and defiant tone you have scattered the wretched crew of calumniators and spies on private life and private intercourse." If Bristow had hoped to mend fences with his political opponent, he was badly mistaken. Blaine attributed the whole sorry mess to a shadowy cabal of Cincinnati newsmen who were sympathetic to Bristow's candidacy.

For the time being, at least, Blaine had managed to evade censure. With the Republican National Convention looming the next week, the exhausted front-runner hoped to forestall further questioning. Three days before the convention was due to begin, Blaine engaged in another round of histrionics. Walking to church on a swelteringly hot Sunday from his Washington home a mile away, Blaine mounted the steps of the

Congregational Church, raised his hand to heaven, cried, "My head, my head!" and swooned gracefully into his wife's arms. Taken home in a cab, he lay unconscious for the next two days, while a steady stream of visitors trudged in and out, muttering darkly about "political assassination" and vowing revenge on the unseen forces. At least one newspaper, the Democratic-leaning *New York Sun*, was unmoved by the dramaturgy. "Blaine Feigns a Faint," it captioned the story.

In Columbus, Ohio, Rutherford B. Hayes, having heard rumors for weeks that he was Blaine's choice to join him on the GOP ticket as the vice presidential candidate, dashed off a letter to the stricken hero. "I have just read with deepest emotions of sorrow the account of your illness," he wrote. "My eyes are almost blinded with tears as I write. All good men among your countrymen will pray as I do for your immediate and complete recovery. This affects me as I was affected by the death of Lincoln. God bless you and restore you." Not to be outdone, Bristow went to call on Blaine in person. He never got past the front door. Blaine's wife, Harriet, was furious with Bristow over an article in a Kentucky newspaper that hinted (correctly, it would seem) that the future Mrs. Blaine had been inconveniently pregnant at the time of her marriage. Rightly or wrongly, she blamed Bristow for the story. Meeting him at the door, Mrs. Blaine said acidly, "Mr. Bristow, you have got your will now; don't come in here." Mortified, Bristow promptly withdrew, but the story of his rebuff quickly made the rounds, and the episode served to stiffen the resolve of Bristow's supporters to block Blaine's nomination by any means possible.

Two days later, like Jairus's daughter in the Bible, Blaine awoke from his slumber, miraculously unfazed by his ordeal. By then the House Judiciary Committee had postponed indefinitely any further hearings on the Mulligan letters. At Blaine's insistence, his son Walker invited Secretary of State Hamilton Fish to go for a carriage ride with his father. Fish agreed, reluctantly, and the news of the ride was immediately telegraphed to Blaine's supporters, who were gathering in Cincinnati for the nominating convention. The candidate himself followed up the news flash with a second cheering telegram: "I am entirely convalescent, suffering only from physical weakness. Impress upon my friends the great gratitude I feel for the unparalleled steadfastness with which they had adhered to me in my hour of trial." The convention would open in a matter of hours.

CINCINNATI, LOCATED DIRECTLY across the Ohio River from Kentucky and Indiana, was not Blaine's personal choice for the site of the convention; he favored Centennial-mad Philadelphia. But the Kentucky-born Bristow, for obvious reasons, wanted the convention held in Cincinnati, and he was joined in his preference by Senator Oliver Morton of Indiana, who nurtured dark-horse presidential dreams of his own. In a tight contest between several evenly matched opponents, geography, not ideology, might carry the day. After a contentious meeting in Washington in January, the Republican National Committee had chosen the Queen City by a one-vote margin, prefiguring the close and suspenseful convention to come. At that point none of the four leading contenders—Blaine, Bristow, Morton, and New York senator Roscoe Conkling—gave even a passing thought to the governor of the convention's host state. But Rutherford B. Hayes, in his own quiet, unassuming way, had been giving them all a great deal of thought. It would not be the last time this political season that he would outthink, outwork, and outgeneral his supposedly more experienced opponents. The fabled "Hayes luck," which had held steady throughout his public life, was about to emerge once again.

For someone supposedly born under a lucky star, Hayes entered the world at a decided disadvantage. Born on October 4, 1822, in Delaware, Ohio, a small farming community in the north-central part of the state, he was a feeble, sickly addition to a family already scarred by tragedy. His father had died before he was born; his mother, Sophia, had buried two other children, both parents, a brother, and a sister before his arrival; and his own brother, Lorenzo, drowned while ice skating when Hayes was two. Not surprisingly, Sophia raised Rutherford and his sister, Fanny, in an atmosphere of free-floating religious dread. Rud, as he was called, was not allowed to do chores around the family farm, play with other children, or engage in strenuous sports until he was nine. Surrounded by doting females, always reminded that he was the only surviving male in the household, Hayes grew into a quietly intense

overachiever, entering Kenyon College when he was sixteen and gradu-
ating with honors three years later. With the generous help of his
mother's wealthy brother, Sardis Birchard, he went on to Harvard to
study law and then returned to Ohio to hang up his shingle. The inner
pressure to be exceptional eventually told on Hayes; in his mid-twen-
ties he suffered a near–nervous breakdown brought on by excessive
worrying that he was losing his mind (there was a family history of
mental illness). He recovered quickly from his "prostrated" mind, but
the experience left him badly shaken. "Health and stimulus" became
his watchwords.

Moving to Cincinnati in 1850 in the hopes of expanding his legal
practice, Hayes wholeheartedly entered the city's burgeoning social
scene. He joined the Eagle Lodge of the International Order of the Odd
Fellows, attended lectures at the Sons of Temperance and the Young
Men's Mercantile Library, and helped to found the Cincinnati Literary
Society, which he described as "a delightful little club of lawyers,
artists, merchants, teachers" who met once a week to debate, converse,
read essays, and eat oysters. In 1852 he courted and wed Lucy Ware
Webb, a doe-eyed, sunny-natured young woman from his hometown
then attending Wesleyan Female College in Cincinnati. The couple's
first three children, sons Birchard, Webb, and Rutherford, followed in
the next six years. In 1858, Hayes was appointed city solicitor after the
current officeholder was struck and killed by a locomotive. His selection by one vote on the thirteenth ballot of the city council was the first
instance of his ineffable luck: the favored replacement had offended too
many special-interest groups, while Hayes, still a neophyte, had offended none. Once in office, Hayes proved an able and popular solicitor,
and his political reputation was such that Abraham Lincoln sought him
out when he came to Ohio in 1859 to campaign successfully for the Republican gubernatorial candidate, William Dennison.

Hayes, in turn, campaigned enthusiastically for Lincoln in the presidential election of 1860, finding the candidate "shrewd, able, and possess[ing] strength in reserve." Lincoln's startling triumph resulted
indirectly in Hayes's own defeat for reelection as city solicitor five
months later, when local Democrats joined forces with members of the
nativist Know-Nothing party to oust Republican officeholders, who they

feared would support a war with the South. Hayes and other Cincinnati Republicans did indeed favor an armed confrontation. "We are all for war," Hayes told his Uncle Sardis. "Anything is better than the state of things we have had the last few months." Following the Confederate bombardment of Fort Sumter, in Charleston harbor, in April 1861, Hayes joined a local militia unit, the Burnet Rifles, and drilled on the courthouse lawn each Sunday morning. Despite his complete lack of military training, he was quickly elected captain of the group.

As a thirty-nine-year-old civic leader and well-connected father of three, with a pregnant wife and an aging mother to support, Hayes might easily have avoided military service. But for a number of personal, professional, and political reasons, he did not want to sit at home while the most epochal event in the nation's history was unfolding around him. Despite assuring his worried uncle that he would not rush into the army, Hayes and an old Kenyon College classmate, Stanley Matthews, immediately began pulling strings to secure commissions in one of the many volunteer units then being formed across the state. Hayes, like many other Americans at the time, was more worried about missing the war than he was about dying in it. As he confided to his diary, "I would prefer to go into it if I knew I was to be killed in the course of it, than to live through and after it without taking any part in it."

In June 1861 he was appointed a major in the 23rd Ohio by Governor Dennison, who remembered Hayes's yeoman work in his successful gubernatorial campaign the previous fall. Hayes surprised everyone, including himself, by falling in love with the military. At Camp Jackson, a converted racetrack four miles west of Columbus, he and Matthews, the regiment's newly minted lieutenant colonel, assumed responsibility for one thousand raw recruits drawn predominantly from northern Ohio. The regiment's colonel, West Point graduate and Mexican War veteran William S. Rosecrans, was often away from camp handling larger administrative affairs, and Hayes and Matthews were left in charge in his absence. "What we don't know, we guess at," Hayes reported to his Uncle Sardis, "and you may be sure that we are kept pretty busy guessing." Despite the new pressures, Hayes enjoyed army life "as much as a boy does a Fourth of July." Soon he was telling his wife, a little tactlessly, "I never enjoyed any business or mode of life as much as I do this."

Hayes and the 23rd Ohio spent the first year of the war fighting guerrillas in West Virginia. It was thankless, often dangerous work, redeemed somewhat by the beautiful natural surroundings. "Our men enjoyed it beyond measure," Hayes told Lucy. "Many had never seen a mountain. We are a great grown-up armed blackberry party." Another midwestern soldier stationed in West Virginia in the fall of 1861, future author and black-humorist Ambrose Bierce, echoed Hayes's praise of the enemy countryside. "Looking back upon it through the haze of near half a century," Bierce wrote in 1909, "I see that region as a veritable realm of enchantment; the Alleghenies as the Delectable Mountains. How we reveled in its savage beauties." Bierce being Bierce, he also remembered a herd of wild pigs eating the faces off a pile of dead bodies, and a fellow soldier named Abbott who was killed by a stray cannonball bearing the foundry imprint "Abbott" that rolled down the mountainside and struck him in the side while he was sleeping. Hayes himself was struck in the knee by a piece of enemy shrapnel during a skirmish near Giles Court House, Virginia, in the spring of 1862, the first of four wounds he would suffer during the war.

In the late summer of 1862, Hayes's regiment was transferred to eastern Virginia, where it took part in the massive Union campaign that climaxed at the Battle of Antietam on September 17. Three days earlier, at South Mountain, Maryland, Hayes was seriously wounded by a Confederate bullet that struck him in the left arm above the elbow, shattered the bone in his upper arm, and severely bruised his ribs. Faint from shock and loss of blood, he doggedly continued directing his regiment's assault while lying down until he began to lose consciousness and had to be carried to safety by one of his men. Thanks in part to his earlier efforts to have his physician brother-in-law, Joseph Webb, assigned to his staff, Hayes received immediate medical attention, which saved his arm and probably his life. After a brief stay in a field hospital, he recuperated at home for several months before returning to the regiment in time to assist in the pursuit and capture of the fabled Confederate cavalryman John Hunt Morgan following Morgan's ill-starred Ohio raid in the summer of 1863.

Promoted to colonel, Hayes commanded a brigade under fellow Ohioan General George Crook in the brutal Shenandoah Valley campaign of 1864, taking part in such vicious battles as Cloyd's Mountain, Kernstown, Berryville, Winchester, Fisher's Hill, and Cedar Creek. At the latter battle, Hayes helped Major General Phil Sheridan famously rally the army after it had been badly surprised by Jubal Early's Confederates. During the battle Hayes narrowly escaped death twice, first when his horse was shot and he was thrown to the ground and knocked unconscious, and later when he was struck in the head by a nearly spent Rebel bullet that, as he somewhat inelegantly told his wife, had "lost its force in getting (I suppose) through someone else." Limping painfully, he barely managed to avoid capture by the onrushing Rebels, hobbling away into the woods with enemy bullets zinging past his head. He rejoined his command in time to witness Sheridan's magnetic arrival on the battlefield—Sheridan had been away from camp and galloped twelve miles back to the front through a jumble of his own retreating soldiers—and heard the army commander cry, "We'll whip 'em yet like hell!" The ensuing Union counterattack, said Hayes, was "glorious," and its crushing reversal of enemy gains "utterly ruined Early" and took all the fight out of the Confederates.

While serving in Virginia, Hayes received word that he had been nominated for Congress by his friends in Cincinnati. Resisting suggestions that he take a furlough from the army to conduct his campaign, Hayes wrote to political confidant William Henry Smith: "An officer fit for duty who at this crisis would abandon his post to electioneer for a seat in Congress ought to be scalped. You may feel perfectly sure I will do no such thing." It was the most effective campaign slogan he could have devised, and a few days before the Battle of Cedar Creek, Hayes learned that he had been elected, one of seventeen Republican congressmen winning office that year in Ohio. He was suitably modest in victory, telling Lucy, "My real share of merit is small enough, I know, but the consciousness that I am doing my part in these brilliant actions is far more gratifying than anything the election brings me." Additional gratification came in December 1864, when Hayes was promoted to brigadier general "for gallant and meritorious services in the battles of Opequon [Winchester], Fisher's Hill, and Cedar Creek."

With Congress not scheduled to reconvene until December of 1865, Hayes served out the remainder of the war on garrison duty at Cumberland, Maryland, leaving the army on June 8, 1865, four years to the day from when he had enlisted. By the time he mustered out, he had participated in fifty separate engagements, been wounded four times—once seriously—had four horses shot from under him, and had nearly been captured on several occasions. He had started the war a politically appointed major and ended it a battle-scarred brevet major general. Not incidentally, he had won his first election to Congress while still on active duty in the army. For Hayes, as it was for thousands of other Union veterans, the Civil War proved to be "the best years of our lives," and he took particular pride in pointing out that he had been "one of the good colonels in the great army."

HAYES ENTERED CONGRESS in December 1865, determined to play a role, however slight, in the political reconstruction of the country. Although beginning his term as a moderate, he soon fell under the spell of the unappeasable abolitionist Thaddeus Stevens of Pennsylvania. Unlike Hayes, who was essentially an affectionate, forgiving person, Stevens was an unregenerate hater of all things southern. He made no secret of that hatred. "The murderers must answer to the suffering race," he said on the floor of the House during the debate to readmit the southern states to Congress. "A load of misery must sit heavily upon their souls. Do not, I pray you, admit those who have slaughtered half a million of our countrymen until their clothes are dried, and until they are reclad. I do not wish to sit side by side with men whose garments smell of the blood of my kindred."

To Hayes, only a few months removed from the war, Stevens possessed "perfect courage, and the sort of independence which long experience, assured position, and seventy years of age gives an able man." As a neophyte congressman, Hayes was more than willing to follow Stevens's lead, even as it led him to a more extreme position on race and Reconstruction than many of his constituents back in Ohio might have desired. Defending his support of the civil rights bill of 1866, Hayes sided with the Radicals, who believed, he said, that "the Rebel states, having gone into insurrection and lost their lawful state governments, it is for the law-making power of the nation to say when (or whether) such new state governments have been set up as ought to be recognized." How this tallied with the long-held views of his idol, Abraham Lincoln, that the southern states had never legally left the Union or lost their inherent rights of citizenship, Hayes did not unduly ponder. As for the still unsettled question of black suffrage, Hayes reported his position as being "suffrage for *all* in the South, colored and white." He added, a little lamely, that he favored universal suffrage "sooner or later in the North also."

During his two terms in Congress—he was reelected in the Republican landslide of 1866—Hayes moved steadily and without apparent soul-searching further into the Radical camp. Following the decision of all but one southern state (Tennessee) to defy the Fourteenth Amendment and remain unrepresented in Congress rather than accept blacks as equal citizens, Hayes supported Stevens's harsh version of the Reconstruction Act of 1867, which repudiated the new southern state governments, divided the South into military districts, called for widespread disenfranchisement of former Confederates, and required the states to draft constitutions embracing universal suffrage and the ratification of the Fourteenth Amendment before being readmitted to the Union. "We agree[d] to disregard the existing state governments in the rebellious states, to institute new ones on the basis of loyalty and colored suffrage and to hold these states firmly in the grasp of military power until the process is complete," Hayes explained to an Ohio legislator. And to his wife's uncle, Scott Cook, he added, "I went with the majority of the party in favor of getting as much power away from Rebels as possible."

Except for Reconstruction matters, Hayes took little interest in his congressional duties, which consisted mostly of running back and forth between various federal departments on behalf of his constituents. "The truth is," he complained, "this being errand boy to one hundred and fifty thousand people tires me." He was therefore delighted when Radical supporters in Ohio engineered his nomination for governor in June 1867, mainly as a way of holding on to the U.S. Senate seat of Thaddeus Stevens's fire-breathing henchman, Benjamin Wade. The gambit failed to protect Wade when Ohio voters elected a Democratic legislature (which had the power to appoint the state's senators), but it worked for Hayes, who won a surprising, razor-thin victory over his opponent, Congressman Allen G. Thurman, by a margin of 2,983 votes out of a total of 484,603. Once again, the vaunted Hayes luck had prevailed.

As a Republican governor saddled with a Democratic legislature, Hayes smoothly reverted to a more moderate stance. He championed such noncontroversial issues as prison reform, humane treatment for the mentally ill, a state-supported home for orphans, and a new geological survey of Ohio. At the same time, he continued to swim against the tide in his own state by supporting the Fourteenth Amendment to the Constitution and increased voting rights for black citizens. When the new legislature voted to rescind the state's ratification of the amendment, Hayes simply ignored the action, as did the federal government. In 1868 he enthusiastically backed Grant for president, and had a "glorious time" celebrating the general's decisive victory. Unlike many other professional politicians within the Republican party, he did not have undue reservations about a politically inexperienced soldier ascending to the presidency. Grant's leadership, he said, was "beyond question." He even held out the hope—ridiculous as it would appear in retrospect—that the new president would bring about civil service reform and raise moral standards in the capital. "If anybody could overthrow the spoils doctrine and practice," Hayes solemnly averred, "Grant is the man."

Hayes enjoyed being governor. "It strikes me as the pleasantest [position] I have ever had," he told his uncle. "Not too much hard work, and plenty of time to read, good society, etc." He was renominated by acclamation at the state Republican convention in June 1869. His Democratic opponent was Senator George Hunt Pendleton, who had run for vice president with General George McClellan in 1864. Pendleton unwisely sought to make Hayes's Civil War record an issue, retailing the unsubstantiated story that his first commander, General William Rosecrans, had once threatened to kick Hayes out of camp for a gross violation of military rules. The charge backfired when Rosecrans, a Democrat himself, declared publicly that Hayes "had both my respect and esteem as an officer and a gentleman, and still retains them." In the subsequent election, Hayes prevailed by 7,501 votes—a total two and a half times larger than his margin of victory in 1867. Even better, from a partisan standpoint, was the fact that the Republicans had regained control of the legislature, making Hayes's continued governance of the state decidedly easier.

Hayes began his second term as governor by leading a successful fight to win legislative approval of the Fifteenth Amendment to the Constitution, which effectively gave blacks the right to vote. The amendment passed in Ohio by the narrowest of margins—two votes in the State House and one in the Senate—and Hayes declared the ratification a "triumph of justice and humanity." Noting with professional satisfaction that the newly enfranchised blacks "vote Republican almost solid," Hayes told a friend that he could now leave politics with a clear conscience, since "the ratification of the Fifteenth Amendment gives me the boon of equality before the law, terminates my enlistment, and discharges me cured." With the adoption of the amendment nationally in 1870, Hayes rejoiced in "the final overthrow of the atrocious system which the Republican Party was organized to oppose. By the adoption of the 15th Amendment the principles of the fathers will be fully recognized in the Constitution."

The rest of his term was largely uneventful, and he left office without regret in January 1872, professing himself to be "a free man and jolly as a beggar." His happiness was short-lived. Despite grave reservations, Hayes reluctantly agreed later that year to stand for Congress in his old district as a way of helping Grant carry Ohio and win reelection. As usual, Hayes's political instincts were acute, and he was soundly defeated by Cincinnati lawyer Henry B. Banning, who ran on the combined Democratic–Liberal Republican ticket. Grant, who scarcely needed Hayes's help to defeat the bumbling Horace Greeley, still showed surprisingly little gratitude after the election, offering Hayes the comparatively minor position of assistant U.S. treasurer in Cincinnati. Hayes brusquely turned down the post, noting with injured justification: "After what I have been and had and done, it would be small potatoes to grasp this crumb. Thanks be given, I am independent of office for my daily bread."

Resettling in Fremont, Ohio, where his Uncle Sardis had died and left him a comfortable country estate, Hayes spent the next two years happily out of politics, remodeling his new home—called Spiegel Grove—and dabbling in real estate investments and local history. At the behest of his Democratic successor as governor, William Allen, he also served on the state board of managers overseeing Ohio's contribution to the upcoming Centennial Exhibition in Philadelphia. In the spring of 1875, worried Republicans pressured Hayes to challenge Allen for re-election, arguing that only a proven vote-getter such as himself could reverse the state's steady slide into the Democratic column. Once again Hayes was reluctant to reenter the political ring, but after he was nominated in June 1875, he found to his surprise that "now that I am in for it I rather like it." He admitted privately that "a third term would be a distinction—a feather I would like to wear. No man ever had it in Ohio."

Hayes's subsequent gubernatorial campaign was the least creditable race of his career. Facing an uphill battle against an equally popular politician, the personally nonreligious Hayes unabashedly played the religion card. Anti-Catholicism had always been present in American politics, and in Ohio it had been reawakened by the controversial decision of the Democratic legislature earlier that year to permit Catholic priests to attend to the needs of their coreligionists in the Ohio Penitentiary and other state correctional facilities. Until then only Protestant ministers had been permitted to serve as prison chaplains, and the sudden ecumenical change, however well intentioned, ignited a firestorm of criticism. Hayes, having fought as governor against state funding for parochial schools, was well versed in such religious controversies. He focused immediately on the issue, noting the day after his nomination: "The interesting point is to rebuke the Democracy for subserviency to Roman Catholic demands." His former protégé in the 23rd Ohio Regiment, Canton lawyer and future president William McKinley, echoed the theme in a letter to Hayes. "We have here a large Catholic population which is thoroughly Democratic, a large Protestant German element that hitherto have been mainly Democratic, they hate the Catholics—their votes we must get."

Thanks largely to his anti-Catholic appeal, Hayes defeated Allen by 5,544 votes out of nearly half a million cast—a minuscule margin of only one percent. His luck still held. Almost immediately, talk began of a Hayes presidential bid. The governor-elect duly recorded in his diary the names of the newspapers booming his candidacy. He had, in fact, been lured back into politics partly by the blandishments of fellow Republicans who "suggest[ed] that if elected governor now, I will stand well for the presidency next year. How wild. Nobody is out of the reach of that mania."

Hayes's interest was piqued further in January 1876 when Ohio senator John Sherman, brother of Civil War general William Tecumseh Sherman, issued an open letter to the press endorsing him for president. Senator Sherman, as combative as his soldier brother, put the upcoming contest in the starkest terms imaginable. "The election of a Democratic president means a restoration to full power in the government of the worst elements of the rebel Democracy," he warned. "If it should elect a president and both houses of Congress, the constitutional amendments would be disregarded, the freedmen would be nominally citizens but really slaves [and] the power of the general government would be crippled." Sherman disavowed any personal preference for the nomination, but said, "I believe the nomination of Governor Hayes would give us more strength, taking the country at large, than any other man. In Genl. Hayes we will have a candidate for president who can combine greater popular strength and greater assurance of success than any other candidate."

Sherman's unsolicited endorsement did not entirely gratify Hayes. The senator, in his letter, went beyond his area of political expertise to critique Hayes's Civil War record. "He was a good soldier, and, though not greatly distinguished as such, he performed his full duty," Sherman wrote, "and I noticed that the soldiers who served under him loved and respected him." Hayes, who had unselfishly refused to run against Sherman for senator in 1872 when a group of dissident Ohio reformers sought to depose the notorious political spoilsman, understandably took offense at the phrase "not greatly distinguished." In his diary he carefully made a list of his various battles and promotions.

Following Sherman's lukewarm lead, the Ohio Republican convention met on March 29 and voted unanimously to support Hayes for president. Professing complete indifference to his chances, Hayes noted privately, "I would be glad if now I could in some satisfactory way drop out of the candidacy. I do not at present see what I can do to relieve myself from the embarrassment of the position I am in." In practice, Hayes did not try very hard to drop out of the race. Although assuring his Democratic friend Guy M. Bryan that "very few Republicans in Ohio are so completely out of the Hayes movement as I am," Hayes nevertheless kept a close eye on political developments within the state's delegation to the Republican National Convention. Hearing that Edwin Cowles, the independent-minded editor of the *Cleveland Leader*, was making noises about switching his vote to James G. Blaine, Hayes immediately fired off a letter to the wavering delegate. "I think I have a right to considerate treatment at the hands of the Ohio delegation," he wrote. "If I am to be voted for at all, and as long as I am to be voted for at all, may I not reasonably expect the solid vote of Ohio?"

These were not the words of a disinterested candidate—even one who could still maintain with a straight face, after whipping Cowles back into line, "I don't meddle." The truth was that Hayes, like countless politicians before him, had caught the presidential bug—the "maggot," as he described it, using the archaic word in the etymological sense of a ridiculous obsession. Hayes was a good writer, and it was precisely the right word for his current state of mind. "It seems to me that good purposes, and the judgment, experience and firmness I possess would enable me to execute the duties of the office well," he noted in his diary. "I do not feel the least fear that I should fail! This all looks egotistical, but it is sincere."

THE REPUBLICAN NATIONAL Committee, by choosing Cincinnati as the site for the party's national convention, had inadvertently given Hayes a huge advantage. Despite the fact that he had lived in the city only briefly in the past eleven years, Hayes still enjoyed the warm support of his adopted hometown. By the time the convention opened, Hayes buttons and banners were everywhere. Still, with all his local advantages, Hayes was given little chance to win the nomination when the 756 Republican delegates and alternates convened at high noon on June 14 inside the barnlike Exposition Hall at the corner of Elm and Fourteenth streets—the same hall where Horace Greeley had won the Liberal Republican nomination in 1872. The wooden building, with its twin towers, exposed rafters, and balcony railings hung with red-white-and-blue flags, resembled "an ambitious and disappointed railroad depot," said the *New York Tribune*, "its decorations those of a country barbecue on a four-acre scale." The delegates' seats, carefully cordoned off into forty-seven separate sections for the individual states and territories, rose sharply from the speaker's platform. Rows of pine tables in front of the stage accommodated a small army of 250 newspapermen ready to dash off dispatches to the adjacent telegraph room.

At first there was little to report. National committee chairman Edwin Morgan of New York opened the convention by needlessly reminding delegates that, for the first time in sixteen years, the presidential nomination was wide open. "There appears to be at the present time no one to whom the unerring finger points as the only candidate," said Morgan. "There seems to be no one man rising so far above all others as to cause exultant voices to exclaim, 'Thou art the man!'" This was not exactly what Blaine's supporters wanted to hear; their strongest appeal was that their man had indeed risen above the other candidates. If so, apparently he had not risen high enough. Hayes's second son, Webb, functioning as his father's eyes and ears at the convention, reported back to Columbus that he had spoken with "a drunken Bristow man" during the first day's proceedings, and that the delegate had confessed, "I'll vote for Blaine before I will vote for a Democrat, but I hate like hell to vote for a man whose shirt tail is covered with shit."

If Blaine was tarred by his own mistakes, the other leading candidates also operated under severe handicaps. Bristow, having permanently alienated Grant and the party's regulars by prosecuting too strongly the Whiskey Ring, had no real chance for the nomination. No one wanted to elect a president who might, as a matter of principle, prosecute them next. Bristow's lack of political experience also weighed against him. John Hay, Abraham Lincoln's former secretary, put it succinctly: "His one sole public act is the prosecution of the Whiskey Ring. It is enough to make him a governor, if he could carry his own state, and might honestly win him the vice-presidency. But twenty men are ready to work for Blaine to one for Bristow. Blaine has shown positive capacity for government and Bristow has not." Bristow knew all too well that he was facing an uphill battle, telling his campaign manager and former law partner, John M. Harlan, on the eve of the convention, "I will make the best fight I can, and, if I must go down will at least fall with my face to the foe."

New York senator Roscoe Conkling's prospects were not much better. Although he presented himself as Grant's handpicked successor, behind the scenes the president privately hoped that Secretary of State Hamilton Fish would get the nomination. As head of the large New York delegation, Conkling could claim with some plausibility that he was the only Republican candidate with a chance to carry the state against the likely Democratic nominee, incumbent governor Samuel Tilden. But Conkling was too closely identified with the corrupt machine politics of the era. When his supporters paraded through the streets of Cincinnati after their arrival in the city, one spectator wondered aloud where Conkling had found the money to bail them out of jail. On the day the convention opened, the *New York Times* reported unhelpfully that "Mr. Conkling is practically out of the convention." And delegates had scarcely taken their seats before fellow delegate George William Curtis, a member of the National Republican Reform Club of New York, rose to denounce Conkling's machine as "an odious and intolerable oligarchy which menaces the very system of our government."

But Conkling, who could read the political handwriting on the wall as well as anyone, was not about to drop out of the race as long as Blaine was still in it. For Conkling it was personal; he hated Blaine with a passion he could scarcely muster for the most unregenerate Democrat. The genesis of that hatred went back a decade, when Conkling was still in the House of Representatives with Blaine. During a debate over a since forgotten bill, Blaine had referred cuttingly to Conkling's "haughty disdain, his grandiloquent swell, his majestic, supereminent, turkey-gobbler strut." The New Yorker was indeed a bit of a dandy, favoring white flannel trousers and flowery waistcoats and combing his flame-red hair into a trademark curl above his eyes. Like many vain men, he was also secretly insecure, and he never forgot Blaine's cruel remark. Years later, at the height of another presidential campaign, he would pointedly decline an eleventh-hour appeal to help Blaine's cause, remarking with long-deferred satisfaction: "No thank you. I have given up criminal practice."

Conkling did not like the other top-level candidate, Oliver Morton, much better than he liked Blaine. From the moment he entered the Senate in 1867, after a fiercely combative reign as war governor of Indiana, Morton had vied with Conkling for the unofficial title of the nation's most radical Republican. His unflagging support for the Union war effort, during which time he had raised twice the number of volunteers that Lincoln had asked for, and his incessant waving of the bloody shirt after the war was over, had earned him the support of southern Republicans, black and white. A convention of African-American officeholders in Nashville two months earlier had overwhelmingly endorsed Morton's candidacy. More temperate Republicans, however, shared Conkling's distrust of the combative Hoosier. Newspaper editor Whitelaw Reid called Morton "an unprincipled demagogue, of large ability and utter unscrupulousness," and John Hay warned that the prospect of a Morton nomination was "positively dreaded by the best men in the party." Blaine, who qualified as something of an expert witness in such matters, considered Morton "extremely ambitious and selfish." The Indiana senator also labored under a serious physical handicap: a severe stroke in 1865 had virtually crippled him, and he walked painfully on crutches, when he walked at all.

The other candidates—with one exception—were strictly favorite sons of their respective states: Governor John F. Hartranft of Pennsylvania and Postmaster General Marshall Jewell of Connecticut. Their nominations were mere formalities, a prelude to the more serious horse-trading between the real candidates. The lone exception was Rutherford B. Hayes. While not as strong as the first-rung candidates, all of whom were better known nationally than he was, Hayes was everyone's choice for second place. Not only was he a proven votegetter, but as governor of Ohio he could virtually guarantee an important state to the Republican party. Even better, in a scandal-weary year, both his public and private lives were unimpeachable. Financially independent thanks to the largesse of his late uncle, Hayes had no inconvenient skeletons rattling about in his closet. Blaine and Bristow had already contacted him indirectly about a place on the ticket, and Morton was also believed to be amenable. Conkling, with true New York City savoir faire, had even commissioned a vaudeville troupe to come up with a catchy campaign song: "Conkling and Hayes / Is the ticket that pays."

But Hayes, as he had already indicated to the leader of the Ohio delegation, was no longer interested—if he ever had been—in the vice presidential nomination. With a superb slate of handlers behind him and a distinct home-field advantage in Cincinnati, he was playing a deep and subtle game for the biggest prize of all. His campaign manager, Edward F. Noyes, made it clear on the first day of the convention that Hayes was going to play rough. Noyes's welcoming speech wasted little time in whacking Blaine. "As to the candidate of this convention," he said, "we of Ohio ask only this. We fight nobody. We assail no man's reputation. Whoever you nominate we will try and help to elect him. All we want is a man, in the first place, who is honest. In the second place, we want a man of comprehension enough to know what is right and what is wrong, and in the third place, we want a man who is brave enough and strong enough to carry out his convictions. Give us a man of great purity of private life and an unexceptionable public record, and count on Ohio next November." In other words, do not give us Blaine, or Conkling, or Morton—and we know you won't give us Bristow. Who else was there? It went without saying.

IN KEEPING WITH long-standing political tradition, neither Hayes nor the other leading candidates attended the convention—it was considered bad form to openly politick for the nomination. Hayes remained in Columbus with his third son, Rud, while a parade of speakers ascended the podium on the first afternoon to praise the Republicans and denounce the Democrats. Two were notable, both for what they said and for what their speeches portended for the upcoming campaign.

Frederick Douglass, the fiery African-American orator, spoke first. There had already been a disagreeable incident at a Cincinnati hotel in which black delegates to the convention had been denied rooms on the basis of race, and Douglass worried that the Republican party as a whole was showing signs of abandoning its newfound commitment to racial equality. "Do you mean to make good to us the promises in your constitution?" he asked bluntly. "You say you have emancipated us. You have: and I thank you for it. You say you have enfranchised us. You have: and I thank you for it. But what is your emancipation? What is your enfranchisement? What does it all amount to, if the black man, after having been made free by the letter of your law, is unable to exercise that freedom, and, having been freed from the slaveholder's lash, he is to be subject to the slaveholder's shotgun?" It seemed, said Douglass, that the Republican party had come to the conclusion that it could "get along without the vote of the black man of the South." The collective shrug that his speech engendered from the delegates was all the answer he required.

The next speaker was Illinois senator John A. "Black Jack" Logan. If Douglass had spoken more in sorrow than in anger, Logan's speech reversed the equation. A former major general in the Union army, Logan was not yet ready to bury the hatchet. Dragging out the well-worn bloody shirt, he lambasted Democrats in general and unreconstructed southerners in particular for being ready to "plunge the dagger of detraction into the very vitals of the men who stand firm against the storms that have been rolling against liberty and freedom in this country." Only a Republican victory, said Logan, would prevent such an underhanded assault.

The next morning the convention heard from a different sort of speaker. Sarah J. Spencer, a leader of the women's suffrage movement, rose to address a gathering that contained not one female delegate. Echoing Douglass's earlier complaint, Spencer noted that "in 1872 the Republican party declared that it had emancipated four million of human beings and established universal suffrage. Where were the ten millions of women citizens of this republic? When will you make this high-sounding declaration true? We ask you for a plank that will place that mighty emblem of power, the ballot, in the hands of ten million American citizens—the wives and daughters of this fair republic."

Spencer's emotional plea for female equality was received with lukewarm applause or outright silence from the exclusively male convention delegates. The gentlemen of the press were even less polite. "The women-folk are dabbling in politics," reported the *Chicago Tribune*. The *New York Sun* preferred to dwell on Spencer's appearance rather than her words. "Mrs. Spencer is a slightly built lady, about forty years," said the newspaper. "She has a high, thin, light voice, inaudible for more than short distances." The *New York Herald*'s report was particularly dismissive. "Mrs. Spencer is a woman of uncertain age, sharp features, acidulous, without distinction in any respect whatever, commonplace in appearance and speech, and when she had spoken her little piece, without anything in it, she wafted herself back to the handiest seat, and that was the end of the incident."

The official party platform, which was reported out of committee following Spencer's speech, promised only to give "respectful consideration" to the demand for women's suffrage. The more pressing issue, said convention chairman Edward McPherson, was the Democratic party—the "enemy"—which was "striped all over with treason and malignity and hate of everything that is national." Continuing the chairman's theme, the platform "deprecate[d] all sectional feeling and tendencies," but noted "with deep solicitude that the Democratic party counts, as its chief hope of success, upon the electoral vote of a united South, secured through the efforts of those who were recently arrayed against the nation; and we invoke the earnest attention of the country to the grave truth that a success thus achieved would reopen sectional strife and imperil national honor and human rights." The Democratic party, "being the same in character and spirit as when it sympathized with treason," had to be defeated again in order to finally achieve, eleven years after the Confederate surrender at Appomattox, the "permanent pacification of the southern section of the Union."

The platform gave the briefest of nods to the reform movement, noting, "We rejoice in the quickening conscience of the people concerning political affairs, and will hold all public officers to a rigid responsibility, and engage that the prosecution and punishment of all who betray official trust shall be swift, thorough, and unsparing." That said, the framers concluded, with no apparent irony, by commending the current administration "for its honorable work in the management of domestic and foreign affairs. President Grant deserves the continued hearty gratitude of the American people for his patriotism and his eminent services, in war and peace."

Having thus disposed neatly of the outgoing president, the convention turned to the more agreeable business of selecting his successor.

The roll call of states commenced at 3:00 P.M. inside the sweltering, smoke-filled hall. Connecticut favorite son Marshall Jewell was nominated first, followed by Indiana's Oliver Morton, whose nomination was seconded by P. B. S. Pinchback of Louisiana. Pinchback, whose brief interim reign as governor of Louisiana in 1872 marked the first time in American history that a black man had been the chief executive of a state, had been elected to the U.S. Senate three years later, but had been refused his seat in an ongoing legal dispute. Morton's election as president, said Pinchback, would "strike terror to the hearts of those monsters in the South who are driving capital from that section and persecuting and murdering black and white Republicans." The order in which Pinchback outlined southern abuses was in itself a subtle acknowledgment of the party's priorities.

Benjamin Bristow was nominated next, by his best friend and campaign manager, John M. Harlan, who told the less than receptive delegates that Bristow's "mode has been to execute the law; and if the Republican party contained offenders who betrayed their trust, or who were thieves, he let them be punished as well as anybody else." It was a noble appeal to conscience, but it was not exactly calculated to rouse the spirits of a partisan political crowd. George W. Curtis of New York, seconding the nomination, sounded a needlessly scolding tone that further depressed the delegates' enthusiasm by reminding them of Bristow's reformist stands: "Let us understand that this government must be purified if the party is to be saved, and that Benjamin F. Bristow is the one man who stands before the country as the embodiment of governmental purification." That was the problem. Many of the delegates in the hall owed their jobs to party patronage and machine politics, and they were not at all convinced that the system needed purifying.

The next nominating speech was the most eagerly anticipated. It was for Blaine, and it was delivered by perhaps the leading orator in America at the time, writer and free-thinker Robert G. Ingersoll of Illinois. Privately, Ingersoll favored Morton; his only interest in Blaine was as a block to Bristow, whom Ingersoll could not abide. After archly skewering Curtis's professions of Bristow's Massachusetts-based support—any Republican could carry Massachusetts, Ingersoll scoffed—the speaker rose (or sank) to the present occasion. The American people, he said, "demand a man whose political reputation is as spotless as a star; but they do not demand that their candidate shall have a certificate of moral character signed by a Confederate Congress." Instead, they wanted "the man who has preserved in Congress what their soldiers won upon the field; the man who has torn from the throat of treason the tongue of slander[,] the man who has snatched the mask of Democracy from the hideous face of rebellion." In case the delegates were unsure who, exactly, this "intellectual athlete" might be, Ingersoll made it obvious for them. "Like an armed warrior, like a plumed knight, James G. Blaine marched down the halls of the American Congress and threw his shining lance full and fair against the brazen forehead of every traitor to his country and every maligner of his fair reputation." To desert such a leader, said Ingersoll, would be like deserting a general on the field of battle. "In the name of the great republic," he closed, "in the name of all her defenders and supporters; in the name of all her soldiers living; in the name of all her soldiers that died upon the field of battle; and in the name of those that perished in the skeleton clutch of famine at Andersonville and Libby, whose suffering he so vividly remembers—Illinois nominates for the next president of this country that prince of parliamentarians, that leader of leaders, James G. Blaine."

Political hokum of the cheapest sort, Ingersoll's speech has been overrated ever since—it has been called the second greatest convention speech of all time, after William Jennings Bryan's "Cross of Gold" peroration in 1896. Its supposed effect on the Republican convention has also been overrated. The speech predictably elicited applause and laughter from the captive audience in Cincinnati, but it changed few if any minds inside the auditorium. (A labored pun quickly made the rounds: "An honest Blaine's the noblest work of Bob.") By ascribing Blaine's well-publicized financial travails to a "Confederate Congress," Ingersoll conveniently overlooked the fact that it was a Massachusetts congressman who had called for an investigation in the first place, after an initial inquiry by a fellow congressman from California. And despite his galvanizing performance on the floor of Congress, more than a few delegates were still unconvinced that Blaine was out of danger, legally or politically. Moreover, the leaders of the stop-Blaine movement at the convention remained united in their opposition to the newly crowned knight. They held firm while the shouting died away, and the subsequent formal nominations of Hayes, Conkling, and Hartranft further allowed them to play for time while tamping down any residual enthusiasm for Blaine within their own state delegations.

By now it was after 5:00 P.M., and the afternoon shadows—to say nothing of the dripping heat inside the wooden building—had settled oppressively over the crowd. An Indiana delegate, citing darkness, moved to adjourn until the next morning. Blaine supporter William P. Frye, pointing to the gaslights inside the hall, wanted to know why that was a problem. "I am informed that the gaslights of this hall are in such condition that they cannot safely be lighted," convention chairman McPherson replied. The convention adjourned. Afterward, various supporters of the other candidates would claim that they had secretly sabotaged the lights to force a postponement of the nominating vote while enthusiasm for Blaine was still running high, but given the tinderbox conditions inside Exposition Hall and the delegates' waning energy level, the chairman's decision seems to have been both spontaneous and well considered.

FOLLOWING THE ADJOURNMENT, the competing camps spent a suspenseful, unquiet night. Edward F. Noyes, who was Hayes's cousin as well as his campaign manager, reached out to Stanley Matthews, an old college friend and wartime comrade of Hayes's who was a leading supporter of Benjamin Bristow. The two agreed that Bristow was unlikely to win the nomination; Hayes had the best, perhaps the only, chance to stop Blaine. At some point during the night it was decided to bring Morton's handlers into the discussion, and the three sides agreed to test their candidates' individual strength for a ballot or two the next morning. Then, if there was no significant movement, the Bristow and Morton camps would throw their support behind Hayes. The deal was finalized with the confidential proffer of a Supreme Court nomination for Bristow's floor manager, John M. Harlan. Webb Hayes passed along the word—if not the details—to his father in Columbus, reporting, "Governor Noyes instructs me to say that the combinations are very favorable." Hayes had predicted what would happen a month earlier, noting in his diary that "the contingency of a union between those who look for availability in the candidate and those who are for purity and reform in administration" would make him the "probable nominee." As usual, his political instincts were right on the mark.

Balloting began at 10:00 A.M. the next morning. A simple majority of 379 votes was needed to win the nomination. Blaine, as expected, forged into the lead, receiving 285 votes on the first ballot. No one else was within 160 votes. The Plumed Knight exhibited the broadest range of support as well, tallying at least one vote from thirty-five of the forty-seven states and territories. Morton was a distant second with 124 votes, all except Indiana's thirty votes coming from the southern states. Bristow had 113 votes, Conkling ninety-nine, and Hayes sixty-one. The balloting continued, largely unchanged, for three more rounds. The most significant event came when a Pennsylvania delegate challenged the unit rule giving all of his state's votes to a single candidate. Chairman McPherson, a Blaine supporter, ruled that the delegates of each state were free to vote their consciences—never again would the unit rule obtain at Republican conventions. Presumably, the ruling would benefit Blaine, who had no large home-state delegation to keep in line, by enabling him to cherry-pick votes from other delegations. It soon transpired, however, that the chairman's ruling did more harm than good.

On the fifth ballot, the deadlock broke when Michigan's badly divided delegation decided to throw its votes to Hayes. Delegation chairman William A. Howard, who earlier had favored Morton, announced the switch. "There is a man in this section of the country who has beaten in succession three Democratic candidates for president in his own state, and we want to give him a chance to beat another Democratic candidate for the presidency in the broader field of the United States," Howard said. "Michigan therefore casts her twenty-two votes for Rutherford B. Hayes of Ohio."

The Michigan movement brought the convention to a fever pitch. "Anything like the scene that followed," wrote the correspondent for the London Times, "I had never, I think, witnessed. The Michigan vote being at once recognized as the first anti-Blaine blow, set more than half the delegates themselves into a state of the most frantic commotion, and the claqueurs (most of them Bristow partisans) being more ready to yell for the 'coming man' than for their falling favorite, the uproar was something terrific. Three long salvos of applause were given before order could be restored."

Moments later the North Carolina delegation, which had been vacillating between candidates in hopes of backing a winner, switched nine of its votes from Blaine to Hayes. Immediately following the Tarheels' action, two Pennsylvania delegates abandoned favorite-son Governor John A. Hartranft in favor of Hayes, who now moved into third place in the balloting. Pennsylvania political boss Simon Cameron, Abraham Lincoln's disgraced secretary of war and the author of the well-known definition of an honest politician as "a man who, when he's bought, stays bought," offered to hand Blaine the Pennsylvania delegation in return for a pledge to put one of Cameron's fellow Pennsylvanians in his cabinet. But Blaine's handlers made a crucial mistake: they interpreted Michigan's abandonment of Bristow as the beginning of a full-scale collapse of all the lesser candidates. They refused Cameron's offer and sat back to await the coming coronation.

Unfortunately for Blaine, the crowning moment never came. On the sixth ballot he rose as high as he would go, receiving 308 votes, seventy-one fewer than he needed to win. But Conkling held fast to the New York delegation, while Morton and Bristow held on to their own. It was obvious to everyone that the next ballot would be decisive. In the alphabetical roll call of votes, Alabama, Arkansas, Florida, Georgia, and Illinois switched twenty-four total votes to Blaine; he seemed headed for the nomination. Then Indiana was called. Chairman Will Cumback walked to the stage and announced dramatically that Oliver Morton had withdrawn his name from consideration; Indiana cast twenty-five votes for Hayes and five for Bristow. This was the signal the other bosses had been waiting for, and the delegates in the hall knew it immediately. "I must leave to the imagination of your readers here and hereafter the scene which followed, lest time and my vocabulary should fail me," observed the giddy London Times correspondent. "They have only to picture from four to five thousand persons, one moment seated in solemn silence to hear a vote given, the next jumping, yelling, stamping, waving arms and hats as if suddenly stricken with raving madness."

Then it was Kentucky's turn, and Harlan, his Supreme Court nomination stashed safely in his back pocket, went to the podium. William C. Cochran, a young observer in the balcony that day, described the subsequent scene to his mother: "Gen. Harlan rose from his place and walked toward the stand, and the people divining his purpose at once set up a great cheer, and it was some time before he could be heard. He stood there, his lips trembling with emotion waiting for the storm of applause to be hushed, and then he spoke grandly"—or not so grandly, as Bristow himself came to believe, feeling that his old friend had abandoned the fight too abruptly. Harlan withdrew Bristow's name from the running and cast Kentucky's twenty-four votes for Hayes, setting off a "scene of wild and tumultuous applause that defies description." The voting continued until it reached New York. It was now clear that the choice was between Blaine and Hayes, which given Conkling's implacable hatred of Blaine was no choice at all. Delegation chairman Thomas Platt, "in the interests of amity and victory," cast sixty-one votes for Hayes to nine for Blaine. Pennsylvania next divided its votes almost down the middle, thirty for Blaine and twenty-eight for Hayes. When the voting concluded, Hayes had won the nomination by a scant five votes. If the unit rule had still been in place, Pennsylvania's bloc vote would have gone to Blaine, giving him exactly the number needed to win. It was that close.

At 5:30 P.M., the balloting was completed, and by six o'clock, as the new Republican presidential nominee informed his son from Columbus, "My hand [was] sore with shaking hands." Back in Cincinnati, the convention quickly wound up its work. In the interest of balancing the ticket with an eastern man as vice president—and perhaps to poke their fingers in the eyes of Samuel Tilden as well—the delegates unanimously selected New York congressman William A. Wheeler, author of the recent Louisiana compromise that had settled the impasse between that state's Republican governor and Democratic legislature. (Ironically, Phil Sheridan, whose draconian actions had necessitated the compromise in the first place, had accurately predicted the Republican ticket months earlier to Hayes, who admitted a little sheepishly to his wife, Lucy, "I am ashamed to say, Who is *Wheeler*?") A personal telegram from Blaine offering his unqualified support and promising to do his utmost to promote Hayes's election "quite unmanned" the nominee, who pledged in his ever-present diary to "try to do in all things more than ever before precisely the thing that is right, to be natural, discreet, wise, moderate, and as firm in the right as it is possible for me to be." The key word, perhaps, was *moderate*.

THE AFTER-THE-FACT explanations of Blaine's defeat were many and varied, ranging from the nonworking gaslights in Exposition Hall to the ill-considered decision by convention chairman McPherson to abolish the unit rule of voting. A bitterly disappointed John Hay, writing to Blaine one day after the convention, blamed "the cowardly good-will of the Ohio and Pennsylvania delegations, who would have voted for you if they had dared to defy the machine lash." One of those well-lashed delegates, Edwin Cowles of Ohio, admitted as much to the nominee. "To be candid," Cowles informed Hayes, "I feel almost conscience-smitten at my having apparently gone back on Blaine after having announced to him three years ago in his library that I was going to trot him out for the presidency and fight for him to the bitter end. My heart was for him but my head was for you."

For his part, Blaine adviser T. C. Crawford believed that Blaine would have won the nomination on the sixth ballot if he had accepted Simon Cameron's offer to hand over the Pennsylvania delegation in return for guaranteeing the state a spot in the cabinet. Massachusetts senator George F. Hoar blamed Mrs. Blaine's Sunday afternoon snubbing of Bristow. Others ascribed the defeat to Roscoe Conkling's personal antagonism, or to Oliver Morton's geographical solidarity—"Men stood together in the Corn Belt." No one wanted to state the obvious, that Blaine's own well-publicized troubles had created just enough residual uncertainty among the delegates to give his opponents the necessary opening to defeat him. Whoever or whatever was to blame, it was inarguably true, as another sorrowful Blainiac put it, that "the hounds pulled down the stag."

In the end, all the explanations missed the most salient point: Hayes had won the nomination at least as surely as Blaine had lost it. His tough and experienced campaign team, led by former Ohio governor Edward Noyes, had played the game perfectly. William Henry

Smith, head of the Western Associated Press and a longtime friend of Hayes's, gave full credit where it was due. "It was of first importance to have such a leader as Edward F. Noyes," he wrote to Hayes five days later. "Better management I never saw. It was able, judicious, untiring, unselfish, inspiring, adroit. If there was a mistake made I did not discover it. His eyes were everywhere and discipline was preserved with as much vigor as on the field of battle." Smith himself had also played a role, meeting secretly with other journalists during the Mulligan letters imbroglio to plot how best to occasion Blaine's downfall, although he may not have divulged that part of his service to Hayes, who preferred at any rate to remain impeccably above the fray. Nor did Hayes necessarily know anything about the Supreme Court tender to Harlan. By letting others do the backroom dealing for him, the candidate could avoid any hint of impropriety, while remaining fully confident that his handlers, in the end, would do whatever needed to be done. Meanwhile, he could say with perfect assurance that he was "in no way conscious of fault in getting [the nomination]."

But if Hayes had stayed for the most part in the background, he still had contributed measurably to his victory. By carefully preserving his political viability while maintaining an Olympian detachment from the fight, he had avoided needlessly alienating anyone, something he had planned from the start. "Be on your guard who you strike," he had warned a supporter weeks before the convention. "You may unwittingly hit a friend." The thing to do was to "behave sensibly, and to do nothing unjust, or uncharitable, even towards [an] opponent." Hayes had also helped his own chances by cannily letting it be known ahead of time that he personally favored Bristow—the one opponent whom he knew for a fact could not get the nomination. It was the sort of poised, professional performance that boded well for the general election.

Reaction to Hayes's nomination was overwhelmingly positive. The staunchly Republican *Chicago Tribune* led the way. "The Republican Party," it said, "has almost miraculously escaped political destruction." George William Curtis, the New York reformer who had defied the Conkling machine from the stage of the convention, was ecstatic. "I cannot help thinking that your nomination at this juncture is as fortunate for the country as that of Mr. Lincoln in 1860," he told the candidate. "The general & joyful response of this state as well as of the country, is due, I am very sure to the feeling that while you are a party man and the candidate of the whole party, yet that your sympathies and purposes are for the purification and elevation of the tone of the government." Even Conkling, the victim of Curtis's direct attack and the helpless onlooker to Hayes's eleventh-hour tidal wave, mustered the grace to tell reporters that "the ticket is an excellent one. Hayes served with me in the House. He has always been a flat-footed Republican, who never apologizes for his party." As for the titular head of that party, outgoing president Ulysses S. Grant was characteristically brief and to the point: "Governor Hayes," he said, "is a good selection and will make a good candidate."

Not everyone was thrilled by Hayes's selection. Joseph Pulitzer, publisher of the *New York World* and a last-ditch supporter of Bristow, found little to crow about. The nominee's chief recommendation, he said, seemed to be that "Hayes has never stolen. Good God, has it come to this?" And from his high-flown perch in Boston, erstwhile reformer Henry Adams dismissed the three-term governor, congressman, and Civil War general as "a third-rate nonentity, whose only recommendation is that he is obnoxious to no one. I hope to enjoy the satisfaction of voting against him."

Meanwhile, Charles A. Dana, editor of the *New York Sun*, basked in his newfound reputation as a prophet: two months before the Republican convention, he had accurately predicted that Hayes would be nominated, in the same way that "Lincoln was nominated in 1860, or Pierce in 1852, or Polk in 1844. He is that kind of neutral man who is always taken when the powerful chiefs can only succeed in foiling each other." But Dana, true-blue Democrat that he was, failed to mention that each of those other "neutral" men had subsequently been elected president of the United States. It remained to be seen if the fourth time around would still be the charm.

CHAPTER THREE

CENTENNIAL SAM

W HILE THE REPUBLICANS were fighting among themselves in Cincinnati to choose a worthy—or at least plausible—successor to Ulysses S. Grant, the Democratic party was preparing to hold its own nominating convention in St. Louis two weeks later. Unlike the fractious Republicans, the Democrats were largely united behind one candidate: New York governor Samuel J. Tilden. Indeed, Tilden's nomination was such a foregone conclusion that the upcoming convention promised to be less a contest among political equals than a carefully orchestrated coronation.

The man about to be crowned was no one's idea of royalty. Samuel Jones Tilden, at sixty-two, looked a good ten years older than his age. Short and slight, with sparse sandy hair, a pale complexion, and a habitually drooping left eyelid, the presumptive nominee gave an appearance of physical frailty that was totally at odds with his workhorse nature. Like his father, Elam, a wealthy store owner and gentleman farmer in upstate New York, Tilden was a congenital hypochondriac. At one time or another in the course of his life he complained of being plagued by such multitudinous but nonspecific afflictions as chills, fever, colds, neuralgia, toothaches, rheumatism, hoarseness, catarrh, arthritis, palsy, corrugated tongue, tremulous hands, pulsations of the head, insomnia, dry mouth, diarrhea, and constipation. His health troubles began at the age of three, when a country physician prescribed laudanum for the toddler's sore mouth. Tilden blamed his subsequent lifelong dyspepsia on the too-liberal use of the powerful drug, which left him with "a weakened stomach and impaired digestive apparatus for the rest of his days."

Perhaps to compensate for his physical shortcomings, Tilden and his father began early in Tilden's boyhood to develop his precociously agile mind. The elder Tilden used the forum of his general store to keep abreast of current events, functioning as a sort of political sounding board for the community. Known locally as "the Oracle of New Lebanon," Elam Tilden became a confidant of various New York politicians, including his son's personal hero, Martin Van Buren, a fellow native of Columbia County. In the urbane, coolly calculating Van Buren, a leading figure in the so-called Albany Regency that controlled New York politics for many years, Tilden found a congenial role model. Van Buren, while unfailingly polite and sophisticated, was also a man who, as one longtime colleague asserted, "rowed to his object with muffled oars." An engaging conversationalist, he preferred to draw out others while keeping his own opinions closely guarded. It was a lesson that young Sam Tilden learned well—perhaps too well.

Besides his father and Martin Van Buren, Tilden acquired his early political leanings—as he acquired everything—from books, particularly his great-aunt's collection of Thomas Jefferson's letters. While other boys were out fishing and hunting, Tilden sat by the fireside poring over Adam Smith's *The Wealth of Nations* and Jonathan Edwards's *Freedom of the Will*. At other times he leaned silently against the counter in his father's store, listening to village elders talk politics with a steady stream of westbound stagecoach travelers (New Lebanon was on the main thoroughfare from New England into the Hudson Valley). Gradually, his father encouraged Samuel to speak his own mind, and family friend William Cullen Bryant, editor of the *New York Evening Post,* noted with amusement that Elam yielded to his son's considered opinions with "comical deference" and listened carefully to "the austere deliberation with which those opinions were unfolded."

Tilden's fragile constitution played havoc with his formal education. He did not attend elementary school until he was eight, and he subsequently spent only three months at Williams Academy in Williamstown, Massachusetts, before returning home to New Lebanon. He dropped out of Yale University, which he entered in 1834 as a twenty-year-old freshman, after a single term, complaining that the food in the university dining hall was impossible for him to stomach. "Day before yesterday morning we had a dish of meat, very fresh bread and butter, coffee, and nothing else whatever," he wrote to his father. "At dinner, we had boiled shad with potatoes, fresh bread and butter and rice pudding . . . for those who could eat such things."

Transferring to New York University in 1835, Tilden managed to attend school sporadically for the next two years, although his growing obsession with politics often called him home in the middle of exams to electioneer for Van Buren and other candidates. Along with his older brother Moses he had been a delegate to the Columbia County convention of 1832 that endorsed the nomination of Andrew Jackson and Martin Van Buren for president and vice president; and in September 1833 he spoke out publicly for the first time, "in a spirited and eloquent manner," at a Democratic-Republican party rally in New Lebanon, denouncing Jackson's particular bugbear, the National Bank. "The capitalist class," Tilden said, sounding more like Karl Marx than Thomas Jefferson, "had banded together all over the world and organized the modern dynasty of associated wealth, which maintains an unquestioned ascendency over most of the privileged portions of our race, and which is now striving to extend its dominion over us."

Tilden's adoption of Democratic ideals was early and absolute. Years later, on the eve of his nomination for president, he explained his reasoning to a fellow Wall Street lawyer who wondered why Tilden, unlike so many other wealthy attorneys, was a Democrat, since "his views [were] not substantially at variance with those held by leading Republicans." Tilden responded that "while it was true that a large majority of men of culture, wealth, and force were to be found in the Republican party, the trouble was that . . . it was a party of self-seekers." To Tilden, such men were so engrossed in the single-minded acquisition of wealth that they inevitably used "their powerful influence so as to shape the legislation of the country in a form which would favor their interests." The Democratic party, by contrast, "held within its ranks a far less number of men of this description—not enough to control its action— and consequently the opinion of its great masses could be more easily shaped and moulded by the mere force of ideas."

The "force of ideas" was the touchstone of Tilden's life, and the key to his elusive personality. A sickly infant and solitary boy who, as his friend and biographer John Bigelow once said, "practically had no youth," Tilden entered public life reluctantly, well aware that he was not a natural-born politician. Unlike Rutherford B. Hayes, a calm, friendly, outgoing individual who seemed genuinely to enjoy the company of others, Tilden had to force himself to make even the slightest gesture of familiarity. It was, in fact, a testament of sorts to his high sense of calling that this most inward of men ever managed to unbend enough to run for anything—much less for president of the United States.

What Tilden lacked in personal magnetism and a backslapping nature, he more than made up for with a brilliant mind. From early childhood he had been trained—and trained himself—in the subtle political skills of grassroots organization, careful vote-targeting, and effective sloganeering. By the time he was eighteen he was already writing sophisticated Democratic party position papers on the National Bank, the anti-Mason movement, and the Nullification controversy, in which South Carolina legislators led by Senator John C. Calhoun attempted unsuccessfully to defy federal authority by nullifying a government tariff on manufactured goods. In 1836, when "Friend Van Buren" ran for president, Tilden sketched a strategy for him to follow to avoid alienating either the Masons or the anti-Masons, who were then a power in New York state. Van Buren's subsequent victory over Whig candidates William Henry Harrison of Ohio, Daniel Webster of Massachusetts, and Hugh Lawson White of Tennessee, who had united in an attempt to throw the election into the House of Representatives, delighted Tilden. In an uncharacteristically gleeful letter, he boasted to his father that "considering the game that was played against [Van Buren], the combination of discordant and powerful factions, the multiplicity of candidates, enlisting in their favor local and sectional interests, artfully calculated to divide and to prevent an election by the people, I must regard such a majority over the whole of them as a more triumphant victory than receiving two-thirds or three-quarters of all the votes against a single candidate."

Returning to New York City in 1837 to study law at NYU and clerk in the law office of the eccentric jurist John W. Edmonds, who claimed to be able to speak to the dead, Tilden continued to immerse himself in Democratic party politics. John Bigelow, a fellow lodger at Tilden's aunt

Polly Barnes's rooming house, found his new friend "wholly engrossed in practical politics." When the Panic of 1837 threw the nation into an uproar over the refusal of banks to convert paper money into gold or silver, Tilden once again rose to the president's aid. At a rally of Democratic working men at Tammany Hall, he assailed the "monarchy and a privileged nobility [who] regulate our affairs" and levy "an indirect tax upon the unprivileged masses for the benefit of the few." A few months later, he took on New York senator Nathaniel P. Tallmadge, who had bolted the Democratic party and joined the Whigs in defiance of Van Buren's soft-money stand. At a Whig party rally, Tilden wittily refuted Tallmadge's charge that the Democratic party had changed while he remained the same. Turning to the chairman of the meeting, Tilden wondered innocently, "Since Senator Tallmadge remains unchanged, I assume it is you, sir, who have changed your views." The question was met with a resounding, "No!" Senator Silas Wright, soon to become governor of New York, warmly congratulated the twenty-four-year-old Tilden for "rebuking a traitor in the midst of his assembled friends" and effectively leading the charge against "lying spirits throughout the state."

Tilden was less successful in the fight to reelect Van Buren president in 1840. The financial downturn occasioned in part by Van Buren's loyal adherence to Andrew Jackson's war on the National Bank put the incumbent in a politically vulnerable position; and the brilliant public relations campaign of "Tippecanoe and Tyler, Too" devised by New York journalist Horace Greeley convinced large numbers of American voters that millionaire planter-general-politician William Henry Harrison had been born in a log cabin on the frontier—not on a grand estate outside Richmond, Virginia, as was actually the case. Tilden did what he could to stem the tide, writing a lengthy pamphlet on European and American financial history that Democrats distributed across the country— even Whig economist William M. Gouge recommended the paper to anyone who knew how "to appreciate the worth of sound doctrine sent forth in clear and intelligible language."

It was not enough. After Van Buren went down to crushing defeat, the ex-president stopped off in New York to discuss the causes of his defeat with his young acolyte, who had already learned the valuable lesson that in the brave new world of mass newspapers and easily accessible printing presses a candidate's carefully manufactured image, however bogus, might trump a lifetime of actual experience. In Ohio, President-elect Harrison's adopted home, another budding young politician, Rutherford B. Hayes, was somewhat less astute, attributing the victory to a "whirlwind" of popular support that had swept irresistibly across the land. "I never was more elated by anything in my life," he told his uncle.

FOLLOWING THE 1840 presidential contest, Tilden completed his legal studies, hung out his shingle at No. 13 Pine Street in New York City, and concentrated on his new career. With customary dedication, the young lawyer took work wherever he could find it, starting at home. He represented his father in a suit against a former tenant who had cut down timber without permission, and helped his Uncle Ward resolve an outstanding $1,500 debt. No case was too small or unimportant; he duly recorded a $1 fee for drawing up a will, along with commissions of $8, $10, and $12.50 for unspecified legal tasks. At the same time, he also won a $17,000 settlement for another client.

With all his lawyering, Tilden still found time to continue his political activities. His practical-minded father wondered aloud if he was "getting any business." Tilden reassured him that "I have nothing to do with politics and meddle no more than is compatible with, if not conducive to, professional success." This was not entirely true. In August 1841 he published an essay in the *Democratic Review* of Washington denouncing the Whigs for attempting to repeal the act discontinuing the National Bank. Later that year he joined forces with William Cullen Bryant at the *New York Evening Post* to investigate and publicize illegal voting in the recent presidential election, a move which he said "made a great sensation" and annoyed the Whigs "amazingly." And as chairman of the Democratic-Republican Young Men of the City and County of New York, he helped elect William C. Bouck governor of the state in a landslide in 1842.

As a reward for his hard work in the trenches, Tilden was appointed corporate counsel of New York City in the spring of 1843. The office was much sought after, and the way in which Tilden campaigned for the appointment revealed both his painstaking approach to politics and the widening reach of his alliances. Besides his old legal mentor, John Edmonds, Tilden marshaled letters of support from New York City mayor Robert H. Morris, the General Committee of the Democratic-Republican Young Men of the City and County of New York, Columbia County judge Aaron Vanderpoel, forty-eight private citizens, and eight prominent Democratic party elders, including James J. Roosevelt, uncle of future president Theodore Roosevelt. He carried the Common Council vote by a 20–6 margin.

Tilden worked hard in his new position, representing the city's interests in a variety of lawsuits, class actions, and ordinance violations. In the first three months of his tenure he handled a staggering 1,200 cases, personally trying between twenty and thirty cases a week. In the official *Complaint Book 1843–44*, he carefully noted some of the many offenses he was called upon to prosecute: encumbering the sidewalk, operating cabs illegally, selling liquor on Sunday, "keeping more hogs than allowed by law," selling decayed oranges, driving too fast (more than five miles per hour), throwing coal ashes into the street, using false weights, parking stagecoaches in front of houses, and shaking carpets in the streets. He complained to his family that his duties prevented him from "get[ting] away a day in the country," but he still found time to show visiting President John Tyler around city hall, try a case before the state Supreme Court, and serve as a delegate to the 1844 Democratic National Convention in Baltimore. He took particular pride in doing what he could to help the common people, "a class of whom the public hears little but of whom I have occasion to know something[,] those who suffer injury and inconvenience from violations of the law and seek its protection at my hands."

Tilden's good deeds did not prevent him from being forced out of office by incoming mayor James Harper, a Whig, in May 1844. By then he had a new project to work on, the *Daily New York Morning News,* a Democratic party newspaper that he founded along with John L. O'Sullivan, editor of the Washington *Democratic Review.* Taking his cue from Horace Greeley's Whig party organ, the *Log Cabin,* which had helped elect Harrison president in 1840, Tilden set out to do the same for Democratic presidential nominee James K. Polk and New York gubernatorial candidate Silas Wright. The campaigns were successful, but Tilden unhappily found himself thrust into a nasty intraparty squabble between the new president and competing factions in New York state. Those factions had gathered around Governor Wright, on one side, and William L. Marcy, Polk's new secretary of war, on the other. Polk, a thin-skinned, combative Tennessean, was well aware that Wright (and Tilden) had fought hard to deny him the presidential nomination in Baltimore. Once in office, he was not particularly disposed to grant their requests for federal patronage. A full-scale political battle erupted between Wright's and Marcy's supporters in New York, and Tilden, at the still young age of thirty, was dispatched to Washington to meet with the president and try to work out a compromise.

Tilden had little luck with Polk, whom he described privately as "weak as dishwater," although he did receive an offer to become collector of the port of New York. Tilden turned down the overture, which might have earned him a good deal of money, because he had resolved to accept no political office unless it was "a post of honor." Such a post came open soon enough. Governor Wright, leading the anti-slavery wing of the Democratic party, the Barnburners, persuaded Tilden to run for election to the state assembly. In the fall of 1845 he was elected— third among thirteen successful candidates on the ballot—and went off to Albany "to help Mr. Wright in a crisis of his administration." At the same time, he divested himself of co-ownership of the *Daily New York Morning News*. Erstwhile partner N. J. Waterbury, foreshadowing some of the criticism Tilden would receive thirty years later in the wake of the 1876 presidential campaign, complained to the governor that Tilden had been ineffective in managing the newspaper. "It was an experiment to push off from the law on an uncertain voyage as an editor," Waterbury said. "Yet when he decided on it, he should have taken the helm boldly; but instead he kept watching the prospect from the cabin-door, and in a few months withdrew; he did [n]either himself [n]or the paper very little good."

In Albany, Tilden quickly established himself as the governor's most valued adviser. Indefatigible as always, he immersed himself in every area of state law, serving on the finance and canal committees and working out a much-praised compromise on the arcane subject of pre–Revolutionary War manorial rights, which had caused disgruntled tenant farmers to band together in defiance of the ancient custom. By instituting ownership taxes on the property and converting the leases into ten-year mortgages, Tilden managed the difficult task of satisfying both the tenants and the landlords—more evidence of his sure-handed grasp of practical politics. He further enhanced his reputation as a reformer by leading the fight to abolish the expensive patronage post of state printer, which by tradition went to the Albany newspaper backing the party in power. The cosy arrangement was complicated by the fact that there were two Democratic factions running the state and two newspapers vying for the printing rights of government documents. Tilden argued that it was not "sound political morals" to pay newspapers with public funds.

Tilden lost the fight over printing contracts, but his lonely stand—both sides opposed doing away with the custom—served to cement his reputation as a man of principle, and led to his selection in 1846 as a delegate to the state Constitutional Convention. Although one of the youngest men at the convention, Tilden so impressed his fellow conventioneers with his encyclopedic knowledge of government that he was offered his choice of running for a seat in Congress or in the state Senate, traditionally a stepping-stone to the governorship. To the surprise of many, Tilden declined to run for either office and chose to return, for the time being at least, to his law books.

FOR THE NEXT few years Tilden stayed off the political stage, devoting himself to his burgeoning legal career. From his new two-room office at 43 Wall Street, he conducted his wide-ranging affairs without the benefit of a partner, explaining to friends who worried that he was working too hard that "I have not been very fortunate in deputizing such business as I have generally had. I am exacting as to the mode in which my clients are served." Partly through his contacts in Albany, Tilden began handling mergers, acquisitions, and reorganizations for a number of northern railroads and industries. He entered into one particularly lucrative arrangement with William B. Ogden, the former Democratic mayor of Chicago, who had become the leading developer of midwestern railroads. Together, the two successfully merged Ogden's Galena & Chicago Union Railroad with the massive Northwestern Railroad. Tilden then managed the purchase of the financially ailing Chicago, St. Paul and Fond du Lac Railroad for over $10 million in stocks and bonds—a deal that became the basis for his growing personal fortune. He would later boast that at one time or another he had as clients over half the great railway companies north of the Ohio and between the Hudson and Missouri rivers.

Tilden's successful rehabilitation of the Chicago, St. Paul and Fond du Lac earned him an industry-wide reputation as a "financial physician" to troubled railroads, and much of his energy in the late 1840s and early 1850s was consumed with reorganizing and reinvigorating other financially challenged transportation lines. At the same time, he also handled personal investments for himself, his brothers, Van Buren, and other clients. His inherent caution, careful planning, and acutely analytical mind—qualities that would sometimes prove to be hindrances politically—combined to make him a peerless stockbroker and investor, someone who invariably made money for himself and his friends.

The rush of business and legal affairs left Tilden little time for outside interests. He did serve as an honorary member of several prestigious organizations, including the American Board of Foreign Missions, the New-York Historical Society, the Metropolitan Museum of Art, the New York Bar Association, and the board of trustees of the New York Medical College. But these were civic groups, not social ones, and although Tilden dined out frequently with friends who were eager to match him up with their daughters, granddaughters, cousins, and nieces, he never allowed himself to be caught matrimonially. As he explained to an older friend, Mrs. Franklin Chase, in 1850: "My life has vibrated between a leisure in which I amuse myself with books, and the greatest activity in public and private affairs. I have never been accustomed to surrender to my inner life." He was thirty-six at the time.

A revealing slip of paper dating from 1852 contains a list of young women who had, at one time or another, briefly attracted his interest: "Miss Butler (17 Washington Place), Miss Hedges (212 Cherry Street), the lady you met on the boat, Miss Butterman, Miss Skinner, Miss Hess, Miss McKern, Miss Smith, Miss Wainwright, the lady who makes your heart thump, the lady with *eyes*." One of these women, perhaps Harriet Butler, the daughter of his friend and former law professor Benjamin F. Butler, engaged Tilden sufficiently to spark rumors of an impending marriage. Martin Van Buren, Butler's longtime law partner, got wind of the rumors and hastened to tell Tilden that he "was happy to hear that you are about to do what you ought to have done long ago . . . you have my ready and hearty consent." For whatever reason, the marriage did not take place, and Van Buren wrote again a few months later to complain: "I see that, in addition to giving up matrimony, you have also abandoned politics. What is to become of you?"

THE FORMER PRESIDENT was right about the broken engagement, but wrong about Tilden's abandonment of politics. In the decade leading up to the election of Abraham Lincoln and the start of the Civil War, Tilden, along with other northern Democrats, found himself fighting a painful inner battle between his personal antipathy toward the institution of slavery and his innate Jeffersonian belief in the primacy of states' rights under the Constitution. It was a conflict that threatened to consume both the party and the country.

Although he preferred to do his fighting in private, Tilden was drawn inevitably into the public battle. As a founding member of the anti-slavery Barnburners, he was an early and enthusiastic supporter of the Wilmot Proviso, a bill first introduced in 1846 to prohibit slavery in any new territories acquired in the ongoing Mexican War. Together with Martin Van Buren and his son John, Tilden helped to write the first Free-Soil manifesto in early 1848, and he was one of the leaders of the National Convention of Free-Soilers that met in Buffalo in August 1848 and nominated Van Buren for president on the Free-Soil—critics called it the Free-Spoil—ticket. In the subsequent election, Van Buren drew off enough disaffected northern votes to deny Democratic nominee Lewis Cass the White House and elect the Whig party candidate, General Zachary Taylor, whose Mexican War exploits had helped raise the issue of new territories in the first place.

Unlike many anti-slavery Democrats, Tilden did not switch his affiliation to the newly formed Republican party in the mid-1850s. Although he considered slavery a "blighting presence" whose spread into the new territories would be "the greatest opprobrium of our age," Tilden was more concerned with preserving the Union than with abolishing slavery. He took no part in the Democratic nominating conventions of 1852 and 1856, and his subsequent relations with Presidents Franklin Pierce and James Buchanan were distant at best. Meanwhile, partly as a result of his anti-slavery views, Tilden's political fortunes ebbed at home. In 1855 and 1859 he lost separate elections for state attorney general and corporation counsel of New York City, and by the end of the decade he professed himself to be, for all intents and purposes, "out of politics."

The ever-worsening political climate, and the remarkable advent of Abraham Lincoln, brought Tilden out of his temporary retirement in the summer and fall of 1860. Somewhat reluctantly, he took part in the Democratic nominating convention in Baltimore, holding the New York delegation in line for Illinois senator Stephen A. Douglas. The angry split between northern Democrats supporting Douglas and breakaway southern Democrats supporting former vice president John C. Breckinridge of Kentucky threatened to give the election to Lincoln. (A fourth presidential candidate, John Bell of Tennessee, was running on the Constitutional Union ticket.) Tilden, hoping to avert a catastrophic Democratic defeat, gave a brief, impromptu speech urging unity at a mass meeting of discontented party factions at the Cooper Union on September 17. The *New York Evening Post,* reflecting editor William Cullen Bryant's switch to the Republican ranks, criticized Tilden's appearance at the rally and offered to print his speech in full so that he could explain "by what process so clever a man has reasoned himself into such bad company."

Tilden took advantage of the tongue-in-cheek offer to publish a thoughtful analysis of the dangers posed by the prospect of Lincoln's election. A Republican triumph, he warned in an open letter to longtime political foe William Kent, would inevitably provoke an angry southern reaction, possibly leading to secession and civil war. "Elect Lincoln, and we invite those perils which we cannot measure," Tilden wrote. "We attempt in vain to conquer the South to an impracticable and intolerable policy. Defeat Lincoln, and all our great interests and hopes are unquestionably safe." But Tilden had little hope of the Democrats defeating Lincoln. "It is too late!" he warned. "We are upon the breakers. My mind is filled, my heart swells with the thought that yon wave which towers above us will engulf more of human happiness and human hopes than have perished in any one catastrophe since the world began."

Tilden's uncharacteristically emotional outburst betrayed the anguish he felt over the looming crisis. That anguish was epitomized by another uncharacteristic display by the normally unflappable Tilden in the offices of the *New York Evening Post* a few days before the election. Dropping by to see William Cullen Bryant, who was not there, Tilden suffered some rough political kidding at the hands of other Republican-leaning newspapermen at the *Post*. "I would not have the responsibility of Bryant and [assistant editor John] Bigelow for all the wealth in the Subtreasury," he said hotly. "If you have your way, civil war will divide this country and you will see blood running like water in the streets of this city." Tilden stormed out of the room, and Bigelow, who had been his friend for nearly three decades, sent one of his assistants after Tilden. "You had better look him up at once and get him home," Bigelow said. "He is very much excited and I fear for his sanity."

Tilden soon recovered his poise, but Lincoln's election, as he foresaw all too clearly, brought the swift secession of South Carolina and other disaffected southern states. Although he considered the president-elect "a frank, genial, warm-hearted man," Tilden doubted that the inexperienced Lincoln could overcome the "chronic sectionalism" upon which his election had been based. At a Democratic party meeting in Albany on January 31, 1861, Tilden supported a resolution calling for a compromise with loyal southerners in the border states and continued patience on the part of the federal government. "I for one would resist, under any and all circumstances, the use of force to coerce the South into the Union," he advised.

With the coming of the Civil War three months later, Tilden loyally pledged his support to the new president, and twice he journeyed to Washington to consult with Lincoln over political and financial matters relating to the war. Although precluded by age and ill health from serving actively in the army, he sometimes delved uninvited into the military side of the conflict as well, counseling Secretary of War Edwin Stanton to rely upon the North's overwhelming numbers to defeat the South. With mathematical logic, Tilden noted that the Union had three times as many men and nine times as many industrial resources as the Confederacy, as well as a great advantage in railroads—his particular area of expertise. The careful concentration of force at critical points, he maintained, would lead inevitably to victory. It was an incisive analysis of the military situation by a decidedly unmilitary man, but Tilden's recommendations were not followed in Washington, and a succession of bumbling generals led the Union forces to one defeat after another during the first two years of the war. Stanton himself told Tilden, a little ruefully, in late 1863, "I beg you to remember, my dear sir, I always agreed with you."

Throughout the war, Tilden walked a thin line between support for the Union and disagreement over how best to preserve basic American liberties. He joined other Democrats in denouncing Lincoln's suspension of habeas corpus and his iron-handed crackdown on internal dissent, which Tilden considered "arbitrary and unconstitutional." He successfully managed fellow Democrat Horatio Seymour's gubernatorial campaign in 1862, and two years later he was instrumental in securing the party's presidential nomination for former Union general George B. McClellan. In helping to defeat the so-called Peace Democrats at the nominating convention in Chicago, Tilden nevertheless exposed himself to charges that he had been outmaneuvered by—or secretly agreed with—leading copperhead Clement Vallandigham, who managed to write into the party platform a controversial resolution calling for the immediate cessation of all hostilities and a negotiated peace with the rebellious South. The peace plank fatally damaged McClellan's presidential hopes and, as Tilden feared, helped Lincoln win reelection. The charge of latent copperheadism would cling to Tilden for years to come, and arise with a vengeance when he commenced his own run for the White House.

WITH THE END of the war in the spring of 1865, Tilden turned his attention to home-state politics, assuming the chairmanship of the New

York Democratic Committee after incumbent chairman Dean Richmond dropped dead of a heart attack in Tilden's new Gramercy Park
home in August 1866. As chairman of the nation's most important
Democratic state, Tilden was closely involved in the backroom wheeling and dealing over the selection of the party's presidential candidate
in 1868. The nominating convention was held in New York City, and
Tilden was accused after the fact of personally engineering the surprise
nomination of his old friend and associate Horatio Seymour, the former
governor of New York. But despite his well-earned reputation as a non-
pareil political operative, Tilden was as shocked as anyone when the
convention stampeded after the twenty-second ballot and nominated
Seymour, instead of pre-convention favorite Salmon P. Chase, the chief
justice of the Supreme Court. Chase's formidable daughter, Kate Chase
Sprague, laid her father's defeat squarely at the feet of Tilden and Seymour, adding sarcastically, "I fear that when the South seceded the
brains of the party went with it."

In the immediate aftermath of Seymour's nomination, there were
even rumors that Tilden had been angling to grab the top spot for himself. Secretary of the Navy Gideon Welles, a last-ditch booster of President Andrew Johnson's forlorn hopes for the nomination, confided in
his diary that he had been told that "Samuel Tilden wanted to be the
candidate of the Democrats for president. It is hardly credible, and yet
in that way, better than any other, can his conduct and that of the New
York Democratic politicians be accounted for." Given the fact that he
had lost his two most recent races for political office in his own state, it
is difficult to believe that Tilden would have entertained presidential
ambitions—however slight—in 1868. Nor is it likely that he would
have been so cynical as to use his good friend Seymour as a glorified
Trojan horse for his own selfish aims. Still, it was a compliment of sorts
to Tilden's growing stature within the party that such rumors could
have arisen in the first place.

As it turned out, Seymour's nomination was a blessing in disguise
for Tilden. Despite his initial reluctance to do so, he served loyally as
Seymour's campaign chairman, crafting a strategy that garnered the
Democratic candidate a surprisingly strong popular vote. But the continuing disarray of the party in the South (and the 650,000 newly en-

rolled black voters there) enabled Republican governments to carry the day for Ulysses S. Grant in Alabama, Arkansas, Florida, Missouri, North Carolina, South Carolina, and Tennessee, providing him with a comfortable margin in electoral votes. Had Tilden won the nomination in 1868, he undoubtedly would have suffered a similar fate, and his presence on the national scene would have ended as quickly as it began. Instead, at no cost to himself, he gained invaluable experience in how to conduct a national campaign, solidified his position as a party power, and, however inadvertently, replaced Seymour as New York's leading Democratic politician following the election.

Tilden used his newfound strength to challenge the ham-fisted hold of the state's most powerful political figure, the almost comically corrupt William Marcy "Boss" Tweed, head of the Democrats' notorious patronage machine, Tammany Hall. With his diamond stickpins, loud checked suits, ruby shirt studs, and bowler hats, the corpulent Tweed was the walking embodiment of big-city corruption. But Tilden, who had known Tweed for over a decade, also understood that he was nobody's fool, outward appearance notwithstanding. In a few years' time, Tweed had risen from the post of lowly bookkeeper and volunteer fireman to the highest level of political power. Bribery, fraud, and physical intimidation had accompanied him every step of his climb. The nexus of his power was the Tammany Hall "wigwam" on East 14th Street. From there he dispatched his "braves" throughout the city—and as far north as Albany—to bribe, coerce, threaten, or cajole anyone wanting to do business with the city, from the lowliest streetsweeper to the highest judge. "Something for everyone" was his motto, beginning and ending with himself. And to those isolated voices who complained about his bully-boy tactics, Tweed had a jeering response: "What are you going to do about it?"

Tweed's power grew out of the arcane inner workings of the Society of Saint Tammany, a fraternal order of craftsmen founded in the late 1780s to protect the rights of working men and women in New York City. Like the legendary chief of the Delaware Indians for whom it was named, the society from the start was slightly bogus (no Saint Tammany is listed in the official rolls of the Catholic Church). Its primary aim was to act as the political go-between for the thousands of Irish immigrants who swarmed into the city during the first decades of the nineteenth century. Their numbers, whether or not they were officially registered on the city's voting lists, carried increasing weight in civic elections, and for a dollar or two per man the Gaelic immigrants could be induced, in Tweed's immortal words, to "vote early and vote often." Since most of the votes went to Democratic candidates, Tammany Hall quickly became the dominant power in New York City politics and, by extension, the state as a whole.

Tweed and his cohorts used that power to undertake the most sweeping and lucrative system of organized corruption ever seen in American politics. Between the years 1863 and 1871, the Tweed Ring stole between $20 million and $200 million from the city and those attempting to do business with it. (The huge discrepancy between the figures is, in a way, a backhanded tribute to the gang's success.) During that time, Tammany Hall elected or bought virtually every post from governor to mayor to Supreme Court judge. Tweed himself was content to stay behind the scenes, using his modest position as deputy street commissioner to dole out contracts for lucrative construction projects in return for kickbacks ranging from 25 percent to 100 percent of the original estimates.

The acme of Tweed's vast peculations was the New York County courthouse, begun in 1862 and completed a full decade later. The scale of the frauds was breathtaking in its shamelessness. The building, which was supposed to cost $250,000, wound up costing the city nearly $14 million, most of it in overcharges by Tweed henchmen. Carpenters were paid $2.1 million for $30,000 worth of work; a Tammany Hall Indian named Andrew Garvey received $1.9 million to plaster the building (earning himself the apt nickname, "the Prince of Plasterers"); the furniture bill was $1.6 million, including $179,729 for three tables and forty chairs; and the bill for carpeting the courthouse was a staggering $4.8 million—enough to carpet the entire city. When an electrician submitted an estimate of $60,000 for fire alarms, Tweed responded, "If we get you a contract for $450,000, will you give us $225,000?" The contract was quickly let. No trick was too small for Tweed. He purchased three hundred benches for $5 each and resold them to the city for $300 each; and when a committee looking into why it was taking so long to complete the courthouse published its report, a Tweed-owned printing company charged the city $7,718 to print its findings.

To insure the survival of the ring, Tweed bought and sold politicians, judges, even journalists. Key reporters were given outside writing commissions or insider stock tips, lucrative advertising contracts were spread among some eighty-seven different newspapers, and when *Harper's Weekly* artist Thomas Nast began drawing his celebrated series of political cartoons depicting Tweed as a voracious tiger devouring the city, Tweed personally offered him $500,000—one hundred times Nast's yearly salary—to go off and study art in Europe. Nast refused, saying he was unable to go to Europe at the present, since "I shall be busy here for some time getting a gang of thieves behind bars." The ring even attempted to purchase the *New York Times* and install one of its lackeys as editor; only a desperate last-minute subscription effort by wealthy reformers prevented the sale by raising enough money to keep the paper afloat.

Tilden, personally incorruptible and independently wealthy, seems not to have realized—or at any rate not given much thought to—the extent to which Tweed and his henchmen were robbing the city. "I had no more knowledge or grounds of suspicion of the frauds of 1869 as they were discovered three years afterwards, than the *Times* or the general public," he maintained, adding that "I never took a favor from these men or from any man I distrusted." Still, as chairman of the state Democratic party, he was forced to consult with Tammany Hall from time to time on political appointments and mutual fund-raising activities, and he held his tongue when Tweed's right-hand man, A. Oakey Hall, forged Tilden's name on a letter to county leaders in the fall of 1868 asking that they telegraph to Tweed their estimate of the vote in the upcoming election—the clear inference being that the Boss would steal the necessary number of votes needed to carry the election. When Tilden's pocket was picked at the state Democratic convention in Rochester two years later, *The Nation* sniped, "We hope he has a realizing sense of the company he keeps, when he opens conventions for Mr. Tweed, Mr. Hall and [Governor John] Hoffman," another Tammany stalwart.

But if Tilden maintained a wary working relationship with Tammany Hall—and as Democratic chairman how could he not?—it is simply untrue that, as various historians have claimed, he did nothing to oppose Tweed and his ring until after the *New York Times* began its famous anti-corruption campaign in late 1870. As early as December 1, 1869, Tilden was calling for a public meeting to organize a New York Bar Association to promote a "reformed judiciary." The next spring he led the fight to elect a slate of uncorrupted judges to the newly formed state Court of Appeals, sending a letter to Democratic leaders that declared unambiguously, "We must elect this ticket." The ticket won, and fellow Democrat Roswell P. Flower congratulated Tilden for his prominent role in the victory. "Three years ago you started with a Democratic mob," said Flower. "Today you have an army."

Tweed, to be sure, considered Tilden an enemy long before the *New York Times* got into the fight. On two separate occasions in 1869 and 1870, he tried unsuccessfully to depose Tilden as chairman of the state Democratic party. At the same time, Tweed associates Sunny Jim Fisk and Jay Gould tried to buy Tilden's goodwill by offering him legal retainers as high as $125,000 to represent their railroad interests—and leave Tweed's alone. Tilden declined, and an enraged Tweed complained: "What does old Sam Tilden want?" Answering his own rhetorical question, the Boss continued, "Sam Tilden wants to overthrow Tammany Hall. He wants to drive me out of politics. He wants to stop the pickings, starve out the boys, and run the city as if 'twas a damned little country store in New Lebanon. He wants to bring the hayloft and cheese-press down to the city, and crush out the machine. He wants to get a crowd of reformers in the legislature who will cut down the tax levy below a living rate; and then, when he gets everything fixed to suit him, he wants to go to the United States Senate."

Tilden further incurred Tweed's animosity when he appeared before the Boss's state Senate committee in the winter of 1870—Tweed had bought himself a Senate seat by then—and opposed the creation of a new charter for the city of New York, a plan that would legally permit Tweed and his fellow foxes not only to raid the henhouse, but to stand guard over it as well by giving them control of the city auditing board and the mayor's office, with the power to appoint their own men to posts previously decided by election. At a point when the *New York Times* was praising the charter and stating flatly that "Senator Tweed is in a fair way to distinguish himself as a reformer," Tilden was crossing swords with Tweed over the same issue in Albany. Appearing before Tweed's Senate committee, Tilden strongly denounced the charter and called for open elections, which he said "would have more purity and more safety." Chairing the committee, Tweed treated Tilden with such contempt that a visibly angry Tilden left the room shaking and told a friend in the hall outside that Tweed would "close his career in jail or in exile."

TILDEN PROVED TO BE right on both counts. In the summer of 1871 a disgruntled Tammany brave, former sheriff James O'Brien, leaked copies of the ring's secret account books to the *New York Times*, which now reversed its previous support of Tweed and began mounting a campaign to topple the Boss and all his minions. Tilden, who had already been in contact with various reform-minded organizations, including the Young Democracy, the Young Men's Municipal Reform Association, and the Executive Committee of the Citizens and Taxpayers, stepped up his own efforts to aid the campaign. Inevitably for Tilden, political as well as moral issues were involved. As he explained to party member Robert Minturn on August 12, "We have to face the question whether we will fall with the wrong doers or whether we will separate from them and take our chances of possible defeat now, with resurrection hereafter."

With Tammany Hall still controlling a majority of the delegates at the state Democratic convention in September, Tilden allied himself with a splinter group, the Apollo Hall Democracy, which nominated its own slate of candidates for the upcoming election—including Tilden, who stood for state assemblyman. He bravely took his stand at the state convention, which Tweed had packed with a gang of insolent New York City thugs. Declaring from the podium that it was "time to proclaim that whoever plunders the people, though he steal the livery of heaven to serve the devil in, is no Democrat," Tilden threw down the gauntlet of reform. "I avow before this convention that I shall not vote for any one of Mr. Tweed's members of the legislature," he said. "And if that is to be regarded as the regular ticket, I will resign my place as chairman of the state committee and help my people stem the tide of corruption.

When I come to do my duty as an elector, I shall cast my vote for hon-est men."

But Tilden did more than simply make speeches. Along with two as-sistants, he spent ten days that October going over Tweed's bank records at the behest of the new city comptroller. The results of his in-vestigation, published in an affidavit entitled "Figures That Could Not Lie," sealed the fate of Tweed and his henchmen. Only someone with Tilden's unique background as a lawyer, politician, and financier could have made sense of the confused welter of payoffs, kickbacks, and bribes contained in Tweed's accounts. As it was, Tilden's affidavit, sub-sequently published in the *New York Times*, helped clarify the people's choice on election day. A week before the election, at a gathering of re-formers at the Cooper Union, Tilden gave perhaps the most eloquent speech of his career. "The million of people who compose our great me-tropolis have been the subject of a conspiracy the most audacious and most wicked ever known in our free and happy land," he said. "A cabal of corrupt men have seized upon the powers of our local government and converted them, not only to the purposes of misgovernment, but also of personal plunder. It is the foremost duty of every good citizen to join with his fellows in the effort to overthrow this corrupt and degrad-ing tyranny. I come before you to advocate a union of all honest men against a combination of plunderers."

In the ensuing election, the reformers won a tremendous victory, voting in all fifteen of their candidates for alderman, thirteen of twenty-one assistant aldermen, two state senators, and six state assemblymen, including Tilden. Tweed, in a last gasp of fraudulent politics, held on to his Senate seat, but was so wounded by Tilden's affidavit that he never physically occupied it—the seat stood vacant his entire term. Indicted on 120 counts of felony, forgery, grand larceny, false pretenses, and con-spiracy to defraud, Tweed fled to California and later to Spain. Other Tammany ringleaders escaped to Canada. Eventually, Tweed was extra-dited back to New York, where he died in prison in 1878, remarking, "I guess Tilden and [Democratic party regular Charles S.] Fairchild have killed me at last. I hope they will be satisfied now."

Tilden's major role in overthrowing the Tweed ring led directly to his election as governor of New York in November 1874. Showing admirable energy for a sixty-year-old, Tilden managed his own campaign, using a statewide organization of key men in each school district to send him weekly estimates of his strength. Analyzing these reports as carefully as he had dissected Boss Tweed's financial records, Tilden was able to predict on election day that he would win by "a little in excess of fifty thousand" votes; the official margin was 50,317.

Once in office, Tilden burnished his credentials as a reformer by forcing through a series of anti-corruption acts aimed at preventing a recurrence of the Tammany Hall scandal. At the same time, he led a successful fight to break the power of the Albany-based Canal Ring, a bipartisan group of state and local officials who had been systematically looting the treasury of millions of dollars by helping dishonest contractors overcharge for unnecessary repairs to the state's system of inland waterways. Denouncing the ring as "sinister, evil, and profligate," Tilden appointed a commission that put an end to the "gross and monstrous frauds" that he estimated had cost the state over $5 million in lost revenues in the past five years alone. Contrasting Tilden's reform-minded efforts in Albany with the ongoing deluge of scandals in Washington, the *New York World* editorialized in early 1876: "Would to God that some Hercules might arise and cleanse *that* Augean stable as the city and state of new York are cleansing." Readers of the newspaper had little trouble guessing the identity of the proposed cleanser.

FROM THE VERY beginning of his term as governor, Tilden gave indications that he was thinking of an even higher office—that of president of the United States. The day after his election, he told the *New York Tribune* that the Democratic landslide across the country demonstrated that the people had awakened to the widespread abuses in Washington, where the "illusion of a false prosperity" had been founded upon "an audacious system of robbery." The election results, Tilden said, clearly indicated that the people had discarded their "present political doctors" in favor of new ones. And in a nod to the southern states where Radical Reconstruction was under increasing attack, the governor-elect observed, "The people are beginning to think that it is time to have a real peace in the United States." He enlarged upon this view in January

1876, devoting fully one third of his annual State of the State address to a ringing denunciation of the evils of Republican mismanagement in Washington and the need for a thorough housecleaning there and in the South. The *New York World,* a Democratic party mainstay, headlined the speech with a simple but powerful phrase that had all the makings of a successful campaign slogan: "Tilden and Reform."

As the Democrats prepared to open their nominating convention in St. Louis on June 27, Tilden had a clear lead in the minds, if not the hearts, of most convention delegates. His recent, much publicized prosecution of the Canal Ring, and his lead role in defanging Boss Tweed and his rapacious Tammany Hall tigers, gave him an invaluable reputation as a reformer, at a time when the American public had sickened noticeably of the nonstop parade of scandals emanating from the nation's capital. Tilden may not have been the most riveting of personalities, but he was as honest as he was nondescript, and that counted for much in the roiling wake of Boss Tweed, Jay Cooke, William Belknap, James G. Blaine, and the other key players in the ongoing immorality play that was American life at the highest echelons of political, governmental, and financial life. As governor of the nation's most populous state, Tilden had the added bonus of thirty-five key electoral votes stashed firmly in his back pocket. The nomination was his to lose.

Despite his obvious advantages, Tilden did not lack for competition. The encouraging prospects of a Democratic victory in November brought out a plethora of would-be candidates. From the U.S. Senate came Thomas F. Bayard of Delaware and Allen G. Thurman of Ohio. Indiana governor Thomas A. Hendricks, a former senator, carried the banner for soft-money proponents. Major General Winfield Scott Hancock, the hero of Gettysburg, was the favorite-son candidate of his native state of Pennsylvania; of all the Democratic candidates, he was the only one with a military background, the only one with a chance to tap into the vast pool of Union veterans who wore the lapel pin of the Grand Army of the Republic. Former Ohio governor William Allen, Senator Thurman's uncle, burned for another opportunity to face Republican presidential nominee Rutherford B. Hayes, who had defeated him a year earlier in a bitterly fought gubernatorial campaign.

Tilden, in his methodical way, already had begun seeding the ground for his nomination. A nationwide advertising campaign touting Tilden's reform record commenced six weeks before the convention in 1,200 rural newspapers. This was augmented by a Newspaper Popularity Bureau, fully staffed with editors, writers, artists, and "advertisement concoctors" who labored diligently to inject human-interest color into the admittedly gray image of their champion. Helpful New York newspapers, including the *Tribune* and the *World,* picked up the staff-written articles, which were reprinted in turn in dozens of publications across the nation. (One dissenting newspaper, the *Cincinnati Enquirer,* complained that Tilden's supporters had reduced the campaign "to the level of a White Pine Extract or a recipe for Stomach Bitters.") A separate Tilden Literary Bureau produced more sophisticated articles designed to educate voters on such topics as civic reform, the abolition of executive patronage, and the popular election of postmasters. The articles were printed on colored paper that was the same size and shape as the ubiquitous railroad timetables carried by travelers everywhere. Finally, clever Tilden cartoons were supplied for those unwilling or unable to read more involved stories. It was a more sophisticated version of the "Tippecanoe and Tyler, Too" campaign that the hated Whigs had used to defeat Tilden's friend and mentor Martin Van Buren in 1840, and it demonstrated Tilden's ability to both remember the past and learn from it.

Nor did Tilden neglect his southern flank. Well aware that he would need the votes of the newly redeemed southern states, and equally cognizant of the fact that his pro-Union stand during the Civil War had not exactly endeared him to the battle-scarred ex-Confederates who increasingly controlled those states, Tilden established a Southern Bureau to help spread the message that he was a friend to the South, despite his earlier statements on slavery, which he now dismissed as mere "youthful indiscretions." His campaign managers made it a point to reach out early and often to such influential sectional leaders as Henry Watterson, editor of the *Louisville Courier-Journal;* Montgomery Blair, scion of the influential Missouri political dynasty; and former Confederate general Richard C. Taylor, son of the late president Zachary Taylor. "Never a leading Southern man came to town who was not seen," Watterson remarked approvingly. "If of enough importance he was taken to No. 15 Gramercy Park. Mr. Tilden measured to the Southern standard of the gentleman in politics."

While Tilden and his team worked tirelessly behind the scenes, hundreds of Democratic delegates, alternates, and hangers-on swarmed into St. Louis in the days leading up to the convention. (One of the latter, sixteen-year-old William Jennings Bryan, shimmied through a side window into the convention hall. Twenty years later, he would mesmerize another Democratic convention with his famous "Cross of Gold" speech on his way to the party's presidential nomination.) Unlike Cincinnati, St. Louis was not the home of any particular candidate. Instead, it owed its selection to a number of subtle political factors. By choosing to hold a national nominating convention for the first time west of the Mississippi River, the Democrats hoped to demonstrate their broad appeal to northerners, southerners, and westerners alike. And although St. Louis was located in a state with widespread Confederate sympathies, it had been a bulwark of Unionism during the Civil War, with its large German population providing thousands of volunteers to the federal ranks. The city's selection to host the convention was a nod to northern patriotism and also, perhaps, a wink to those who had worn the gray. Moreover, Missouri was the home of Carl Schurz, the father of the modern reform movement, whose manifold appeal the Democrats hoped to ride all the way to the White House.

More problematically, the West was also the center of the soft-money movement, and despite the fact that the convention front-runner was a notorious hard-money Democrat and a friend of the much-hated railroad interests, the party knew that it would have to retain the support of recalcitrant greenbackers if it had any chance of winning the election. The division between the two camps was deep and ominous. The debate over the nation's monetary policy had its roots in the Civil War, when the financially strapped Lincoln administration issued $300 million worth of government bonds to help pay for the war. Printed in green ink, the new paper money immediately became known as greenbacks, and rapidly replaced gold coins as the national currency of choice. Since they were not backed by gold reserves, the greenbacks theoretically were less valuable;

it took more of the so-called soft money to purchase equivalent goods and services. Western farmers, hit particularly hard by the Panic of 1873, had seen the value of their own goods plummet. They wanted the government to issue more greenbacks as a way of increasing consumers' buying power and thus easing the crisis. Many of the farmers had borrowed heavily during and after the war, and the eastern bankers who were their chief creditors did not want more greenbacks flooding the marketplace, to be used in turn by the farmers to pay down their debts. The Republican party was firmly in favor of specie resumption, or a return to the gold standard, and so was Samuel Tilden, who believed adamantly that a policy of hard money was needed to put the national economy back on a solid footing. The best the Democrats could hope to do in St. Louis was to agree to disagree.

Harper's Weekly, a reliable Republican party mouthpiece, lampooned the Democrats' spread-eagled catholicity in a cartoon depicting a be-robed Irish priest, a Ku Klux Klansman, a well-fed eastern millionaire, a rag-doll baby symbolizing soft-money westerners, and a Tammany Hall Indian brandishing a tomahawk. Although no one in the East knew it yet, a more indigenous group of Indians—Sioux, Cheyenne, Blackfeet, and Arapaho—had made their presence felt a few days earlier, in decidedly less comical circumstances, on the grassy slopes of the Little Bighorn River in southern Montana. There, on Sunday, June 25, while Democratic party delegates were streaming into St. Louis for the nominating convention, Lieutenant Colonel George Armstrong Custer and 263 troopers under his command in the U.S. 7th Cavalry had been wiped out by a much larger force of Indians led by the totemic Sioux medicine man Sitting Bull and the charismatic warrior-chief Crazy Horse.

Custer, who had ridden his hell-for-leather reputation all the way to a major generalship in the Civil War, had reverted after the war to his Regular Army rank of lieutenant colonel. His personal and professional standing had dropped as well. Transferred to the West to fight Indians, Custer, like the rest of the army, had endured a series of frustrating campaigns against the elusive and dangerous enemy. He had managed to win a victory over the Cheyenne at the Battle of the Washita River in western Oklahoma in November 1868, but even that success had been marred by charges that he had massacred mainly old men, women, and children, and had also abandoned a smaller force of troopers to the malign embrace of a returning war party. In the meantime, Custer had been court-martialed and nearly cashiered from the service for taking an unauthorized leave of absence to visit his wife; and he had gained the tireless hatred of his commander-in-chief, Ulysses S. Grant, for having the nerve to testify twice before the House committee investigating Secretary of War William Belknap and the trading post scandal. Only the personal intercession of his western commander, Lieutenant General Phil Sheridan, had enabled Custer to reclaim his field command—just in time to ride off in search of Sitting Bull and Crazy Horse, both of whom he found soon enough in the Valley of the Greasy Grass beside the Little Bighorn River.

After Custer's death, absurd rumors arose that the impetuous young cavalryman had attacked the seething Indian village in the hopes of somehow stampeding the upcoming Democratic convention into giving him its presidential nomination. Like most high-ranking career officers, then and now, Custer was something of an amateur politician as well as a soldier, and his widely publicized appearance before the Clymer Committee had earned him the appreciation and respect of his fellow Democrats. But the only suggestion that Custer entertained fatal presidential aspirations was the statement of an Arikara Indian scout, thirty-seven years after the fact, that Custer had told him on the day of the battle that a victory over the Sioux would make him the Great Father in Washington. That was as much a forlorn hope as his ill-advised frontal assault on Sitting Bull's camp: given Tilden's viselike grip on the nomination, it would have taken Custer far more than the 263 troopers he led to their doom to wrest the prize from Tilden's hands.

UNAWARE OF CUSTER'S shocking demise—it would take several days for the news to reach civilization—prideful Democrats thronged the downtown streets of St. Louis, which were illuminated at night by strings of Chinese lanterns and limelights. Giant American flags and red-white-and-blue bunting hung from storefronts, lampposts, and hotel awnings. The Republican-leaning *Chicago Tribune* reflected both a political and an intercity bias in its headline, "A Dull Town Agog," adding,

"Good rooms are scarcer than snakes in Ireland, and, in fact, are not to be had for love or money." Southern delegates congregated around the Southern Hotel and a Mississippi riverboat, the *Great Republic*, which had been chartered to accommodate overflow guests. "Honest John" Kelly, Boss Tweed's slightly more reputable successor, led 150 Tammany Hall braves quartering at the Lindell Hotel, scene of Orville Babcock's notorious liaisons with the sylphlike Louise Hawkins of Whiskey Ring infamy. From their second-floor headquarters the rebellious New Yorkers hung a large banner proclaiming: "The City of New York, the Largest Democratic City in the Union, Uncompromisingly Opposed to the Nomination of Samuel J. Tilden for the Presidency Because He Cannot Carry the State of New York." Tilden's brother Henry led a second New York delegation that loudly begged to disagree.

The focal point for the delegates was the four-story Merchants Exchange Building near the river, where the nominating convention was gaveled into order at noon on June 27 by Augustus Schell, chairman of the Democratic National Committee. As an immediate sign of who truly controlled the proceedings, Schell turned the chair over to Henry Watterson, one of Tilden's chief lieutenants. Well aware that Tilden's personality was not the type to inspire spontaneous outbreaks of emotion or galvanic excitement, Watterson advised the 983 delegates—not one of whom was black or female—"It is the issue, not the man, that should engage us." That issue, said the journalist, was reform. "We are called together to determine by our wisdom whether honest government, administered by honest men, shall be restored to the American people." Watterson also sounded the notes of a second Democratic campaign theme. "Hard times, vacant houses, neglected fields, closed factories, and idle hands are all about us," he said, adding that the cause for that economic distress was "partisan misrule and sectional misdirection"—a subtle dig at Reconstruction. "We are here," Watterson concluded, "to make the people's fight for a free and honest government—for reform, home rule, economy, and a chance for all men."

The resolutions committee, which had the responsibility of drafting a campaign platform, was headed by Lieutenant Governor William Dorsheimer of New York, another Tilden acolyte. Dorsheimer had the uncomfortable task of drawing up a document that would reflect his candidate's immovable hard-money stand while somehow managing to avoid alienating the large number of soft-money Democrats, mostly westerners, who were calling loudly for the repeal of the Specie Resumption Act of 1875. The committee met throughout the night, first adopting a resolution calling for repeal of the act, then reversing itself an hour before the convention was reconvened on June 28 and voting for a slippery-worded compromise that opposed both inflation and the "sham" resumption of specie payments. Dorsheimer, reflecting the strain of the intraparty struggle, fainted as he left the committee room. Indiana delegate James "Blue Jeans" Williams, a leading soft-money proponent, was unsympathetic. "If I had had the triumph that man has had," he said of the unconscious Dorsheimer, "I'd get good and drunk, too."

The mood of the convention was lightened considerably by the appearance of local suffragist-lawyer Phoebe Cousins, who made her way to the platform to speak in behalf of women's voting rights. Remembering the unchivalrous treatment the less attractive Sarah Spencer had received at the Republican convention two weeks earlier, the suffragists had chosen the younger, more appealing Miss Cousins to champion their cause in St. Louis. Eschewing the severe widow's black favored by Susan B. Anthony and other matronly leaders of the movement, Cousins wore a tasteful brown dress for her convention debut. She referred wittily to the fact that 1876 was a leap year, noting: "In the good old days of our ancestors, it was deemed an unpardonable offense if the leap year privileges accorded to women were not acquiesced in." She urged the delegates to "say 'yes' to the sweet maiden's coy wooing [and] give heed to the warning from out of the gates of Paradise—'It is not good for man to be alone'—and accept for your companions in the political household she who blends all discord into the divine harmony of sweet nature's better half." The male conventioneers, by and large, were unmoved by the appeal, and the party platform promised only to give financial aid to the widows of soldiers and sailors, failing even to match the Republican party platform's wan salute to "the substantial advances recently made toward the establishment of equal rights for women."

With convention niceties out of the way, the delegates got down to serious business. The first task at hand was the reading and approving of the Democratic platform. Before that event could take place, Honest

John Kelly rose to his feet, waving a piece of paper in the air. The paper, he said, had been signed by New Yorkers who were unalterably opposed to Tilden's nomination. He asked for the privilege of reading the names out loud to the convention. A blizzard of "cat calls, Indian yells, applause, hisses, stamping feet, and clapping hands" greeted Kelly's request, and permanent convention chairman John McClernand, a former Union general, banged away with his gavel for several minutes, unable to restore order, until the house band broke into an inspired medley of "Yankee Doodle" and "Dixie." Kelly lost his temper and used "minatory language toward several gentlemen" before retiring from the stage.

Dorsheimer, recovered from his earlier faint, read the proposed platform in a booming voice that carried to every corner of the sweltering hall. Applause built steadily as he read aloud the nine planks embedded in the document, each beginning with the words, "Reform is necessary." By the time he reached the final plank, the words had become a veritable revival meeting call-and-response. The section earning the loudest cheers was the one assailing Reconstruction and the myriad frauds of the Grant administration: "Reform is necessary to rebuild and establish in the hearts of the whole people of the Union, eleven years ago happily rescued from the danger of a secession of states, but now to be saved from a corrupt centralism which, after inflicting upon ten states the rapacity of carpetbag tyranny, has honeycombed the offices of the federal government itself with incapacity, waste, and fraud; infected states and municipalities with the contagion of misrule; and locked fast the prosperity of an industrious people in the paralysis of 'hard times.' . . . [T]he first step in reform must be the people's choice of honest men from another party, lest the disease of one political organization infect the body politics, and lest by making no change of men or parties we get no change of measures and no real reform."

It was, as such things go, a fairly stirring document. No less a judge than James G. Blaine—himself one of the targets skewered by it— judged the Democratic platform "the most elaborate paper of the kind ever put forth by a National Convention." The platform's chief sticking point, the disagreement between hard- and soft-money advocates, was bluntly put to rest by Dorsheimer, who warned that no Democrat could be elected president without carrying New York, and no one could carry

New York on a soft-money platform. "This announcement was like an electric shock to the convention and sent a thrill through the entire assemblage," the *New York World* reported the next day. "From that moment there was no doubt of the result." The inflationary plank was defeated 515–219, and the convention turned immediately to the selection of a presidential nominee.

First to be nominated was Delaware senator Thomas F. Bayard. The heir to a long-standing family tradition of political service—his grandfather, father, and uncle had all been United States senators—Bayard was one of Ulysses S. Grant's harshest critics. His opposition to all things military extended to the use of army troops in the South. That opposition, and the fact that Delaware had been a slave state prior to the Civil War, made him the favorite candidate of southern Democrats, who nevertheless recognized that Bayard could not win the general election as "a Confederate candidate." Bayard himself admitted as much to Virginia congressman Eppa Hunton, late of the House Judiciary Committee's investigation into the doings and misdoings of James G. Blaine. "The man of our party who combines [the] most capacities for obtaining the confidence & support of the Northern & Western States should in my opinion be accepted by the South whether they would under other circumstances have preferred him or not," Bayard wrote. He was speaking, of course, of Tilden.

The next nomination was for Indiana governor Thomas A. Hendricks, the leader of the soft-money wing of the party. Hendricks's name was greeted by "howling applause from the wild men of the West," sniffed the correspondent for the *New York Herald*. "[T]he Hendricks supporters spouted a rigmarole of half knowledge and financial nonsense." Like Tilden, the fifty-six-year-old Hendricks had the advantage of being governor of a large northern state whose electoral votes would be crucial in a close national election. The defeat of the soft-money plank, however, put a damper on Hendricks's hopes, as did persistent rumors that he had certain unsavory links to Tammany Hall and the Canal Ring—rumors that Tilden's floor leaders did nothing to suppress. The bully-boy tactics of Honest John Kelly, Hendricks's most vociferous supporter, did not help the Hoosier's chances.

Following the favorite-son nomination of New Jersey governor Joel

Parker, it was New York's turn in the roll call of states. Senator Francis Kernan took the stage. "The great issue upon which this election will be lost or won is the question of needed administrative reform," he said. "If we have a man who has laid his hand on dishonest officials, rooted out abuses, lowered taxes and inaugurated reforms, and if we are wise enough to select him as our leader, we will sweep the Union." The convention hall erupted with deafening cheers. In the midst of the Tilden demonstration, Kelly rushed the stage and began to speak. By rights, the next speaker should have been Tilden's seconding delegate, but Kelly did not stand on ceremony. Once again he urged the convention to nominate Hendricks and repeated his implausible charge that Tilden could not carry New York. A chorus of boos drowned out his words. Someone cried, "Three cheers for Tilden!" Kernan graciously stepped forward and urged the delegates to let Kelly continue, but the impromptu speech dribbled out with an exchange of curses between the burly New Yorker and the restless crowd.

After Kelly's outburst the other nominations, for former Ohio governor William Allen and General Winfield Scott Hancock of Pennsylvania, were anticlimactic. The balloting began immediately. From the start it was a Tilden landslide. Needing 492 votes for the nomination, Tilden amassed 401½ on the first ballot, to 140½ for Hendricks, seventy-five for Hancock, fifty-four for Allen, a surprisingly few thirty-three for Bayard, eighteen for Parker, and a mainly complimentary sixteen Missouri votes for home-state candidate James O. Broadhead. Following the tally the convention band broke out with another rendition of "Dixie," although it was unclear who, exactly, they were saluting.

On the second ballot, each of the first eight states in line unanimously cast their votes for Tilden, giving him an uncatchable lead of ninety-eight votes before anyone else received a single nod. The landslide continued. At the end of the balloting, Tilden was a scant dozen votes short of the necessary two-thirds majority. A flurry of strategic delegate switches put him over the top, and Pennsylvania's chairman moved successfully to make the nomination unanimous. It was 8:30 P.M., local time.

Back east, in Albany, the Democratic party's presidential nominee for 1876 was quietly sipping tea with his widowed sister, Mrs. Mary

Pelton. He had spent the day attending to official business at his home on Eagle Street. A private telegraph line had been installed in the governor's office on Capitol Hill, but Tilden preferred to stay close to home, working on a lawsuit with his personal attorney, James C. Carter. Late in the afternoon the two went for a long carriage ride, and Tilden betrayed a slight case of nerves by talking incessantly and driving so carelessly that Carter "was in constant fear of a catastrophe." The younger man suggested that Tilden might return home to find a telegram informing him of his nomination. Tilden said, "No, not until about half-past nine." Eventually, they did return to the governor's mansion, and at almost exactly 9:30 Tilden's aide, W. C. Newell, rushed into the parlor and read a new telegram from St. Louis: "Tilden nominated on second ballot." The governor looked up from his tea. "Is that so?" he asked mildly.

News of Tilden's nomination spread rapidly across Albany, and victory bonfires sprang up everywhere on Capitol Hill. An organization of Democratic working men, the Jackson Corps, serenaded the nominee from his front yard to the boisterous strains of a full brass band. Coming onto the porch, Tilden thanked the men for their salute, but warned that the lengthy national depression had left "the wolf at the door of nearly every home in the land, gaunt and hungry." He denounced wasteful government spending, increased taxes, and widespread corruption. "In the public administration everywhere," he said, "[are] abuses, peculations, frauds and corruption, till we are almost becoming ashamed of the institutions of our country, and instead of holding them up as examples for the imitation of the oppressed people of other countries, we are confessing them as a scandal in the eyes of mankind. The government no longer exists for the people. The people exist for the government. Our centennial products are the evils, license, and wrongs to escape [from] which our ancestors abandoned their homes in the Old World and planted themselves in a wilderness." What was the remedy? he wondered rhetorically. "The election of Tilden!" someone shouted. The candidate had a different answer. "It is comprised in one word," he said. "Reform."

Back in St. Louis, the convention wound up its business the next morning, unanimously approving Thomas Hendricks as Tilden's running mate, despite the two men's unresolved differences on monetary policy. John Kelly was so moved by the choice that he went to the speaker's rostrum yet again, this time pledging to do everything in his power to assist the upcoming campaign. He did not tell the delegates how strongly he had been forced to twist Hendricks's arm to get him to accept the second spot on the ticket in the first place.

The Democratic ticket was greeted largely with approval, although wits in the Republican press likened it to a kangaroo, "with all its strength in its hind legs." Soft-money Democrats in the Midwest grumbled about the nomination of a known Wall Street man for president. Hendricks discussed the greenback question with local Democratic leaders during a stopover in Cleveland a few days later, and wired Tilden to warn him that thousands of Ohio votes would be lost without his prompt support for the repeal of the Resumption Act. Tilden ignored the jittery telegram, just as he ignored the doleful frettings of old-line liberal Charles Francis Adams, who informed the nominee that he wanted desperately to support him, but that Hendricks's public statements "make my position wholly untenable. You, without any platform and with a nobody for a Vice President I could see my way to support aggressively. Cannot you throw some of the weight off?" When an industrious reporter cornered Tilden in his garden and asked him about his potentially burdensome running mate, the candidate merely pointed to a rose bush. "A week ago," he said, "that was covered with flowers. How quickly they fade." As every gardener knew—and Tilden was an avid gardener—the bloom quickly left the rose. The wise man, like Candide, tended his own garden, and kept an eye on the approaching weather.

CHAPTER FOUR

A HOT AND CRITICAL CONTEST

FOLLOWING THE CONVENTIONS in Cincinnati and St. Louis, the two parties began preparing immediately for the general election. For the first time since 1860 the White House was truly up for grabs, and experienced observers in both camps expected a close, contentious campaign.

Rarely, in peacetime, had the stakes been higher. Like the pivotal election of 1860, the upcoming political contest promised to be a referendum on the very essence of American government. The Republicans, buoyed by four straight presidential triumphs and undergirded by a small army of partisan federal employees who owed their livelihoods to party patronage, wanted to expand the reach and power of the central government. They viewed themselves, with some justice, as the saviors of the Union and the conservators of individual liberties. Those liberties, which included especially the free workings of the capitalistic marketplace, had been extended—on paper at least—to the millions of black Americans physically liberated by the Civil War. Republicans, particularly southern Republicans, saw the protection of black voting rights as a primary function of the federal government, and a vital, if symbolic, representation of a mighty nation's inherent goodness.

For millions of Democrats, in the North as well as the South, the federal government seemed less the protector of liberty than the chief impediment to personal freedom. The scandals surrounding the Grant administration, though petty in scope and banal in details, represented to Democrats a powerful argument for reducing and reforming the government itself. "Retrenchment and reform" was the new Democratic catchphrase, and "corrupt centralism" was the party's bugbear. The sins of the federal government in Washington—wasteful spending, excessive taxation, economic mismanagement, and personal scandals—were mirrored in Democratic minds by the abuses of Reconstruction in the South. Decentralization was one way to rein in the government, reducing the myriad temptations to abuse power that Thomas Jefferson had foreseen by diffusing that power among the individual states. If that meant returning control of the southern states to the white Democrats who made up their social and political elites, then so be it. It was time to restore the proper relation between the federal government and the states. The South, as Mississippi congressman Lucius Q. C. Lamar had said, "must be part of the government or held in duress under it." Reconstruction must end so that reunion might begin.

The inevitable waning of Reconstruction was accepted, for the most part, by large majorities in both parties—southern Republicans excepted. Indeed, the two parties agreed to a surprising degree on most of the major issues of the upcoming campaign: the need for governmental reforms; the requirement for a solid, gold-based currency; the legal and moral responsibility to safeguard black Americans' civil rights as called for by the Fourteenth and Fifteenth amendments. In support of those issues, the parties had nominated fiscally conservative, reform-minded governors from large northern states, men who were similar philosophically, if not politically. Neither Rutherford B. Hayes nor Samuel Tilden was likely to disturb too violently the national mood. Both were solid, well-grounded individuals with a firm sense of right and wrong, and both had the virtue of quiet self-composure, a much-needed quality in any president hoping to successfully lead the captious, still somewhat fragile nation successfully into its second hundred years.

But the overall similarities between the parties and their nominees concealed some fundamental differences. Heading into the election, each candidate had particular strengths and weaknesses that the opposing side hoped to negate or exploit. For Hayes and the Republicans, the chief advantage lay in their widespread identification as the party of Lincoln, the party that had saved the Union. For millions of former "Boys in Blue," the Republican party had an unbreakable hold on their affections, and not even the steady stream of scandals flowing out of

Washington could lessen their determination, as the popular phrase had it, to "vote as they shot." If anything, the ongoing collapse of Reconstruction governments in the South only sharpened northern animosity toward the ever-troublesome region.

Barely a decade after the end of the Civil War, men who had suffered and bled for the Union cause naturally resisted the notion of handing over the federal government to the Democratic party, which rightly or wrongly they still identified with slavery, treason, and disunion. In every election since the war—local, state, or national—Republican speakers had made sure to remind them of that identification, vigorously fanning the flames of simmering intersectional discord. Hayes, a veteran himself, understood completely the power of the bloody shirt. *"The danger of giving the Rebels the Government* is the topic people are most interested in," he emphasized to Ohio congressman James A. Garfield. And to Maine senator James G. Blaine, who would prove to be one of his most forceful and effective spokesmen during the campaign, Hayes urged keeping in mind that "our strong ground is the dread of a solid South, rebel rule, etc., etc. I hope you will make these topics prominent in your speeches. It leads people away from 'hard times,' which is our deadliest foe."

Added to the appeal of the bloody shirt was the residual power of incumbency. Except for the accidental interregnum of Andrew Johnson, a Democrat who had run with Lincoln on the short-lived Union party ticket, Republicans had held the presidency for the past sixteen years—virtually a lifetime in politics—and thousands of federal employees owed their very livelihoods to patronage. Government workers earning over $1,000 a year were expected, in return, to contribute a strict 2 percent of their salaries to the Republican party campaign fund; those who refused would find their names on a list of uncooperative individuals forwarded to their immediate superiors. Such strong-arm tactics had long been a feature of American politics, but during the Grant administration they had been raised to the level of an art form. Despite pressure from liberal Republicans such as Carl Schurz to disavow the forced assessments, Hayes did nothing to stop the practice. "If what [you advise] so earnestly were carried into effect," he explained to Schurz, "it would be a surrender of the campaign." He settled instead for a mild

For the first time since the election of Abraham Lincoln in 1860, the White House was truly up for grabs in 1876, and the Republican and Democratic parties offered balanced, experienced tickets led by the governors of two of the nation's most influential states: Rutherford B. Hayes of Ohio and Samuel J. Tilden of New York.

3

4

The United States in 1876 was far from the "American Mecca" envisioned by boosters of the Centennial Exhibition in Philadelphia. When President Ulysses S. Grant and Brazilian emperor Dom Pedro appeared before the great Corliss engine to open the exhibition in May 1876 (above), Grant was already a lame-duck president, beset by such scandals as the forced resignation of Secretary of War William Belknap (left) and the ongoing debate over reconstruction policies in Mississippi governor Adelbert Ames's state (opposite, top). Throughout the South, determined white resistance to black voting rights sometimes led to "Death at the Polls" (opposite, bottom), a problem that persisted long after the election of 1876.

5

6

The two presidential candidates followed very different paths to their parties' much-coveted nominations. Samuel Tilden, seen at left as a young corporation lawyer and at right in 1876, amassed a fortune as an attorney for financially threatened railroads before entering New York state politics as a crusading legislator and implacable foe to "Boss" Tweed's corrupt Tammany Hall ring. Rutherford B. Hayes, shown below in the uniform of a Union army major and opposite following the election, parlayed his valorous Civil War service—he was wounded four times—into two terms in the U.S. House of Representatives and three terms as governor of Ohio.

9

10

The politically adept Tilden faced little effective opposition in his determined march to the Democratic party's 1876 presidential nomination. Hayes, on the other hand, was a comparative dark horse who had to beat back challenges by Maine congressman James G. Blaine (left), the Republican party's putative frontrunner, and treasury secretary Benjamin H. Bristow (below), the darling of the reform-minded wing of the party.

11

12

When Tilden broke out to a lead of 260,000 votes on election night, the contest seemed to be over. Both Democratic party chairman Abram S. Hewitt (left) and Republican party chairman Zachariah Chandler (below) went to bed believing that Tilden had been elected president. Chandler took a bottle of whiskey to bed with him for consolation.

13

14

One of the few politicians who refused to believe that Tilden had won was former Union general Daniel B. Sickles (left), whose swift telegrams to Republican governors of three undecided southern states—Florida, Louisiana, and South Carolina—set into motion a series of events that would throw the entire nation into a turmoil. Republican National Committee secretary William E. Chandler (below) followed Sickles's telegrams with his own canny advice to party officials to hold on to their states for Hayes, despite the gloomy initial returns.

15

16

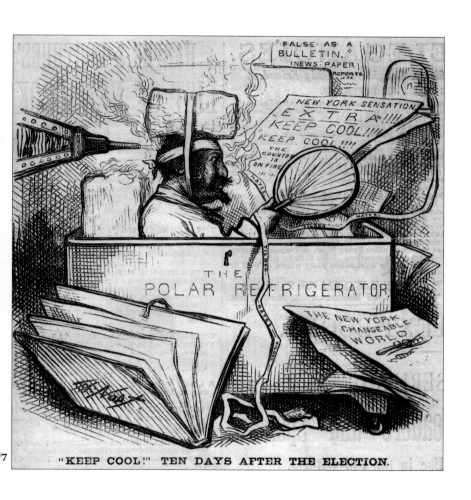

"KEEP COOL!" TEN DAYS AFTER THE ELECTION.

Although Tilden needed just one more electoral vote to seal the election, the Republicans insisted that their candidate had won. The lack of a clear-cut winner on election day raised tensions and temperatures across the country. *Harper's Weekly* political cartoonist Thomas Nast, a hard-core Republican partisan, lampooned the unsettled national mood by depicting himself sitting in an ice chest, reading the latest news bulletins and trying unsuccessfully to "Keep Cool" ten days after the election. Several more months of rancorous indecision lay ahead.

GO SOUTH, YOUNG MAN.
The latest and most reliable news.

18

19

Political operatives of both parties were urged to "Go South" after the election to oversee the vote counts in three disputed states. Democratic candidate Wade Hampton (left) was claiming the governor's chair in South Carolina, but the presidential vote in all three states was too close to call. Ohio senator John Sherman (opposite, top) and Ohio congressman James A. Garfield (opposite, middle) pressed Hayes's case in Louisiana, but visiting statesman Francis Barlow (opposite, bottom) was less convinced of the righteousness—or legality—of Hayes's case in Florida.

20

1

22

A TRUCE—NOT A COMPROMISE, BUT A CHANCE FOR HIGH-TONED GENTLEMEN TO RETIRE GRACEFULLY FROM THEIR VERY CIVIL DECLARATIONS OF WAR

23

In the face of rising tensions and the threat of violence by political hotheads in both parties, Congress devised a special 15-man Electoral Commission to decide the winner of the disputed ballots. The solution offered "A Truce—Not a Compromise," and averted any immediate resort to arms by those chanting "Tilden or Blood." The fact that neither presidential candidate favored the commission was irrelevant—they had effectively lost control of the contest. Meanwhile, President Grant took all necessary military precautions, pulling extra soldiers into Washington, D.C., to safeguard strategic forts and bridges.

24

For the next several weeks, the members of the Electoral Commission held a series of tortured hearings in the Supreme Court's chambers on Capitol Hill, studying returns from the three contested southern states and Oregon, where a single presidential elector's vote was still up in the air. Meanwhile, Democratic Speaker Samuel Randall (right) fought hard to keep angry congressmen from physically attacking each other on the floor of the House, where partisan emotions ran high.

25

THE PRESIDENCY—MR. FERRY ANNOUNCING THE RESULT OF THE COUNT.—FROM A SKETCH BY THEO. R. DAVIS.—[SEE PAGE 203.]

With the help of a compromise between Republican leaders and southern Democrats, a last-minute filibuster threat was averted, and the electoral count was completed peacefully. Finally, at 4 A.M. on March 2, 1877, after eighteen straight hours of deliberation, Republican Thomas W. Ferry, the Senate's president pro tempore, announced to the assembled members of the House and Senate that Hayes had been officially elected president and Representative William A. Wheeler of New York had been elected vice president. The nation's long wait for its nineteenth president was over.

After being secretly sworn in as president on March 3 at the White House to avoid any last-minute actions by Tilden and his congressional supporters, Hayes publicly repeated his oath of office two days later on the steps of the Capitol, drawing to a close the most unsavory and corrupt presidential election in American history. Twenty thousand onlookers—but few elected Democratic officials—heard Hayes call for a renewed sense of national unity based on "the loving devotion of a free people." The new president would find such unity in short supply.

"ANOTHER SUCH VICTORY, AND I AM UNDONE."—Pyrrhus.

Despite being an adamant Hayes supporter, *Harper's Weekly* cartoonist Thomas Nast spoke for millions of Americans when he depicted a bruised and battered Republican party elephant visiting the grave of the Democratic "tiger" and lamenting dispiritedly, "Another such victory and I am undone." The brutal election and its unseemly aftermath had nearly undone the country once again, only a dozen years after the end of a civil war that had torn it apart and sent 600,000 Americans to an early grave.

remonstrance to party officials that such assessments were "a plain departure from correct principles, and ought not to be allowed." Always a careful writer, Hayes's choice of the word *ought* left a good deal of room for differing interpretations.

The selection of Secretary of the Interior Zachariah Chandler as chairman of the Republican National Committee was a clear indication of the sort of bare-knuckles campaign the party intended to run. A coarse, unpolished midwesterner, Chandler was known for his ruthless fund-raising tactics. *Cincinnati Commercial* reporter Wilson J. Vance nicely summarized Chandler's professional reputation. "That Zachariah Chandler is personally honest nobody disputes, notwithstanding the fact that he began life as a post-trader or sutler at Fort Wayne, Detroit," Vance wrote. "There is nothing in his public life or his private life so far as known, to justify the assertion that he ever stole a cent to put into his private pocket. On the other hand there is nothing in his public career to justify the assumption that he would not steal any specified sum provided it could safely be done, for the use and benefit of his party." Whatever the state of Chandler's ethics, under his direction the Republican party—with Hayes's tacit support—would raise some $200,000 in campaign assessments from federal employees in 1876.

The Republicans' heavy emphasis on fund-raising was influenced to a great extent by what they saw as an enormous advantage for the Democrats: the deep pockets of their own presidential nominee. Samuel Tilden, it was widely believed, would spare no expense to bankroll his campaign. A political cartoon by Tilden's erstwhile ally, Thomas Nast, showed him emptying "Uncle Sammy's bar'l" of cash directly into a ballot box; the caption read: "Shotgun policy for the South and the barrel policy in the North." Actually Tilden, whose net worth was between $5 and $10 million, would contribute relatively little of his own money to the campaign, believing as a matter of principle that other Democrats—rich and poor alike—should help to fund the party's efforts. Would-be supporters felt just as strongly that someone as wealthy as Tilden should be willing to loosen his purse strings in his own behalf. Tilden's unwillingness to do so would put him frequently at odds with his party's national leadership, and would prove to have serious consequences in the upcoming campaign.

Even more than Tilden's money, Republicans feared his intellect. William Henry Smith, the Western Associated Press chieftain and long-time Hayes supporter, warned the Republican candidate at the start of the campaign that "the enemy to be met is no common enemy. He is the embodiment of human craft and the experience in cunning of genera-tions of Tammany." Fellow journalist Joseph Medill, editor of the *Chicago Tribune*, echoed Smith's warning. "We have a hard fight ahead of us," he told Hayes. "Your opponent is a tireless worker, a wonderful organizer, a shrewd, crafty, able man. He makes no mistakes." Still another Republi-can journalist, Whitelaw Reid of the *New York Tribune*, called Tilden "the most sagacious political calculator I have ever seen." Even Hayes's own running mate, New York congressman William A. Wheeler, joined the chorus of Tilden admirers. The Democratic nominee, said Wheeler, was "a wonderful organizer and manipulator, has large wealth and is utterly unscrupulous in its use." Given such dire forecasts, it is no wonder that Hayes considered the race from the outset "a hot and critical contest." The opening odds—five-to-two for Tilden in most betting parlors—accu-rately reflected the view in both camps.

As proof of Tilden's organizational skills, Republicans needed to look no further than New York City, where the "perfect system" that Tilden had built for his drive to the Democratic nomination remained in place. Tilden's nephew, Colonel William T. Pelton, took charge of the Literary Bureau at 59 Liberty Street, installing a printing press in the basement and beginning to pump out millions of pieces of campaign lit-erature—five mailings apiece for every eligible voter by the end of the campaign. Along with the Literary Bureau, which mainly printed leaflets touting Tilden's political career and speeches made by leading Democrats, a Speakers Bureau was set up to coordinate the appearances of Tilden spokesmen in the hinterland, and a Bureau of Correspondence was created to handle requests for campaign material and information. A. M. Gibson, the Washington correspondent for the *New York Sun*, helped prepare the 750-page *Campaign Text Book*, which exhaustively catalogued Republican corruption great and small. The *Text Book* was distributed free of charge to party workers across the country, and friendly newspapers were encouraged to reprint choice selections of Democratic rhetoric on their own editorial pages.

If the Republicans had a tough, wily campaign chairman in Chandler, the Democrats had an altogether more refined and gentlemanly leader in New York congressman Abram S. Hewitt. The differences between the two men mirrored the differences in their respective campaigns. Chandler was a battle-tested veteran of the political wars, a longtime friend of Ulysses S. Grant's, and a consummate Washington insider. At various times in his career he had been a store owner, a sutler, a lumberman, a United States senator, a national committeeman, and secretary of the interior. In political terms, he knew where all the bodies were buried. Hewitt, on the other hand, was a courtly, soft-spoken patrician who had struck it rich in the manufacturing business; one of his most grateful partners was Samuel Tilden, whom he had induced to invest in various iron and coal companies before the Civil War. But Hewitt was also a comparative newcomer to politics. At Tilden's urging he had run for Congress in 1874, and somewhat to his surprise he had been swept into office on the Democratic tidal wave that November. With less than two years of public service under his belt, Hewitt's lack of practical political experience would eventually come back to haunt the Tilden campaign.

Hewitt had played a leading role in securing Tilden's nomination in St. Louis, and he was intensely loyal to his Gramercy Park neighbor. But in accepting the party chairmanship, Hewitt fully expected Tilden to take charge of the day-to-day campaign, and it was not long before he was complaining about the candidate's surprising lack of personal involvement. "To tell the truth," Hewitt wrote to Delaware senator Thomas Bayard, "I am so annoyed at the position in which I am placed, and the demands that are made upon me which I would be glad to meet but am utterly powerless to recognize, that I would be glad to be consigned for the next sixty days to any purgatory which I have ever heard described— so long as it would relieve me from this one." Hewitt also labored under an unusual handicap for a presidential campaign manager: his eighty-five-year-old father-in-law, Peter Cooper, was running for president as well, as the quixotic candidate of the tiny Greenback party.

Despite his lack of contact with Tilden, Hewitt worked hard to implement on a national scale Tilden's proven system of voter identification. A circular letter went out to all state Democratic chairmen in early

July, just after Tilden had won the nomination, urging them "to make a thorough and immediate canvass of your state including the name of every voter of all parties, with the political complexion of each. Full sets of canvass books and blanks for the organization of clubs will be furnished by the national committee for each polling district." Organizers were to be appointed for each district, which would be broken down further into fifty-voter subdivisions. "By using these books and blanks in accordance with the directions given, the whole country will be organized on a uniform system, and we shall have, in a few weeks, a complete record of every voter in the United States," Hewitt assured the chairmen. "By the use of this system we will, on Election Day, secure every vote to which we are entitled. With such an organization of the Democratic party defeat will be impossible." In Illinois alone, some fifteen hundred canvass books and eighteen thousand subdivison sheets were distributed to district workers.

Hewitt and his forty-man staff labored heroically to organize the canvass, but it would prove impossible to implement, in a few weeks' time, a system that Tilden had needed years to devise in New York. Nor could Hewitt rally the troops with overly strident partisan appeals. At Tilden's insistence, the campaign was to be run on a high moral plane; it would not do for the candidate of reform to engage in petty mudslinging. Admirably if unrealistically, Tilden envisioned a campaign of ideas and ideals, one in keeping with his lifelong dedication to good, honest government. Reform, as he had reminded supporters on the night of his nomination, was what the country wanted most. All that was needed was to educate the voters about their hearts' desire and spell out his program for giving it to them. No one, he thought, wanted a repeat of the past eight years.

Tilden may have wanted to run an elevated campaign, but in his reformist zeal he forgot one crucial point—in politics, unlike war, few campaigns are ever won by taking and holding the high ground. The Republicans, on the defensive after eight long years of scandal, depression, and moral drift by Grant and his cohorts in Washington, intended to mount a smear campaign exceeding even the gratuitously cruel and vindictive race they had run against Horace Greeley in 1872. Tilden was no stranger to character assassination—Boss Tweed played as roughly as anyone—but not even a politician as canny and experienced as Tilden could foresee the lengths to which the Republicans were prepared to go in order to maintain their grip on power.

On a purely practical level, too, Tilden's hopes for a high-toned campaign were quickly dashed. Despite the blizzard of speeches, newsletters, handbills, and cartoons mailed out by his indefatigable headquarters staff, it would not be possible to make a sophisticated policy argument to restless voters in the four months remaining before the general election. Tilden's reluctance to spend his own money in the campaign, however noble it may have been as an expression of democratic ideals, saddled Hewitt and campaign treasurer Edward Cooper, Hewitt's brother-in-law and the son of third-party candidate Peter Cooper, with the constant need to raise ready cash to defray postage and printing costs. At the same time, the lack of experienced campaign workers severely hindered efforts to reach voters individually. The candidate, too, contributed to the problem. Intellectual, rational, and a bit aloof, Tilden failed to connect viscerally to prospective voters. He simply did not realize that his broad appeal was based not on a bloodless concept like reform, but on a much more basic human emotion. His supporters did not want reform—they wanted revenge.

The thirst for revenge cut across sectional lines, uniting Democrats in a way that they had not been united since the heady days of Andrew Jackson. Northern Democrats, who had seen their patriotism and loyalty consistently impugned since the Civil War by Republican accusations of copperheadism, wanted to strike back at their flag-waving accusers. Small farmers, shopkeepers, and humble working men and women, who had seen their life savings swallowed up by the Panic of 1873, wanted to lash out at the physical instruments of their suffering—the bankers, brokers, and financiers who controlled and exploited the nation's wealth behind a miserly bulwark of high tariffs, high taxes, and hard money. Southern Democrats, who had lost the flower of a generation on Civil War battlefields and had then returned home to find their state governments dominated by carpetbaggers, scalawags, and former slaves, wanted to reclaim their old way of life. And honest, hardworking Americans on both sides of the Mason-Dixon line, who had endured eight years of unparalleled corruption at the very seat of power, wanted simply to throw the rascals out—not as a function of political reform, but as an expression of personal disgust. Almost without realizing it Tilden was leading a popular revolt, but the book-lined study of his Gramercy Park mansion was a world away from the barricades.

WHILE THE TWO parties worked industriously behind the scenes to prepare for the traditional start of the upcoming general campaign on Labor Day, most Americans' attention was focused on the nation's gala one hundredth birthday festivities. In a replay of the Centennial Exhibition's opening day ceremonies, 200,000 visitors descended on Philadelphia on July 4 for a daylong round of speeches, concerts, parades, and fireworks celebrating the country's propitious birth. Conspicuously missing from the scene was President Grant, who apparently had endured all the civic ballyhoo he could stand at the grand opening of the exhibition two months earlier. Citing physical exhaustion caused in part by the nonstop crush of tourists dropping by the White House to shake his hand en route to the festivities in Philadelphia—he estimated sourly that between five hundred and six hundred "centennial pilgrims" imposed themselves upon him each day—Grant stayed home on the Fourth, sending Michigan senator Thomas W. Ferry, the president pro tempore of the Senate, to speak in his place. (Vice President Henry Wilson, his usual stand-in, had died of a stroke the year before.)

Grant's failure to appear was duly noted. "General Grant," complained local diarist James McCabe, "remained in Washington, preferring his selfish ease to a little patriotic exertion. His absence was generally remarked and severely condemned by his countrymen." *Atlantic Monthly*'s Philadelphia correspondent was equally scathing. "The president's absence put the finishing touch to the sum of his offenses," the journalist wrote. "It was the most condensed yet crudest statement of his estimation of the dignity of the country, the occasion, and his office. The credit of the day and nation could only gain by his absence."

By prior arrangement with the Centennial Commission, the Fourth of July celebration was held in Independence Square instead of Fairmount Park. A smartly dressed contingent of cadets from the United States Military Academy at West Point came down for the festivities, joining militia units from many of the states, as well as a special Centennial Legion comprised of marchers from the thirteen original colonies. In a spirit of intersectional reconciliation, the legion was commanded by former Confederate general Henry Heth, whose Rebel division had opened the fighting at Gettysburg, 143 miles away, almost exactly thirteen years earlier. On the reviewing stand outside Independence Hall were army commander William Tecumseh Sherman, Emperor Dom Pedro of Brazil, Prince Oscar of Sweden, Lieutenant General Asaigo of Japan, Centennial Commission chairman Joseph Hawley, Senator Ferry, and a beaming assortment of governors—but not the two presidential nominees, who remained carefully out of the limelight.

The biggest stir was caused by women's rights activist Susan B. Anthony, who led a group of fellow suffragists onto the reviewing stand and insisted on presenting to the befuddled Ferry a copy of their revised Declaration of Independence, which insisted that all men *and women* had been created equal. The women then retired to the musicians' platform on the opposite side of the square, where Anthony proceeded to read the declaration aloud while Philadelphia poet Bayard Taylor struggled manfully to recite his centennial ode on the main stage. Accompanying Anthony for moral support were Sarah Spencer and Phoebe Cousins, who had crashed the Republican and Democratic conventions a few weeks earlier. Adding to the din was a steady rumble of cannon fire from Fairmount Park, the U.S. Navy Yard, and Brazilian, Swedish, and American warships anchored offshore in the Delaware River, as well as the hooting of a giant foghorn that supposedly could be heard sixty miles away. At Ferry's suggestion, the increasingly restless crowd was encouraged to join him in reciting the Hundredth Psalm, which begins, "Make a joyful noise unto the Lord, all ye lands."

Elsewhere across the nation, the Fourth was marked by a variety of equally raucous observances. In Montgomery, Alabama, the first capital of the Confederacy, a thirteen-gun salute was fired—whether in honor of the original thirteen colonies or the thirteen stars in the rivalrous Confederate banner, no one could say. In Richmond, Virginia, the second and longest-lived Rebel capital, the American flag and the state flag were hoisted together for the first time since 1860. A less conciliatory attempt to raise a Confederate battle flag in Oronogo, Missouri, was met by threats from an angry crowd to gun down the perpetrators of the studied slight. Meanwhile, in Lawrenceburg, Kentucky, a Confederate flag was successfully suspended from the county courthouse alongside a banner bearing the names and likenesses of the Democratic party's presidential and vice presidential candidates, neither of whom presumably would have been pleased by the unhelpful linkage of political causes.

FARTHER SOUTH, in Hamburg, South Carolina, across the Savannah River from Augusta, Georgia, another explosive Fourth of July celebration would prove to have a far-reaching effect on the presidential campaign. That afternoon two young white farmers, Thomas Butler and Henry Getzen, passed through Hamburg on their way to their homes in Edgefield County. Despite being located in the Deep South, Hamburg was a far from typical southern town. It owed its odd Teutonic name to its German founder, who christened the hamlet after the city of his birth. By 1876 the town's founding father and most other whites had left Hamburg, and it had become the center of an unusually outspoken black community and the home, as well, of a large cattle-rustling ring. Hamburg's leaders included militia commander A. L. "Doc" Adams, a former resident of Augusta who had moved across the river in search of a more congenial political environment; his chief lieutenant, A. T. Attaway, a member of the state legislature who had publicly advocated the forced removal of the entire white population of South Carolina; and town marshal James Cook, who was notorious for fining white visitors to Hamburg for various petty offenses, ranging from the unauthorized use of the public water fountain to failing to yield the right of way.

As part of the Fourth of July festivities, the town militia was conducting a spirited close-order drill when Butler and Getzen came clattering inconveniently down Main Street in their buggy. Accounts differ on what happened next. Either the men brusquely demanded that the armed militia stand aside and let them pass, or else the marchers, led by Adams, surrounded the wagon and menaced the unoffending pair in loud and racially charged language. At any rate, angry words were exchanged before the militia parted ranks and permitted the men to go on their way. The next day, Butler's father went into Hamburg and swore out a complaint against Adams for obstructing a public thoroughfare. Trial justice Prince Rivers, a political rival of the militia leader, summoned Adams to his chambers for questioning. There, Adams apparently lost his temper and threatened the justice with bodily harm; Rivers charged him with contempt of court. A hearing was set for Saturday, July 8.

In the meantime the Butlers hired a famous attorney to handle their case, former Confederate general Matthew Calbraith Butler. M. C. Butler—no relation—had commanded a troop of horsemen in fellow South Carolinian Wade Hampton's legendary cavalry division during the Civil War, and had been renowned for leading his troops into battle armed only with a silver-tipped riding crop. He had lost a foot at the Battle of Brandy Station but had served through to the bitter end, returning home to find his plantation in ruins and his net worth reduced to $1.50. Rebuilding his life and his legal practice, Butler had become a leading figure in the state Democratic party—there had even been talk earlier in the year of him running for governor against incumbent Republican Daniel H. Chamberlain.

The hiring of Butler added another combustible element to the already simmering situation. When the ex-calvaryman returned to Hamburg on the day of the trial, he was accompanied by an armed escort. Adams, seeing the white force ride into town, took refuge with his followers in the town's two-story brick armory. After waiting fruitlessly for Adams to appear in court, Butler crossed the Savannah River into Augusta later that afternoon and began spreading the word that "a collision between the whites and blacks was imminent." Soon, a force of several hundred armed Georgians rode into Hamburg and took up positions near the armory alongside their South Carolina counterparts.

Justice Rivers made a last-ditch appeal to Adams and his men to surrender their arms; Adams replied that he would surrender only to a legal representative of the state militia. Sometime after dusk gunfire erupted, with each side claiming the other had fired first. For over an hour the skirmish continued, and one young white man was killed after peering incautiously around a wall. Meanwhile, more whites poured into Hamburg from Augusta, bringing with them a large-caliber cannon. After several thumping artillery rounds had struck the armory, Adams and his men climbed down ladders at the rear of the building and attempted to escape. Marshal Cook, either siding with the militia or attempting futilely to keep the peace, was shot and killed as he tried to jump a fence, and several other militiamen were wounded. Adams somehow managed to get away, but twenty-seven of his followers were captured. Shortly afterward, a disputed number of blacks—four, five, six, or eight, depending on the account—were shot and killed "while attempting to escape." M. C. Butler, who might have preserved some semblance of order, had already left the scene after the crowd began "committing depredations." One month later a grand jury indicted seven white men for murder in connection with the deaths at Hamburg, but no one was ever convicted in the case.

News of the violence, immediately dubbed the Hamburg Massacre by the Republican press, spread rapidly across the country. Northerners, already sensitized to the word *massacre* by lurid accounts of the recent Custer debacle, denounced the incident as yet another instance of southern lawlessness. Governor Chamberlain, seeking to shore up his waning support among the state's black majority, recklessly fanned the flames by portraying the gunfight—a mutual explosion of long-festering local grievances—as a purely political attack on black Republicans by white Democrats. He appealed to Grant for federal assistance, warning the president that the killings at Hamburg were merely the beginning of an organized "campaign of blood and violence" on the part of Democrats to recapture political control of the state. Grant promised to "give every aid for which I find law or constitutional power," but mindful perhaps of the avalanche of criticism he had received two years earlier for sending troops to Louisiana, he held off dispatching more federal soldiers into another sovereign southern state.

Chamberlain's blatant politicizing of the Hamburg incident was a huge personal miscalculation. Already unpopular with the state's Republican leadership for attempting to institute a few mild reforms, he had seen his appeal rise among moderate South Carolina Democrats, who had declined that spring at their state convention to nominate an opponent to run against him. In the wake of his appeal for federal intervention, however, outraged Democrats reconvened in August and swiftly nominated Wade Hampton for governor (M. C. Butler moved his nomination). Overnight, hundreds of pro-Hampton "rifle clubs" sprang up across the state, their members sporting bright red shirts to mock the Republicans' wearisome bloody-shirt appeals. Many were former Confederate soldiers, and they quickly organized themselves into a formidable paramilitary force. What had seemed like a sure victory for Chamberlain—and by extension Rutherford B. Hayes—had become, quite literally, a battleground.

For Tilden and his advisers, the Hamburg incident was an unexpected and unwanted political dilemma. The steady drumbeat of northern denunciations made the Tilden camp distinctly uncomfortable. Worried supporters urged Tilden to keep his distance from the South. "All [the Republicans] want is to get up two or three such riots to put the military over them and control the election," one Pennsylvania Democrat warned. "I wish we could keep them [i.e., white southerners] quiet." The outcry grew so shrill that Hewitt nervously contacted Mississippi congressman L. Q. C. Lamar, a leading southern moderate, and asked him to use his influence to keep the peace. "I trust there will be no outbreaks in the South no matter how great the provocation may be," Hewitt said, "for the people of the North will resist turning over the government to any party which inherits the odor of rebellion; and the Republican speakers are making the most of this fear." Southern whites, sensing a lack of support from their party's presidential nominee, began distancing themselves in turn. Hampton, whose post-nomination efforts to coordinate his campaign with that of Tilden were pointedly ignored, made his own position clear. "It is not Tilden we are working for," he said, "so much as relief from the rule of the robbers here at home. I am not in the big fight. I am in this little fight to save South Carolina." Tilden, he implied, would have to save himself.

BY TRADITION, the two presidential candidates began their campaigns with a formal acceptance letter outlining their political philosophy and endorsing the platforms adopted by their parties at the nominating conventions. Since neither candidate was expected to campaign actively for his election—the fiction being that the office sought the man, not the other way around—the letters were avidly read by the voting public for their runic revelations of presidential character and intent. In 1876 each candidate faced a complex letter-writing task. For Hayes, the main problem was how to rally party regulars—many of whom had supported his opponents for the nomination—while distancing himself, however gently, from the increasingly unpopular Grant administration. At the same time, he hoped to address at least indirectly the palpable hunger for political reform. Finally, he needed to say something about the South, where conditions in some states verged on anarchy and the last fraying bonds of Reconstruction seemed to be unraveling day by day.

In his July 8 letter, Hayes worked hard to address those disparate aims. He formally endorsed the Republican platform, including the hard-money plank calling for the resumption of specie payments, but ignored suggestions that he name a specific date for such resumption. In a nod to Schurz and other reformers, he denounced the spoils system of civil appointments for fostering "extravagance and official incapacity," and called for its "thorough, radical, and complete" reform. Then, in a classic case of overreaching, Hayes declared it his "inflexible purpose, if elected, not to be a candidate for a second term," lest his reelection be secured by the same discredited spoils system he was sworn to root out. Hayes's unexpected pledge made him, in essence, a lame-duck president before he had even been elected. It was a rare political misstep for the normally sure-footed candidate, and it unwittingly angered the current president, who saw it as an implicit criticism of his own two terms in office. Within a week Grant dispatched a personal emissary to Columbus to inform Hayes in no uncertain terms of his displeasure. Hayes immediately sent back a labored explanation, maintaining that his only aim had been to reassure the loyal supporters of his convention opponents that he "would not be in their way four years from now." Sulkily, Grant waited a month before acknowledging, if not necessarily accepting, Hayes's belated apology.

The longest section of Hayes's letter dealt with conditions in the South. There was no mention of the Hamburg incident, which had occurred too recently to be included in the letter, even assuming that Hayes would have wanted to touch on such a sensational topic in the first place. Instead, like the careful politician he was, he offered suitably bland generalities. What the region needed most, Hayes declared, was "an intelligent and honest administration of government, which will protect all classes of citizens in their official and private rights." Then, after "a hearty and generous recognition of the rights of all by all," he could foresee using the federal government in a purely beneficent way "to promote the efforts of the people of those states to obtain for themselves the blessings of honest and capable local government." *Local government,* as Hayes well knew, was a code phrase for states' rights, and he may have been trying to send a signal to the growing numbers of northern voters who were heartily sick of Reconstruction that he, too, was ready to move on with his life and leave the South to its own devices. Whatever his long-range plans for the region, embattled white Republicans and their black allies in the South were thoroughly disheartened by the candidate's unfortunate choice of words and, like their Democratic counterparts, began distancing themselves from their party's inconstant presidential nominee.

Despite its unfavorable reception by southern Republicans, Hayes's letter elicited a generally positive response in the rest of the country. "The tone and grasp of the letter are alike most striking, for they show unmistakably that it is not the work of a politician but of a very different person," New York reformer George William Curtis assured Hayes. (The fact that the letter was precisely the work of a politician, in both a positive and a negative sense, was lost on the idealistic Curtis.) Whitelaw Reid gushed to Hayes that "if it had been specially designed to enable *The Tribune,* and those for whom it speaks, to make their support of you effective it could not have better accomplished the purpose." The candidate himself, who seldom evinced anything less than complete approval of his own actions, considered it "a bold and honest letter of acceptance. It will offend some and cool the ardor of others, but it is sound and I believe will be strong with the people."

While Hayes was busy congratulating himself, Tilden continued to put off publishing his own acceptance letter. Weeks went by before Tilden sat down to compose his response. Besides his characteristic caution, Tilden was also preoccupied by the recent death of his older brother Moses, whose passing had burdened him with legal and finan-

cial problems regarding Moses' estate. His health, too, was problemati-
cal. A slight stroke the year before had weakened his left side and
caused his left eyelid to droop; more than ever he looked like a man in
desperate need of a good night's sleep. Equally vexing on a political
level was how to reconcile his own hard-money position with the infla-
tionist philosophy of his midwestern running mate. Twice during the
month of July, Tilden met privately with Thomas Hendricks at Saratoga
Springs, New York, to talk over their economic differences. In the
meantime, rumors spread that one or the other of them was planning to
drop off the ticket.

Finally, on August 4, Tilden released his letter. In it he carefully
straddled the currency question, denouncing the Specie Resumption
Act while seeming to accept its inevitability. He sought common
ground with Hendricks by recommending the creation of a "central
reservoir" of coins from which to redeem paper money. Only then, by
means of "gradual and safe processes," should full specie resumption
take place. The bulk of the letter outlined at tedious length the financial
and historical issues underlying the currency controversy. Few men
outside the rarefied confines of a Wall Street stockbrokerage or the inner sanctum of a bank president's office had either the knowledge or
the patience to wade through the persiflage. One reader complained
that "Tilden writes like a schoolmaster of finance. His letter is like a
chapter from some German work in metaphysics . . . able, learned, wise,
but so far as the masses are concerned, above the clouds." But Tilden,
as usual, had a reason for his actions. When the editor of the *New York
Star* complained that the letter was too long for people to read, Tilden
replied tartly, "It was not intended for *people* to read." The titans of finance would take his point.

As expected, Tilden called for a systematic reform of the federal government, although not as strongly, perhaps, as his supporters might
have wished. Rather than address directly the multifarious scandals of
the Grant administration, Tilden settled instead for a bloodless con-
demnation of "excessive governmental consumption," "mismanagement of the currency," and "inefficiency, peculation, fraud, and
malversation of the public funds." On the issue of civil service reform,
he was even less forceful than Hayes, who after all had been criticizing

his own party. While denouncing the "political mercenaries" who controlled the federal government, Tilden called merely for raising the standards by which civil servants were appointed and the dismissal of "untrustworthy or incapable subordinates." Merit testing of office-seekers, "wherever practicable," might come later, he suggested, as might the single-term limitation on the presidency that Hayes had already imposed unilaterally on himself.

On the subject of Reconstruction, Tilden was carefully equivocal. Leery of Republican charges that he and other northern Democrats had been lukewarm defenders of the Union during the war, and assuming perhaps that the South was already his for the asking, Tilden issued a vaguely worded plaint decrying "the systematic and insupportable misgovernment imposed on the states of the South." Somewhat pleadingly, he tied conditions in the South to the general "distress in business" that was affecting the country as a whole, and called for a removal of "every obstacle to a complete and durable reconciliation between kindred populations once unnaturally estranged." He appealed to "the moral influence of every good citizen to establish a cordial fraternity and good-will among citizens, whatever their race or color," pledging at the same time to enforce the laws and the Constitution to protect "every political and personal right" of all citizens. There was not one word in the entire 4,400-word letter addressing the Hamburg incident. A few days later, *Harper's Weekly* published a savage cartoon by Thomas Nast depicting Tilden standing over a pile of murdered blacks beneath a sign that read: "Niggers reformed at Hamburg, S.C." The caption had Tilden saying blandly, "It is not I, but the idea of reform which I represent."

Like Hayes's statement on the subject, Tilden's position on the South pleased no one, particularly those who were living there. Many southern Democrats, already suspicious of Tilden's northern roots and pro-business background, read the letter with a resigned grimace and committed themselves ever more fiercely to winning the gubernatorial elections in their own states. As one perceptive South Carolinian noted of his fellow Democrats: "If by trading him [Tilden] off to certain defeat they could get control of South Carolina they would cheerfully do it. It is hard to say what they would not trade off to get South Carolina under their control once more. All they want is to get it once, knowing very well that they can hold it forever." When Hewitt told Tilden, "Your letter gives general satisfaction," his choice of adjectives was more apt than he realized. For southern Democrats, the letter was a good deal more general than it was satisfying.

AFTER THE CANDIDATES had released their letters, the campaign ground along sluggishly for several weeks. "A flat and tame campaign," the *New York Herald* complained on August 19, "the canvass is at a dead halt." In an effort to stir up news, the paper sent a reporter to Tilden's New Lebanon birthplace, but the visit was a boring bust. "No one remembered his robbing an apple orchard, or his running away from school to go swimming, or playing hooky to go fishing, horse racing, hiding his grandmother's spectacles or indulging in any other pastimes for which country boys are generally noted all over the land," the newspaper reported. "He enjoyed his books and his studies, was a good mathematician, the marvel of his teachers, and the admiration of his fellows."

As for Hayes, *The Nation* complained: "No ingenuity of interviewers was sufficient to extract from him any expressions of opinion on any topic having the remotest bearing on the presidential contest. He recognized nothing, and neither authorized nor repudiated anybody. According to the newspaper accounts he would hardly go further in political discussion than to accede to the proposition that there was a republican form of government and that this was the hundredth year of the national government." San Francisco–based journalist Ambrose Bierce, who had served in West Virginia with Hayes during the Civil War, swiped at his former comrade from afar. "There was enough of Lincoln to kill and enough of Grant to kick," wrote Bierce, "but Hayes is only a magic-lantern image without even a surface to be displayed upon. You cannot see him, you cannot feel him; but you know that he extends in lessening opacity all the way from the dark side of [Ohio senator] John Sherman to the confines of space."

Hayes's innate caution extended to his official biographer. Novelist William Dean Howells was married to Hayes's cousin Elinor Mead—indeed, the candidate had introduced the couple sixteen years earlier—but Hayes did not entirely trust his fellow Buckeye's political instincts.

Howells had written a well-received campaign biography of Abraham Lincoln in 1860; it had gotten him out of military service and into a safe position with the U.S. consulate in Venice, Italy. But as Howells began assembling material for a similar biography of Hayes, the candidate felt constrained to warn him: "Be careful not to commit me on religion, temperance, or free-trade." He allowed Howells to consult his diaries, but adjured him: "No quoting of anything on political or semi-political topics capable of being turned to account by the adversary." Silence, he said, was the only safety.

As usual, Hayes's political instincts were sharp, even if those of his personal secretary were not. Two days after Hayes released his acceptance letter, the virulently anti-Catholic American Alliance had notified his office of its unqualified support. Hayes never saw the letter, but Alfred E. Lee, his secretary, responded fulsomely in his behalf. "Governor Hayes desires me to acknowledge receipt of your valued favor," Lee reported, "and to say in reply that he is deeply gratified by this expression of confidence." Lee went on to promise the alliance "such aid and cooperation as seems to be advisable." Hayes, burdened with his own anti-Catholic baggage, would soon have cause to regret his secretary's polite but ill-considered response.

CONTROVERSY OF A DIFFERENT sort ensnared Tilden in late August, when the *New York Times* published an article accusing him of cheating on his income taxes during the Civil War. Zachariah Chandler, in his dual role of secretary of the interior and chairman of the Republican National Committee, had called for an investigation into Tilden's finances within days of his nomination. The *Times* obligingly publicized the unfounded allegations under the blaring headline: "Is Mr. Tilden a Perjurer?" The newspaper charged that in 1863, at the height of the war, Tilden had filed a fraudulent tax return, claiming only $7,118 in income for the previous year, instead of $108,000, which the article alleged was the proper amount.

The accusations caused a sensation, particularly in the North, where Tilden's supposed financial transgressions were viewed as still more evidence of his patent failure to support the war. Tilden was furious about the allegations, but he was unable to locate the fourteen-year-old records dealing with his finances. Several weeks went by while the candidate, with the help of Hewitt and Tilden's former law clerk, Judge James P. Sinnott, worked on a detailed response to the charges. In the meantime, the *Times* and other Republican newspapers hammered away unmercifully at the candidate, accusing Tilden of paying the employees of his Michigan-based mining company with worthless "shinplasters," of wrecking a Pennsylvania railroad for his own selfish profit, and of making huge stock profits "on the street." An obscure New York City policeman, B. E. Buckman, produced a garbled account of Tilden's supposed railroad dealings, *Samuel J. Tilden Unmasked*, a ghostwritten pamphlet that denounced its subject as nothing less than "the farmer's foe, a perfidious attorney, a sycophant of corporations, a corrupter of the press, a dangerous demagogue, an enemy of state schools and the Erie Canal, a traitor to the Democratic party, a disgrace to the state of New York and a menace to the United States." At least Tilden, being unmarried, was not accused of beating his wife.

As Tilden's delay in answering the charges continued—the generally favorable *Nation* called his reticence "an ugly flaw"—his strongest supporters waited and worried. Old friend Samuel Barlow wrote to Hewitt: "I cannot express to you the anxiety that Gov. Tilden's friends feel about the charge of non-payment of his income [tax] and it is as certain as anything ever was that the delay in answering these charges is doing great harm. The Govr. does not seem to understand how dangerous our position is." Fellow New Yorker William C. Whitney urged Tilden to "sacrifice personal feeling and delicacy for the sake of the party. You must yourself personally come before the scenes and make a sensation." At length Tilden's closest friend, John Bigelow, was enlisted to help the candidate focus on the issue, which, Bigelow confided to his diary, had "worried the governor until he is scarcely fit or able to do anything. He can't write or control himself. He finds fault with everyone about him & makes the most childish complaints of others for his own omissions & commissions." Tilden's seeming paralysis over the issue made Bigelow wonder "whether he will prove equal to the labors of the presidency."

Finally, in late September, Tilden issued a statement effectively refuting the allegations by showing that most of his income-producing property in 1862 had been comprised of railroad stocks and bonds on which the taxes had already been paid, and that he had further incurred large business losses in a drug company based in his hometown of New Lebanon. Democratic newspapers trumpeted the response as a total vindication, and even the Republican-oriented *Chicago Daily News* found it "complete and satisfactory." Tilden's old Republican friend William Cullen Bryant denounced the *Times* for its "shameful" and "slanderous" attacks, while the punctilious *Nation* pronounced Tilden's returns "as full as men of his class were accustomed to make." Nevertheless, the charges and the long delay in answering them undoubtedly hurt Tilden in several northern states where he could ill afford to lose a single vote.

HAYES, FOR HIS PART, kept quiet about Tilden's tax problems, perhaps because he had a potentially larger problem of his own. On September 4 he rather plaintively asked George William Curtis, "What is there in the charge that Tilden by perjury swindled the government of its income tax? If false it ought to be dropped." Ten days later, Hayes confided in his diary: "As an offset to what is said of Gov. Tilden's income returns mine have been examined. It appears that in 1868 & 1869 I made none at all." The Democrats may have heard something about the oversight. Hewitt requested a copy of Hayes's tax statements from the Treasury Department, but Zachariah Chandler effectively blocked release of the documents. On September 6 the *Chicago Times*, which supported Tilden, published a vaguely worded article regarding Hayes's alleged transgressions, but the story was ignored by Republican newspapers. At the same time, friendly journalists Murat Halstead and James M. Comly dissuaded the still worried Hayes from making a public response to the charges, probably because they felt that he had no real explanation to give.

Disturbed and angered by the charges against Tilden, Democrats urged him to take the offensive. One supporter, J. S. Douglas, sent him a list of issues on which to attack Hayes, including the Republican's questionable tax returns; his supposedly excessive army pay; his unreported legal earnings; his undervalued paintings, books, and jewelry;

his unacknowledged bequests from his late Uncle Sardis; and his radical record as a congressman and governor. The list concluded with the sensational question: "Did Hayes shoot his mother in a fit of insanity?" Tilden declined to pursue these matters, preferring to keep his campaign on a higher, if less exciting, plane. He favored the inoffensive ditties published in *The Tilden Illustrated Campaign Song and Joke Book,* including a takeoff on "Yankee Doodle" that solemnly pledged: "Sam Tilden is a gentleman, / A true and honest man, sir; / And when we call for honest work / He's just the chap to answer." It was not exactly red meat for the masses.

Hayes, too, took the high road—or at least stayed out of the running gutter. Newspaper accounts assured the public that he was preoccupied with state affairs, "every day and all day quietly and steadily attending to his duties as governor of Ohio." He was praised for his "stainless character [and] his church-relationship"—which managed to overlook the inconvenient fact that Hayes did not belong to any church and was, in fact, something of an agnostic when it came to religion. Meanwhile, those same newspapers kept up a ceaseless stream of abuse against Tilden, ranging from the public to the personal. A paragraph from the *Chicago Tribune* that August was representative of the overall level of Republican political discourse. Tilden, said the *Tribune,* "is weazened, and shrimpled, and meanly cute. There is nothing about the man that is large, big, generous, solid, inspiring, powerful, or awakening. He's a small, lazy, odorous, ungainly, trickling stream, winding along and among the weeds that have grown up in the track of the great river, long since dried up. He is as cold as 32 degrees below zero. O that face!— that left eye!—that mouth."

Assessing the Republican smear campaign, *The Nation* complained later that Hayes had been ill-served by his supporters. "All sorts of bad characters were usefully employed in the service of a candidate of spotless reputation," the journal noted, "under an ingenious arrangement by which he profited by their activity without incurring any responsibility for their rascality." Personally, Hayes could afford to remain above the fray: he had a small army of surrogates already doing the dirty work for him. With the notable exception of New York senator Roscoe Conkling, who had taken to his bed with an attack of "malarial fever" follow-

ing the Republican National Convention, all of Hayes's former opponents campaigned for him that fall. James G. Blaine led the charge in
New England, Benjamin Bristow came out of forced retirement (Grant
had sacked him as attorney general immediately after the Republican
convention) to tour Kentucky and the upper South, and Indiana senator
Oliver Morton canvassed the Midwest.

At Hayes's behest, Blaine prevailed upon his old convention champion, Robert G. Ingersoll, to pick up the gauntlet as well, and Ingersoll
responded in late September with the campaign's most electrifying
speech. Speaking to a convention of Union veterans in Indianapolis, Ingersoll achieved the pinnacle of bloody-shirt oratory. A veteran himself—he had served in an Illinois cavalry regiment before being wounded
and paroled at Shiloh—Ingersoll brought the old soldiers to their feet
with a thunderous address that gained in impact what it lacked in sub-
tlety. "I am opposed to the Democratic party, and I will tell you why," Ingersoll declared. For the next two hours he did just that. "Every state
that seceded from the United States was a Democratic state," he roared.
"Every ordinance of secession that was drawn was drawn by a Democrat.
Every man that endeavored to tear the old flag from the heaven that it
enriches was a Democrat. Every man that tried to destroy this nation
was a Democrat. Every enemy this great republic has had for twenty
years has been a Democrat. Every man that shot Union soldiers was a
Democrat. Every man that denied to the Union prisoners even the
worm-eaten crust of famine was a Democrat. Every man that loved slavery better than liberty was a Democrat. The man that assassinated Abraham Lincoln was a Democrat. Every man that raised bloodhounds to
pursue human beings was a Democrat. Soldiers, every scar you have on
your heroic bodies was given you by a Democrat."

Ingersoll crisscrossed the country during the last six weeks of the
campaign, giving more or less the same speech to tens of thousands of
appreciative Republicans and winning for himself in the process the
lifelong nickname, "the Centennial Spread Eagle." Along with his familiar litany of Democratic crimes, Ingersoll savaged Tilden personally,
in a way that raised questions about the candidate's presumed sexual
preferences. "I am opposed to him first," Ingersoll said of Tilden, "because he is an old bachelor. Any man that will live in this country for

sixty years, surrounded by beautiful women with rosy lips and dimpled cheeks, in every dimple lurking a cupid, with pearly teeth and sparkling eyes—any man that will push them aside and be satisfied with the embraces of the Democratic party, does not even know the value of time." Tilden, he smirked, was "a little, dried-up old bachelor [who] courted men because women cannot vote."

The implication was clear to the audience: Tilden was a homosexual. Much was made of his clean-shaven appearance, fastidious dress, and tastefully decorated mansion, and his lifelong bachelorhood was contrasted negatively to the virile, bearded virtues of his married opponent, with his plump, smiling wife and their five well-brought-up children. The never-subtle Thomas Nast frequently sketched Tilden wearing a dress. Tilden ignored the cruel gibes, just as he ignored the seemingly contradictory charge that he was syphilitic, but his handlers were sufficiently concerned about the attack to put out the rumor, however unpersuasive, that he was planning to get married after the election. So many different women were mentioned in the press as possible mates that one newspaper editor joked that the sixty-two-year-old must also be planning to become a Mormon.

Along with the aid of professional rabble-rousers like Ingersoll, Hayes received support from some unlikely sources. One of the most unlikely was author-humorist Samuel Langhorne Clemens—or Mark Twain, as he was known to much of the civilized world. Clemens, who was living the comfortable life of a well-fed pillar of the community in Hartford, Connecticut, was William Dean Howells's best friend. He had just finished his latest novel, *The Adventures of Tom Sawyer*, a book whose high-spirited, all-American hero was about as far away from Samuel Tilden's own sheltered boyhood as it was possible to be. At Howells's urging, Clemens agreed to say a few words at a Republican campaign rally in Hartford on September 30.

Modestly declaring himself "the humblest member [of] the literary tribe," Clemens began his speech by wondering aloud why it was that most writers seemed to be "march[ing] under the banner of Hayes and Wheeler. I think these people have come to the front mainly because they think they see at last a chance to make their government a good government because they think they see a chance to institute an honest and sensible system of civil service. Our present civil system, born of General Jackson and the Democratic party, is so idiotic, so contemptible, so grotesque, that it would make the very savages of Dahomey jeer and the very gods of solemnity laugh." He was just getting warmed up. With congressional candidate Joseph Hawley, the erstwhile Centennial Commission chairman, looking on unhappily, Clemens proceeded to lambaste the long-accepted system of political spoils. "We serenely fill great numbers of our minor public offices with ignoramuses," he said. "We put the vast business of a custom-house in the hands of a flathead who does not know a bill of lading from a transit of Venus. We put oceans of money and accompanying statistics through the hands and brain of an ignorant villager who never before could wrestle with a two weeks wash bill without getting thrown. We send creatures all over the world who speak no language but their own, and even when it comes to that, go wading all their days through floods of moods and tenses and flourishing the scalps of mutilated parts of speech."

Not surprisingly, given the Republican makeup of the audience, Clemens's maiden political speech fell flat. The *Boston Evening Transcript* groused that "somebody should have led him off the platform by the ear." It did not seem to have occurred to Clemens—or perhaps it did—that many in the crowd were creatures of the same "idiotic" civil service system that he was decrying so energetically. Howells loyally described the speech as "civil service reform in a nutshell," but it was Clemens's first and last campaign appearance. Nevertheless, he avidly followed the course of the campaign, reassuring Howells on October 11 that Hayes "is as bound to go to the White House as Tilden is to go to the devil when the last trumpet blows." And when Tilden supporters, perhaps misled by his Hartford speech, asked Clemens for advice in "raising the Tilden flag," he responded curtly, "Don't raise it."

A fellow humorist who shared both Clemens's Republican leanings and a famous pen name of his own was David Ross Locke, editor and publisher of the *Toledo Blade*. Under the expansive moniker Petroleum Vesuvius Nasby, Locke regularly lambasted Democrats in general and Tilden in particular. His literary conceit was to write and speak in the manner of a low-born Irish immigrant. In the guise of Nasby, Locke produced a suggested rallying cry for Democrats: "Rally agin hard money in the West. Rally agin soft money in the East. Rally agin offishls uv a corrupt administrashun. Rally agin the military power, which prevents us from killin niggers as we please. Rally agin nigger in the concrete. Rally agin nigger in the abstract. Rally for victory and postoffices. P.S. I forgot to say we might ez well rally for reform."

In his heavy-handed way, Locke may have been on to something—reform, the Democrats' prized campaign issue, had indeed become something of an afterthought. Tilden's old friend, former New York governor Horatio Seymour, was one high-ranking Democrat who was glad that it had. "The word 'reform' is not popular with the workingmen," he warned the candidate. "To them it means less money spent and less work." He advised Tilden instead to play up Hayes's palpable hostility toward the Irish, as demonstrated most recently in his anti-Catholic campaign for governor. Whether or not Seymour's warning had any direct effect, a copy of the letter from Hayes's secretary to the American Alliance was leaked to the *New York World* in early October, and Democratic newspapers throughout the country quickly reprinted it. Hayes's journalist-friend William Henry Smith warned him that something of a panic had broken out among Republicans in Chicago and other midwestern cities with large Irish Catholic populations. But Hayes, who was truly obsessed with "sectarian interference" in public schools, refused to be pressured into retracting the letter. "The K.N. [Know Nothing] charges are more than met, (*not* by denial or explanation) but by charging Dems with their Catholic alliance," he assured Smith. The Republican National Committee, unconvinced, printed a number of leaflets in German maintaining solemnly that Hayes had no real objection to naturalized Americans voting or holding public office—just to operating their own schools.

A second Democratic charge against Hayes was more easily blunted. On September 30, the same day that Clemens was touting Hayes's candidacy in Hartford, the *Chicago Times* printed an article denouncing Hayes for allegedly pocketing $1,000 in cash that a soldier in the 23rd Ohio Regiment had given him for safekeeping before the Battle of Winchester in 1864. The soldier, Nelson J. LeRoy, had been killed in the battle, and his father, James LeRoy, had periodically badgered Hayes for years to return the supposedly stolen money. James LeRoy claimed that he possessed signed affidavits from wartime eyewitnesses and personal letters from Hayes that proved his guilt. The candidate was sufficiently worried to dispatch his son Rud to the family home in Fremont to retrieve his papers relating to the affair. With the help of old tax records obtained from the ever-obliging Treasury Department, Hayes prepared a lengthy legal defense demonstrating that Nelson LeRoy had never even possessed $1,000—much less given it to Hayes for safekeeping. William Henry Smith used his Western Associated Press connections to flood the northern states with Hayes's denial, and the issue quickly died away. A Nast cartoon smugly depicted Hayes as an impregnable iceberg, floating serenely on political waters while a ship labeled the Democratic party smashed itself to pieces against his side.

Where true reformers were concerned, the cartoon was all too accurate: Hayes's nomination had effectively eliminated reform as a viable campaign issue. Disregarding the fact that Hayes had been a consistent and enthusiastic supporter of the Grant administration, Liberal Republicans on the whole returned to the party banner in 1876. To justify their newfound allegiance, they pointed to Hayes's many years of honest service as governor of Ohio, far from the quicksands of Washington, as well as his stated support of civil service reform and his selfless pledge to serve only one term. "Unless I am very much mistaken," Carl Schurz had assured fellow liberal Charles Francis Adams, Jr., in July, "Cincinnati has nominated our man without knowing it." Adams and his brother Henry were not convinced. In an article in the *North American Review* that October, the Adamses agreed that Hayes had been a "faithful though uninfluential" congressman and a "respectable, though not brilliant" governor. But they questioned the wisdom of turning over the country to any man "on merely supposed virtues or rumored ability," especially since the Democrats had nominated their "most distinguished reformer" for president.

For most liberals, however, Hayes was a perfectly acceptable alternative to the Democratic nominee, and the reformist zeal that Tilden had hoped to tap into largely dissipated as the campaign wore on. In its place, as Hayes foresaw, the bloody shirt continued to hold a paramount position in the hearts and minds of northern voters. To make sure that it remained there—at least for another two months—he jotted down in September a list of helpful catchphrases for his spokesmen to use on the stump, all revolving around the central question: "Are you for the Rebellion, or are you for the Union?" It was a coarse, even cynical reduction of the campaign to a single divisive issue, but Hayes had not won three statewide elections for governor and two terms in Congress by being overly subtle or idealistic. Besides, as his advisers told him, he had little hope of winning any southern states anyway. He would be better served by shoring up his base of support in the East and Midwest—and that meant waving the bloody shirt as long and hard as he possibly could.

THE CONTINUING MISBEHAVIOR—real and imagined—of southern Democrats was used to justify Hayes's course. In the three unredeemed states that Republican governors still controlled—Florida, Louisiana, and South Carolina—the campaign was marred from the outset by mutual charges of fraud, corruption, and intimidation. It was only a taste of what was to come.

In Florida, the Republicans were split into two factions—those supporting incumbent governor Marcellus L. Stearns, a late-coming carpetbagger and former Freedmen's Bureau official from Maine, and those supporting incumbent U.S. senator Simon B. Conover, who was seeking to unseat Stearns in November. When the state convention renominated Stearns, Conover's supporters angrily walked out, and for the next three months Conover campaigned for governor as an independent, threatening to split the Republican vote. By contrast, the Democratic nominee, George F. Drew, was a well-liked political moderate whose great success in the lumber industry—friends called him Millionaire Drew—excited universal admiration among humble Floridians. At the same time, Drew's prewar opposition to secession also appealed to crossover voters, many of whom had relocated to Florida from the North in the decade following the Civil War.

With more white voters than black ones in the state, there was no need for Florida Democrats to resort to physical violence. Instead, they relied on unsubtle economic suasion to influence undecided voters.

Democratic landowners and merchants warned black sharecroppers that their credit would be adversely affected by a vote for Hayes. The Monticello, Florida, Democratic Club resolved "to give the first preference in all things to those men who vote for reform; and to give second preference in all things to those who do not vote at all." Those suspected of voting Republican would be charged a 25 percent surtax by local landlords, shopkeepers, doctors, and lawyers. Likewise, the Florida Central Railroad Company handed out numbered ballots to its employees, with the pointed admonition that the ballots had better turn up on election day. Conversely, the state-run Jacksonville, Pensacola and Mobile Railroad summarily fired any of its employees who attended Democratic campaign rallies, and levied a political assessment on its remaining workers. When all else failed, votes could be bought in the black community (so it was said) for $5 apiece, or a new pair of shoes.

Some violence, mild by southern standards, was reported in Florida in the weeks leading up to the election. In Columbia County, an armed group of white men waylaid a smaller group of blacks outside Lake City, placed nooses around their necks, and calmly discussed the most efficient way to go about hanging them. Eventually, they released their shaken captives in return for their promise to quit the Republican party. That November the county went Democratic for the first time since 1868. In the state capital of Tallahassee, another group of Democrats paid a call on Governor Stearns. Former Confederate colonel Robert H. Gamble, the group's spokesman, told the governor bluntly, "We have come, sir, to put you on notice that if a single white man is killed in Leon County on election day, there are three hundred of us who have sworn that your life shall pay for it." Stearns, described without apparent irony as being "white as a sheet," immediately issued a ringing proclamation calling on all citizens to "temper their zeal with discretion."

In response to Democratic intimidation, Florida Republicans relied on crude scare tactics to rally black voters. Stearns warned that a victory by Drew would result in nothing less than another Civil War. L. G. Dennis, the Republican boss of Alachua County, ominously advised his black constituents to carry guns when they went to the polls on election day. William Watkins Hicks, the state superintendent of public education, urged blacks to vote "early and often"; otherwise, he said, they ran the risk of being returned to slavery by the triumphant Democrats. The most sensational charge came from Malachi Martin, chairman of the Republican state executive committee, who reported two weeks before the election that armed bands of Georgia Democrats were preparing to invade Florida on election day. (The only Georgia band to invade the Sunshine State that fall was the Thomasville Cornet Band, which attended a Drew-Tilden rally in Monticello on October 28.) A Democratic railroad superintendent neatly reversed the geographical threat by sending a number of black workers northward into Alabama to repair the roads, where their train conveniently broke down and stranded them—and their votes—until after the election.

IN LOUISIANA, TOO, there was surprisingly little violence before the election. Indeed, Louisiana Democrats made a concerted and somewhat successful effort to appeal to black voters who had grown increasingly disgusted by years of Republican misrule and neglect. The Democratic nominee for governor, former Confederate general Francis R. T. Nicholls, had impeccable credentials for making such an appeal—he had lost his left arm at Winchester and his left foot at Chancellorsville. (As he was being carried from the field following his second wound, Nicholls joked gallantly that his lifelong ambition to be a judge had been ruined, "as henceforth I shall be a one-sided man.") Ennobled by his suffering, Nicholls could afford to reach out to black voters without fear that he would appear weak or traitorous to his white supporters. One similarly wounded veteran assured the candidate, "General, all what's left of me is going to vote for all what's left of you."

Nicholls's interparty appeal was helped by the fact that his Republican opponent, United States Marshal Stephen B. Packard, was widely disliked by a large segment of his own party, black and white. One impartial outside observer, Charles Nordhoff of the *New York Herald*, called Packard "the most dangerous politician in the state . . . a man of unflinching courage, strong will, and no scruples." The *New Orleans Democrat*, whose name revealed its political affiliation, adjudged Packard "the most complete and personal political representative of U.S. Grant that the hideous phantasmagoria of the past eight years has produced." As leader of the so-called Custom House Gang in New Orleans, Packard had helped Grant's brother-in-law James F. Casey and his cohorts systematically loot the state of millions of dollars—a Louisiana judge estimated at the beginning of 1876 that "$100,000,000 in gold would fail to compensate for the robberies and injuries that have been inflicted upon Louisiana by the villainous politicians who have been kept in power by Grant's illegal use of Federal troops when they had been defeated at the polls."

One consequence of the Custom House Gang's financial misdoings was the loss of state tax revenues for public schools, which many black Louisianans later cited as the primary reason they had switched over to the Democratic side. Others pointed to the increased efforts of Nicholls and his followers to court black voters with joint barbecues, concerts, integrated political clubs—1,200 Zouave-style marching uniforms were sent to Bayou Sara for black Democrats to wear, just like their white counterparts—and the promise of equal justice for all under a more enlightened Nicholls regime. At the same time, many blacks complained of disinterest, if not outright disdain, on the part of state Republicans. Henry Rivers, a black Republican leader in East Feliciana Parish, explained later why he had switched camps: "The reason," he told a congressional committee, "was that the Republican party had fallen into a weak place, and she seemed like she was busted up anyhow. The men who ought to come here and enlighten these people as they did before would not come among us, and it looked like we were left to paddle our own canoe." A white army officer stationed in East Baton Rouge underscored Rivers's observation. "One thing was quite apparent," he told the committee. "The Democratic side worked hard to induce colored men to vote their ticket, while but little effort was perceptible on the part of their opponents."

Louisiana Republicans may have taken the black vote for granted because they still controlled the state returning board, which was empowered to certify all ballots cast in the upcoming election. In both the gubernatorial election of 1872 and the legislative election of 1874, the board had shamelessly overturned apparent Democratic majorities, causing a controversy that reached all the way to the White House, and no one doubted that they were prepared to do so again, should the need arise. Incumbent governor William P. Kellogg, himself a creation of the most recent overturning, indicated as much a few days before the election, when he told the *New Orleans Daily Picayune,* "It would be suicide for them [the Democrats] to raise a tumult, for the vote of every poll and every parish where there are disturbances will certainly be thrown out by the returning board." In response, the Democratic state committee circulated a confidential memo to parish organizers warning them to "be careful to say and do nothing that can be construed into a threat or intimidation."

Despite the warning, some violence was reported in Louisiana in the weeks leading up to the election, although it was not always clear exactly who was attacking whom. Conflicting accounts of alleged abuses in Ouachita Parish, where the most serious pre-election violence occurred, variously attributed the killing of a Republican organizer named John H. Dinkgrave to local Democratic gunmen or to a family of Texans with a long-standing personal grudge against the victim. When Republican leaders sought to avenge the killing by rallying black supporters at Monroe with the dire warning, "The war has begun," white rifle clubs began patrolling the district each night. Tensions ran high, but in the end no shots were exchanged between the two sides, and a number of parish blacks later converted to the Democratic cause. In East Feliciana Parish, Republican supervisor James E. Anderson was also ambushed (but suspiciously not injured) while registering black voters, and it was widely rumored that he had arranged the shooting himself as a pretense to throw out the parish vote, which he feared would lean heavily Democratic in the coming election. For their part the Democrats, having worked hard to recruit black support in East Feliciana, paid Anderson an additional fee to stay on and complete his work. It would not be the last time that Anderson sought to be rewarded for simply doing his job.

The most sensational episode of Louisiana violence took place three days before the election, when a black man living in Ouachita Parish, Henry Pinkston, was brutally murdered one night in his home. Again, the identity of the killer (or killers) was not determined. Republicans accused local Democrats of the crime; Democrats attributed the killing to another black man who had been in a fight with Pinkston a few months before. Pinkston's wife, Eliza, who should have been the ulti-mate witness, gave highly conflicting testimony about the event, which one local resident called "a put-up job to make political capital in favor of the Republican party." Mrs. Pinkston reported first that her husband had been killed by a band of thirty to forty white men who invaded their home and shot him down, declaring that "if Henry voted the Republi-can ticket, he would do so in hell." Her employer, however, later testi-fied that Mrs. Pinkston burst into his house on the morning after the murder and told him that her husband had been killed by a small band of blacks.

Mrs. Pinkston's testimony was weakened further when Republican authorities replaced her initial account of the murder with a second document accusing entirely different persons of the crime, including some local Democrats who were able to prove conclusively that they had been miles away at the time of the murder. Nor was she helped by the testimony of black neighbors who reported that she had already murdered at least three people herself, including two of her own infant children, and had been heard to threaten her husband publicly on nu-merous occasions. Against the swirl of innuendoes was the indis-putable fact that Mrs. Pinkston had also been wounded in the attack and her infant daughter killed. Three other blacks reportedly were at-tacked that same night by marauding whites, including one man whose disemboweled body was thrown into a bayou. Whatever the truth of the matter, Henry Pinkston's murder was used by Republicans to dis-credit their opponents, and Mrs. Pinkston would repeat her accusations again, to sensational effect, after the election was over.

While exploiting the Pinkston murder for maximum political ad-vantage, Louisiana Republicans also worked hard behind the scenes to insure the victory of Packard and Hayes. The week before the election, 29,000 advertising flyers from the so-called Southern Charm Sewing Machine Company were mailed to registered Democrats in New Or-leans, with postmen given express instructions to return promptly all flyers they could not deliver in person. Anyone not receiving a flyer was stricken immediately from the voting rolls, with no time left to reapply. In all, some eight thousand Democrats were cut from the rolls, includ-ing some of the oldest and most respected residents of the city. The

Daily Picayune filled one entire page of its November 3 edition with the names of disqualified voters listed in fine print. It was later revealed that the "Sewing Machine Swindle" was the brainchild of three Republican functionaries operating secretly out of the statehouse.

IN SOUTH CAROLINA, as in Louisiana, the Democratic candidate for governor made a concerted effort to appeal to black voters. Like Francis Nicholls, Wade Hampton was a much wounded former Confederate general who did not have to rely on nakedly racist appeals for support. Instead, realizing that black voters outnumbered white voters in the state by a three-to-two margin, Hampton took pains to reach out to black Republicans, assuring them that he intended to be a governor for both the races. His first campaign speech, at Abbeville on September 16, made his position plain. "The only way to bring prosperity in this state is to bring the two races in friendly relations together," Hampton said. "If there is a white man in this assembly who believes that when I am elected governor that I will stand between him and the law, or grant to him any privileges or immunities that shall not be granted to the colored man, he is mistaken, and I tell him so now."

Hampton had been one of the first prominent southerners to publicly advocate black voting rights—he believed that all voters should be subject to the same literacy and property-owning requirements—and his speech at Abbeville was printed and distributed to black communities throughout the state. At the same time, black members were integrated into Democratic political clubs, and Hampton passed the word to his white supporters that he expected each of them personally to recruit at least one black man into the Democratic ranks, to induce him to "cross over Jordan," as such party-switching was called. One of the first to do so was black community leader Martin R. Delany, a former Union soldier and Freedmen's Bureau official who took to the stump for Hampton and Tilden. By early November there were eighteen separate black Democratic clubs in the state, and hundreds of black supporters donned the distinctive red shirt and marched alongside their white counterparts in elaborate campaign processions that snaked across the South Carolina countryside beneath banners proclaiming "Peace and

Prosperity to All Classes" and "Honest and Good Government for All."

Not all white Democrats welcomed the black converts with open arms. In the westernmost counties of the state, where Hamburg was located, M. C. Butler and his close associate Martin Gary, another former Confederate general, directed a campaign of physical and psychological intimidation modeled after the Mississippi election a year before. The plan, known variously as the Edgefield, Straight-out, or Shotgun policy, also called for individual whites to control one black vote apiece, "by intimidation, purchase, or keeping him away" from the polls. As outlined in Gary's self-authored "No. 1 Plan of the Campaign," Democrats were advised to "never threaten a man individually. If he deserves to be threatened, the necessities of the times require that he should die. A dead Radical is very harmless." The extent and impact of the Straight-out Policy have been debated by historians ever since, and one scholar has argued persuasively that Gary exaggerated his role in the election as a way of downplaying black support for Hampton. Nevertheless, complaints filtered into the governor's office on a regular basis decrying white violence in the western part of the state. One, signed by "the Colored Citizens of Laurens," reported that Democratic threats "were being put into execution almost daily. No week passes without some of our people are either whipped, shot at by the night riders[,] don't know that we can call them KKK but we are certain that they are Democratic desperadoes."

Hampton openly disavowed such attacks, saying he favored "force without violence" and wanted above all to avoid federal intervention before the election. In the place of outright violence, Hampton's followers boycotted Republican-run businesses, refused to sell goods, loan money, or rent land to their political opponents, and demanded equal time for their speakers at Republican campaign rallies. If such a "division of time" was not permitted, Democratic rifle club members resorted to the simple but effective method of "hacking"—riding about noisily, firing their weapons into the air, and generally making a nuisance of themselves. Governor Daniel H. Chamberlain, after a few such disruptive experiences, refused to campaign in public and remained out of sight in the executive mansion.

By no means was all political intimidation in South Carolina confined to white Democrats. Indeed, the most serious episodes of violence during the campaign were carried out by black Republicans apparently infuriated by the inroads Hampton had made among members of their race. On September 6, in Charleston, a mob attacked two black speakers following a meeting of the Hampton and Tilden Colored Club at Archer's Hall. White Democrats rushed to the speakers' aid, and a full-scale riot spilled into the streets. White and black Democrats were assaulted, stores were looted, and two reporters for the *Charleston News and Courier* were badly beaten in a night-long reign of terror. The city's predominantly black police force did little to quell the disorder. Two weeks later, at Ellenton, a small town twenty miles downriver from Hamburg, another riot broke out after two black men were arrested for robbing and beating a white woman in her home. Following an erroneous report that the men had been lynched, armed bands of both races poured into town, and for the next three days the two sides sniped at each other in the surrounding countryside. At least seventeen partisans, black and white, were killed in the fighting before a company of U.S. infantry arrived on the scene to restore the peace.

The worst outbreak occurred in mid-October at Cainhoy, a tiny hamlet twelve miles outside of Charleston. There, a joint Democratic and Republican campaign rally turned violent after a group of young white men discovered a cache of shotguns and rifles hidden in a shed near the speaker's stand. As the men were attempting to remove the weapons, one of the firearms discharged accidentally, and overeager partisans on both sides pulled their guns and began shooting indiscriminately. The badly outnumbered whites retreated toward the river, pursued by a party of blacks who killed five of the fugitives and wounded at least fifteen others. One black man was killed, possibly by accident, and three other blacks—all Democrats—were wounded before the whites managed to escape to Charleston by boat.

The ultimate effectiveness of the Democratic outreach to black voters in Louisiana and South Carolina cannot be measured accurately. Many observers, then and now, questioned both the motives and the good faith of the efforts, seeing them as mere window dressing for a traditional southern campaign of violence and intimidation. And it was undoubtedly true, particularly in isolated rural communities in the western part of South Carolina, that some white Democrats resorted to less pacific methods to win the election—the whip and the shotgun still played a role. At the same time, many Republican claims of abuse were invented or exaggerated after the fact for purely political purposes, used to justify their own campaign misdoings. The general consensus seems to be that the 1876 election, on balance, was less violent than either the 1868 or 1872 contests, when Republican governments still controlled the majority of the southern states. Whether the reduced violence was the result of a successful effort by Democrats to include black voters in the political process, or was merely evidence of a more subtle form of racial intimidation, lies as always in the eye of the beholder.

IGNORING EVENTS in the volatile South, the two parties looked to a handful of northern states as the keys to winning the election. The candidates' home states, New York and Ohio, obviously were crucial, as was Indiana, which was the home of the Democratic vice presidential nominee. Illinois, too, was considered a toss-up, given the fact that the Republican candidate for governor, Shelby M. Cullom, had been implicated in the Whiskey Ring scandal the year before. And in Wisconsin, a normally Republican state that in 1873 had elected its first Democratic governor in nearly a generation, the Democrats were mounting a well-organized campaign that included circulating written materials in English, German, and Norwegian. In Massachusetts the grand old Augustan, Charles Francis Adams, Sr., agreed to run for governor on the Democratic ticket, although his entire campaign contribution consisted, in the end, of writing two public letters supporting Samuel Tilden. Other states where the outcome seemed too close to call were Connecticut, New Jersey, Delaware, and Maryland.

The newest state in the Union, Colorado, was one that both sides expected to carry. The Centennial State, as it inevitably was called, had just been admitted to the Union on August 1. Statewide elections were held nine weeks later. The Democratic majority in the U.S. House of Representatives could easily have delayed Colorado's admission until after the presidential election, but the party was misled by the territory's lone congressional delegate, fellow Democrat Thomas Patterson, who assured them that the state would vote Democratic in 1876. Subsequently, little attention was paid to Colorado by either party, and it was a surprise to everyone when Republicans swept the governorship and the state legislature. To spare the cost of holding two separate elections less than a month apart, Congress had already authorized the new legislature to choose the state's presidential electors, and Hayes was accorded the state's three electoral votes—the first such votes to be entered in either candidate's column. At the time, a mere three votes did not seem particularly significant.

Colorado's election may have received scant attention in the East, but other western events periodically captured the public's eye. On August 2, James Butler Hickok, better known as Wild Bill, was shot and killed while playing cards in a Deadwood, South Dakota, saloon. His assailant, one Jack McCall, was later lynched for the crime, which was said to be the work of professional gamblers worried that Wild Bill, a former U.S. marshal, would either agree to put his badge back on and clean up the town, or else use his lengthy experience at the gaming tables to cut into their poker winnings. (The hand that Hickok was holding at the time he was murdered—a pair of aces and a pair of eights—became known ever afterward as the "Dead Man's Hand.") One month later an equally famous badman nearly came to a similar end. Jesse James, a former Confederate guerrilla, led an audacious daylight bank robbery in the unlikely town of Northfield, Minnesota. Along with his brother Frank, their cousins Cole, Jim, and Bob Younger, and assorted other desperadoes, Jesse shot it out with an impromptu posse of outraged Northfield shopkeepers, barely managing to get away in one piece—which was more than could be said for the rest of the gang, his brother excepted, who were either killed or wounded by the alert townsfolk in ten short minutes of intense gunplay.

A third incident that summer also dominated eastern newspapers. Three weeks after the Custer massacre, another flamboyant western plainsman, Buffalo Bill Cody, won national fame with a well-choreographed bit of real-life drama. On the morning of July 17, Cody was serving as a scout for General Wesley Merritt's 5th Cavalry Regiment, which was patrolling eastern Wyoming in search of Sitting Bull, Crazy Horse, and other hostile Indians. Cody had already achieved a measure of notoriety as the titular hero of a series of dime novels by the pulp writer Edward Z. C. Judson, or Ned Buntline, as he signed himself. Together, they had toured the East in Buntline's melodrama *Scouts of the Prairie; or, Red Deviltry As It Is*. On the day in question, Cody led a surprise attack on a party of Indians hiding in a ravine near War Bonnet Creek. In the subsequent fighting, he shot and killed a young Cheyenne warrior named Hay-o-wai, or Yellow Hand. Then, with a showman's practiced flair, he scalped the fallen Indian while intoning portentously, "The first scalp for Custer!" Widely reported in the eastern press, Cody's feat became the basis for a sensational new Wild West show, which began touring to packed houses later that year.

Back in the more sedate East, the two presidential candidates continued to maintain determinedly low profiles, although both found it necessary to make the obligatory pilgrimage to the Centennial Exposition. Tilden went first, on September 21, which had been designated New York Day at the fair. Attendance topped 135,000—the largest crowd for any of the individual state occasions—with several special trains making the trip south from New York City. The crowd was so vast that Tilden was two hours late getting to the New York Building for a scheduled reception. Bowing and smiling, the candidate stopped on his way inside to shake hands with well-wishers. Soon the line of supporters snaked around the building and up State Avenue; Tilden never made it into the reception. Finally, in mid-afternoon, he ascended to the front balcony of the building, where he was greeted with a tremendous ovation. Doffing his hat, he thanked the people for coming to see him, assured them a little unpersuasively that "my right arm is not wearied with the hearty and friendly grasp of the thousand whom I have had the pleasure to meet and shake by the hand," and praised the exhibition for its demonstrated "moral power." That said, he tendered the crowd his "cordial and complete salutation," and bowed his way gracefully offstage. There was no need for a political speech: the tumultuous reception spoke for itself.

The crowd for Hayes's October 26 visit was not nearly as large—Columbus, Ohio, after all, was a good deal farther away from Philadelphia than was New York City. Still, like Tilden, Hayes shook hands with supporters for several hours, including a large contingent of the nation's leading business executives, who were in town for a supposedly nonpartisan professional convention. During the course of his daylong visit Hayes made four brief speeches, saying nothing of note, and even the pro-Republican *New York Times* found little to praise in the candidate's performance—not even his mode of dress. "Truth to say," the newspaper reported, "His Excellency's personal appearance was more informal than any of those who crowded to pay their respects to him, for he wore a dreadfully shabby coat and a shockingly bad hat, all brushed up the wrong way." He looked, someone said, like an old-fashioned country doctor. That night, arriving late for a political reception, Hayes suffered the acute embarrassment of being turned away at the door by hired security guards who failed to recognize the guest of honor. Only the timely intervention of Philadelphia mayor William S. Stokley averted a complete social disaster. Hayes, to his credit, accepted the misunderstanding with good-humored grace.

IF THE CROWDS at the Centennial Exhibition were any indication, Tilden had a slight but measurable lead going into the last days of the campaign. He was reported to be completely confident of victory. Republicans, on the other hand, were said to be cowed by Tilden's organization in New York state and less than thrilled by their chances in many other contested states. A series of state elections in the weeks leading up to national election day contained mixed portents for both camps. Maine and Vermont, as expected, went Republican; West Virginia favored the Democrats. In Indiana, the Democrats' rather Lincolnesque candidate, sixty-eight-year-old congressman James D. "Blue Jeans" Williams, drawled his way to victory over former Union general Benjamin Harrison, the grandson of President William Henry Harrison. Williams's victory was not unexpected, given the state's soft-money leanings and the disarray within the Republican camp after the forced resignation of gubernatorial nominee Godlove S. Orth, a former congressman and minister to Austria who had quit the race after refusing to answer accusations of influence peddling. The sour-faced Harrison— dubbed "Kid Gloves Harrison" and "the Human Iceberg" by the Democratic press—was no match for the folksy Williams, who crisscrossed the state in his trademark light-blue denim suit, dispensing droll bits of country wisdom and showing off his enormous feet, which he boasted were the largest in the entire Wabash Valley. He carried the state by five thousand votes.

That same day, October 10, Hayes's home state of Ohio elected a Republican secretary of state, the highest contested position on the ballot, by a margin of 6,600 votes, thereby underscoring Hayes's astute prediction that "October will not decide the election unless both Ohio and Indiana go the same way." Three days later, Republican National Committee secretary William E. Chandler advised Hayes confidentially that he could only count on carrying fourteen states, largely in the East and Midwest, with a total of 144 electoral votes. The other forty-one electoral votes needed for victory would have to come from somewhere else, and neither of Chandler's best-case scenarios was overly optimistic. In order to win the election, Chandler said, Hayes would either have to carry New York and Wisconsin, or else he would have to win Wisconsin, California, New Jersey, Indiana, and Nevada—a tall order, given that Indiana was the home of the Democratic party's vice presidential candidate and New Jersey was right across the river, geographically and politically, from New York. As for his chances in the South, committee finance chairman Richard McCormick warned Hayes on October 16, "We should be prepared for a solid South for Tilden." Hayes agreed. "The contest is now with the East," he said.

In the Democratic camp, the numbers were about the same, although neither New York nor New Jersey was considered to be in much danger from the Republicans. Counting the ticket's home states and the Solid South, Tilden could depend on 181 nearly sure electoral votes— only four shy of the total needed to win. The neighboring states of Connecticut and New Jersey, together with the border states of Delaware and Maryland—both former slave states—would give him another twenty-six electoral votes, for a grand total of 207. Clearly, Tilden had more of a margin for error than Hayes, who would have to draw the equivalent of a political royal flush to pull out a victory on November 7.

Such estimates, of course, were subject to revision, particularly in a year as unstable and unpredictable as 1876. Back in Washington, the current occupant of the White House did not intend to simply sit on his hands and do nothing while Tilden marched inexorably to victory. On October 17, one week after Indiana had gone Democratic and two days after the riot at Cainhoy, Grant dispatched hundreds of additional troops to South Carolina. Declaring the state to be in a condition of virtual insurrection, the president acted with his old wartime alacrity. Despite the fact that the army's district commander in South Carolina, Brigadier General Thomas H. Ruger, had assured Grant that the situation had quieted down and that he had enough troops on hand to meet any future emergencies, Grant nevertheless pulled 1,144 additional soldiers from outposts in Virginia, New York, Rhode Island, Connecticut, Massachusetts, and Maine and hurried them south to preserve the peace.

The introduction of more federal troops to South Carolina did not go uncriticized in the North. On October 19 *The Nation* strongly condemned the armed intervention, noting perceptively: "The soldiers who are now making arrests for 'intimidation' in South Carolina, and who are to preserve order at the polls on Election Day, are really an armed force in service, and acting under the orders of, one of the parties to the political contest." And in Indiana, Judge Walter Gresham, a loyal Republican, worried that "the use of bayonets in connection with the election [is] a dangerous thing. How long will it be before the same thing is resorted to in the North?"

For the time being, the only troops being deployed in the North were the small army of federal marshals and supervisors—more than sixteen thousand, at a cost to taxpayers of $291,000—that moved into place in the final days of the campaign to monitor the election. In New York City alone, there were 2,300 deputy marshals and 1,144 supervisors, all operating under the obsessive eye of federal election watchdog John I. Davenport. The thirty-two-year-old Davenport, a former Union intelligence officer during the Civil War, was a true believer; he spent thousands of dollars of his own money to pay a battalion of overworked clerks to count the number of registered voters on each block and even (Davenport boasted) the number of houses, stories, and rooms on each block. To keep up with the ever-shifting populace of the nation's largest and most protean city, Davenport required his minions to bring their four thousand registration books to his home each night for checking, and the house was so overrun with election officials that his family was forced to move into a hotel. On the eve of the election, Davenport assured Hayes that "there will not be 100 fraudulent votes polled in the city." Hayes, noting the huge registration in New York City, was not reassured. He fully expected to lose the state and, with it, the election, no matter how zealously Davenport and his deputies watched the polls.

IN THE FINAL DAYS of the campaign, as a mark perhaps of desperation, the Republicans revived old charges that Tilden, as president, would agree to honor southern claims for damages suffered during the Civil War. The unmerited allegation predictably thrummed northern emotions; exaggerated estimates put the total of "Rebel claims" at anywhere from $6 million to $2 trillion. (An enterprising Alabama newspaper, the *Auburn News and Democrat,* found no such southern claims on the books, but it did locate thirteen separate northern claims, ranging from $3,395 to $270,000, by various individuals.) Maine senator James G. Blaine solemnly advised listeners that there was "nothing in the world to prevent" such reimbursements, conveniently ignoring the fact that the Fourteenth Amendment specifically prohibited either the federal government or any state government to "assume or pay any debt or obligation incurred in aid of insurrection or rebellion against the United States. [A]ll such debts, obligations, and claims shall be held illegal and void."

Once again Tilden wanted to ignore the allegations, but campaign chairman Abram Hewitt finally prevailed upon him to issue a brief letter addressing the charges. The letter, published in the October 25 edition of the *New York World,* seemed conclusive. In it Tilden said flatly that "no rebel debt will be assumed or paid. No claim for the loss or emancipation of any slave will be allowed. No claim for any loss or damage incurred by disloyal persons, arising from the late war will be recognized or paid. I shall deem it my duty to veto every bill providing for the assumption or payment of any such debts, losses, damages, [or] claims." Even that categorical denial did not satisfy the Republican-leaning *New York Times,* which argued obtusely that Tilden had only said that he would consider it his duty to veto any war claims bill—not that he would actually do so.

Overlooked in the uproar about Tilden's intentions was the letter's touching final paragraph, in which the candidate exhibited a depth of sympathy and understanding that augured well for a Tilden presidency. It was a rare stab at oratory by this most quiet of politicians, and an even rarer glimpse at the private face behind the public mask. "The calamities to individuals which were inflicted by the late war are for the most part irreparable," Tilden wrote. "The government cannot recall to life the million of our youth who went to untimely graves, nor compensate the sufferings or sorrow of their relatives or friends. It has no safe general rule but to let bygones be bygones; to turn from the dead past to a new and better future; and on that basis to assure peace, reconciliation, and fraternity between all sections, classes and races of our people." It would have made a great inaugural address.

WHETHER OR NOT Tilden would get the opportunity to deliver such an address remained to be seen. On Tuesday, November 7, eight and a half million Americans went to the polls, fully two million more than had voted in the presidential election of 1872. It was Democratic weather—raw and windy in Hayes's home state of Ohio, overcast and cold in Tilden's New York—and the polling places were quiet, even in the South. Both candidates affected to follow their regular routines, but their differing demeanors seemed to suggest the likely outcome. Hayes, who as a gesture of good sportsmanship never voted for himself, spent the day secluded inside his home in Columbus, jotting down dire predictions of electoral calamity and pronouncing himself at peace with events. Meanwhile Tilden, flashing an uncharacteristic, bright-red carnation on the lapel of his coat, went to the polls early in New York City, then lingered for hours at Democratic headquarters, shaking hands and accepting congratulations, before rushing off to receive another round of well-wishers at his Gramercy Park residence. After dinner he returned to party headquarters to monitor last-minute events, riding past crowds of excited onlookers who were happily reading the latest returns on chalkboards posted outside newspaper offices. Everywhere he went he was showered with cheers.

But even as Tilden was completing his royal progress and retiring for the night as the nation's presumptive president-elect, an unlikely trio of supporting actors—a controversial former general, an openly pessimistic political operative, and a bitterly partisan journalist—was preparing to make its entrance onto the stage. And with the subsequent dispatching of a few well-chosen telegrams to Republican functionaries in a handful of questionable southern states, those three bit players— Daniel E. Sickles, William E. Chandler, and John C. Reid—would set into motion a chain of events that would effectively stall Samuel Tilden's long-anticipated victory march and stifle the cheers in millions of Democratic throats. Over the course of the next few days Americans would come to realize—with conflicting emotions of anger, elation, and disbelief—that the presidential election of 1876, far from being over, in many ways had just begun.

CHAPTER FIVE

IT SEEMED AS IF THE DEAD
HAD BEEN RAISED

T HE NATION AWOKE on November 8 to a welter of conflicting newspaper headlines purporting to show conclusively what could not, in fact, be shown at all: who had won the presidency. Most of the nation's major newspapers assumed that Samuel Tilden had carried the day. The *New York Sun,* which under the direction of crusading editor Charles A. Dana had given the Democrats their most effective campaign slogan—"Turn the rascals out"—declared flatly: "Tilden Is Elected." The *New York Tribune,* another Democratic newspaper, was more expansive. "Ave! Centennial Sam!" it exulted, "Complete Democratic Victory." The *Louisville Courier-Journal,* helmed by Tilden's closest southern supporter, Henry Watterson, crowed: "Thank the Lord! Boys We've Got Em." Farther west, the *Chicago Tribune,* a Republican party organ, was inconsolable: "Lost. The Country Given Over to Democratic Greed and Plunder," it said; "Tilden, Tammany and the Solid South Are to Rule the Nation." The Chicago paper attributed "the terrible defeat we have experienced" to what it termed "Grantism." Thousands of normally loyal Republicans had voted for Tilden, said the *Tribune,* "because they were sick and tired of the corruption and jobbery which have found countenance in Washington."

Two newspapers that morning stubbornly refused to name a winner. The *New York Times* continued to nurture, through its various editions, the seeds of a self-fulfilling prophecy: "A Doubtful Election." The *New York Herald* followed suit. "The Result—What Is It?" the *Herald* puzzled. "Something That No Fellow Can Understand. Impossible to Name Our Next President. The Returns Too Meager." Even so, the newspaper conceded, "Returns seem to indicate that Governor Tilden has been elected."

Those returns, in a less technologically advanced age, were slow to trickle in and far from complete. The westernmost states had not yet been heard from, although there seemed to be little doubt that the Republicans had carried them all. Nevertheless, by midmorning on November 8, both parties had a fair assessment of the final results from most of the states. The Democrats, under Tilden, could count firmly on seventeen states with a total of 184 electoral votes. The Republicans could claim eighteen states, with 166 electoral votes. That left three states, with nineteen electoral votes between them, still unaccounted for: Florida, Louisiana, and South Carolina, the last remaining southern states where Republican governors still held office. It was there that the election ultimately would be decided, although not in a way that anyone could have anticipated.

Few persons outside the murky recesses of the *New York Times*'s editorial office had any real doubts that morning about Tilden's election— not even the typically cautious man himself. Why should he have doubted? On the face of the admittedly incomplete returns, it seemed apparent that he had won. In the North, he had carried New York by more than thirty-three thousand votes, New Jersey by more than twelve thousand, Indiana by five thousand, and Connecticut by three thousand. Every undecided border state—Delaware, Maryland, Kentucky, West Virginia, and Missouri—had gone Democratic as well. There was even some question about the electoral vote in Republican-leaning Oregon, where one of Hayes's electors was in danger of being disqualified by the state's Democratic governor for violating federal election laws. The South was solid, or nearly so. Even if he lost two of the three states the *New York Times* persisted in claiming were doubtful—Florida, Louisiana, and South Carolina—Tilden would still win the election. His lead in the popular vote exceeded 263,000, or better than 3 percent, and his aggregate total, 4,300,590, was nearly three quarters of a million votes more than Ulysses S. Grant had polled against the ineffectual Horace Greeley in 1872. Returning home from Democratic headquarters that afternoon, the presumptive president-elect gave a brief statement to the *New York World*. "My election was due to the issues," Tilden said. "I received a great number of Republican votes. I did not expect a large majority in the Electoral College."

That closing qualification contained, perhaps, a trace of uneasiness. The *Times*'s refusal to concede the election was worrisome, possibly reflecting some secret knowledge, and Tilden and his advisers spent several hours at Democratic headquarters the day after the election, going over the figures state by state. They found when they emerged from the meeting that the *Times*, in the wake of managing editor John C. Reid's predawn intervention at the Fifth Avenue Hotel, had changed the totals on the bulletin board outside its office; by its unofficial count of all 369 electoral votes, Hayes now led Tilden, 185 to 184. If those figures were correct, then Hayes, not Tilden, had won the election. To help make that journalistic leap of faith a political reality, Republican party chairman Zachariah Chandler sent off another round of messages to the governors of the three disputed southern states, urging them to take control of the fluid situation and promising bluntly that, as he told Marcellus Stearns in Florida, "Troops and money will be furnished." Slowly, almost imperceptibly, the tide was turning.

ONE GOVERNOR WHO had not yet gotten the message was Rutherford B. Hayes. The morning after the election Hayes awoke refreshed and, so he reported, "contented and cheerful" with his lot. Like most of his follow citizens, he assumed he had lost the election. The first thing he saw when he came downstairs was a telegram from the New York manager of the Western Associated Press informing him that "dispatches indicate New Jersey [has] gone Democratic[,] leaving no further doubt of Tilden's election." Maintaining his regular schedule along with his dignity, Hayes went to his office at the usual hour, betraying no outward signs of disappointment. He immediately sat down and wrote a letter to his son Rud, who was away at college in Ithaca, New York. Hayes assured Rud that he and the rest of the family were "cheerful and philosophical" about his defeat; he only regretted that he would not be able "to establish Civil Service reform, and to do a good work for the South. But it is decreed otherwise and I bow cheerfully to the result."

Throughout the day a steady stream of visitors dropped by Hayes's office to offer condolences. "The ordinary habitue of the Capitol could not tell from his appearance whether he was a candidate for any office or not," the *Ohio State Journal* reported. "He received those who called in his usual cordial manner, and was very unconcerned, while the greatest office on the American continent was trembling in the balance." Hayes confided to a reporter for the *Cincinnati Times* that he had little hope for a last-second reversal of fortune. "I don't care for myself," he said, "and the party, yes, and the country, too, can stand it; but I do care for the poor colored men of the South." In the wake of the election, he predicted, white southerners "will practically treat the constitutional amendments as nullities, and then the colored man's fate will be worse than when he was in slavery, with a humane master to look after his interests."

Later that afternoon, Hayes met with a group of reporters at his office. He was remarkably frank about his assessment of the election. "I think we are defeated," he told the journalists, adding, "I am of the opinion that the Democrats have carried the country and elected Tilden, as it now seems necessary for the Republicans to carry all the states now set down as doubtful to secure even a majority of one." He asked the press not to send out any more "encouraging dispatches," since such reports might "mislead enthusiastic friends to bet on the election and lose their money." He made it clear that he was keeping his own money firmly in his pocket.

On balance, Hayes seemed to be taking his apparent defeat better than were his friends. Stanley Matthews, who had joined the 23rd Ohio Regiment alongside Hayes in 1861, reverted to quasi-biblical language to describe the depths of his despondency. "I seemed all day to walk through the valley of the shadow of death," he wrote to his old comrade-in-arms. "I felt as if a great conspiracy of ignorance, superstition, and brutality had succeeded in overthrowing the hopes of a Christian civilization as represented and embodied in the Republican party. . . . I sincerely hope that the later and more encouraging news may be verified and that our fears may be removed. I shall rejoice with joy unspeakable and full of gladness."

Matthews was referring, perhaps, to reports reaching Columbus early on the evening of November 8 that Hayes, implausibly, had carried New York. Excited supporters thronged the streets and marched to the governor's house, calling happily for the "president." Hayes himself was not persuaded. Appearing at his door, he signaled for quiet. "If you will keep order for one half minute," he urged the crowd, "I will say all that is proper to say at this time. In the very close political contest, which is just drawing to a close, it is impossible, at so early a time, to obtain the result, owing to the incomplete telegraph communications through some of the southern and western states. I accept your call as a desire on your part for the success of the Republican party. If it should not be successful, I will surely have the pleasure of living for the next year and a half among some of my most ardent and enthusiastic friends, as you have demonstrated tonight." It sounded very much like a concession speech.

IN NEW YORK CITY, Zachariah Chandler was not conceding anything. Later that same night he issued a statement to the press that left—or attempted to leave—no doubt about the election's outcome. "Dispatches received at these headquarters report that Louisiana, Florida, South Carolina, Wisconsin, Oregon, Nevada and California have given Republican majorities," Chandler announced. "There is no reason to doubt the correctness of these reports and if confirmed the election of Hayes is assured by a majority of one in the Electoral College." Except for a possible legal challenge to one of the three Oregon electors, Democrats had already conceded the last four states on Chandler's list to the Republicans—they had no bearing on the 184 undisputed electoral votes that Tilden already claimed. But the three southern states, as Chandler well knew, had not been conceded to anyone—certainly not to Hayes. Indeed, there were unconfirmed reports that the governors of Florida and Louisiana had already told Chandler confidentially that the Democratic ticket had carried their states. If so, Chandler simply disposed of the inconvenient telegrams like the wily political operative he was and declared an unconditional victory, trusting his friends in the Republican press to put the best construction on things.

The *New York Times* needed no additional encouragement. The next morning it ran a banner headline: "The Battle Won. A Republican Victory in the Nation—Gov. Hayes Elected President and William A. Wheeler Vice-President." The body of the story claimed twenty-one states for Hayes, including all three of the disputed southern states. "The latest intelligence points to the certain election of Gov. Rutherford B. Hayes to the presidency, and a Republican victory in the nation," the report concluded. The *New York Sun* was equally, if oppositely, convinced: "Tilden Is Elected. The Democrats Jubilant." Other leading newspapers remained uncertain. The *New York Herald* deemed the election: "Neck and Neck." The previously despairing *Chicago Tribune* suddenly found reason for renewed optimism. "Hope!" said its headline, followed by a dizzying cascade of clichés: "It Is Nip and Tuck. Never Give Up the Ship—Don't Pass in the Chips Yet Awhile. While There's Life There's Hope."

While the partisan press fought over the outcome with streaming banners and black-bordered columns, political operatives behind the scenes began laying the groundwork for a long and potentially bloody siege. Chandler followed up his grand victory pronouncement of the previous night with a confidential telegram to President Grant, asking him to send additional troops to the contested southern states to protect the local canvassing boards. At the same time, he arranged for various party functionaries to begin heading to the disputed states to render whatever assistance—moral, political, or financial—was needed on the ground. The first to go, fittingly enough, was the ubiquitous William E. Chandler, who left for Florida that very night. En route, Chandler wrote a brief letter to Hayes, detailing his role in the dramatic election-night events at the Fifth Avenue Hotel. "When our people came around this morning," he bragged, "it seemed as if the dead had been raised." Still, he cautioned, the outcome was very much in doubt. "One majority is as good as twenty if we hold it but we are more liable to be cheated out of it." Chandler promised to do everything in his power to prevent that from happening.

WHILE ZACHARIAH CHANDLER was adroitly claiming the election for Hayes, his Democratic counterpart, Abram Hewitt, was unaccountably slow in formulating an effective response. Hewitt, like others in his frequently disappointed party, was emotionally spent. He had gone home at midnight on election night, exhausted but happy, stopping to buy a copy of the *New York Tribune* from an urchin on the street that proclaimed in bold type: "Tilden Elected." The next morning he had awakened to the *New York Times*'s call of a doubtful election. As the day went on Tilden's lead had dwindled visibly, even as the candidate was busy accepting congratulations and hearing himself addressed as "Mr. President." Hewitt, for his part, was not convinced. Tilden was used to outwaiting his opponents; he had spent years preparing to move on Boss Tweed. He saw no great danger in the swirl of conflicting reports in the newspapers. "The fiery zealots of the Republican party may attempt to count me out," he conceded, "but I don't think the better class of Republicans will permit it. It would be a bad precedent to set. The popular majority must have its effect in the way of counteracting any attempt at upsetting the honest result of the election."

Hewitt did not share Tilden's optimism. He began drafting a statement for the candidate to release, calling on the American people to assemble at various points around the country "to protest against the frauds which have been committed, and to express their determination that the people should not be robbed of their choice for president." Tilden struck out the passage concerning public assemblies on the grounds that it might encourage violence, then chose not to issue the statement at all, telling the dumbfounded Hewitt that "it would be safe to trust to the sense of justice which sooner or later would show itself in the public mind and make the consummation of the fraud impossible."

Tilden also rejected the advice of party stalwart Henry Watterson, who wrote from Louisville on November 8 to encourage him to meet with Hayes and arrange for a joint committee of "eminent citizens" from both parties to go to Louisiana to oversee the count. Tilden's nephew, Colonel William T. Pelton, breezily assured Watterson that "the returns from Florida, Louisiana and South Carolina show all three for Tilden and Hendricks. Their election is now conceded by intelligent Republicans. The people of New York are wild with enthusiasm." Watterson was not concerned about the reaction of New Yorkers, however enthusiastic it might be—it was Louisiana he was worried about. He set out on his own for New Orleans the next day, wiring Tilden urgently that "our friends in Louisiana need moral support and personal encouragement. You must reinforce us."

Again Tilden failed to act. Stymied, Hewitt resorted to sending letters of his own to prominent northerners—Republicans as well as Democrats—inviting them to go to the disputed southern states to insure a fair vote count. He found no takers in the opposing party. President Grant, staying at his friend George Childs's Philadelphia estate preparatory to the formal closing of the Centennial Exhibition on November 10, had already followed Zachariah Chandler's lead and asked prominent Republicans to hurry south to monitor the vote. "Everything depends now upon a fair count," he told the press, neglecting to mention that he believed personally that such a count, when completed, would show indisputably that Tilden had won the election. Among those reached by Grant was Ohio senator John Sherman, who stopped off in Columbus to confer with Hayes on his way to New Orleans. According to Sherman, Hayes "expressed in the strongest language his opposition to any movement on the part of anyone to influence the action of the Returning Board in his favor. He said if Mr. Tilden was elected he desired him by all means to have the office." As Sherman well knew, *if* was a big word in politics.

Hayes's instructions to Sherman reflected his continuing belief that he had lost the election. "The election has resulted in the defeat of the Republicans after a very close contest," he wrote in his diary on November 11. The next day he expanded on that thought, noting that "figures indicate that Florida has been carried by the Democrats. No doubt both fraud and violence intervened to produce the result. But the same is true in many southern states. We shall—the fair minded men of the country will—history will hold that the Republicans were by fraud and violence and intimidation, by a nullification of the 15th amendment, deprived of the victory which they fairly won. But we must, I now think, prepare ourselves to accept the inevitable."

IRONICALLY, HAYES'S OPPONENT in New York seemed to be thinking much the same thing. On the afternoon of the tenth, Tilden went for a long buggy ride with his friend John Bigelow. The two discussed the possibility of the election being overturned in the disputed southern states, and agreed that "whether he had been elected or not, there was nothing to reproach him with in his defeat. The result shows that nothing but the reform issue he had made saved the ticket and that [Senator Thomas] Bayard or anyone else could have made no head at all against the cry of the bloody shirt which has been after all the piece de resistance of the Republicans in this canvass." Privately, however, Bigelow was not so philosophical. "Another civil war may be the consequence of this state of things," he fumed in his diary, "and we may enter upon the next century under a different form of government from that of which for nearly a century we have been boasting." The tortured wording was all too indicative of his unhappy state of mind.

Other Democrats shared Bigelow's view. Telegram after telegram chattered over Tilden's private wire, urging him to act swiftly to secure his victory. Former Confederate general Gideon J. Pillow, writing from Memphis, warned Tilden: "You are the only man who can save the government, preserve the Constitution and the liberties of the people. You must act." Others spoke of "bloody revolution" and "liberties best preserved by the sword." North Carolina governor-elect Zebulon Vance fretted to a friend, "Only the most prompt and determined resistance can avert the utter destruction of constitutional government." Through it all, Tilden kept his head. "Be satisfied with the reflection that the people are too patriotic, too intelligent, too self-poised," he assured Bigelow, "to allow anything perilous to be done that may disturb or destroy our peculiar form of government. Don't be alarmed." It was not advice that was easy to take.

Some historians have interpreted Tilden's initial, unemphatic reaction to the sudden turn of events as proof that he never truly expected to be inaugurated anyway as president. Certainly his actions in the days immediately following the election were not the firm, decisive steps of a man who was convinced beyond a shadow of a doubt that he had an unassailable claim on the White House. They were, however, entirely characteristic of Tilden's personality. "He rides a waiting race," an opposing newspaper had said many years earlier, and it was an apt metaphor for the cerebral, self-contained little man whose "wonderful self-control [betrayed] no anxiety," in the words of the *New York Tribune*.

He was, at any rate, more lawyer than politician, and he probably believed that the election ultimately would be settled in court, where he had a decided advantage, personally and legally, over anyone the Republicans could array against him. Moreover, he was also a realist, and he knew that no matter how many impassioned letters he received from angry zealots vowing to take matters into their own hands, the Republicans still controlled the White House, the Senate, the Supreme Court, and the army. Tilden had no intention of starting a fight that he had no chance of winning—however justified such a fight might be.

Tilden's calm demeanor did not assuage all of his loyalists. Dark rumors spread that Democratic forces were arming themselves to march on Washington and install Tilden by force. "Tilden or Blood!" was a popular cry. The Albany, New York, *Argus* spoke grimly of the "prospect of war in every street and on every highway of the land." Shadowy forces such as the Knights of the Golden Circle and the Sons of Liberty were said to be organizing in the Midwest, and several Tilden-Hendricks Minutemen clubs openly rallied to the Democratic banner. Most of this was bluster, a way for angry partisans to let off steam, but Tilden was sufficiently concerned about the potential for armed confrontation to meet privately with Hewitt and Bigelow in mid-November and discuss the possibility of naming former Union general George B. McClellan as his military "adjutant." The idea was dropped as quickly as it was raised, but various other Civil War–era generals, among them William B. Franklin, John M. Corse, and Winfield Scott Hancock, were floated as possible commanders of the phantom Democratic army.

In the meantime, the nation's current commander-in-chief, Ulysses S. Grant, his mettle long since proven at such places as Shiloh, Cold Harbor, and Petersburg, had already taken steps to prepare for any armed threat to the government. Seven additional companies of soldiers rolled into Washington from Baltimore and assumed positions around the federal arsenal. At the same time the USS *Wyoming* sailed up the Potomac to cover the approaches to the Anacostia Bridge into Maryland and the Long Bridge into Virginia. A company of marines began patrolling a third strategic span, the Chain Bridge, while army engineers inspected long-abandoned Civil War forts with an eye toward their emergency use. Commanding general William Tecumseh Sherman somewhat unconvincingly described the maneuvers as purely precautionary. "We must protect the public property, you know, and we must guard the arsenals," he said. Leading Democrats saw the moves as less precaution than provocation, but there was nothing they could do, legally or politically, to stop them.

With troops massing in the capital and "visiting statesmen" descending on the South from all directions, Grant sent Sherman an uncharacteristically wordy order, one whose fulsome homilies suggest that it was intended for public consumption. "Instruct General [Christopher] Augur, in Louisiana, and General [Thomas] Ruger, in Florida, to be vigilant with the force at their command to preserve peace and good order, and to see that the proper and legal Boards of Canvassers are unmolested in the performance of their duties," the president commanded. "Should there be any grounds of suspicion of fraudulent counting on either side, it should be reported and denounced at once. No man worthy of the office of President would be willing to hold the office if counted in, placed there by fraud; either party can afford to be disappointed in the result, but the country cannot afford to have the result tainted by the suspicion of illegal or false returns."

No one, in good faith, could argue with Grant's sentiments. The sticking point was what constituted "illegal or false returns." That uncertainty was the main reason why the southbound trains to Columbia, Tallahassee, and New Orleans were packed with distinguished-looking gentlemen from both parties in the days immediately following the election. And as the northern visitors would quickly learn, in the South legality was in the eye of the beholder, and truth was a readily negotiable concept.

EACH OF THE THREE disputed states represented a different set of circumstances. In South Carolina, where there had been the worst pre-election violence, the presidential race was complicated by an even more bitter governor's race. Helped immeasurably by the influx of additional federal troops in the two weeks prior to the election, Hayes's sworn electors had carried the state by anywhere from six hundred to one thousand votes, a slender but seemingly sufficient margin. The problem for the Republicans lay in the fact that Democratic gubernatorial candidate Wade Hampton apparently had won the election by an even wider margin. It looked odd, to say the least, for winners of the top two offices to be on different tickets in the same election. Even worse, Republican governor Daniel H. Chamberlain was refusing to concede that he had lost the race; his refusal threatened to throw the state into even greater turmoil. If, as seemed likely, the Republican-dominated state canvassing board threw out enough votes to keep Chamberlain in office, Hampton and his Red Shirts might feel compelled to take matters into their own hands. For the time being, the former Confederate general held his restless troops in check, but nerves were fraying by the hour in the always edgy Palmetto State.

The outcome of the election in Florida was even less clear-cut than it was in South Carolina. Initial returns gave Tilden a victory in the presidential race and Democratic candidate George F. Drew a victory in the gubernatorial contest—but both by such razor-thin margins that the slightest puff of air might blow them away. In the presidential contest, Tilden appeared to have carried the day by ninety-one votes; Drew's lead was 497 votes. Republicans, however, were crying foul, complaining loudly of fraud, intimidation, and pre-election violence. When a train carrying returns from the western counties of the state derailed en route to Tallahassee on November 8, Governor Marcellus Stearns charged—without providing any proof—that the train had been "ku-kluxed," and petitioned the president for additional troops. (The Democratic-leaning *Savannah Morning News* had a different view of the incident; it attributed the wreck to divine providence.) Hard-traveling General Thomas Ruger, who had been stationed recently in South Carolina, left immediately for Florida at the head of twelve infantry and artillery companies. When he arrived in Tallahassee, the city was so quiet that the soldiers simply set up camp near the statehouse, stacked their rifles and bayonets, and passed the time in more congenial pursuits—hunting, fishing, napping, and loafing.

Meanwhile, squadrons of Republican and Democratic statesmen arrived in Tallahassee and checked into the City Hotel and the less opulent but equally crowded Warwick Hotel near the capitol. Leading the Republican contingent was William Chandler; he was joined by former

Ohio governor Edward F. Noyes, who had stage-managed Hayes's drive for the presidential nomination in Cincinnati, former Union generals Francis Barlow and Lew Wallace, Iowa congressman John A. Kasson, and various lesser lights, including a dozen federal investigators helpfully dispatched from Washington by Secretary of the Treasury Lot M. Morrill, Attorney General Alphonso Taft (father of future president William Howard Taft), and Postmaster General James N. Tyner. Democratic statesmen, who unlike their Republican counterparts had to pay their own way to Florida, included Manton Marble, former editor of the *New York World*, Pennsylvania politicians C. W. Woolley and John F. Coyle, Massachusetts party activist Leverett Saltonstall, and former governor Joseph E. Brown of Georgia. Chandler and Marble, the leaders of the two opposing camps, came armed as well with secret cipher codes to communicate with party headquarters back in New York. The canny Chandler also brought along a carpetbag stuffed with $10,000 in ready cash.

Across the Gulf of Mexico in New Orleans, another group of visiting statesmen moved into place in mid-November. On the face of the initial returns, the outcome of the presidential race in Louisiana did not seem to be in any doubt. Tilden's electors had leads of anywhere from 6,300 to 8,957 votes—surely enough to withstand any challenge from the Republicans. Nevertheless, both sides knew that in the past the state returning board had shown a marked propensity for reversing decisions of the ballot box, and Louisiana governor William P. Kellogg had set the stage for just such an eventuality two days before the election when he sent a detailed report of alleged Democratic abuses to Republican National Committee chairman Zachariah Chandler (the allegations subsequently were reprinted in *The New York Herald*).

Given the state's recent history with disputed elections, both sides assumed that 1876 would be no different, and accordingly sent some of their most experienced politicians to New Orleans. The Republicans, led by Senator John Sherman, included Ohio congressman James A. Garfield, former U.S. attorney general William M. Evarts, longtime Hayes friend Stanley Matthews, former Union generals William Stoughton, James Van Alen, and Lew Wallace (who shuttled back and forth between Louisiana and Florida), and Chicago party activist Charles B. Farwell, reputed to be "the ablest politician and wisest coolest head in Illinois." The Democrats, with Henry Watterson as their self-appointed leader, included Senators J. E. McDonald of Indiana and John W. Stevenson of Kentucky, Congressman Samuel Randall of Pennsylvania, former Illinois senator Lyman Trumbull, former governors John A. Palmer of Illinois and Andrew G. Curtin of Pennsylvania, Mississippi congressman L. Q. C. Lamar, former Confederate general Edward Walthall, and Judge J. R. Stollo of Cincinnati. In all, the Republicans sent twenty-five statesmen to Louisiana, the Democrats twenty. "Within a week," Watterson joked, "the St. Charles Hotel might have been mistaken for a caravansary of the national capital."

The makeup of the three boards did not inspire much confidence in Democratic hearts. In South Carolina, the state board of canvassers was composed of five elected officials: Secretary of State H. E. Hayne, Attorney General William Stone, Comptroller General T. C. Dunn, Inspector General H. W. Purvis, and Treasurer F. L. Cardozo. All were Republican partisans, three were black, and Hayne, Cardozo, and Dunn were candidates for reelection who ultimately would rule on their own cases. In Florida, the state canvassing board was composed of Secretary of State Samuel B. McLin, Comptroller Clayton A. Cowgill, and Attorney General William Archer Cocke. McLin and Cowgill were Republicans, and besides a common party affiliation they shared another, less salubrious distinction—they were both suffering from tuberculosis, and had moved to Florida a few years earlier for their health. McLin, a native Tennessean, had abandoned the Confederate army during the Civil War to become editor of the *Tallahassee Sentinel*, one of the most influential and pro-Republican newspapers in the state. Cowgill, a Delaware native, was a trained physician who had served in the war as a Union surgeon; he had moved to St. Johns County in 1867 to grow oranges and sit in the sun. Cocke, a former Whig, had been one of the few Florida Democrats to support U.S. Grant against Horace Greeley in 1872, an apostasy that won him an appointment as state attorney general under Republican governor Ossian B. Hart. When Hart died in office, his successor, Marcellus Stearns, attempted unsuccessfully to rescind the appointment, thereby ensuring Cocke's unrelenting animosity.

If the South Carolina and Florida boards seemed ripe for partisan manipulation, they were pillars of Athenian probity and good governance compared to the Louisiana returning board. Members of that board, all Republicans, included James Madison Wells, Thomas C. Anderson, Louis M. Kenner, and Gadane Casanave. A fifth board member, Democrat Oscar Arroyo, had resigned two years earlier, charging the board with rampant corruption. According to state law, the other four members should have filled Arroyo's position, but for obvious reasons they did not. Arroyo's resignation was scarcely the worst problem facing the Democrats. While the South Carolina and Florida boards were composed of generally respected, if partisan, individuals, the Louisiana tribunal mirrored the worst aspects of Reconstruction-era politics.

The board chairman, Madison Wells, was a case in point. A former two-term governor, Wells had a background that was byzantine even by Louisiana's notoriously twisty standards. Before the Civil War, he had been a prosperous cotton planter, owning over a hundred slaves. When the tides of war shifted to the Union side, he smoothly switched sides himself, organizing and leading a group of pro-Union guerrillas to prey on his former associates. Entering the governor's office in 1865 as a Radical Republican, Wells did an abrupt flip-flop when large numbers of former Confederates began returning to politics after receiving presidential pardons from Andrew Johnson. With the help of a large anti-black vote, he managed to hold on to office alongside a Democratic-controlled legislature that speedily enacted a repressive vagrancy law aimed at disempowering Louisiana blacks. One year later he switched sides again after congressional Radicals had regained the upper hand, leading the drive for a constitutional convention to rewrite the state bylaws and expand black voting rights. The ensuing turmoil resulted in a bloody riot in the streets of New Orleans in September 1866, with nearly two hundred citizens—most of them black—killed or wounded. Eventually, Wells was removed from office by district commander Phil Sheridan in a raging dispute over federal patronage. Wells, said Sheridan, was "a political trickster and a dishonest man [whose] conduct has been as sinuous as the mark left in the dust by the movement of a snake." The *New Orleans Times,* speaking for thousands of citizens, black and white, punned happily after Sheridan's action: "All's well that ends Wells."

To its dismay, the newspaper quickly found that it had spoken too soon. With the advent of Republican governor William P. Kellogg's disputed administration in 1875, Wells returned to public life, becoming surveyor of the port of New Orleans and an integral part of the Custom House Gang. As an indication of his renewed political clout, he was selected as chairman of the returning board by his three fellow board members, none of whom could match his extensive political pedigree. Anderson, the other white man on the board, was a scalawag state senator who in the past had used his legislative position to extract a hefty contract from the state for a navigation company in which he had a controlling interest. Like his counterparts in South Carolina, he was also up for reelection. The two black members of the board, Kenner and Casanave, had their own image problems. Kenner, a former servant in a New Orleans gambling house, had been fired for stealing from his employers; only a public apology kept him out of jail. Undeterred, he opened a combination faro parlor and bawdy house a few doors down from the capitol. Casanave, an undertaker by profession, generally was considered the most honest member of the board, but he was also considered the most ignorant member as well, evincing, said one newspaper, "such indifference to the obligation of an oath as warrants the conclusion that he would be a willing accomplice in any rascality by which he might profit." These were the men who would rule on Louisiana's eight electoral votes.

THE THREE CANVASSING boards set about their deliberations in mid-November under the tense, watchful eyes of the visiting statesmen. By law, each board had a limited amount of time to entertain, investigate, and otherwise rule on any legal challenges placed before it. For all three boards, the clock was ticking: the Electoral College electors were due to meet on December 6 in the capitals of the thirty-eight states and formally cast their votes for president. (Under the Constitution, presidents were chosen by electors who had sworn to vote for them in the Electoral College. Despite various attempts—one as recently as 1875—to amend the Constitution and permit the direct election of the president by popular vote, the archaic system remained in place, with critical implications for the current election.)

South Carolina's board went to work first, convening on November

10 in Columbia. The atmosphere was rife with potential violence. One day earlier, in Charleston, a mob of blacks had set upon a group of whites who were reading the latest election returns posted in the windows of the *Charleston News and Courier*. A taut standoff ensued after a black policeman fired two pistol shots at the white men, and other black police officers armed with bayonet-tipped rifles moved to disperse the angry crowd. Army colonel Henry Hunt, whose hastily massed artillery had helped turn back Pickett's Charge at Gettysburg, rushed to the scene with a contingent of soldiers. Along the way, Hunt passed the headquarters of a Hampton rifle club; inexplicably, he invited the Red Shirts to join his column. The union of northern soldiers and southern Democrats was a novel scene in downtown Charleston, and served to disperse the grumbling crowd, but it did not set well with Hunt's superiors. When word got back to Washington, the erstwhile war hero was quickly removed from command for giving the appearance of a pro-southern bias.

The initial returns in South Carolina gave Hampton a 1,134-vote lead over Chamberlain in the governor's race, while Hayes's electors also led the balloting by a narrow margin. Under existing law, the state legislature was empowered to declare the winner of the gubernatorial contest, while the board of canvassers ruled on the other races. Returns seemed to indicate that the Democrats had carried just enough seats to win a one-vote majority in the legislature, meaning that Hampton would be certified governor when the body reconvened on November 26. But the makeup of the new legislature was called into question when Republicans charged that Democratic margins in the always troublesome western counties had been tainted by violence and voter intimidation. As proof, the Republicans cited the returns from Edgefield and Laurens counties, where Republican majorities in 1874 had turned into sizable Democratic margins two years later. Not coincidentally, those counties were controlled by Straight-out Democrats Martin Gary and Matthew C. Butler. The Republicans demanded that the board invalidate the election in the affected counties and decertify their newly elected Democratic legislators, thus preserving a seven-vote Republican majority in the legislature.

The Democrats protested bitterly, petitioning the state Supreme

Court to prohibit the board from doing anything other than merely sanction the existing vote totals. Surprisingly, the all-Republican court agreed, issuing an order to that effect on November 17. Hampton, sensing victory, released a statement "offering our people my heartfelt congratulations and gratitude for the grand victory they have won," and asking them "to prove themselves worthy of it by a continued observance of good order and a rigid preservation of peace." In the meantime, unrest continued on the streets of Charleston, where blacks suspected of voting for the Democratic ticket were set upon and beaten by their fellow blacks, while in the remote South Carolina countryside barn burners on both sides of the political fence settled long-standing grudges at the smouldering end of a match.

Chamberlain, fighting for his political life, retailed lurid stories of Democratic misdeeds, but numerous army officers stationed at the affected polling places testified later that they had witnessed little if any violence on election day. Colonel A. W. Randall, commanding seven companies of troops in Edgefield County, later told a congressional committee that he had "visited this same precinct several times during the afternoon and toward evening, and I saw nothing in the way of disturbance or intimidation, or anything else." Randall added that the town itself "was remarkably quiet. I have seen elections in the North ten times more noisy." Lieutenant H. G. Litchfield, stationed at Winnsboro, testified that he had "never witnessed a more quiet election in any country." And Captain James Stewart, commanding the federal troops in Laurens, said flatly that he had observed no sign of disturbance or intimidation during the polling on November 7. Supporting the soldiers' stories was the inarguable fact that none of them had been called upon to intervene by Republican officials on election day.

Despite the lack of hard evidence—and in defiance of the state Supreme Court's earlier ruling—the canvassing board reconvened on November 22 and threw out the returns for Edgefield and Laurens counties, citing wholesale fraud and intimidation. At the same time, it ignored similar charges leveled against Republican-controlled counties in the so-called black belt around Charleston, where no soldiers or federal marshals had been stationed on election day, despite repeated requests by the Democrats. The board then certified the state's seven

Electoral College votes for Hayes, changed just enough votes to elect the Republican candidates for comptroller and superintendent of education, and let stand without comment the elections of all other candidates, Democrats and Republicans alike. The board disregarded a second Supreme Court order to provide an official vote count for the presidential electors, a requirement that Democrats hoped might salvage at least some of the electors for Tilden, by allowing the court to "go behind" the returns and investigate complaints. Instead, the board simply declared itself formally adjourned and thus out of the reach of any further legal mandates. Secretary of State H. E. Hayne protested the actions of his fellow board members, but was quickly voted down. Outraged, the Supreme Court had the five members of the board arrested that night for contempt of court, but a fast-acting Republican magistrate soon released them from custody.

The situation quickly degenerated into farce. Four days after the canvassing board had disbanded, the state legislature met to certify the new governor. Fearing trouble, a company of soldiers was stationed in the capitol. Attempting to enter the house chamber, eight newly elected Democratic representatives from Edgefield and Laurens counties were denied entrance by the Republican sergeant at arms for not having the proper election certificates. Bayonet-wielding soldiers backed the Republicans. In a show of sympathy, the remaining Democratic legislators walked out of the chamber and set up headquarters a few blocks away at Carolina Hall. Meanwhile, the Republicans, although lacking a legal quorum, organized for business as usual and prepared to formally certify Chamberlain's election. Outside, in the streets of Columbia, thousands of heavily armed Hampton supporters began massing for trouble.

Two days later the Democratic legislators returned to the capitol and stormed back into the assembly hall. For the better part of a week the state was treated to the spectacle of two separate governing bodies attempting to occupy the same small room. While the legislators took turns braying at each other at the top of their lungs and passing resolutions designed to prove their exclusive legitimacy, rumors flew that Chamberlain had imported a gang of black toughs from Charleston, the mysterious "Hunkidories," and intended to set them loose on the Democrats. Eventually, at Hampton's urging, the Democrats went back to

Carolina Hall to await a new Supreme Court ruling on which of the two legislatures was the state's official representative body. The Republicans, not waiting for the ruling, continued preparing for Chamberlain's inauguration.

IN THE MIDST of the standoff in South Carolina, Democratic party chairman Abram Hewitt turned his gaze across the country to Oregon, where another legal controversy was brewing. Both sides conceded that Hayes had carried the state by a little over a thousand votes, but whether he was entitled to all three of the state's electoral votes was very much an open question. One of the three designated Hayes electors, John W. Watts, was a postmaster (fourth-class) in Yamhill, where he earned the unprincely annual sum of $268 for his troubles. The fact that Watts was a postmaster, and hence a federal employee, clearly violated the Constitution, which declared unambiguously that "no Senator or Representative, or Person holding an Office of Trust or Profit under the United States, shall be appointed an Elector."

Watts, apparently, was aware of the disqualifying clause. Before the election, he had asked Oregon senator John Mitchell for advice on the subject. But Mitchell, no constitutional scholar, had told him that he could simply resign after the election and carry out his duties as an elector—presumably with the understanding that he would then be reappointed to his post by the new, happily predisposed president. Hewitt read the law differently. "Upon careful investigation, the legal opinion is that the votes cast for a federal office-holder are void, and that the person receiving the next highest number of votes should receive the certificate of appointment," he informed Democratic governor Lafayette Grover. "This will force Congress to go behind the certificate, and open the way to get into merits of all cases, which is not only just, but which will relieve the embarrassment of the situation."

Hewitt denied later that he had any ulterior motive in writing to Grover, but the last sentence of his telegram spelled out plainly the Democrats' gambit and seemed to indicate the current thinking inside the Tilden camp about the probable outcome of the vote count in the three disputed southern states. If, as expected, the Republican-dominated canvassing boards ruled in favor of Hayes, then a clear inducement to "go behind" the certificate in Oregon would enable the Democrats to reexamine the boards' decisions in South Carolina, Florida, and Louisiana as well. Hewitt—and by extension Tilden—was convinced that such a reopening would cause any temporary Republican lead to disappear. Postmaster General James Tyner apparently shared the Democratic view, hastily accepting Watts's resignation one week after the election and complaining to Hayes confidant James M. Comly: "How any people could commit such an act of folly as to elect such men to positions of such responsibility, is beyond my comprehension; but then you know there have been fools in all the past, and there will be fools for at least thirty years yet."

Although Oregon law mandated that any vacancy in the state's electors should be filled by the other electors, Governor Grover was deluged with demands from Hewitt and other Democrats that he take it upon himself to fill the vacancy with the next-highest vote-getter, E. A. Cronin, a Democratic elector who was pledged to Tilden. At the same time, a shadowy Nebraska mining official named J. N. H. Patrick went to Oregon at the behest of the Democratic National Committee to oversee the efforts to unseat Watts. "If Tilden is president, he will give you anything you want," Patrick assured Cronin. Secret cipher telegrams flew back and forth between Patrick and Colonel William Pelton, Tilden's nephew, discussing the terms for a possible bribe—figures ranged from $3,000 to $10,000—to replace the Republican elector with a Democrat. Tilden himself had no knowledge of the discussions, which apparently involved a forged message from Governor Grover, in Patrick's handwriting, purporting to "decide every point . . . in favor of the highest Democratic elector."

The situation simmered for the next two weeks, while Grover heard conflicting arguments about his legal right to name a new elector. In the end, he decided that since Watts had not been eligible to appear on the ballot at the time of the election, his subsequent disqualification had not created a vacancy for the other two electors to fill. Instead, Grover reasoned, any votes cast for Watts were simply invalid, and the next-highest elector, Cronin, was the true choice of the Oregon people. It was an ingenious if not altogether convincing solution, and Cronin prepared to take his seat with the other two electors when the Electoral College convened on December 6.

WHILE OREGON'S GOVERNOR wrestled with what to do about the federal-postmaster-turned-presidential-elector in his state, the Louisiana returning board convened in New Orleans on November 17 to begin its own procrustean deliberations. Democratic visiting statesmen immediately requested that the Republicans join them in calling for a fair and public canvassing of votes. The Republicans, through their spokesman, Ohio senator John Sherman, declined. They were not there, Sherman explained a little disingenuously, to interfere with the official proceedings, but merely to serve as witnesses, "without power or legal influence over the result, or over the means by which, under the laws of Louisiana, the result is to be determined." As both Sherman and his Democratic counterparts were well aware, Louisiana law gave the returning board the absolute authority to decide which votes to count and, more important, which votes to throw out. One could almost see the satisfied smirk behind Sherman's further assurance that "we join heartily with you in counsels of peace and in the expression of an earnest desire for a perfectly honest and just declaration of the results of the recent election in Louisiana by its lawfully constituted authorities, and we may add that we know of no reason to doubt that such declaration will be made."

Despite Tilden's seemingly unassailable lead, the Democratic leaders in New Orleans were anything but confident as the returning board began its work. Former Union general James McQuade, a New York Democrat, told Tilden frankly, "I am convinced they will count you out." Henry Watterson concurred. "Well-organized plans supported by troops to cheat us in count of votes," he telegraphed Tilden. "Our majority seventy seven fifty seven [7,757]. The whole case one-sided in every particular." (It was revealed later that every telegram sent to Tilden by his Louisiana representatives was intercepted by Republican partisans at Western Union and forwarded to the Republican National Committee in New York.) Another visiting statesman, George W. Julian of Indiana, advised his wife: "It is believed here the board will turn us all out in a day or so, go into secret session, & declare the result in favor of Hayes. If so we can only make an appeal to the country & go home."

As a sop, perhaps, to public opinion, the board agreed to allow five statesmen from each side to observe its deliberations, but refused eight separate appeals by the Democrats to appoint another board member, as required by law, to replace the previously resigned Arroyo. Board chairman Madison Wells explained the refusal by saying first that the remaining members could not agree upon another member to appoint, and then by declaring that the Democrats, by dint of Arroyo's resignation, had forfeited the right to another representative. A similar disregard for legal niceties extended to the handling of parish returns, which the law required the fifty-six individual registrars to mail to the capital immediately after the election. Wells, for reasons that would soon become clear, permitted the various registrars to hand-deliver the returns, in some cases several days after the fact. At the beginning of the board's deliberations, only thirty-seven sets of returns had been received, and twenty of these had been delivered to the Republican-controlled customhouse instead of to the board itself.

The board began its deliberations by agreeing first to rule openly on the ballots from all uncontested parishes, while reserving the right to go into secret session any time one of the members so desired. The Democrats immediately protested, and even Republican congressman James A. Garfield, one of the visiting statesmen, worried that such secrecy might "serve to inflame the public mind with suspicion that the board were determined to count a Republican majority right or wrong." The board, which was indeed so determined, ignored the protests and began its work on November 20, canvassing eleven parishes and setting aside five sets of contested returns. The other six returns were handed over to the board's clerks to be tabulated privately in a back room. All the clerks were Republicans, five were under indictment in criminal courts at the time, and two others had been cleared recently of charges ranging from perjury to murder. In their hands rested the electoral fate of all state officials except the governor and the presidential electors.

The Republican visiting statesmen, led by Sherman, proved more determined—or at any rate more efficient—than their Democratic counterparts. They quickly divided the contested parishes among themselves and set out to investigate, interview, and in some cases coach prospective witnesses to alleged Democratic campaign abuses. Under existing state law, their labors should have been rendered moot from the outset: only protests filed by mail within one day of the election, supported by sworn affidavits by three eyewitnesses and attached to the official returns "by paste, wax, or some adhesive substance," were supposed to be allowed. The returning board simply ignored the law, permitting parish registrars to deliver their returns and protests by hand, open and examine various returns, and insert new affidavits in some of the packages a week or more after the fact. When challenged by the Democrats, the board airily dismissed the violations as mere "clerical errors."

Meanwhile, Republican investigators, aided by soldiers, rounded up some three hundred witnesses to alleged Democratic abuses. Of that number, a total of 157 subsequently testified before the returning board in New Orleans, at a cost to the federal government of some $10,000. Most of the testimony centered on Ouachita Parish, where Tilden had won a comfortable majority. The most explosive, if not necessarily persuasive, testimony came from Eliza Pinkston, the widow of Henry Pinkston, who appeared before the board on November 28. Mrs. Pinkston, borne into the meeting room by two burly attendants and accompanied by a lady-in-waiting armed with a handy bottle of "restoratives," gave a lurid account of her husband's death at the hands of unidentified assailants three days before the election. Mrs. Pinkston's testimony, which even a sympathetic observer later admitted was "embellish[ed] with details that were evidently fictitious," was accepted as fact by the returning board, which also accepted without qualm the supporting affidavit contesting the parish's returns, even though the affidavit had been filed more than two weeks after the election. Again the Democrats protested, apparently with good cause, since a subsequent congressional investigation determined that Mrs. Pinkston's testimony was, at best, too confused and contradictory to be believed. For the time being, however, the grieving widow's testimony stood as uncontroverted proof that the Democrats had gone to murderous lengths to influence the election—although why, exactly, they would want to murder Pinkston, who was widely reputed to have been a "good Negro" and a Democrat to boot—no one bothered to explain.

That same congressional investigation also uncovered serious if ultimately unproven allegations that the Republican party, in general, and
Senator Sherman, in particular, had conspired to bribe certain Louisiana
election officials to help deliver the state's eight electoral votes to Hayes.
East Feliciana Parish election supervisor James E. Anderson testified before Congress that Sherman, in the midst of the returning board's deliberations, had endeavored to get Anderson and West Feliciana supervisor
D. A. Weber to throw out enough Democratic votes in their respective
parishes to tilt the outcome to the Republicans. Anderson claimed to
have received both oral and written assurances from Sherman that he
and Weber would be "taken care of" by Hayes after the election. (Unfortunately for Weber, he was taken care of first by unknown assailants who
shot and killed him in broad daylight outside the courthouse in St. Fran-
cisville, three days after the new president was inaugurated in March
1877.) Anderson's case was weakened when he could not produce a
copy of Sherman's letter—he said he had given it to Weber for safekeeping—and Sherman testified, a little lamely under the circumstances, that
he did not remember having written such a letter, but that he did not believe he had ever done so.

Despite Sherman's pallid disavowal, Anderson subsequently had
managed to get in to see Hayes on three different occasions at the
White House, and later had been offered separate appointments as U.S.
consul to Madeira and as a federal customs inspector in Baltimore,
Boston, or Philadelphia. Anderson turned down both appointments,
but later got a job at the Republican-leaning *Philadelphia North American*
newspaper. No copy of Sherman's alleged letter was ever produced, but
another former visiting statesman to Louisiana, Stanley Matthews, did
write to Hayes recommending Anderson for a government post—all of
which proved nothing, perhaps, except that Anderson was an industrious office-seeker who had met Sherman and Matthews during the post-
election imbroglio and had tried to trade on his brief connections.
Nevertheless, Hayes was sufficiently troubled by the allegations to de-
vote several pages of his private diary to a personal examination of his
own professedly brief relations with Anderson following the election.

Other serious allegations of bribery arose at the time of the
Louisiana deliberations. Henry Watterson reported that he had been

approached by an unnamed state senator who claimed to be acting on behalf of the returning board. How much did the board want to rule in favor of Tilden, Watterson wanted to know. "Two hundred and fifty thousand dollars," the senator said. "One hundred thousand each for [Madison] Wells and [Thomas] Anderson and twenty-five thousand apiece for the niggers." Watterson declined to negotiate, but Wells apparently offered, through another intermediary, to sell himself to the Democrats for $1 million—later marked down to $200,000. John T. Pickett, a shady soldier of fortune who previously had sold the Confederate government's archives to the federal government, traveled to New York to meet with Hewitt, but Tilden's campaign manager turned down the offer. William Pelton, Tilden's nephew, was less squeamish about such matters and gave the offer serious thought, but in the end the interested parties were unable to complete the deal. A brief but tantalizing reference one year later to visiting statesman Charles Farwell's role in the proceedings by Hayes confidant William Henry Smith praised Farwell as "our right hand man" and noted that "his wealth supplied the means when no other could be reached," suggesting that Wells may have found a willing buyer for his services after all.

Hayes, in his office in Columbus, Ohio, was a long way removed from the seamy vote-selling in Louisiana, but he probably had a general idea about the overall tenor of the deliberations. At any rate, he felt the need to caution Sherman to maintain at least the appearance of propriety. "We are not to allow our friends to defeat one outrage and fraud by another," he wrote. "There must be nothing crooked on our part. Let Mr. Tilden have the place by violence, intimidation and fraud, rather than to undertake to prevent it by means that will not bear the severest scrutiny." Sherman took pains to reassure the candidate. "Wells was a Union man from the time the war broke out, and although he suffered greatly by it in the loss of property, he never faltered in his devotion to the Union cause," he advised Hayes. "His experience in public life has been great and varied, and his capacity to discharge the duties assumed cannot be questioned." Furthermore, said Sherman, "I have formed a high opinion of Governor Wells and [Thomas] Anderson. They are firm, judicious, and, as far as I can judge, thoroughly honest and conscientious." Garfield, who two years earlier had declared Wells and his associates "a graceless set of scamps," now professed to his wife that "my opinion of the Returning Board is far better than it was before I came." He assured Hayes that a fair vote in Louisiana undoubtedly would have gone his way, and "I will be able to draft a paper on the state of affairs which will show our northern people how justly the vote can be thrown out."

Garfield may have genuinely believed that Hayes's cause was just, but his assumption that the Republicans would necessarily have won a fair election rested on the debatable proposition that the number of registered black voters in Louisiana far exceeded that of white voters, and that all black votes, as a matter of course, would have gone to Hayes and Stephen B. Packard, the Republicans' unpopular gubernatorial candidate. A careful comparison of the state's 1870 and 1880 census figures later revealed that there were considerably fewer black voters in 1876 than had been claimed at the time by the Republican administration in New Orleans (a similar study of South Carolina's census figures found much the same thing in that state as well). Nor did Garfield take into account the concentrated efforts by Louisiana Democrats to reach out to black voters disillusioned by years of misrule by the Republican party in the state.

These factors—a smaller gap between the number of black and white voters, and Democratic inroads among at least a minority of black voters, to say nothing of the messianic zeal of the Democrats to recapture control of the state government—were enough to explain the large leads enjoyed by Tilden and gubernatorial candidate Francis R. T. Nicholls. Indeed, the Democratic margin was so wide in both races that an earlier plan by the Republicans to contest merely five allegedly "bulldozed" parishes bordering Mississippi and Arkansas had to be scrapped by the returning board and replaced by a much wider and more involved canvassing of the vote in other selected parishes.

One frequently cited example of alleged Democratic misconduct involved the returns from East Feliciana Parish. In 1874 Republican candidates for state office had received 1,688 votes. Two years later, not a single Republican ballot was cast—concrete proof that black voters in the parish had been demoralized and intimidated, according to the Republicans. In fact, no Republican votes were cast for the simple fact that no Republican ballots were provided for the parish, which party leaders knew to be leaning heavily toward the Democrats. In this way, it was hoped that the seemingly dramatic drop in Republican votes would give the returning board all the excuse it needed to throw out the parish's entire vote.

Besides East Feliciana, the board focused on the parishes of West Feliciana, Ouachita, East Baton Rouge, and Morehouse. Witness after witness appeared before the canvassers to testify how he was prevented from casting his desired votes for Hayes and Packard. An additional 4,500 pages of written testimony was introduced as supporting evidence. Democratic protests were disallowed. The identities of many of the witnesses were never formally ascertained, and several others who were located testified later that they had never made the statements attributed to them or signed the affidavits bearing their signatures. (Many were illiterate, and could not have signed anything had they wanted.) On November 27, the board called for a brief adjournment to allow investigators to concentrate on other unbulldozed parishes after it determined through preliminary computations that the loss of the bulldozed parishes alone would not be enough to prevent Tilden from claiming two of the state's eight electoral votes—one more than was needed to push him over the top nationally.

On December 1 the board ended its public hearings and went into secret session to complete its work. The Republican statesmen drafted a report to President Grant upholding the work of the returning board and left New Orleans en masse for Cincinnati, confident that their efforts had borne the necessary fruit. Garfield, for one, "did not think it altogether wise to say so much as was said in regard to the personnel of the Returning Board," but Sherman defended his uncritical praise as being necessary "to resist the determined purpose manifested in the newspapers to break down the confidence of the people in the justice of the board." The Democratic observers, who had seen enough of the board's peculiar form of justice to have their own confidence already broken down, stayed on through the bitter end.

Three days later the board announced its findings in the friendly pages of the *New Orleans Republican*. Citing "systematic intimidation, murder, and violence toward one class of voters, white as well as black, of such a character as to have scarcely a parallel in the history of this state," the board threw out the entire votes from East Feliciana and Grant parishes, as well as sixty-nine partial returns from twenty-two other parishes. In all, the board disallowed a total of 15,623 votes, 13,211 of which were Tilden's (Hayes's 2,412 lost votes were mainly from parishes he had failed to carry anyway). In the allegedly bulldozed parishes, fewer than 1,500 registered voters who had cast ballots in 1874 failed to do so in 1876, a shortfall more than explained by the 1,688 missing Republican ballots from East Feliciana alone. Before leaving New Orleans, the Democratic statesmen issued a statement denouncing the board's actions as "arbitrary, unfair, and without the warrant of law." Local newspapers, long accustomed to such post-election misadventures, nevertheless were stunned by the blatant injustice of the actions of the "Overturning Board's" decision.

IN FLORIDA, the task facing the Republican-controlled State Canvassing Board was less daunting, but in a way more complicated, than that facing its counterpart in Louisiana. Both sides agreed that the voting had been very close, and both quickly dispatched trainloads of partisans across the state to prepare affidavits challenging or justifying the paper-thin margins in the contested counties. The chief difficulty facing the canvassing board was the sheer closeness of the numbers, which were subject to challenge—and manipulation—by both sides. A plausible case could be made for either Tilden or Hayes (Republican gubernatorial candidate Marcellus Stearns, who had run behind Hayes in nearly every county, had a less convincing claim to victory, but even he was not prepared to concede defeat to his Democratic rival, George F. Drew). The three members of the canvassing board thus confronted a challenge of near-Solomonic proportions, made infinitely more difficult by the national repercussions their decision would have, whichever way they decided in the end.

Soon after his arrival in Tallahassee, William Chandler, the leader of the Republican visiting statesmen, warned Hayes to "be prepared for an unfavorable result." Although Chandler believed, on the face of questionable early returns from northern Florida, that Hayes had narrowly carried the state, he nevertheless was concerned by the logistics of getting Republican investigators into distant counties where, he said, Democratic election officials could alter the returns just enough to tilt the election in their favor. "How can we, within ten days, get there and back in a hostile region and prove it?" he asked rhetorically.

The first thing to do, Chandler decided, was to get the board to postpone any official canvassing of the vote for as long as possible. State law gave the board thirty-five days to complete its work, and Chandler and his assistants pressured the board to take the full length of time allotted. The Democrats, by contrast, wanted the board to begin certifying the results immediately; they were concerned about rumors that Governor Stearns planned to count the votes himself and unilaterally certify the state's four presidential electors for Hayes. To prevent this from happening, the Democrats applied to Circuit Court Judge Pleasant W. White for a writ of mandamus ordering the board to convene immediately. Chandler complained that the court had no jurisdiction over the governor, who, Chandler said, was not planning to count the votes anyway. Whatever Stearns's original intent, the Democrats' legal maneuver alarmed the canvassing board enough to induce it to begin counting the ballots on November 27, ten days before the Electoral College was due to meet. The board agreed to canvass the presidential votes first, postponing its decision on the governorship and other state offices until later. In doing so, it was apparently following the directions of Chandler, who worried that a too-sweeping effort in favor of Stearns might open the board to a future legal challenge.

As in Louisiana, the canvassing board decided to allow some of each party's visiting statesmen to witness its deliberations. Five representatives from both sides crowded into Secretary of State McLin's tiny office in the statehouse, along with Governor Stearns, Democratic gubernatorial candidate George F. Drew, and General John M. Brannan, who had replaced Thomas Ruger as the army's commander in Tallahassee when Ruger was recalled to South Carolina. A ruling by Attorney General William Cocke two years earlier had reserved for the board the right to exclude any returns that were found to be "irregular, false, or fraudulent," and challenges were made immediately to the returns from all thirty-eight counties—even sparsely populated Dade County, whose announced totals of nine votes for Hayes and five for Tilden brought peals of laughter from both sides of the room.

A tactical mistake by Democratic state chairman Samuel Pasco at the very outset of the counting proved costly, if not fatal, to Tilden's chances of carrying the state. After opening the returns from Baker County, McLin announced the figures as 130 votes for Hayes, 89 votes for Tilden. The county was reliably Democratic in its leanings, and Pasco leaped to his feet in protest. But despite information that McLin had more than one set of returns from Baker County in his possession, Pasco permitted the total to be recorded officially, subject to a formal challenge later. The initial vote count, when completed later that day, showed Hayes with 24,337 votes, Tilden with 24,294. Republican newspapers immediately reported that Hayes had carried Florida, giving his claim to the White House enhanced plausibility across the nation. A subsequent examination of the ballots from Baker County revealed that the newly appointed county election board, consisting of three Republican officeholders named by Stearns three days after the election, had summarily thrown out two of the county's four precincts after hearing rumors that a handful of illegal votes had been cast. McLin admitted that two other sets of complete returns, showing identical 238–143 totals in favor of the Democrats, were correct, and they were officially recorded in the state's tally, giving Tilden a 94-vote lead. But by then much of the nation already had read that Rutherford B. Hayes had carried Florida.

Under extreme pressure from partisans on both sides, the canvassing board spent two full days examining the returns from Alachua County in north-central Florida. The predominantly black county had gone for the Republicans, as expected, but Democrats challenged the returns from one precinct, which they said contained 219 Republican votes added after the polls had closed. Testimony revealed that the ballot box in question had been kept overnight at the Gainesville home of Republican county chairman L. G. Dennis, and two poll inspectors admitted later that they had been bribed to sign the erroneous returns, but the board ruled that there was "insufficient proof" to reject the county's vote. When Republican spokesman Edward Noyes asked Dennis to testify in the matter, Dennis refused, saying he would not take the stand unless Noyes was prepared to lose his case.

The Alachua case was too much for one Republican visiting statesman to stomach. Brooklyn-born General Francis Barlow, a twice-
wounded Civil War hero, had been in charge of the initial investigation
in Alachua County. The forty-two-year-old Barlow, whose clean-shaven
looks and youthful appearance had marked him, along with George
Armstrong Custer, Wesley Merritt, and Elon J. Farnsworth, as one of
the Union's famous "Boy Generals," had a good deal of experience in
criminal investigations. As New York state attorney general, he had
brought the first formal charges against Boss Tweed, and later had
worked hand in hand with Samuel Tilden to successfully prosecute the
case. Barlow's previous connection with Tilden, and his stint as editor
of the Democratic-leaning *New York Tribune,* might have disqualified him
from the ranks of visiting statesmen, but the Republicans apparently
wanted his untarnished reputation—he was one of the founders of the
American Bar Association—to lend credibility to their efforts in
Florida. If so, they badly misjudged their man. After looking into the
Alachua County case, Barlow was convinced that the Democrats had a
winning argument. He conveyed his feelings to canvassing board member Clayton Cowgill, who was sufficiently swayed by Barlow's argument to tell an incredulous Marcellus Stearns that he could not in good
conscience rule in favor of the Republicans.

Somehow, Chandler learned of Barlow's reservations and hastily recalled him to Tallahassee. At the same time, Chandler instructed
Stearns to whip Cowgill back into line. Barlow, disgusted, headed back
north, his reputation as an honest man loudly trumpeted by the Democrats, but his once-promising political career within the Republican
party ruined. Barlow's "idiosyncrasies," said the wondering Chandler,
were "not capable of a reasonable explanation." As for Cowgill, a fellow
Florida Republican gave Chandler a decidedly backhanded endorsement of their fellow party member. "Cowgill," Chandler was told, "is an
extraordinary person and we very narrowly escaped the odium of having two lunatics on our board."

Another former Union general turned Republican visiting statesman, Indiana native Lew Wallace, was also troubled by the vote-
changing efforts in Florida. "I scarcely ever passed a week under such
depression of spirits," he told his wife, Susan, on November 27. "It is

terrible to see the extent to which all classes go in their determination to win. Conscience offers no restraint. Nothing is so common as the resort to perjury, unless it is violence—in short, I do not know whom to believe. If we win, our methods are subject to impeachment for possible fraud. If the enemy win, it is the same thing exactly—doubt, suspicion, irritation go with the consequence, whatever it may be." Whatever his personal doubts, Wallace managed to keep them within the family. Publicly, he praised the canvassing board for its "observance of legal forms," and pointed out, a little legalistically, that the Democrats in Florida "had not denied the jurisdiction of the board." In due time, Wallace was rewarded for his efforts, being appointed territorial governor of New Mexico in 1878, where he subsequently completed writing his best-selling biblical novel, *Ben-Hur*, and tricked no less an outlaw than Billy the Kid into testifying against his former compadres in return for Wallace's (unkept) promise of a gubernatorial pardon.

With time running out before the Electoral College was due to convene on December 6, the board focused its attention on six remaining counties—Jefferson, Duval, Manatee, Hamilton, Jackson, and Monroe—where serious questions existed about the legality of the voting. Allegations ranged from ballot-tampering to illegal participation by black juveniles to improperly filed returns. In each case, the board ruled in favor of the Republicans. The net result was the addition (or addition by subtraction from Tilden's rightful tally) of several hundred votes for Hayes.

As in Louisiana, there were rumors of an attempt to sell the board's decision to the highest bidder. Testimony taken two years later by the congressional committee looking into alleged election frauds revealed that Democratic visiting statesmen Manton Marble and C. W. Woolley had mentioned the possibility of a bribe, variously set at $50,000 or $200,000, to deliver the Florida board for Tilden. The board member in question apparently was Chairman McLin, whose political availability, Marble said, was public knowledge at the time. Negotiations broke down before a deal could be made. (McLin later was appointed to the New Mexico Supreme Court by President Rutherford B. Hayes in 1877, but his appointment was quashed by Florida senator Simon B. Conover, a longtime political enemy. McLin died a short time later, complaining that in his home state he was widely regarded as "enormously wicked, in greater discredit than a traitor, with an infamy equal to arson and murder combined.")

While the board met in secret session through the night on December 5, a restive crowd gathered in the streets of Tallahassee. An armed detachment of soldiers moved onto the capitol grounds to guard against any outbreak of violence. Shortly after one o'clock word spread that Hayes had carried the state by a margin of 924 votes. In arriving at that total, the canvassing board had thrown out more than twice that many votes for Tilden. Former Georgia governor Joseph E. Brown spoke for his fellow Democratic visiting statesmen when he observed: "The dark deed of infamy is done by throwing out Democratic counties and precincts in the teeth of the evidence and in shameless violation of the law." Someone had cut the telegraph wires in Tallahassee, but an enterprising young reporter for the *Atlanta Constitution* named Henry Grady commandeered a wagon and a team of horses to race to a nearby village to report the scoop to the waiting country.

THE NEXT DAY, December 6, as prescribed by law, the chosen members of the Electoral College met in the capitals of the thirty-eight states to formally record their votes for president and vice president. In thirty-four of the states, the voting was unexceptional. But in each of the four contested states—South Carolina, Florida, Louisiana, and Oregon—two separate election certificates were filed. In South Carolina, where neither Daniel Chamberlain nor Wade Hampton had been formally declared governor, Chamberlain in his post as incumbent governor signed the certificate in favor of Hayes. The certificate supporting Tilden, bereft of official signature, was forwarded to Washington as well by the rump Democratic legislature. In Florida, where the canvassing board had not yet completed its count of the gubernatorial vote, incumbent governor Marcellus Stearns, by virtue of his unrelinquished powers, signed the Republican certificate. Attorney General William Cocke, wearing two hats and ruling, in essence, against himself, signed the Democratic certificate in favor of Tilden. In Louisiana, outgoing governor William Kellogg signed the Republican certificate in favor of Hayes;

John F. McEnery, the onetime Democratic claimant to the governorship, emerged briefly from political obscurity to endorse the conflicting certificate for Tilden.

In Salem, Oregon, a seriocomic charade took place. Democratic governor Lafayette Grover, following up on his ruling that Republican elector John W. Watts was ineligible to serve since he had been a federal postmaster at the time of the election, issued official elector's certificates to Republicans William H. Odell and John C. Cartwright and Democrat E. A. Cronin. Secretary of State Stephen F. Chadwick, who two days earlier had signed rather matter-of-factly the initial election returns showing Watts as one of three chosen electors, hand-delivered the governor's certificates to Cronin. When Cronin refused to hand over the certificates to the two Republicans, Odell and Cartwright simply declared themselves in session and appointed Watts to fill his own vacancy. They then cast three electoral votes for Hayes. Meanwhile, Cronin summoned two fellow Democrats into the chamber and, as planned, recorded two electoral votes for Hayes and one—his own—for Tilden. Governor Grover signed Cronin's certificate, which Cronin transported immediately to Washington, while Odell took the original return, bearing the secretary of state's signature, to the nation's capital.

At the end of the day the votes of the 369 Electoral College members, like the votes of eight million individual Americans one month earlier, were maddeningly inconclusive. Tilden still had the 184 electoral votes he had won unofficially on election day; Hayes had the 165 votes he had started with. The remaining twenty votes, alternately supported or contradicted by separate election certificates signed by various governors, governors-presumptive, secretaries of state, or, in the case of South Carolina's Democratic certificate, no one at all, were claimed by both candidates. The standoff continued.

That night, in Columbus, Ohio, Rutherford B. Hayes and his family awaited reports from the other thirty-seven state capitals. It was, he said, "a lively happy little gathering," made even livelier and happier by the encouraging news from Florida, Louisiana, and South Carolina. Overwhelmed by visitors congratulating him on the results, Hayes still took the time to dash off a quick note to longtime supporter Carl Schurz. "I have no doubt," he told a skeptical Schurz, "that we are justly and legally entitled to the presidency. My conversations with Sherman, Garfield, Stoughton and others settled the question in my mind as to Louisiana." Hayes was still worried about the Oregon dispute, which he feared might develop into a crisis "perhaps fatal to free government," but he trusted that "the Oregon fraud," as he termed it, would eventually be "thrown aside without dissent." On the whole, he remained convinced that he had been "fairly, honestly and lawfully elected," and he fully expected "a general acquiescence in the result among judicious men of all parties."

His opponent in New York had an understandably different reaction. "Our presidential election," said Samuel Tilden, "has been subverted by a false count of the votes cast by the presidential electors, founded on a substitution of pretended votes known at the time to be fraudulent or forged, and to have been manufactured for that particular use." The entire government, he warned, was in danger of "degenerat[ing] into a bad copy of the worst governments of the worst ages." As usual, Tilden's political instincts were razor-sharp, but not even he could have foreseen just how bad, personally and politically, things were about to get.

CHAPTER SIX

EIGHT VILLAINS TO
SEVEN PATRIOTS

IN WASHINGTON, where Congress had reconvened on December 4 to formally receive the Electoral College certificates from the thirty-eight states, the political spotlight shifted onto Michigan senator Thomas W. Ferry, the acting president of the United States Senate. Ferry, forty-nine, had ascended to the post in 1875 after the death of Vice President Henry W. Wilson, who had held the position during Grant's second administration. (Grant's first vice president, Schuyler Colfax, had been dumped from the ticket in 1872 following his implication in the Crédit Mobilier scandal.) As Senate majority leader, Ferry had assumed Wilson's largely ceremonial role. In his current position, it was Ferry's constitutional duty to open the electoral certificates on the second Wednesday in February and then—do what? That was the burning question of the day, and no one, least of all the irresolute Ferry, had the slightest inkling of how to respond.

The Constitution itself was maddeningly vague about the operational specifics of Ferry's duties. Under the provisions of the Twelfth Amendment, passed in 1804 in the wake of the contested election of 1800 between Thomas Jefferson and Aaron Burr, the president of the Senate was directed "in the presence of the Senate and House of Representatives [to] open all the certificates, and the votes shall then be counted." The wording was opaque: did the framers mean that the president of the Senate should open the certificates and count the votes himself, or merely that he should open the certificates, whose contents would then be counted by someone else—presumably the assembled members of the two houses of Congress? And if Ferry was supposed to count the votes, did that also imply that he had the authority to decide, in the case of competing electoral certificates, which set of votes to count?

The Republicans naturally inclined toward the view that Ferry was the final arbiter of the competing certificates, in which case he would inevitably decide to accept those favoring Hayes from the three contested states—Florida, Louisiana, and South Carolina. Together with Oregon's three electoral votes (one of which was still in dispute), that would make Rutherford B. Hayes the winner of the presidential election by one electoral vote, 185 to 184. The Democrats, just as naturally, held that Ferry could only open the certificates and announce the results, after first setting aside all multiple certificates. With neither candidate having a majority of the remaining electoral votes, the contest then would be thrown automatically into the House of Representatives, as specified by the Twelfth Amendment. Because the Democrats controlled the House, Samuel Tilden would become the next president.*

Senate Republicans had taken steps the previous January to prevent just such an unhappy occurrence when they voted to "recede," or withdraw, from the Twenty-second Joint Rule, which had been in place since 1865. The Joint Rule permitted either the Senate or the House to throw out any electoral votes it considered invalid, something that had been done five separate times in the presidential elections of 1864 and 1872. Then, however, both houses of Congress had been controlled by the Republicans, and it was Democratic votes in the South that were being thrown out. But after the Democrats recaptured the House in 1874, the Republicans realized that such a rule would, in effect, give the Democrats the power to do the same thing to them in 1876. And so they had backed out of the existing agreement, despite the best efforts of Indiana senator Oliver Morton to preserve the rule by changing its wording to

---

*Under the provisions of the amendment, the House would elect the president by a vote of the states, with each state having one vote, based on a majority of its congressional delegation, rather than by a vote of the individual House members. The Senate, meeting separately, would elect the vice president by a vote of all the senators. In 1877, given the Democratic majority in the House and the Republican majority in the Senate, this would have resulted in the election of Samuel Tilden as president and William A. Wheeler, Hayes's running mate, as vice president.

require both houses to agree on any electoral challenges. For the Republicans it was an inspired decision, and it prevented the House, at least temporarily, from installing Tilden as president by disallowing enough electoral votes for Hayes—no matter which way Ferry decided—to throw the election into its lap.

The practical effect of the Senate's decision was to create a stalemate between the two houses of Congress. The Republicans, controlling the Senate, insisted that Ferry had the sole right to count the votes; the Democrats, in charge of the House, argued that it was ultimately their responsibility. Neither side could afford to budge; any concession of its assumed prerogative to decide the winner would virtually guarantee the election of the other side's candidate. The painful memories of Abraham Lincoln's divisive election in 1860, and the failure then of the northern and southern states to reach a workable political compromise on the issue of slavery, loomed large in every legislator's mind. No one, least of all the southern members of Congress who had seen their region devastated by war, wanted a replay of the winter of 1860–61, when the country had slid ineluctably into chaos. But largely because of those still unassuaged memories, neither party was willing to concede the current election, particularly one that had devolved, with depressing inevitability, into yet another national referendum on the staying power of the bloody shirt.

Clearly, something had to be done to break the logjam, and on December 7 Iowa congressman George W. McCrary, a moderate Republican, introduced a resolution calling for a special bipartisan committee in the House of Representatives to devise "such a measure, either legislative or constitutional," to resolve the crisis by "determining questions that may arise as to the legality and validity of returns made of such votes by the several states." Following the resolution's approval one week later, four Democrats and three Republicans were chosen to serve on the advisory committee, including McCrary and Tilden's former campaign manager, New York congressman Abram S. Hewitt. McCrary's resolution also called for the creation of "a tribunal whose authority none can question and whose decision all will accept as final."

On the same day that McCrary introduced his resolution in the House, as if to underscore the need for some sort of comprehensive congressional action, South Carolina Republicans inaugurated Daniel B. Chamberlain for a second term as governor, ignoring a ruling by the state Supreme Court that sought to block the ad hoc inauguration. Rebellious Democrats, in turn, inaugurated their own champion, Wade Hampton, on December 14, and Hampton immediately demanded that Chamberlain hand over the great seal of the state and the keys to his office in the statehouse. Chamberlain refused. The state now had two presumptive governors as well as two presumptive legislatures, and the rightful recipient of South Carolina's disputed electoral votes remained very much an open question.

One day after McCrary's resolution passed in the House, the Senate approved the creation of its own bipartisan committee to study ways of resolving the election. Four Republicans and three Democrats comprised the panel, neatly reversing the makeup of the House committee. The creation of the Senate and House committees reflected a growing sense of unease by both parties over the relative strength of their political positions. The Republicans worried that there were enough potential defectors in the Senate to deny Ferry the formal resolution he required before he would agree to rule unilaterally on the ballots. The Democrats feared that any move on their part to throw the election into the House of Representatives would compel Ferry to rule immediately in favor of Hayes, counting on a Republican president and Republican-dominated Supreme Court to back him up. In any case, neither side was sure how the American people would react—with a resigned shrug of their shoulders, or a furious dash to the barricades?

WHILE THE LEGISLATIVE stalemate continued in Washington and separate Senate and House investigative committees headed south to begin hearings over alleged election abuses in the three disputed southern states, the two presidential rivals in New York and Columbus reacted to the crisis in characteristic and revealing ways.

Samuel Tilden devoted most of his energy in the month of December to overseeing the preparation of a massive, book-length study of previous presidential elections. *The Presidential Counts*, a copy of which would be placed on the desk of every senator and congressman, was a masterful summation of electoral procedures followed by Congress in the previous twenty-two presidential elections. In the book Tilden made a compelling argument against allowing the president of the Senate to decide which electoral votes to count from a contested state. Instead, he maintained that the Senate and the House had the ultimate right to examine the ballots and decide which, if any, of the disputed ballots to accept. In the event the two legislative bodies could not approve a majority of the electoral votes for either candidate, the election should be thrown into the House of Representatives, as prescribed by the Constitution. A workable precedent for this procedure had been set in the election of 1824, when neither Andrew Jackson nor John Quincy Adams had obtained a majority in the Electoral College and Adams subsequently had been chosen president by the House. Then, however, none of the states had sent in multiple electoral certificates, which made the process a good deal more straightforward and manageable.

Congressional Republicans were not persuaded by Tilden's logic, and even his erstwhile campaign chairman, Abram Hewitt, believed that Tilden "accomplished little of value by this work." Furthermore, said Hewitt, "It was absurd for the head of the party to labor on it to the neglect of more vital tasks." Hewitt's criticism reflected his growing estrangement from Tilden's inner circle, but it neglected to give Tilden credit for helping to blunt Republican claims for Ferry's unilateral vote-counting authority. Indeed, had Hewitt and the other Democratic leaders in the House followed Tilden's lead and insisted on their own constitutional right to decide a deadlocked election, it is entirely possible that the precedent set in 1824 would have carried the day, and Tilden would have been elected president.

But party leaders were unaware of Tilden's book-writing activities—a Democratic congressman spent several weeks working on a similar study of precedents—and the lack of communication between New York and Washington pointed up a larger problem faced by the Democrats: the lack of a focused, carefully orchestrated plan to seat their candidate in the White House. Belying his reputation as a master manipulator, Tilden seemed increasingly disinterested in the day-to-day details of the Democratic efforts on Capitol Hill. Whether from an exaggerated sense of political courtesy or a deeply ingrained reluctance to bring other people into his confidence, Tilden maintained a discreet distance, literally and figuratively, from party leaders in Washington. And when Democratic politicians made the pilgrimage to New York to consult with him, as they did several times in December, they inevitably came away from the meetings puzzled, frustrated, and angry at the governor's unwillingness to act in his own behalf. "Oh, Tilden won't do anything; he's cold as a damn clam," an unidentified legislator told the *New York Tribune* after leaving one such inconclusive meeting.

Georgia senator John B. Gordon, who had served under Robert E. Lee in the Civil War and thus was accustomed to more forceful and daring leadership, made a special return trip to New York to chastise Tilden for his lack of direction. As Gordon later reported to their mutual friend Samuel Barlow, he told the gentlemanly candidate that "I thought we were being robbed of our victory by our own supineness. If the Democrats would through speeches, resolutions, the press and mass meetings let the country know that it was their purpose to inaugurate the men whom the people had elected, we should at once see these desperate leaders of the Republican party forsaken by the masses behind them. If we announce by our silence beforehand that we intend to acquiesce in any outrage they may perpetrate, we only invite aggression from them and prepare our own friends for a degrading submission."

Another former Confederate, newly elected Kentucky congressman Henry Watterson, also urged Tilden to act forcefully to assert his rights. Concerned by the "intense quietude of our side," Watterson traveled north from Louisville to meet with Tilden and finalize plans for a speech calling for a mass convention of 100,000 "peaceful citizens" in Washington. The new congressman, who had been one of the Democratic visiting statesmen in Louisiana the previous month, had no great faith in such an appeal, particularly after it had been toned down by Tilden and the site of its delivery moved from the floor of Congress to—of all places—Ford's Theatre, where Abraham Lincoln had been fatally shot by John Wilkes Booth. After Watterson made the speech, its effect was minimized by Republican ridicule, including a drawing by Thomas Nast in *Harper's Weekly* showing an impassioned Watterson being drenched with ice water by a disapproving Republican.

An increasingly exasperated Hewitt appealed again to Tilden to issue a personal call for mass meetings "in every city, town and hamlet" on January 8, when Democrats traditionally celebrated Andrew Jackson Day. Again Tilden refused. Plans were made independently to hold protests in Illinois, Ohio, Indiana, Virginia, and the District of Columbia, but Tilden showed little interest in promoting the gatherings. Illinois Democratic party chairman Cyrus McCormick was told by a Tilden aide in no uncertain terms: "When the time comes for a public popular demonstration then the signal will be given from here and the whole country will act coherently and effectively. Until such signal is given all should remain quiet and trust in the wisdom of our leader."

Not content to wait for such a Jovian signal, Hewitt in his role as national committee chairman issued his own statement on December 13 declaring that Tilden had been elected president with a rightful claim to 203 electoral votes. Like Watterson's fiery call to arms, this, too, was met by derisive laughter from the Republicans. The *New York Herald* jeered in an editorial the next day: "There is a gentleman in Utica, the inmate of a public institution, who regards himself as the Emperor of China, and issues edicts by the score, but we have never heard that he enjoys the revenues of the Celestial kingdom." In the game of political one-upmanship, the Republicans seemed to hold a distinct advantage.

GIVEN THE DISORGANIZATION, if not the downright demoralization, of the Democratic party, the Republicans could well afford to laugh. Ohio congressman James A. Garfield, who had been one of the party's visiting statesmen to Louisiana the previous month, watched the opposing side closely in the first days of the new legislative session. "The Democrats are without a policy or a leader," he reported to Hayes on December 8. "They are full of passion and want to do something desperate but hardly know how to get at it." Reassured by Garfield's words, as well as those of Senator John Sherman and the other Republican visiting statesmen who had stopped by to visit him on their way home from Louisiana, Hayes now was convinced that a fair election in the South would have given him a clear majority of the region's electoral votes and a decided preponderance of its popular vote. He was totally at peace with his legal and moral claims to the White House. "I fully expect to be inaugurated," he announced on December 12.

Hayes owed his newfound optimism, at least in part, to a series of behind-the-scenes meetings he and his advisers had initiated with various southern Democrats who were no longer convinced—if they ever had been—that Tilden had won the election on November 7. While Tilden spent his time compiling reams of legal precedents that were as nonbinding as they were well reasoned, Hayes chose the more direct route, reaching out to individuals who might materially affect his chances of becoming president. In the post-election campaign to assert his right to the presidency, Hayes was far busier and more effective than Tilden—one might almost say that his actions were presidential.

Hayes had met with one self-appointed representative of southern interests even before the Electoral College certificates arrived in Washington. Colonel William H. Roberts, managing editor of the *New Orleans Times,* called on the governor in Columbus on December 1 to sound out his views regarding the South. During the course of the three-hour-long meeting, Roberts professed to speak for Wade Hampton, John B. Gordon, Lucius Q. C. Lamar, and other leading southern Democrats. All thinking southerners, he said, were anxious to avoid any further conflict with the North. "If we felt that you were friendly to us," Roberts told Hayes, "we would not make that desperate personal fight to keep you out that we certainly will make if you are not friendly."

According to Roberts, Hayes responded favorably to the overture, remarking that "carpetbag governments had not been successful; that the complaints of the southern people were just in this matter; that he would require absolute justice and fair play to the Negro, but that he was convinced this could be got best and most surely by trusting the honorable and influential southern whites." Hayes did not remember making any such sweeping statements to Roberts; he said he had only referred his visitor to his acceptance letter, which he said "meant all it said and all that it implied." But Hayes did recall in his diary that the southern newsman had assured him: "You will be president. We will not make trouble. We want peace."

The particulars of the meeting, including Hayes's explicit disavowal of Republican carpetbag regimes, were reported the next day in the

Cincinnati Enquirer, which was edited by Hayes's close friend Murat Halstead. A follow-up story was printed two days later in the *New York Herald,* clarifying Hayes's position, but nothing that had been reported earlier was specifically disclaimed or disavowed. It was a clear sign to disaffected southerners that Hayes was disposed to hear them out, and the political implications were troubling to Tilden's supporters. Democratic congressman R. B. Bradford of Ohio cautioned Tilden on December 18: "I am in intimate relations with many southern members, and I am convinced if we fail to secure them the victory they have assisted us in obtaining they will make conditions with Hayes, who has already assured them of his intention to admit them into his confidence and provide for them in the highest places of his administration." Bradford added that he had attended a meeting of forty or fifty southern congressmen, where "the sentiment of all who spoke freely was to abandon the democracy if there was a failure to maintain every right in the present contest." Bradford's warning echoed an earlier admonition to Tilden from visiting statesman Charles Gibson of Missouri, who complained that "the entire democracy of the South feel more than ever that they are leaning on a bag of mush when they look for aid and comfort from the North."

Following Hayes's lead, some of his most trusted lieutenants began to reach out to other southerners. William Henry Smith, head of the Western Associated Press, used his journalistic contacts to begin a dialogue with Tennessee newspaper editor Andrew J. Kellar, a member of the WAP's board of directors. Kellar, a prewar Unionist who had reluctantly joined the Confederacy out of state loyalty and had risen to the rank of brigadier general, had run for Congress as an independent in 1874, siphoning off enough Democratic votes to help elect the Republican candidate. A political gadfly who was unpopular with a large segment of the population in his own hometown of Memphis, Kellar would seem to have been an odd choice for interparty bridge-building, but his close connections with Pennsylvania railroad mogul Tom Scott gave him an entrée to the highest Republican political circles. Kellar proposed using regional support for Scott's long-delayed Texas and Pacific Railway to detach some thirty to thirty-six southern congressmen from the Democratic majority in the House of Representatives, in return for a promise by Hayes to provide generous federal subsidies to the railroad after he became president.

The Republican party, as a matter of principle, had long opposed financing any such chimerical "southern route" from Texas to California. Nor did northern Democrats, including Tilden, support such a potentially budget-busting project. Scott's proposed rail line had languished, unfinanced and unbuilt, for the past five years, while rival developer Collis P. Huntington, of transcontinental railroad fame, offered to build his own line from Los Angeles to Fort Worth without any federal assistance whatsoever. Kellar, who was a director of Scott's company, hoped to checkmate Huntington's designs by enlisting Hayes in a deal to underwrite the Texas and Pacific instead. From the start, Hayes was leery of Kellar's plans. "I am not a believer in the trustworthiness of the forces you hope to rally," he told William Henry Smith in the midst of Kellar's machinations. The furthest Hayes would go toward committing himself to the project was to promise to be "exceptionally liberal about internal improvements of a national character" in the South. Even then, he insisted, "We must rely on our own strength to secure our rights. With firmness it can be done."

At the same time that he was reaching out to southern Democrats, Hayes was keeping a worried eye on potential defectors within his own party. Chief among them was the ever troublesome Senator Roscoe Conkling of New York, who had lost the presidential nomination to Hayes in Cincinnati, and thereafter had done virtually nothing to help him win the general election. A leader of the Stalwart wing of the Republican party, which supported both the continued practice of political patronage and the preservation of carpetbag governments in the South, Conkling feared that Hayes was "in the hands of the Reform element" and might very well threaten Conkling's base of power in New York by replacing Conkling's political appointees with his own reformist candidates. Feeling, perhaps, that it would be easier to deal with an old Tammany Hall veteran like Tilden than the unpredictable, squeaky-clean Hayes, Conkling had asked a Tilden associate whether the Democrats "meant to act upon the *good-boy* principle of submission, or whether we mean to have it understood that Tilden has been elected and by the Eternal he shall be inaugurated." If he were a Democrat, Conkling said, that was the position he would take.

Hayes was sufficiently concerned by Conkling's perceived disloyalty to meet with the senator's "intimate personal friend" Albert D. Shaw, American consul general to Toronto, on December 17. Shaw bluntly warned Hayes that his reformist tendencies might cost him "the friendship and support of enough senators to change the result of the presidential election, and bring in Mr. Tilden." Hayes, who insisted that Ferry alone had the constitutional right to rule on the competing electoral certificates, needed all the support he could get from Republican senators to enforce that debatable proposition. Nevertheless, he was unwilling to offer Conkling any guarantees that he would leave the senator's New York political machine untouched after he became president. As Hayes informed Senator John Sherman immediately after the meeting with Shaw: "I told him I was in no way committed to persons or as to policies except as the public knew—that I would try to deal fairly and justly by all elements of the party." Conkling, for his part, continued to insist that Ferry did not have the unilateral right to count the ballots. He was prepared to see Tilden chosen as president, if it came to that, before he cooperated in an act that he considered "a political Hell Gate, paved and honeycombed with dynamite."

Conkling was not Hayes's only worry. Ulysses S. Grant had also let it slip, through various sources, that he believed on balance that Tilden had won the election. In a meeting with Abram Hewitt on December 3, the president repeated his earlier statement to the cabinet that he felt that Tilden had carried Louisiana. Grant told Hewitt that the returning board there "was in very bad odor with the public; that the people had no confidence in it; and even if it did right, it would not be credited with honest intentions." Grant thought it "not unreasonable" to assume that Louisiana's electoral votes might be thrown out again, as they had been in 1872. If that were the case, "he did not expect there would be any serious trouble." Hewitt, who spent much of the interview flattering Grant, obtained assurances from the president that he would not intervene, either politically or militarily, in the crisis. He left the meeting convinced that Grant, at the very least, was willing to see Tilden peacefully inaugurated if that was what Congress eventually decided.

Word of Grant's meeting with Hewitt got back to Hayes, who dispatched his old Civil War comrade, James M. Comly, to Washington to remonstrate with the president. Comly, who had replaced Hayes as commander of the 23rd Ohio Regiment, was editor of the *Ohio State Journal*, which had functioned during the campaign as one of Hayes's most reliable mouthpieces. Comly met privately with Grant for two hours at the White House on January 4, during which time he emphasized Hayes's "staunch friendship" for Grant and insisted that Hayes would do whatever he could "to avoid anything that could seem to be a reflection upon the president or a censure of his administration." Still nettled by Hayes's acceptance letter, which had seemed to be an unsubtle criticism of his own administration, Grant was studiedly noncommittal about what he intended to do until Comly assured him that "there was not one chance in a million" that Hayes would offer a cabinet appointment to former treasury secretary Benjamin Bristow, whom Grant loathed. "At this point in the conversation," Comly reported, "he drew the friendly cigars from his pocket and tendered one to me as he settled down to a quiet smoke and a confidential talk."

Grant, who was leaving public life forever in a matter of weeks, could afford to be expansive; Republican senators in the three disputed southern states could not. Reports continued to reach Hayes that many of the imperiled carpetbaggers were planning to side with Conkling and vote against the right of Ferry to count the votes. Republican National Committee secretary William E. Chandler, for one, could not blame the carpetbaggers for being worried. As he informed Hayes: "They have no future in their states; all they can hope for is what consideration & patronage the administration may give them." As for Conkling, Chandler considered the flamboyant New York senator "bitter, determined, excited, and I now think [he] means to defeat Hayes & Wheeler." Chandler concluded gloomily that Conkling probably had enough senators in his camp to defeat any attempt to have Ferry singlehandedly count the votes.

Despite the warning, Hayes rejected Chandler's advice to send a personal representative to Washington to meet with Conkling and the southern Republicans. Instead, he left it up to his Ohio supporters already in the capital "to organize and unitize the Hayes strength." The Ohio cabal included U.S. Attorney General Alphonso Taft, Senator John Sherman, Congressman James A. Garfield, former governor William

Dennison, and James M. Comly of the *Ohio State Journal*. Dennison, whose 1858 campaign for governor had first brought Hayes into political prominence, offered to meet with the southerners. Sherman, who had just spent several days in Louisiana observing that state's returning board in action, absolutely refused to have anything further to do with such men. "I will do anything I can, but I'll be damned if I do that," he told Dennison. "I can't talk with those fellows—don't know how to get at them. Somebody else must do it." Attorney General Taft volunteered to help. As head of the Justice Department, he said, he "had occasionally found it in his power to be serviceable to the Republicans of the South"—mainly by sending federal investigators into the region, at taxpayer expense, to help ferret out examples of alleged Democratic campaign abuses. Garfield, too, offered "to confer with doubtful senators, and confirm their courage."

Not all the doubtful senators were from the South. In addition to Conkling, Vermont senator George F. Edmunds, who had sponsored the creation of the Senate committee looking into ways of resolving the crisis, wanted the Supreme Court to intervene and count the votes, with the chief justice empowered to open the ballots. Such a move, Edmunds told former Missouri senator Carl Schurz, would be "the anchor of our safety," both legally and politically. The reform-minded Schurz agreed, urging Hayes to endorse the Edmunds plan publicly. "We must look the undeniable fact in the face," Schurz wrote to Hayes, "that the Republican party is today morally very much weaker than it was on the day of election, and it will grow weaker still in the same measure as it countenances arbitrary acts of power." But if the Supreme Court counted the vote, he insisted, "the result will be accepted as legal, just and legitimate by every American citizen." Hayes, who was not at all convinced that his position was morally weak—much the opposite, in fact—ignored Schurz's recommendation and let the reformer's follow-up letters go unanswered.

BEFORE GARFIELD and the other members of Hayes's Ohio brain-trust could meet with the southerners, other behind-the-scenes discussions combined to make such meetings unnecessary. In early

January the separate Senate and House special committees studying the standoff agreed to merge into a single Joint Committee on Electoral Count. The fourteen-man panel, evenly divided between Democrats and Republicans, immediately began discussing plans to name an independent Electoral Commission to adjudicate the crisis and decide who should be the next president. Initially, the Republicans on the committee wanted the board to consist of Supreme Court Chief Justice Morrison R. Waite and four associate justices drawn by lot. The Democrats insisted on dropping Waite, an admitted Republican partisan and family friend of Hayes's, and including members of the House and Senate on the commission. An amended version of the proposal called for ten legislators and five Supreme Court justices (the names of six proposed justices would be placed in a hat, and the one drawn out would be eliminated from the panel). Discussions continued until January 17, when the two sides reached a tentative agreement on the fifteen-member commission.

A heightened sense of urgency surrounded the ongoing discussions. Besides the political damage being done to the country as a whole by the lack of a clear-cut presidential winner, the business community was worried about the possible effect on the nation's economy, and foreign governments were increasingly perplexed by the American electoral impasse. Wild rumors persisted of plots by the Republicans to "bulldoze" New York with the help of General Phil Sheridan, federal troops, and warships; to throw Democratic leaders into Fortress Monroe; and to install Senator John Sherman as president of the Senate and his brother, General William Tecumseh Sherman, as commander-in-chief. Democrats, conversely, were said to be making plans to have southern rifle clubs descend on Washington and seat Tilden at gunpoint, and Tilden Minutemen clubs were rallying in the Midwest to assist in the desperate, last-ditch endeavor. In northern states, the Democratic Veteran Soldiers Association put its members on notice that they might have to put their old uniforms back on soon and fight again for freedom and justice. Meanwhile, in Washington, the veterans' former commanding general, Ulysses S. Grant, felt it necessary to declare that "any demonstration or warlike concentration of men threatening the peace of the city or endangering the security of public property or treasure of the government would be summarily dealt with." If he had to do so, Grant warned, he would declare martial law in Washington.

On Jackson Day, Henry Watterson, as planned, issued his public call for 100,000 Democrats to assemble peaceably in Washington and insist on Tilden's right to be inaugurated. *New York World* publisher Joseph Pulitzer, who followed Watterson to the stage at Ford's Theatre, was less pacific. He called on Democrats to "come fully armed and ready for business." In Indianapolis, former Quaker abolitionist George W. Julian warned the Republicans that "millions of men will be found ready to offer their lives as hostages to the sacredness of the ballot as the palladium of our liberty." Apparently, Julian's recent stint as a Democratic visiting statesman in Louisiana had converted him to violence. Speaking in quasi-religious terms, Julian urged his listeners, "Whosoever hath a sword, let him gird it on, for the crisis demands our highest exertions, physical and moral."

Conspicuously missing from the calls to arms were the voices of Samuel Tilden and leading southern Democrats, the very individuals whose lives would be most directly affected by an adverse decision by the Electoral Commission. Tilden, as he had done throughout the election, called for calm. In response to a statement by Ohio Democratic senator Allen G. Thurman that the party had three alternatives—"We can fight, we can back down, or we can arbitrate"—the governor was adamant about his preference. "It will not do to fight," he said. "We have just emerged from one Civil War, and it will never do to engage in another; it would end in the destruction of free government. We cannot back down. We can, therefore, only arbitrate." Southern Democrats, many of them Confederate veterans of the Civil War, were equally loath to consider violent measures to install Tilden. They noted that most of the calls for "Tilden or blood!" came from northern Democrats, men who, as Georgia congressman Benjamin Hill said cuttingly, had been "invincible in peace and invisible in war." Such men, Hill added, "had no conception of the conservative influence of a 15-inch shell with the fuse in [the] process of combustion."

Southern Democrats had fought hard for Tilden during the election, even South Carolina gubernatorial candidate Wade Hampton, whom Tilden had studiously ignored in the wake of the Hamburg Massacre. But the southerners were on the horns of a political dilemma: it seemed increasingly likely that Tilden would be counted out, either by the president of the Senate or by the proposed Electoral Commission. At the same time, southern Democratic fortunes were flourishing on the gubernatorial level. Hampton had been inaugurated as governor by his fellow Democrats—even though South Carolina Republicans had inaugurated Daniel Chamberlain—and Louisiana's Democratic gubernatorial claimant Francis Nicholls, whose supporters controlled the streets of New Orleans and much of the surrounding countryside, was insisting on his right to be similarly anointed. In Florida, Democrat George F. Drew had been sworn into office on January 2 after the state Supreme Court upheld his challenge to the canvassing board's decision one month earlier to award the election to incumbent Republican governor Marcellus Stearns.

Given Drew's legally mandated ascension to office and the brightening prospects of Hampton and Nicholls, southern Democrats increasingly felt that they had achieved their main goal in the campaign, the political redemption of the last three southern states controlled by Reconstruction governments. There was no way they were going to go to war again, for the second time in sixteen years, simply because a northern Republican had been elected president. If, by some improbable circumstance, Tilden was confirmed as president, they would be glad to have a fellow Democrat in the White House; if not, Rutherford B. Hayes, by his artful outreach, had persuaded many of them that he was a man with whom they could do business. As Colonel William H. Roberts, managing editor of the *New Orleans Times,* admitted later, the southern position at the time was that no matter what the Electoral Commission ultimately decided, "We have got to see that, whatever horse loses, our horse wins."

Hewitt, although not privy to the earlier discussions between Hayes's representatives and southern Democrats, could not help but notice the decidedly unmilitant position the southerners had taken in party councils. With that in mind, Hewitt returned to New York in mid-January to confer with Tilden over the makeup of the proposed Electoral Commission. It was not a pleasant meeting. Tilden still favored having the election thrown into the House of Representatives. When

Hewitt told him the Democratic senators on the joint committee—Thomas Bayard of Delaware, Allen Thurman of Ohio, and Matthew Ransom of North Carolina—had already agreed in principle to an Electoral Commission, Tilden lost his temper. "Is it not rather late, then, to consult me?" he asked.

"They do not consult you," Hewitt responded with equal heat. "They are public men and have their own duties and responsibilities. I consult you."

Tilden tried to reason with Hewitt. Pointing out that there was still one month left before the electoral certificates were slated to be opened by Senator Ferry before the assembled members of Congress, he wanted to know the reason for the Democrats' unseemly haste. "Why surrender now?" he asked. "You can always surrender. That is all you have to do after being beaten. Why surrender before the battle, for fear of having to surrender after the battle is over?"

Without mentioning the possible defection of southern Democrats in the House and Senate, Hewitt pressed Tilden to agree to the rough outline of the proposed Electoral Commission. Still Tilden demurred. "I can't advise you to agree to the bill," he told Hewitt, "but I will advise you as to details." He was particularly opposed to the way the Supreme Court justices on the panel were to be selected. "I may lose the presidency, but I will not raffle for it," he said. For once, the New York Times was on Tilden's side. In a contemporaneous editorial, the newspaper derided the "Dice-Box vs. Ballot-Box" method of selection, and scoffed that the two candidates might just as well cut cards for the presidency. "I am afraid that we are giving up too much, but I do not see that we can do anything else," Tilden told his friend Judge John P. Daly after Hewitt had left.

Hewitt returned to Washington without Tilden's approval of the Electoral Commission, but he gave other Democrats the distinct impression that the candidate favored some sort of congressional plan. The joint committee went back to work hammering out a compromise agreement. After three days of vigorous, sometimes bitter debate, the committee arrived at a consensus recommendation: the Electoral Commission would be composed of five Democratic congressmen and senators, five Republican congressmen and senators, two Democratic

Supreme Court justices, two Republican Supreme Court justices, and a fifth justice chosen by the other four. The fifth justice was expected to be political independent David Davis of Illinois, who had been named to the court in 1862 by his longtime legal associate, Abraham Lincoln. Hewitt believed the proposed agreement was the best arrangement the Democrats could make, given the very real threat that Senate president Thomas Ferry could always decide to count the ballots for Hayes and then fall back on the support of Grant and the army. Ever-combative Democratic congressman Henry Watterson disagreed. "The only effect of the Electoral Commission bill," he complained to Hewitt, "will be to put Mr. Hayes into office with the color of a title, whereas otherwise he will have to be inducted by the Senate, General Grant, and the army."

Despite the reservations of Tilden, Watterson, and others in the governor's inner circle, the bill creating the fifteen-man Electoral Commission passed out of committee on January 18 and came before the two houses of Congress. Debate over the proposal dragged on for another week. From Columbus came word that Hayes opposed the commission, believing it to be "a surrender, at least, in part, of our case." John Sherman, James A. Garfield, William Dennison, and Edward Noyes—Hayes's closest advisers—also fought against it. To agree to arbitration by a newly created commission when Senator Ferry already had the right to rule on the electoral certificates, Garfield complained, was tantamount to the "surrender of a certainty for an uncertainty."

Carl Schurz, ever the idealist, counseled Hayes to accept the commission. Noting the failure of Sherman, Garfield, and the other Republican visiting statesmen in Louisiana to insist on appointing a Democrat to the state returning board to remove the well-founded suspicions of blatant partisanship, Schurz warned that if the Republicans defeated the Electoral Commission bill and managed to have Hayes declared president by Ferry, "the sentiment of the country will be so overwhelmingly against you that, if the House sets up Tilden as a counter-president, as it then will certainly do, it will be no mere puppet-show." Hayes, for his part, was not convinced. He opposed the bill, he somewhat lamely told Schurz on January 23, because "the appointment of the Commission by Act of Congress violates that part of the Constitution which gives the appointment of all other officers 'to the President.'"

In the end, neither candidate's wishes proved to be a deciding factor when Congress finally voted on the measure on January 26. The Senate acted first, approving the Electoral Commission bill, 47–17. That afternoon the House gave its consent as well, by a margin of 191–86. Most Democrats in Congress voted for the bill (186 for and 18 against), while most Republicans voted against it (85 against, 52 for). But Democratic joy—if that was what it was—proved painfully short-lived. That same afternoon it was learned that David Davis had just been elected to the Senate by the Illinois legislature. The legislature, which had been deadlocked for weeks over the issue of picking a new senator, chose Davis over incumbent Republican senator John A. Logan by a narrow margin, with the Democrats uniting with eight members of the upstart Greenback party to give Davis the victory. Republicans immediately charged that Davis had cut a deal with the Democrats to serve on the Electoral Commission in return for his election to the Senate. If that was the case, Davis quickly turned the tables on his alleged supporters by announcing that under no circumstances would he consent to serve on the commission, even though he was not planning to resign his seat on the Supreme Court until March 5—the day of the scheduled inauguration of the president.

At first, neither party knew what to make of Davis's decision. As the only declared independent on the Supreme Court, the three-hundred-pound jurist had always been seen as something of a wild card. No one, perhaps not even Davis himself, knew which presidential candidate he preferred; it was public knowledge that he had not even voted in the recent election. As the fifteenth and deciding vote on the commission—the congressional members were universally expected to toe the party line—Davis would have had the singular power to decide the presidency by himself. That was the rub. Having long entertained presidential ambitions of his own, Davis knew that he would inevitably alienate one of the two parties with his decision, thus cutting in half his own chances of ever reaching the White House. Under the circumstances, he was only too glad to let the cup pass untasted from his lips.

In Davis's place, the last seat on the Electoral Commission was taken by Republican justice Joseph P. Bradley of New Jersey. Bradley had been appointed to the Supreme Court in 1870 by President Grant, and had played a key role in the court's surprising decision (*United States v. Cruik-shank*) earlier in 1876 to limit the federal government's power to enforce the Fifteenth Amendment protecting blacks' civil rights, a decision that earned him a great deal of favorable comment in the South. Although Abram Hewitt considered him "entirely satisfactory" and southerners adjudged him racially sound, Bradley had a very large skeleton in his closet. While serving as a judge for the United States Circuit Court for the Western District of Texas in 1870, he had issued a tortuous legal ruling that transferred ownership of the bankrupt Memphis, El Paso, and Pacific Railroad Company to Pennsylvania monopolist Tom Scott, as part of his scheme to build a new railroad from Texas to the Pacific coast. With Scott's forces in Washington now leading the push for a rapprochement between southern Democrats and Rutherford B. Hayes, there was every reason to assume that Bradley would look out for Scott's best interests on the Electoral Commission. The always canny William E. Chandler suspected as much, assuring Hayes that Bradley was "as safe as either of the other Republican judges." Hayes's son Webb agreed with Chandler. On January 31 he wired his father from Washington: "The bets are 5 to 1 that the next president will be Hayes."

IN ADDITION TO BRADLEY, the Electoral Commission consisted of Democratic representatives Eppa Hunton of Virginia, Henry Payne of Ohio, and Josiah Abbott of Massachusetts; Democratic senators Thomas Bayard of Delaware and Allen Thurman of Ohio; Republican representatives James A. Garfield of Ohio and George Hoar of Massachusetts; Republican senators George Edmunds of Vermont, Frederick T. Frelinghuysen of New Jersey, and Oliver Morton of Indiana; and Supreme Court justices Nathan Clifford and Stephen Field, Democrats, and William Strong and Samuel Miller, Republicans. Most, but not all, of the legislators had served on the earlier Joint Committee on Electoral Count. One notable absence was that of New York senator Roscoe Conkling, who recognized the opposition of Hayes supporters to his presence on the commission and gracefully stepped aside, declaring— no doubt truthfully—that "the duties would be inconvenient if not distasteful" to him.

Under the provisions of the act, the official date for opening the electoral certificates was pushed forward from February 14 to February 1 to allow adequate time for deliberations. At 1:00 P.M. on the day in question, the members of the Senate filed solemnly into the hall of the House of Representatives, preceded by their flag-bearing sergeant at arms. House members rose to their feet to greet them. The visitors' gallery was overflowing with high-ranking dignitaries, including English foreign minister Sir Edward Thornton, the foreign ministers of Germany and Japan, various other foreign representatives, General William Tecumseh Sherman, Secretary of War James D. Cameron, and historian George Bancroft. An air of nervous anticipation hung over the crowd as Senator Ferry mounted the speaker's podium and called the meeting to order.

In front of the podium was a polished mahogany box containing the official electoral certificates from all thirty-eight states. One by one, in alphabetical order, Ferry pulled out the ballots from Alabama, Arkansas, California, Colorado, Connecticut, and Delaware. Twenty-five electoral votes were recorded for Tilden, twelve for Hayes. When Ferry came to Florida, the room fell silent. There were now three sets of returns from the state: one certificate signed by former governor Marcellus Stearns on December 6, giving Florida's four electoral votes to Hayes; a second certificate signed on the same day by Florida attorney general William Cocke, claiming the electoral votes for Tilden; and a third certificate, signed on January 19 by newly sworn governor George F. Drew, that also gave the state to Tilden on the basis of a careful recanvassing of returns.

Objections were raised immediately to the multiple ballots. Ferry referred the objections to the Electoral Commission and adjourned the joint session, which had lasted little more than an hour. The stage was set for the next round of fighting.

The commission began its deliberations the next day in the Old Senate Chamber, which served as home to the Supreme Court. Associate Justice Nathan Clifford, by virtue of seniority, acted as president of the body. The seventy-three-year-old Clifford had previously served as United States attorney general under President James K. Polk, in which role he had helped conclude the Treaty of Guadalupe Hidalgo ending the Mexican War. He had subsequently been appointed to the Supreme Court by James Buchanan in 1858. Not wanting to usurp the majesty of the court, commission members crowded around a briefing table on the floor of the chamber, while the justices' nine chairs sat empty above them, looking down on the proceedings from a raised platform in the center of the room.

For the next four days batteries of lawyers argued the pros and cons of the Florida case. New York congressman David Dudley Field, a confidant of Tilden's since their days together in the anti-slavery Barnburners movement in the late 1840s, made the Democratic presentation. It was patently obvious, said Field, that Tilden had carried the Florida election; only "a sort of jugglery" by a corrupt returning board had reversed the decision of the ballot box, allowing a defeated and discredited governor to knowingly sign a false electoral certificate. Citing specific election abuses in Baker County, where returns from two of the county's four precincts had been thrown out illegally by Republican officials appointed three days after the election, Field asked the commission to go behind the returns and investigate the true facts of the case, which he was certain would support the electoral certificates filed for Tilden.

As everyone in the room clearly understood, this was the crux of the matter—not just for Florida but for the entire election. The actions of the returning boards in Florida, South Carolina, and Louisiana would not bear close scrutiny; any reasonably impartial board was likely to reverse the findings, particularly those from Louisiana, where no amount of Democratic intimidation could possibly have equalled the wholesale disqualification of more than thirteen thousand votes for the Tilden-Hendricks ticket. Iowa Congressman John A. Kasson, who had been a Republican visiting statesman in Florida after the election, sought to stave off any such inquiry by the Electoral Commission. Piously decrying federal intrusion into Florida's sovereign affairs, Kasson said that the Republican position was based strictly on "the face of the returns," which he said had been examined by the duly appointed returning board and signed by the sitting governor of the state on the date required by federal law. The commission had no right to go behind the official return, Kasson reasoned, because the Constitution left it up to the individual states to certify their own returns. Furthermore, the Electoral Commission could not go behind the returns in a particular Florida county without opening itself up to similar challenges in other counties. There was simply not time to investigate all such challenges before the March 4 deadline. The commission, said Kasson, had no choice but to accept the official certificate signed by Governor Stearns.

The hearings droned on through February 6, when the commission went into executive session to begin its private deliberations. Abram Hewitt, who had been present for the opening arguments, believed that the Democrats had made a good case, particularly since there was recent precedent to justify going behind a state's returns. In 1873, under the aegis of the Twenty-second Joint Rule, the Republican-controlled Senate had gone behind the returns in Louisiana and thrown out that state's electoral votes. Hewitt believed the 1873 decision confirmed the right of the Electoral Commission to undertake similar action in 1877. As a member of the joint committee that had created the commission, Hewitt also believed that a clear majority of the committee had agreed to the premise "that the action of the Returning Boards must be inquired into and should be reversed if substantial justice should seem to demand such action." Unfortunately for the Democrats, Hewitt had neglected to get the agreement down in writing, and the Republicans now denied subscribing to any such principle. When Hewitt attempted to broach the matter before the commission, Republican commissioner George F. Hoar joked dismissively that Hewitt had "a screw loose somewhere" if he truly believed that had been the basic understanding.

Everything hinged on Bradley's decision. At 2:13 P.M. on February 7, Bradley rose from his chair at the conference table and began reading his opinion. For ten minutes the other commission members held their breath as the jurist went over the various points made by both sides. All the members were lawyers, and when Bradley began citing Chief Justice John Marshall's famous 1810 decision in *Fletcher v. Peck*, in which the great jurist had declined to go behind an act of the Georgia legislature on the basis of "slight implication and vague conjecture," it suddenly dawned on them that Bradley was going to vote in favor of the Republicans. "The two houses of Congress, in proceeding with the count, are bound to recognize the determination of the state board of canvassers as the act of the state and as the most authentic evidence of the appointment made by the state," Bradley said. "While they may go behind the governor's certificate, if necessary, they can only do so for the purpose of ascertaining whether he has truly certified the results to which the board arrived. They cannot sit as a court of appeals on the action of that board."

A few minutes later, voting strictly along party lines, the commission voted eight to seven not to receive any more evidence in the Florida case. There would be no further investigation of the state canvassing board. Florida's four electoral votes would go to Hayes, and so—barring a miraculous change of heart by Bradley or another Republican commissioner—would the electoral votes of the other three contested states. Critics immediately denounced the ruling as an outrageous bullying act by "eight villains to seven patriots."

The Democrats were stunned, none more so than Hewitt. In an unhappy echo of election night, when he had gone to bed with the *New York Tribune*'s headline—"Tilden Elected"—dancing before his eyes, Hewitt had retired for the evening on February 6 with the assurances of a mutual friend that Bradley was going to rule in favor of the Democrats. John G. Stevens, an attorney from Trenton, New Jersey, was staying with Hewitt in Washington. He returned about midnight from a visit to Bradley's home to report that he had just read Bradley's opinion and that it was "in favor of counting the vote of the Democratic electors" in Florida. Stevens did not say how, exactly, he had come to read Bradley's decision, but he was absolutely convinced that the justice would come down in favor of Tilden.

In the wake of Bradley's sudden reversal, outraged Democrats immediately charged that the justice somehow had been "reached" in the lonely hours between midnight and dawn. The *New York Sun* claimed later that "during the whole of that night, Judge Bradley's house in Washington was surrounded by the carriages of visitors who came to see him apparently about the decision of the Electoral Commission. These visitors included leading Republicans as well as persons deeply interested in the Texas Pacific Railroad scheme." As many as seventeen carriages at a time were seen outside Bradley's home, the newspaper reported. According to Hewitt, two of the spectral carriages belonged to

Senator Frederick T. Frelinghuysen and Secretary of the Navy George M. Robeson, fellow New Jerseyans who had practiced law alongside Bradley for several years.

Except for the questionable propriety of visiting another commission member on the night before a crucial vote, Frelinghuysen, a future secretary of state under Chester A. Arthur, was untouched by scandal. Indeed, in the judgment of English foreign minister Edward Thornton, the senator looked and acted like a Methodist parson. His own cousin, Secretary of State Hamilton Fish, considered him "unexceptional." Robeson was a different matter. He had served as Grant's secretary of the navy for the past seven years, during which time he had somehow managed to deposit—on a salary of $8,000 a year—over $320,000 in savings. A congressional committee investigating his financial transactions a few months earlier had found a great deal of circumstantial evidence linking his sudden wealth to the grateful largesse of Philadelphia grain merchant A. G. Cattell & Company, which had been awarded a hefty government contract not long after Robeson took office. The navy secretary was accused of gross misconduct and corruption, but he managed to escape impeachment for the simple reason that Congress was already busy impeaching Secretary of War William W. Belknap, a far more tempting target than the little-known Robeson.

According to Hewitt, Frelinghuysen and Robeson begged Bradley to change his position on the Florida question. They were joined in their urging by Bradley's wife, "a highly religious woman and a strong partisan," who came downstairs in her dressing gown and prayed over the matter with her faltering husband. Bradley, for his part, stoutly denied that he had been visited by anyone on the night in question, and his son Charles supported his father's contentions, saying the insomniac jurist had gone to bed at eleven and gotten back up at three. The younger Bradley felt constrained to add, however, that his father was "as staunch a Republican as any of those members of the commission who were deliberately selected by reason of their own political predilections." (Charles Bradley, too, was a staunch Republican, and later received a lucrative job with the New York customhouse at the behest of the Hayes administration.) Obviously, someone was lying, and it is difficult to see why Stevens would have made up such an easily refutable story. The Bradleys, on the other hand, had some motive to lie. And Bradley's subsequent admission that he had, indeed, written down a decision favorable to the Democrats—he said it was merely an old lawyer's trick to test which side of an argument was stronger—indirectly supported Stevens's story.

Whatever the truth about Bradley's visitors, Democrats in Congress lambasted the justice. Threats were made against his life and an armed guard was posted around his home. Missouri senator Lewis V. Bogy led the charge from the floor of the Senate, declaring that "the name of that man who changed his vote upon that commission from Tilden to Hayes, Justice Bradley, will go down to after ages covered with equal shame and disgrace. Never will it be pronounced without a hiss from all good men in this country." In New York, Tilden told his friend John Bigelow that someone had offered to sell him Bradley's vote for $200,000. Recalling previous invitations to bribery in the three southern states, Tilden joked lightly, "That seems to be the standard figure."

Bradley's decision, however it was reached, was a grievous blow to Tilden's chances. As stipulated by law, the commission reported its findings to the House and Senate, which then withdrew to consider the report separately. It was a strictly pro forma exercise: under the provisions of the Electoral Commission Act, both houses of Congress would have had to reject the board's finding to render it invalid. The Democratic majority in the House went through the motions of doing just that, but the Republican majority in the Senate, as expected, found the Florida ruling entirely appropriate. The decision stood. In Columbus, Ohio, Hayes began drafting his inaugural address and penciling in members of his proposed cabinet. In New York City, Tilden began making plans for a lengthy trip abroad.

IN WASHINGTON, Hewitt and other Democratic leaders put their last hopes on an unlikely savior—Republican senator Roscoe Conkling. From the start, Conkling had questioned Hayes's right to Louisiana's eight electoral votes. He had also questioned the authority of the president of the Senate to rule unilaterally on the contested electoral certificates. On the morning after the Florida decision was announced,

Hewitt met privately with Conkling, who promised to give a speech before the Senate defending Tilden's right to Louisiana, as "there could be no doubt as to the election having been in favor of Tilden by a large majority." Had Conkling made such a speech on February 12, when the Louisiana electoral certificates were opened in Congress, there is good reason to believe he would have carried the day. The *Brooklyn Eagle* and the *Philadelphia Press* both conducted surveys later of the other senators and found that Conkling controlled enough votes to force acceptance of the Democratic certificate and prevent the Electoral Commission from receiving the case. Instead, for reasons never fully explained, Conkling conveniently absented himself from the Senate on the day the Louisiana certificates were opened and took a train to Baltimore.

Three competing certificates, two signed by outgoing Republican governor William Kellogg and the other signed by presumptive Democratic governor John F. McEnery, went before the commission. Members were not told that one of the forms signed by Kellogg was a forgery, although Thomas Ferry knew it at the time. When the original certificate was delivered to Ferry by Louisiana returning board member Thomas Anderson, the Senate president noticed that the form had not been signed by all the electors, as required by law. Ferry improperly permitted Anderson to take a copy of the certificate back to Louisiana, where the two missing signatures were forged and backdated to December 6 by an official in Kellogg's office. To draw attention away from the forgery, the Republicans arranged to have a fourth certificate presented to the commission as well, this one received by mail from "John Smith, bull-dozed governor of Louisiana," certifying the state's electors for Greenback party candidate Peter Cooper, Abram Hewitt's father-in-law. As such things went, it was a pretty good joke.

The commission debated the merits of the Louisiana case for four full days. Again, Democratic lawyers implored the members to go behind the certificates and investigate the obvious corruption of the state returning board. Again, the commission refused. On February 16 the panel met for a marathon eleven hours to reach its decision. For commission member James A. Garfield, it was "a day of the most nervous strain and anxiety I have ever passed since Chickamauga"—a reference to the bloody Civil War battle in 1863, when then-general Garfield had made a famous ride back to the battlefield to deliver a message to General George H. Thomas on Snodgrass Hill. The message itself was unimportant and the ride was largely without incident, but the feat was later romanticized into an act of such death-defying proportions that Garfield rode it all the way into the White House, where an assassin's bullet rode him out again after only six months as president. That unhappy event was still four years in the future, and Garfield now imagined that he could hear the watches ticking away in each commissioner's pocket as Bradley announced his vote in favor of Hayes.

Once again the Democrats were outraged. When the results were reported to the joint session of Congress on February 19, furious cries of "Fraud!" and "Conspiracy!" echoed through the House chamber. The emotional outburst did no good. The Senate, without disagreement from the ineffable Conkling, voted to accept the Electoral Commission's finding and award Louisiana's eight electoral votes to Hayes. Democratic senator Samuel Bell Maxey of Texas took the floor to denounce the decision, which he said "in effect exalts fraud, degrades justice, and consigns truth to the dungeon." Delaware senator Thomas Bayard continued the theme. "Deep indeed is my sorrow and poignant my disappointment," he said. "Not only does this decision of these eight [Republican] members destroy and level in the dust the essential safeguards of the Constitution . . . but it announces to the people of this land that truth and justice, honesty and morality, are no longer the essential bases of their political power." In the House, New York congressman Samuel S. "Sunset" Cox attempted to read a passage from Psalm 94, verse 20: "Shall the throne of iniquity have fellowship with thee, which frameth mischief by a law?" Republican congressman William D. Kelley of Pennsylvania immediately objected. The Bible itself, Cox responded, must be objectionable to the Republicans.

Two Massachusetts congressmen, Republican Henry Pierce and Independent Julius Seelye, refused to endorse the Louisiana decision. Announcing his principled opposition, Seelye, the longtime president of Amherst College, made a brief but cogent speech that aptly summed up the entire post-election muddle. "It seems to me perfectly clear that the charges made by each side against the other are in the main true," Seelye said. "No facts were ever proved more conclusively than the fraud and corruption charged on the one side and the intimidation and cruelty charged on the other. Which of the two sides went the further would be very hard to say. The corruption of the one side seems as heinous as the cruelty of the other side is horrible, and on both sides there does not seem to be any limit to the extent they went, save only where the necessities of the case did not permit or the requirements of the case did not call for any more. I find it therefore quite impossible to say which of the two sets of electors coming up here with their certificates voices the true will of the people of Louisiana in the late election, and therefore equally beyond my power to assent to the propriety of counting either."

Ohio senator John Sherman, one of the most intransigent of Hayes's supporters, angrily refuted the Democratic charges. "A good deal is said about fraud, fraud, fraud—fraud and perjury, and wrong," Sherman railed. "Why, sir, if you go behind the returns in Louisiana, the case is stronger for the Republicans than upon the face of the returns. What do you find there? Crime, murder, violence, that is what you find. While there may have been irregularities, while there may have been a non-observance of some directory laws, yet the substantial right was arrived at by the action of the returning board."

In the end, all the speeches were beside the point. The Senate accepted the commission's decision, the House rejected it, and the decision stood. Eight more electoral votes went into the Republican column.

Following the Louisiana decision, Tilden came under renewed pressure to do something dramatic. "I would not consent to this damnable fraud," one supporter told him bluntly. Tilden was urged to do everything from writing a public letter protesting the action to simply declaring himself president. Resurgent calls of "Tilden or blood!" came from the North and Midwest; the South remained strangely quiet. Tilden's nephew, Colonel William Pelton, wired from Washington to denounce the "outrageous proceeding" and to beseech his uncle, a little weakly, "If you have anything to suggest, send by messenger Saturday night." John Bigelow thought his friend was showing a little more "disposition to consult" with other Democrats, now that the presidency was slipping away, but Tilden still ventured no public criticism of the Electoral Commission. As for suggestions that he name himself president, Tilden found the notion ludicrous. If the House of Representatives had made a formal declaration early on, before the Electoral Commission was created, he later told a reporter, he would have gone immediately to Washington and taken the oath of office, even if he had been arrested and shot. As it was, "After the electoral scheme, which I always opposed, was complete, I never entertained the idea of taking the oath of office either in Washington or in New York or elsewhere. It would have been ridiculous. I had no evidence of title then—no claim—no warrant."

SLOWLY BUT SURELY, Rutherford B. Hayes was acquiring just such "evidence of title." The day after the Louisiana decision was announced, the electoral count resumed and the votes were recorded from Maine, Maryland, Massachusetts, Michigan, and Nevada. Oregon's two competing certificates, with their varying claims for or against the eligibility of one of the three Republican electors, were referred to the Electoral Commission. Despite the fact that the commission had refused to go behind the official certificates signed by the governors of Florida and Louisiana, Republican lawyers now argued that Oregon governor Lafayette Grover's similar certification should be overturned. Grover, they said, had acted improperly when he voided the election of Republican elector John W. Watts on the grounds that Watts's position as a postmaster had disqualified him as a candidate. A great deal of debate ensued over the eligibility or ineligibility of Watts as an elector, as well as Grover's right to certify the candidate with the next highest number of votes, a Democrat, to take Watts's place as an elector. In the end, the inexplicable decision of Oregon's Democratic secretary of state, Stephen F. Chadwick, to sign a separate return certifying Watts as an official elector gave the commission the opening it needed to ignore the certificate signed by the governor of Oregon and accept the one signed by the secretary of state— a ruling that was exactly the opposite of what the commission had decided in the Florida case.

While the commission was debating the merits of the Oregon case, the two sides continued jockeying for position outside the meeting room. The Democrats, not expecting the Oregon ruling to be any more favorable to their side than the commission's earlier votes, began discussing other ways to prevent Hayes's likely inauguration. In a caucus of congressional Democrats on the night of February 19, House Speaker Samuel Randall suggested, for the sake of argument, that the House could pass an amendment to the Presidential Succession Act of 1792 and name Secretary of State Hamilton Fish acting president until a new election could be held. Or, said Randall, the Democrats could simply filibuster through March 4, when the Electoral Commission's formal mandate expired, thus preventing the commission from completing its work by blocking any further House votes on its rulings. With no new president named by that date, the House could then arrange for a new election to take place under existing laws. Noting the recent pas de deux between southern Democrats and Hayes supporters, Randall also warned the southerners not to believe everything they were told. There was no assurance, he said, that Hayes would keep—or even recognize—the promises being made in his behalf. Instead, the former Union general was likely to revive bayonet rule in the South and institute policies "of such a character as to overwhelm any southern man in ruin who aided in carrying out their agreement in good faith."

Immediately after the caucus adjourned—no action would be taken until after the Oregon issue was decided—concerned southern Democrats hurried to the home of Republican congressman Charles S. Foster, who represented Hayes's district in Ohio. As Foster later described it to Hayes, "The Southern people who had agreed to stand by us in carrying out the electoral law in good faith were seized with a fright, if not a panic." They wanted Foster to counteract Randall's "violent speech" with a speech of his own from the floor of the House, reassuring their fellow southerners that Hayes's policy would not be "that of the bayonet towards the South." After conferring with Hayes's Ohio friend Stanley Matthews, James A. Garfield, and former U.S. attorney general William M. Evarts, Foster agreed to make the speech without waiting for the candidate's formal approval.

On February 20, while the Electoral Commission continued to debate the Oregon question, Foster rose from his seat in the House chamber. "Representing as I do the district in which Governor Hayes resides, and being a lifelong acquaintance of his, I say that his administration will be wise, patriotic, and just," Foster began. "I feel certain that I shall be sustained by his acts when I say that his highest ambition will be to administer the government so patriotically and wisely as to wipe away any and all necessity or excuse for the formation of parties on a sectional basis and all traces of party color lines; that thereafter and forever we shall hear no more of a solid South or a united North. The flag shall float over states, not provinces, over freemen, and not subjects."

Foster's carefully noncommittal speech was long on platitudes and short on specifics—much like Hayes's campaign had been. It promised nothing beyond the scope of Hayes's well-worn acceptance letter, which Conkling, Grant, and other Stalwarts had tacitly repudiated. Nevertheless, it temporarily reassured the southern Democrats at whom it was aimed—very temporarily, as it turned out. Two days after Foster's speech, an article appeared in James M. Comly's *Ohio State Journal* attacking Louisiana's white Democrats as drunken loafers and calling on Grant to use the army to forcibly seat Republican gubernatorial claimant Stephen B. Packard. Besides being one of Hayes's closest friends, Comly had been intimately involved in wooing southern Democrats, and his sudden change of heart seemed to prove Randall's point about the basic untrustworthiness of the Republicans. A copy of the article quickly appeared on the desk of every Democratic member in the House.

Once again Hayes's supporters scrambled to reassure the jumpy southerners, who held in their hands the fate of any successful filibuster. A hasty telegram to Comly demanded to know how such an inflammatory article could have been published in his journal. Comly replied that he had been home, sick in bed, when a young reporter at the office mistakenly ran the article without his knowledge. A lengthy explanation was printed in the *Washington National Republican* two days later, the same day the Electoral Commission announced its invariable eight-to-seven decision for Hayes in the Oregon case. On the floor of the House, where some members had begun wearing pistols for their protection—James A. Garfield, for one, had heard rumors that he might be assassinated so that his place on the commission could be filled by a less partisan congressman—intense discussions resumed among Democrats over whether or not to begin a filibuster. Abram Hewitt, after giving a speech simultaneously denouncing the commission and reminding his fellow party members that they, too, had supported its creation, engineered a weekend recess until February 26, when Congress would have a mere six working days left in which to complete the electoral count.

On the morning of the twenty-sixth, Edward A. Burke, chairman of Louisiana's Democratic state committee, met privately with President Grant in the White House. Burke, a shadowy adventurer who had arrived in New Orleans six years earlier from parts unknown and somehow had worked his way up from a penniless day laborer to a political power broker, was in Washington as the personal representative of Louisiana gubernatorial hopeful Francis Nicholls. In the pursuance of his duties Burke already had met with Stanley Matthews and Ohio congressman Charles Foster, seeking guarantees that Hayes would drop his support for Packard's carpetbag regime. In return for such a guarantee, Burke promised to deliver the goodwill of his southern friends in Congress. Otherwise, he warned, there would be a last-ditch filibuster, and Hayes would never be inaugurated.

Matthews and Foster could scarcely commit Hayes to such an understanding—particularly since Packard had received several thousand more votes for governor than Hayes had received for president in Louisiana—but Grant had no problem agreeing, at least in principle, to Burke's demands. The president had felt all along that Tilden and Nicholls had carried the state, and he told Burke "unequivocally that he is satisfied that the Nicholls government is the government which should stand in Louisiana and that the sentiment of the country is clearly opposed to the further use of troops in upholding a state government."

Burke went immediately from the White House to Capitol Hill, where he met with Matthews, Senator John Sherman, and former Ohio governor Edward Dennison in a locked committee room. Sherman wanted to know Burke's terms for helping to block the filibuster. Burke replied that the three Republicans should go to Grant and encourage him to remove all remaining federal troops from Louisiana. When Sherman refused, saying the president would never agree to such a move, Burke dramatically produced a signed statement from Grant agreeing, in essence, to do just that. Sherman, who had just returned from a trip to Columbus, where Hayes had promised him a seat in his cabinet, caved in without a fight. All he wanted, said Sherman, was a promise from Burke that the Democrats in Louisiana would not unleash a new reign of terror on the state's Republicans, black and white, whom the national party was abandoning to their fates. It would also be helpful, Sherman said, if the Democrats would not challenge the recent election to the Senate of the state's outgoing Republican governor, William P. Kellogg. Burke agreed. The final pieces were falling into place.

While Burke and the Republican principals were meeting behind closed doors, the electoral vote count proceeded in the House chamber. Pennsylvania and Rhode Island were counted for Hayes, and at 6:00 P.M. on February 26, South Carolina's two competing returns were submitted to the Electoral Commission for review. That same night a gathering was held at Washington's landmark Wormley Hotel on the corner of 15th and H streets, NW, to ratify the various discussions that had been taking place for the past several days between Hayes's inner circle and the Democrats under Burke's alleged control. Among those present at the meeting in former United States attorney general William M. Evarts's hotel room were Evarts, Matthews, Sherman, Garfield, Foster, Dennison—the Ohio braintrust—and Burke, Louisiana congressmen E. John Ellis and William M. Levy, and Kentucky congressman Henry Watterson, who had been asked to attend the meeting by future senator Matthew C. Butler of South Carolina to represent the interests of the Palmetto State.

The meeting got off to an unfortunate start when Garfield, who had not been privy to the earlier negotiations, balked at committing Hayes to any hard-and-fast agreements, particularly at what was virtually the election's eleventh hour. "Nobody has any authority to speak for Governor Hayes beyond his party platform and letter of acceptance," Garfield said, "and it would be neither honorable nor wise to do so, if any one had such authority." The natural politician in Garfield took over long enough for him to add that "the whole nation would honor those southern men who are resisting anarchy, and thus are preventing civil war; but neither they nor we could afford to do anything that would be or appear to be a political bargain." Getting the distinct impression that Matthews, for one, did not approve of his remarks, Garfield put on his hat and left. The others remained behind to repeat their earlier assurances regarding the removal of federal troops in Louisiana and South Carolina and the derailment of any Democratic filibuster in the House.

Historians have argued ever since about the relative importance of the Wormley Hotel Conference. C. Vann Woodward devoted much of his influential 1951 book, *Reunion and Reaction,* to a painstaking recreation of the events leading up to the conference, only to conclude that the meeting itself "added nothing to the agreements reached earlier in the day, but merely went over the same ground for the benefit of new participants." Nevertheless, a popular legend has developed of a shadowy cabal of white politicians cynically selling out the futures of four million black southerners in return for Rutherford B. Hayes's ascension to the White House. One suspects that the legend endures, at least in part, because of the irresistible irony of such a plot being hatched in a hotel owned by one of the wealthiest black entrepreneurs in Washington. At any rate, it is difficult to see how any agreement so sweeping and long lasting could have been concluded without the approval of the one man who stood to gain the most by the deal—Hayes himself. But Hayes, whatever his faults, would never have agreed to such an arrangement, particularly when the scent of victory was in the air. Nor could a lone lobbyist such as Edward Burke, however well connected he claimed to be, have controlled enough votes in Congress to effectively shut off a Democratic filibuster if that was the prevailing will of the House. Like many other high-level political deals, the Wormley agreement was more a mutual concession of the obvious than a device for controlling larger events. Even Burke admitted later that the various discussions between him and the Yankees had been little more than "a bluff game." The end of the electoral crisis was already in the works, and it did not depend on any secret deals.

ON FEBRUARY 28 the Electoral Commission voted, eight to seven, to award South Carolina's seven electoral votes to Hayes. The Senate concurred. All three disputed southern states had gone to the Republican candidate, as had the one contested elector in Oregon. Former secretary of state Jeremiah S. Black, the Pennsylvania Democrat who prior to the

Civil War had advised President James Buchanan not to go to war to preserve the Union, denounced the commission in terms that matched his given name. "If this thing stands accepted and the law you have made for this occasion shall be the law for all occasions, we can never expect such a thing as an honest election again," Black warned. "If you want to know who will be president by a future election, do not inquire how the people of the states are going to vote. You need only to know what kind of scoundrels constitute the returning boards, and how much it will take to buy them." Eventually, he said, divine justice would strike the Republicans with an iron hand.

After South Carolina's votes were recorded for Hayes, the electoral count continued before the joint session of Congress, with Tennessee and Texas going into Tilden's column. A brief flurry arose over Vermont's five electoral votes when Abram Hewitt produced a second electoral certificate, which he said Ferry had refused to accept. The two houses separated to consider whether to challenge the state's official certificate. Hewitt knew that the second certificate was spurious, but he forced an overnight delay in the vote count, he later claimed, to extract more satisfactory assurances from Hayes's representatives concerning the removal of troops in the South and also, conversely, to allow enough time "to obtain Tilden's explicit approval of the abandonment of the contest." Hewitt claimed to have House Speaker Samuel Randall's approval for the move, which some Republicans feared was the beginning of the long-dreaded master plot they had been expecting from Tilden all along.

Whatever Hewitt's ulterior motives, the unexpected parliamentary delay ratcheted up tensions to the breaking point. The next morning, March 1, the House chamber was packed with congressmen, lobbyists, newspaper reporters, and onlookers, including almost the entire Senate, when the House resumed deliberations on the Vermont certificates. After Hewitt announced that the second certificate somehow had gone missing, pandemonium ensued. Roaring members leaped onto their desktops, some clutching pistols, as Randall gaveled unsuccessfully for order. Motion followed motion, with Randall refusing to entertain any new business. Spectators cheered and applauded as though they were at a boxing match. Texas congressman James W. Throckmorton and

New York congressman David Dudley Field, both Democrats, almost
came to blows at one point. "I don't care to reply to you, sir," Field told
the enraged Texan. "No, you don't dare reply, you ____!" Throckmorton
shouted. "There isn't a dog in the land that would stop to ____ you!"
When a Virginia congressman similarly sought to confront Mississippi
congressman Lucius Q. C. Lamar, he suddenly found himself looking
down the barrel of Lamar's drawn derringer. "Take him away," Lamar
told startled onlookers, "or I'll present him to a cemetery!" Randall implored the lawmakers to remember "that they are members of the
American Congress."

At length the missing certificate magically reappeared, and some
semblance of parliamentary order was restored. Louisiana congressman
William Levy, one of the Wormley Hotel conspirators, took advantage
of the lull to gain the floor. He had been in contact with Francis
Nicholls in New Orleans, Levy said, and he thus could speak with some
authority. "The people of Louisiana," he assured his fellow Democrats,
"have solemn, earnest, and I believe truthful assurances from prominent members of the Republican party, high in the confidence of Mr.
Hayes, that, in the event of his election to the presidency, he will be
guided by a policy of conciliation toward the southern states, that he
will not use the federal authority or the army to force upon those states
governments not of their choice, but in the case of these states will
leave their own people to settle the matter peaceably, of themselves."
He called on other Democrats to join him in allowing the vote count to
be completed.

Levy's carefully calibrated speech broke the back of the would-be
filibusterers. Vermont's bogus return was rejected, 148–116, and the
House accepted the original certificate. The Green Mountain State
passed into Hayes's column. The joint session resumed, and Virginia
and West Virginia were counted for Tilden. Only one more state, Wisconsin, remained. A challenge arose to one of the state's electors on
the grounds that he was a government pension officer. Again the two
houses separated to consider the validity of the state's certificate. In
the House, Texas congressman Roger Q. Mills introduced a motion to
have the lower body suspend the count and move immediately to elect
a president on its own—something Samuel Tilden had been demand-

ing for the past four months—but Speaker Randall tabled the resolution without a vote.

It was now just past midnight on Friday, March 2. Kentucky congressman Joseph C. Blackburn, a former Confederate colonel, followed Mills to the well of the House. "Mr. Speaker," he said, "the end has come. There is no longer a margin for argument, and manhood spurns the pleas of mercy, and yet there is a fitness in the hour which should not pass unheeded. Today is Friday. Upon that day, the savior of the world suffered crucifixion between two thieves. On this Friday constitutional government, justice, honesty, fair dealing, manhood, and decency suffer crucifixion amid a number of thieves."

Wisconsin Republican congressman Charles Grandison Williams, who had spent the war years safely practicing law in Madison, could not let Blackburn's remarks pass unchallenged. "I do not desire to retort in the spirit indulged in by the gentleman who has just taken his seat," said Williams, "but if I did I might remind him and this House that this is not only Friday but hangman's day; and that there could be no more fitting time than just after the hour of midnight . . . that this bogus, pretentious, bastard brat of political reform, which for the last twelve months has affronted the eyes of gods and men should be strangled to death, gibbetted higher than Haman." So much for grace in victory.

After a final bit of parliamentary business, the Senate formally marched back into the House chamber and Wisconsin's ten electoral votes were recorded for Hayes. Randall, who a few minutes earlier had received a telegram from Tilden urging him to complete the count, surrendered the speaker's chair to Ferry. It was now 4:10 A.M.; the House had been in session for a marathon eighteen straight hours. After indulging in a last bit of self-congratulatory back-patting—the election and its aftermath had been "worthy of the respect of the world," Ferry said, presumably with a straight face—he announced the final vote totals: 185 electoral votes for Hayes, 184 for Tilden. "Wherefore, I do declare that Rutherford B. Hayes, of Ohio, having received a majority of the whole number of electoral votes, is duly elected President of the United States for four years, commencing on the 4th day of March, 1877. And that William A. Wheeler, of New York, having received a majority of the whole number of electoral votes, is duly elected Vice-

President of the United States for four years, commencing on the 4th day of March, 1877."

In New York, a weary Samuel Tilden took the news stoically. "It is about what I expected," he said. Back in Washington, Abram Hewitt collapsed on the House floor from nervous exhaustion. When he regained consciousness three days later, Rutherford B. Hayes was president.

EVEN BEFORE THE VOTE was concluded, the nation's new president-elect was already en route to Washington, riding in comfort aboard a luxury train provided free of charge by Tom Scott and the Pennsylvania Railroad. The night before, much like Abraham Lincoln had done when he left his hometown of Springfield, Illinois, sixteen years earlier, Hayes had delivered an emotional farewell address to his friends and supporters from the rear platform of his train. "My fellow citizens," he said, "I appear to say a few words in bidding goodbye to you. I understand very well the uncertainty of public affairs at Washington; I understand very well that possibly next week I may be with you again to resume my place in the governor's office and as your fellow citizen." He said he was reminded of a similar leave-taking in the summer of 1861, when he marched down High Street with his Ohio regiment en route to the Civil War. "Of my comrades, one third and over never returned to their homes," he noted solemnly. "They perished in the discharge of their duty, that the Republic might live." But there was something that mere military force could not do, Hayes remarked. "We would have our Union to be a union of hearts, and we would have our Constitution obeyed, not merely because of force that compels obedience, but obeyed because the people love the principles of the Constitution. I do hope, I do fervently believe, that by the aid of divine providence we may do something in this day of peace, by works of peace, toward reestablishing in the hearts of our countrymen a real, a hearty attachment to the Constitution as it is and to the Union as it is."

Accompanying Hayes on the trip east were his wife, Lucy, children Scott, Fanny, and Webb, his late sister, Fanny's, daughter, Laura, and a small group of friends, including future president William McKinley and William Henry Smith of the Western Associated Press. The party had been warned of possible violence, especially when passing through Baltimore, and Hayes had taken the added precaution of keeping his time of arrival out of the press. The threat of assassination was real enough: a few weeks earlier, as Hayes and his family were sitting down to dinner in Columbus, someone had fired a bullet through the plate glass window in the parlor. The incident was hushed up to avoid enflaming the American public, and no one was ever arrested for the crime.

For the sake of appearances, Hayes did not want to reach Washington before the electoral count was formally completed, and the train stopped for the night outside Harrisburg, Pennsylvania. Just after dawn on Friday, March 2, he was awakened and handed a telegram informing him that, four months after the presidential election of 1876 had been conducted, he had officially been declared the victor. His sons commenced to whoop it up. "Boys, boys, you'll waken the passengers," Hayes admonished them.

Despite his wish for secrecy, Hayes's arrival in Washington at 9:00 A.M. was met by two thousand delighted supporters. Senator John Sherman and his brother, army general William Tecumseh Sherman, were among those on hand to greet the president-elect. After a short breakfast at Senator Sherman's home, Hayes hurried to the White House to pay his respects. Betraying, perhaps, a touch of emotion, Hayes took President Grant's hand in both of his and "seemed for a moment too overcome for expression." Grant, as usual, was taciturn. "Governor Hayes," he said, "I am glad to welcome you." He showed Hayes a copy of the telegram he was preparing to send to Stephen Packard in Louisiana, advising him not to count on any more political support and ordering the immediate withdrawal of federal troops from the state. Hayes ventured no overt disagreement, but in private he passed along word to General Sherman not to be in any hurry to carry out the order. Despite what his friends had said at the Wormley Hotel Conference and behind locked doors on Capitol Hill, Hayes did not feel any immediate obligation to honor their commitments. He would wait to see how the southerners behaved.

The next evening the Grants hosted a gala dinner for the Hayeses at the White House. Before sitting down to eat, Grant quietly ushered Hayes into the Red Room, where Secretary of State Hamilton Fish,

Chief Justice Morrison Waite, and Navy Secretary George Robeson—Joseph Bradley's late-night visitor—stood waiting. Although Grant's term ended on March 4, a Sunday, the official inauguration would not be held until Monday, March 5. To forestall any doubts about who was really president during the unavoidable one-day interregnum—who knew what Samuel Tilden might decide to do?—Hayes was sworn into office secretly. No one at the dinner was told of the scheme.

Two days later, before a crowd of thirty thousand unsuspecting onlookers, Rutherford B. Hayes took the oath of office again on the front steps of the Capitol. It was all a sham—he was already president—but perhaps, given the circumstances, it was only fitting.

I STILL TRUST THE PEOPLE

RUTHERFORD B. HAYES'S political honeymoon, a tradition for all incoming presidents, was considerably shorter than the length of time it had taken him to reach the White House. Even before his public inauguration, Democratic newspapers across the country had begun decrying his suspect election. On March 3 the *New York Sun,* Samuel Tilden's most ardent supporter, appeared on the newsstands with a thick black border cloaking its front page. "These are the days of humiliation, shame and mourning for every patriotic American," *Sun* editor Charles A. Dana grieved. "A man whom the people rejected at the polls has been declared President of the United States through processes of fraud. A cheat is to sit in the seat of George Washington." Dana called on "every upright citizen [to] gird himself up for the work of redressing this monstrous crime. No truce with the guilty conspirators! No rest for them and no mercy till their political punishment and destruction are complete." When Hayes visited New York a few weeks later, the newspaper printed his picture with the letters F-R-A-U-D inscribed across his forehead.

The theme of fraud was picked up and expanded upon by the nation's Democratic newspapers, which vied among themselves for the honor of giving the new president the catchiest and most demeaning nickname. Among the most popular were "His Fraudulency," "Rutherfraud," "Old Eight to Seven," and "Returning Board Hayes." Even in his adopted hometown, Hayes was lambasted by the press. On March 2, the *Cincinnati Enquirer* intoned in bold type: "It is done. And fitly done in the dark. By the grace of Joe Bradley, R. B. Hayes is 'Commissioned' as President, and the monster fraud of the century is consummated."

As a parting shot across Hayes's bow, the House of Representatives on March 3 passed a resolution officially declaring that Tilden had been "duly elected President of the United States" with a total of 196 electoral votes. Florida and Louisiana were counted in Tilden's column, while Oregon and South Carolina were counted for Hayes. Ten congressmen signed an accompanying telegram to Tilden announcing the resolution and affirming their belief that the toothless parliamentary action, in and of itself, had made him president. Tilden did not see it that way. Diehard friends such as Manton Marble, New York legislator Smith M. Weed, and Edward Cooper urged him to take the oath of office, but Tilden refused, telling John Bigelow that the House resolution "created no warrant of authority." Marble was so angered by Tilden's refusal that he slammed the door in his old friend's face. Henry Watterson, who had reversed his initial opposition to the Electoral Commission and fought against a last-minute filibuster, thought that Tilden might have "carried all before him" by taking sudden, decisive action. But, Watterson observed, Tilden lacked "the touch of the dramatic discoverable in most of the leaders of men." He was no William of Orange, Louis XI, Oliver Cromwell, or George Washington, said Watterson, and "he had none of the audacious daring" of even James G. Blaine.

Perhaps Watterson was right about Tilden's lack of daring, but it did not necessarily follow that he was lacking in courage. A man capable of publicly denouncing Tammany Hall before an audience of handpicked New York City toughs, as Tilden had done at the state Democratic convention of 1871, was no coward. Neither did he rely on the easy courage of other people's shared convictions. Had Tilden agreed to be sworn in as president solely on the strength of the House declaration, it might well have occasioned an outbreak of violence in assorted northern and midwestern states, but it would not have succeeded in putting him in office. From the beginning of the deadlock, Ulysses S. Grant had signaled his willingness to use whatever force was necessary to maintain order. He controlled the army, and no cobbled-together force of rebellious civilians would have been a match for his military brilliance. Southern Democrats, who had discovered that fact for themselves during the Civil War, were consistently unwilling to test it again. Besides, any public outbreak of violence undoubtedly would have resulted in the retention of Republican regimes in Louisiana and South Carolina—the last thing in the world that most southerners wanted to happen. Tilden recognized this, even if some of his fire-breathing followers did not, and he placed the welfare of the nation above his own personal political ambitions. It was an act of supreme patriotism on the part of a man who had won, if not the presidency, at least the election.

ONCE INSTALLED IN the White House, Hayes found himself confronted by members of his own party as well as Democrats. This was due partly to his campaign promise to serve only one term as president, and partly to the reformist tilt of his cabinet selections, which infuriated old-line Stalwarts such as Roscoe Conkling and Zachariah Chandler. Keeping his promise to Grant, Hayes did not nominate Benjamin Bristow for a cabinet post, but he did the next best thing by choosing former Missouri senator Carl Schurz as secretary of the interior. Zachariah Chandler, whom Schurz replaced, had guided Hayes to victory in the presidential race, partly by pressing political appointees to contribute some $200,000 in forced assessments to Hayes's campaign. Now, said Chandler, "Hayes has passed the Republican party to its worst enemies."

Equally unpopular with the Republican rank and file were the appointments of former Tennessee senator David M. Key as postmaster general and former United States attorney general William M. Evarts as secretary of state. Key, a southern Democrat and an ex-Confederate, was the protégé of Texas and Pacific Railroad lobbyist Andrew J. Kellar, and his selection to the most powerful patronage position in the government was widely viewed as a payoff to both the railroad lobby and the southerners in Congress who had helped forestall a last-minute Democratic filibuster. Evarts, who had defended President Andrew Johnson during his 1868 impeachment trial, had been one of Hayes's most eloquent lawyers before the Electoral Commission, but many Republicans still blamed him for Johnson's one-vote acquittal in the Senate, and they remembered as well his vocal opposition to the use of army troops in Louisiana in 1875.

Other cabinet appointments went to men who, directly or indirectly, had helped Hayes successfully press his case before the Electoral Commission. Iowa Republican George McCrary, author of the bill creating the commission, was named secretary of war. Charles Devens, Hayes's pick as attorney general, was the law partner of Massachusetts congressman George F. Hoar, who had also served on the commission and consistently voted the eight-to-seven line. Richard W. Thompson, the new secretary of the navy, was a longtime associate of Indiana senator Oliver Morton, who had championed the right of Senate president Thomas Ferry to declare Hayes president unilaterally. And Ohio senator John Sherman, Hayes's choice as secretary of the treasury, had been a visiting statesman in Louisiana and a party to the Wormley Hotel Conference between leading Republicans and southern Democrats in the chaotic last days of the electoral vote count.

For both personal and political reasons, Hayes was in no hurry to keep the pledges made in his behalf concerning the removal of federal troops from the South. Personally, Hayes did not feel honor-bound by any such pledges, however broadly he may have agreed with them in principle. From the time of his nomination, he had always insisted that the removal of troops was contingent upon the proven good behavior of southerners in the affected states, specifically their demonstrated commitment to protecting the civil rights of their black fellow-citizens. He would not be pushed into acting prematurely. As he put it in his inaugural address: "The inestimable blessing of wise, honest, and peaceful self-government is not fully enjoyed [in the South]. . . . But it must not be forgotten that only a local government which recognizes and maintains inviolate the rights of all is a true self-government."

Politically, the new president also felt constrained to move slowly on the southern question. A dozen Republican congressmen from the South had been returned to Congress, and they warned loudly that they would bolt the party if Hayes abandoned too precipitately the carpetbag regimes in Louisiana and South Carolina. Playing for time, Hayes professed himself to be "too crowded with business to give thought to these questions." Instead, he appointed a commission—much like the erstwhile visiting statesmen—to travel to Louisiana and advise him on the case. In the meantime, southern patience was wearing thin. Mississippi Democratic congressman Lucius Lamar took the extraordinary step of writing personally to the president and reminding him, in no uncertain terms, of his previous commitments. "It was understood that you meant to withdraw the troops from South Carolina and Louisiana," Lamar wrote on March 22. "Upon that subject we thought you had made up your mind; and indeed, Mr. President, you told me that you had. We cannot willingly acquiesce in the delay which is to be prolonged at the expense of so much suffering and in the face of so much danger."

Lamar's letter apparently did the trick: the next day Hayes summoned South Carolina gubernatorial rivals Daniel Chamberlain and Wade Hampton to the White House to discuss the situation personally. Chamberlain, who remained convinced that he had won the election fairly and squarely, refused to resign voluntarily, and Hayes was forced to withdraw the federal troops surrounding the state capitol before Chamberlain conceded the obvious. This he did on April 10, after issuing a public statement to the Republican voters of South Carolina informing them that "by the order of the President whom your votes alone rescued from overwhelming defeat, the government of the United States abandons you, deliberately withdraws from you its support, with the full knowledge that the lawful government of the state will be speedily overthrown." One day later Wade Hampton moved into the governor's office, nearly four months after he had been inaugurated as governor by the Democrats.

Chamberlain's stubborn refusal to abdicate his position put him in bad light with the administration, and he received no comfortable sinecure for his troubles (an earlier offer of the post of American minister to Switzerland was quickly withdrawn). The same could not be said for Louisiana gubernatorial claimant Stephen Packard, who voluntarily relinquished his position to his Democratic rival, Francis Nicholls, on April 24, after pronouncing himself "wholly discouraged by the fact that, one by one, the Republican state governments of the South have been forced to succumb to force, fraud, or policy." Despite his defiant words, Packard received an appointment from Hayes to head the American consulate in Liverpool, where he lived high and ate well off the profits of a lucrative shipping concession that far exceeded the president's own $50,000-a-year salary.

Other principals in the post-election jumble were also rewarded for

their service to the party. William Kellogg, the former Louisiana governor who had signed the official returning board certificate giving the
state to Hayes and the Republicans, ascended to the United States Senate as part of the deal between Senator John Sherman and Louisiana
lobbyist Edward Burke. Marcellus Stearns, the outgoing governor of
Florida who likewise had endorsed his state canvassing board's questionable findings, was named federal commissioner at Hot Springs,
Arkansas. Florida canvassing board chairman Samuel McLin was appointed to the New Mexico Supreme Court. General Lew Wallace, one
of the Republican visiting statesmen in Florida, was named territorial
governor of the same western territory. James Madison Wells, the chairman of the Louisiana returning board who supposedly had offered to
sell his goodwill to the highest bidder, became collector of the port of
New Orleans; his board colleague Thomas Anderson served as deputy
collector. Louis Kenner, a third board member, was appointed deputy
naval officer of the port; and the fourth member of the board, Gadane
Casanave, had a brother named to a post in the city customhouse. In
all, no fewer than sixty-nine of the men involved in the Louisiana election received federal appointments, most through the good offices of
Treasury Secretary John Sherman.

THE WITHDRAWAL OF federal troops from the statehouses in South
Carolina and Louisiana represented the symbolic end of Reconstruction. (Ironically, the troops left New Orleans on the fifteenth anniver-
sary of the Union capture of the city in 1862.) Whether it was part of a
cynical bargain by Hayes and his supporters, as critics charged, or
merely the inevitable result of a political process that had been going on
at least since President Grant refused to intervene in the Mississippi
election of 1875, the end of Reconstruction would prove to have catastrophic and far-reaching effects on the four million black Americans
living in the South. Many of them realized it at the time. Said
Louisiana-born Henry Adams (not the Massachusetts historian of the
same name): "The whole South—every state in the South—had got
back into the hands of the very men that held us as slaves." South Carolina freedman William T. Rodenbach lamented to former governor

Daniel Chamberlain: "To think that Hayes could go back on us, when we had to wade through blood to help place him where he is now." An unidentified South Carolinian wrote passionately if ungrammatically to the president: "I am a unprotected freedman. . . . O God Save the Colored People."

Not all of Hayes's critics were black. Former Ohio senator Benjamin F. Wade, who had seconded Hayes's nomination in Cincinnati, announced that he felt "deceived, betrayed, and humiliated" by the president's actions. John A. Martin, chairman of the Kansas Republican state committee, complained that the new administration policy seemed to imply "Carpetbaggers to the rear, and niggers take care of yourselves." Old-line abolitionist William Lloyd Garrison accused Hayes of making a cowardly compromise with the "incorrigible enemies of equal rights and legitimate government." And Amos T. Akerman, the former United States attorney general who had helped prosecute hundreds of Ku Klux Klan members in the early years of the decade, derided the policy for its "peculiar logic of curing lawlessness by letting the lawless have their own way," and warned that it was "suicide for the purpose of a glorious resurrection. Such ends do not come from such means."

But Hayes's critics, black and white, were far outnumbered by the thousands of southern Democrats and northern Republicans who fully supported the end of Reconstruction. Ohio congressman Charles Foster, one of the attendees of the Wormley Hotel Conference and the author of a crucial speech on the floor of Congress during the emotional electoral debate, assured Hayes that he was "extremely happy" at the "undoing of the S.C. & La. muddle. Here & there, a Republican may be found who takes the Ben Wade view of the situation, but, generally speaking, the people of both parties are rejoiced to know that your policy has been a success, and that a genuine peace is to again grow up between the North & South." *The Nation*, which fancied itself the journalistic conscience of the country, ventured the confident prediction that "the negro will disappear from the field of national politics. Henceforth, the nation as a nation, will have nothing more to do with him." Even Grant allowed that the Fifteenth Amendment giving blacks the right to vote had been a mistake, one that "had done the Negro no good, and had been a hindrance to the South, and by no means a political advantage to the North." Black orator Frederick Douglass, newly appointed by Hayes to the powerful post of U.S. marshal for the District of Columbia, saw the removal of the troops as regrettable but unavoidable. "What is called the President's policy," he said, "might rather be considered the President's necessity. Statesmen often are compelled to act upon facts as they are, and not as they would like to have them."

The dismantling of Reconstruction, and the consequent political and social disempowerment of the region's sizable black minority, set the stage for nearly a century of de facto and legalized segregation, culminating in the notorious Jim Crow laws of the early 1900s that formalized the social, political, and economic marginalization of southern blacks begun in earnest three decades earlier. The right to vote, so recently received, was abruptly snatched away again—figuratively if not literally—from the former slaves. Redeemer governments across the South quickly wrote new laws into the books, similar to the infamous Black Codes of the late 1860s, that severely curtailed blacks' ability to vote in sufficient numbers to measurably influence elections on the local, state, or national level. Previously black districts were gerrymandered or otherwise broken up to dilute their strength, and poll taxes, literacy tests, and complicated registration laws further reduced black voter participation, making good on a southern newspaper's boast that while the Fourteenth and Fifteenth amendments "may stand forever . . . we intend to make them dead letters on the statute-book."

The reduction of black voting power was reinforced by restrictive new laws diminishing their rights to own and sell property, obtain credit, serve on juries, become policemen, or educate their children. Almost overnight, the Republican party in the Deep South disappeared as an effective political force. The Solid South, which for most of the next century would mean the solidly Democratic South, was the ironic, unforeseen result of Hayes's conciliatory policy toward the region. He had envisioned, no doubt too optimistically, a new political partnership between northern Republicans and "the best sort" of southerners to create a new, enlightened white majority in the South. That policy proved to be a grievous political mistake, as Hayes himself conceded in 1878, after the midterm elections had witnessed renewed violence and fraud in South Carolina, Louisiana, and other southern states. "I am reluctantly forced to admit that the experience was a failure," he told the *Washington National Republican* on November 13, 1878. "The first election of importance held since it was attempted has proved that fair elections with free suffrage in the South are an impossibility." Black historian W. E. B. Du Bois put it more succinctly. "The slave went free; stood a brief moment in the sun; then moved back again toward slavery," he wrote half a century later, summarizing the entire Reconstruction experience.

HAYES'S HISTORICAL IMAGE has been tarnished ever since by the way in which he entered the White House and by his perceived abandonment of blacks in the South. In both cases, however, he was more a captive of large events than he was himself a controller of those events. He went to bed on election night believing—with good reason—that he had lost the presidency to Samuel Tilden, a belief he held on to for several days. It was only after party leaders had assured him that he was morally obligated to accept the victory in behalf of the thousands of black southerners who had been deprived of their voting rights that Hayes became convinced of his claim to the White House. Once convinced, he never wavered in this belief. And although he may have turned a blind eye to the post-election abuses in Florida and Louisiana, it is also true that he had been told by people he trusted that he had a rightful claim to the electoral votes in those states. Such misdeeds as were done in his name by partisan Republican election officials were done without his personal knowledge. Whether he should have known about them in the first place is another question altogether.

As for the popular legend that Hayes singlehandedly ended Reconstruction, it is simply incorrect. Ulysses S. Grant, for all his inconsistent statements on the subject, had clearly begun the psychological, if not the physical, withdrawal of troops from the South as early as 1875, when he refused to intervene in the violent state election in Mississippi. Furthermore, the House of Representatives already had acted in March 1877 to forestall future troop deployments by blocking the annual military appropriations bill, and there was no money available to pay the troops. Hayes's politically astute wife, Lucy, referred to this fact when she later told a critic of her husband's policies, "Why, what could Mr. Hayes do but what he did? He had no army." Nor did he have the backing of the courts. The Supreme Court, in such landmark decisions as the *Slaughterhouse Cases* (1873) and *U.S. v. Cruikshank* (1876), had rolled back the authority of the federal government to intervene in state and local civil rights cases, and state courts in the South increasingly arrogated to themselves the power, if not necessarily the need, to rule on such matters in the foreseeable future. Finally, the withdrawal of troops did not occur in a political vacuum. The people of the North, with few exceptions, were as eager for Reconstruction to end as were their fractious cousins in the South. In pulling back the troops, Hayes was reflecting the will of the people, as presidents normally are expected to do. On paper, at least, he managed to extract promises from the new Democratic governors of South Carolina and Louisiana to protect the civil rights of their black citizens—which was more than his predecessor had done when the other southern states were similarly redeemed.

Still, the mantle of illegitimacy clung to Hayes throughout most of his single term of office. (He consistently rejected friends' advice to renege on his campaign promise and run for reelection in 1880.) It was only after the 1878 revelation of the so-called Cipher Telegrams between Tilden's supporters and corrupt officials in the disputed southern states that Hayes was, partially at least, rehabilitated in the public eye. These telegrams, illegally obtained by the Western Union Telegraph Company, purported to show Tilden's nephew, William Pelton, and others of his closest associates bargaining to bribe election officials in the three disputed southern states. A congressional committee subsequently interviewed Tilden in New York City, and the former candidate adamantly denied any prior knowledge of the attempted bribery. Despite the best efforts of Republican members of the committee to link Tilden to the bribes, he was cleared of any personal wrongdoing. Still, the allegations effectively destroyed his claims to moral superiority by lowering him, in effect, to the level of the Republicans. And although Tilden himself was at least as blameless as Hayes for the sordid dealings and double-dealings done in their names, the mere suggestion that he had bargained for the presidency made him suspect in many people's eyes. If Tilden was no better than Hayes, then Hayes was no worse than Tilden. The groundswell of sympathy for Tilden in the wake of the 1876 election subsided for good after the revelation of the Cipher Telegrams, and the once loud chorus of catcalls denouncing "His Fraudulency, Rutherfraud B. Hayes" dwindled away to a dissatisfied grumble. Once again, the fabled Hayes luck had won out.

Given the criticism Hayes endured for refusing to keep federal troops stationed in in the South, it was more than a little ironic that the most sensational event of his presidency involved the use of government troops in the North to put down the great railroad strike of 1877. Confronted by a rapidly spreading strike that threatened to stop train traffic throughout the Northeast and Midwest, and recalling the bloody Paris Commune six years earlier that had given rise to a new political epithet, *communism*, Hayes sent U.S. Army troops into West Virginia, Maryland, Pennsylvania, Illinois, New York, and Missouri to help local police and state militia restore the peace. In the end, between one hundred and two hundred people were killed and another one thousand injured, but the railroad bosses, including Hayes's old friend Thomas Scott, were saved from ruin. The widespread support for Hayes's strike-breaking was too much for the normally tight-lipped Grant to bear. "During my two terms of office," he said, "the whole Democratic press, and the morbidly honest and 'reformatory' portion of the Republican press, thought it horrible to keep U.S. troops stationed in the southern states, and when they were called upon to protect the lives of negroes—as much citizens under the Constitution as if their skins were white—the country was scarcely large enough to hold the sound of indignation belched forth by them for some years. Now, however, there is no hesitation about exhausting the whole power of the government to suppress a strike on the slightest intimation that danger threatens."

Grant's implicit criticism notwithstanding, Hayes left office in 1881 as a relatively popular president, particularly considering the way he had entered the White House four years earlier. His teetotaling wife, dubbed "Lemonade Lucy" by the national press for her ban on alcohol at White House functions, probably rivaled him in popularity. Capital wits may have joked good-naturedly about formal state dinners where "the water flowed like wine," but her pleasant face and winning disposition made Mrs. Hayes a positive asset to her more solemn husband.

Hayes's mild attempts to institute civil service reform, although they failed to win a majority in Congress, were also popular with the millions of American voters who in 1876 had overwhelmingly endorsed some type of political reform; and his unexceptionable private life proved a much-needed change from the noxious scandals of the Grant administration. When Hayes entered retirement in 1881—he would live until 1893—one Democratic constituent joked to Delaware senator Thomas Bayard that "he has done so well that I sometimes almost wish he had been elected."

THE HISTORICAL LEGACY of Samuel Tilden is more elusive. Once numbered among the most famous politicians of his age, Tilden today is virtually unknown to the general public, and he rarely receives more than a passing mention in the standard academic surveys of the era. In a way, he had begun the reductive process himself, soon after he awoke on November 8, 1876, to find that it was not enough to have won the election by more than 260,000 votes—one had to win the grimy post-election scramble as well. Unwilling to bargain for the presidency, and unable to muster the moral and physical energy needed to take charge of the struggle and lead his disorganized supporters in Congress, Tilden reacted the way most people react under stress: he reverted to type. While Rutherford B. Hayes was subtly but industriously directing the various efforts to install him as president—consulting with party leaders, meeting with southern spokesmen, keeping close tabs on his surrogates in Washington—Tilden was poring over his dusty law books in the privacy of his New York City mansion. A brilliant lawyer, he produced in time a brilliant legal brief, one that might have persuaded any court of law to rule in his favor on the facts of the case. In his own mind, at least, he had done all he could do to defend his rights.

Unfortunately for Tilden and for the millions of humble working men across the country who had voted for him, the presidency is primarily a political position, even if it is also a legal one. When Congress was unable to decide legally who deserved the disputed electoral votes, it acted politically to decide the question, and Tilden knew at once that he had been beaten. With little trust in the wisdom or courage of Democratic leaders in Washington, he increasingly withdrew from the post-election struggle. Able enough politically to rise to the top of New York politics and easily capture the Democratic presidential nomination, Tilden was either unwilling or unable to delegate political responsibilities to others. In the end, his presidential aspirations foundered amid a dismaying tangle of misunderstandings, miscommunications, and fatally crossed purposes. To his credit, he refused to blame others for his defeat, even staying on good terms with his ill-starred campaign chairman, Abram Hewitt, whom more than a few of their fellow Democrats did, indeed, blame for Tilden's loss. A realist and a patriot, he stoically played the hand that fate had dealt him, but he refused to draw out the game indefinitely. When the time came, he walked away from the table with grace and dignity, remarking with some relief, "I can retire to private life with the consciousness that I shall receive from posterity the credit of having been elected to the highest position in the gift of the people without any of the cares and responsibilities of the office."

What sort of president Tilden might have made, and how his policies might have differed from those of Hayes, is purely a matter of speculation. Like Hayes, he would have removed the troops from the South and recognized the Democratic governors of Louisiana and South Carolina. (Had he embraced their candidacies wholeheartedly from the start, rather than shying away from their support for fear of appearing too much like a copperhead, he—and they—probably would have avoided the whole post-election imbroglio in the first place.) He also would have insisted on the continued protection of blacks' civil rights, and his personal commitment to honest government might have served to moderate the most blatant political abuses of the new southern regimes. Still, it is doubtful that Tilden, a budget-minded northerner, would have had much more influence over the South than Hayes had, at least at first, when southerners were still counting on Hayes's support for increased patronage positions and a new railroad link to the West. (Once in office, Hayes quickly withdrew his support of the Texas and Pacific Railway.) And without the residual threat, weak though it was, of a Republican president deciding at some future date to send federal troops back into the region, Tilden might have had even less influence on southern affairs than Hayes did. At any rate, given the prevailing temper of the times, the political future of black southerners would have remained bleak, regardless of who was sitting in the White House.

In the area of governmental reforms, it is entirely possible that Tilden, a proven reformer and a much superior bureaucrat to Hayes, would have enacted more sweeping and effective changes in the federal government. To begin with, he would have had a working majority in the House of Representatives, and he probably would have avoided the politically damaging fight that Hayes endured with fellow Republican Roscoe Conkling in the Senate over the control of patronage positions in New York state. Given the moral mandate for change that Tilden's election would have carried with it, the "general reform of administration" that he envisioned might well have ensued, and a merit-based civil service might have been instituted several years before the Pendleton Act mandated such a change in the wake of President James A. Garfield's assassination by a deranged office-seeker in 1881.

In his handling of the economy, Tilden, like Hayes, would have supported the Resumption of Specie Act of 1879 that called for the gold-based redemption of all existing greenbacks by the federal government. Both men were hard-money advocates, and Tilden, too, would probably have vetoed the Bland-Allison Act of 1878, which required the government to mint millions of dollars' worth of silver to help alleviate the mountains of debt faced by farmers and small business owners. At the same time, Tilden was vigorously committed to frugality in government, and given the 1876 Democratic platform's opposition to "the profligate waste of public lands," it is likely that he would have cut back on the unrestrained granting of public land to already bloated railroad companies. Whether he would have been able to avert, through consultation and conciliation, the great railroad strike of 1877, it is impossible to say. Tilden had much closer ties, personally and professionally, to the leading railroad magnates than Hayes had—he had made his fortune in railroad speculation—and he might have been able to convince them not to reduce their workers' salaries so drastically in the first place. But it is also unlikely that Tilden, as president, would have sent federal troops into sovereign northern states to gun down strikers who were, after all, overwhelmingly Democratic in their politics.

However they might have compared as presidents, the one major advantage that Tilden would have enjoyed over Hayes—and it would have been a crucial distinction—was in the perceived legitimacy of his claim to office. Without the election-night interference of a few unregenerate Republicans and the subsequent actions of partisan returning boards in the three disputed southern states, Tilden would have assumed the presidency with a clear majority of both the popular and electoral votes and a broad base of intersectional support. The manifest desire of the American public for political reform, embodied in the person of the country's best-known reformer, might well have led to a restoration of the people's badly damaged trust in government, something that orators had called for at wearying length throughout the tumultuous centennial year. Instead, at an immeasurable cost to public confidence and civic morale, the nation got a personally decent but fatally compromised president, an unremarkable career politician who, as the popular if somewhat inaccurate joke then had it, "came in by a majority of one and goes out by unanimous consent." By any reasonably impartial judgment, that hardly seems like a fair exchange.

THE BLATANT MANNER in which he was denied the presidency made Tilden a formidable front-runner for the same office four years later. Even with the revelation of the Cipher Telegrams and the concomitant damage to his previously unsullied reputation, the Democratic party's 1880 presidential nomination was still Tilden's for the asking. But the physical, mental, and emotional strain of the 1876 campaign had exacted a heavy toll on the governor's health, and at the age of sixty-six he was now a prematurely old man. The certainty of another unrelenting Republican assault on his personal morals and private life, together with the lingering aftereffects of the stroke he had suffered five years earlier, compelled Tilden to forgo the race. When Republican congressman James A. Garfield, one of the visiting statesmen to Louisiana in 1876, defeated Democratic nominee Winfield Scott Hancock by less than one tenth of one percent of the popular vote, it was widely believed by both sides that Tilden would have won the election easily.

Four years later, in 1884, many Democrats again clamored for Tilden to run for president, but his physical infirmities were so pronounced that he reluctantly withdrew from the race in favor of New York governor Grover Cleveland, whose subsequent victory over Republican senator James G. Blaine afforded Tilden and his loyalists a long-deferred triumph, if only by proxy, over the shopworn forces of the shredded ballot and the bloody shirt.

Two years later, Tilden died. After what amounted almost to a state funeral at his country estate in Yonkers, New York, the old campaigner was laid to rest in the family plot in New Lebanon, the tiny upstate village where he had learned the art of politics at his father's general store. Those lessons, together with a brilliant mind and a true reformer's heart, had carried him ultimately to the gates of the White House, where the reins of power were snatched from his grasp at the very moment of triumph. If he was embittered by his remarkable experience, unique in the annals of American politics—a virtual coup d'etat deposed him before he had even taken office—Tilden never showed it by word or deed. He remained, to the end, a committed patriot. In one of his few public appearances after the election, at the Manhattan Club in June 1877, at a testimonial dinner for his former running mate, Thomas Hendricks, he spoke less of heartache than of hope. "Everybody knows that, after the recent election, the men who were elected by the people were counted out; and the men who were not elected were counted in and seated," Tilden said. "If my voice could reach throughout the country and be heard in its remotest hamlet, I would say: Be of good cheer. The Republic will live. The institutions of our fathers are not to expire in shame. The sovereignty of the people shall be rescued from this peril and reestablished."

He took that faith with him to the grave. Inscribed on his headstone, above his name, is the poignant and pointed valediction: "I Still Trust the People."

NOTES

Prologue: Election Night, 1876

PAGE

7   *Tilden shared a quiet dinner:* Alexander Clarence Flick, *Samuel Jones Tilden: A Study in Political Sagacity* (New York: Dodd, Mead, 1939), p. 323.

8   *"The contest is close":* T. Harry Williams, ed., *Hayes: The Diary of a President, 1875–1881* (New York: David McKay, 1964), Nov. 1, 1876, pp. 45–46. Hereafter cited as *Diary.*

8   *"I shall find many things":* Claude Moore Fuess, *Carl Schurz, Reformer* (New York: Dodd, Mead, 1932), p. 229.

8   *"Democratic chances [are] the best":* Diary, Nov. 7, 1876, p. 47.

8   *"Tilden is really going":* Keith Ian Polakoff, *The Politics of Inertia: The Election of 1876 and the End of Reconstruction* (Baton Rouge: Louisiana State University Press, 1973), p. 198.

8   *"After sixteen long years":* Ibid.

8   *"contested result":* Diary, Oct. 22, Nov. 7, 1876, pp. 44–46.

9   *The small group of family and friends:* Diary, Nov. 11, 1876, pp. 47–48.

10   *"From that time I never":* Diary, Nov. 11, 1876, p. 48.

10   *"soon fell into a refreshing":* Diary, Nov. 11, 1876, p. 48.

10   *"Devil Dan" Sickles:* Edward Longacre, "Damnable Dan Sickles," *Civil War Times Illustrated* (May 1984), pp. 16–25. For a fuller account of the Key murder, see Nat Brandt, *The Congressman Who Got Away with Murder* (Syracuse: Syracuse University Press, 1991).

11   *"That looks like the election":* Jerome L. Sternstein, ed., "The Sickles Memorandum: Another Look at the Hayes-Tilden Election-Night Conspiracy," *Journal of Southern History* 32 (August 1966), pp. 342–57.

11   *"rouse the old Republican":* Ibid., p. 353.

11   *"a bloody shirt campaign":* J. Kilpatrick to R. B. Hayes, August 21, 1876,

in Rutherford B. Hayes Papers, Rutherford B. Hayes Presidential Center, Fremont, Ohio.

11 *"proceeded to take only"*: Sternstein, "Sickles Memorandum," p. 354.

11 *Returning to his home:* Ibid.

12 *"You will find them"*: Ibid.

12 *"After a careful scrutiny"*: Ibid.

12 *"With your state sure"*: Ibid., p. 355.

12 *"If you advise it"*: Ibid.

13 *The Democrats in question:* Mark D. Harmon, "The New York Times and the Theft of the 1876 Presidential Election," *Journal of American Culture* 10 (1987), pp. 35–41. For Barnum, see Flick, *Tilden,* p. 282.

14 *"Please give your estimate"*: Harmon, "The New York Times," p. 38.

14 *John C. Reid:* Curiously, most accounts have Reid being imprisoned at Libby Prison, but his file clearly states that he was held at Andersonville, Georgia, which makes more sense since he was captured outside Atlanta on August 27, 1864, while serving with Company E, 10th Ohio Cavalry. John C. Reid Military Service Records, National Archives. See also John C. Reid Pension Records, National Archives, File No. 655848.

14 *"not a pleasant or popular person"*: Charles J. Rosebault, *When Dana Was the Sun: A Story of Personal Journalism* (New York: R. M. McBride and Company, 1931), p. 218. See also Elmer Davis, *History of the New York Times, 1841–1951* (New York: J. Little & Ives, 1921), pp. 131–40.

14 *"A Doubtful Election"*: *New York Times,* November 8, 1876.

15 *Reid hurried off to Republican headquarters:* Reid's personal account of the night's adventures was published in the *New York Times,* June 11, June 15, 1887.

16 *"All right"*: Sternstein, "Sickles Memorandum," p. 356.

16 *"Damn the men"*: *New York Times,* June 11, 1887.

16 *William Chandler could speak:* For Chandler's background, see Leon Burr Richardson, *William E. Chandler, Republican* (New York: Dodd, Mead, 1940).

17 *"Look at this"*: *New York Times,* June 15, 1887.

Chapter One: American Mecca

19 *one fifth the entire population:* Robert W. Rydell, *All the World's a Fair: Visions of Empire at American International Expositions, 1876–1916* (Chicago: University of Chicago Press, 1984), p. 10.

20 *"an athlete of steel and iron"*: William Dean Howells, "A Sennight of the Centennial," *Atlantic Monthly* 38 (July 1876), pp. 93–107.

20   *"unstudied harmony of dissimilarity"*: John D. McCabe, *The Illustrated History of the Centennial Exhibition* (Philadelphia: National Publishing Company, 1876), p. 345.

20   *"a most offensively Frenchy negro"*: Howells, "Sennight of the Centennial," p. 93.

20   *a sort of adjunct fair*: McCabe, *Illustrated History*, pp. 302–15.

21   *"Dear Mother, Oh! Oh!!"*: Rydell, *All the World's a Fair*, p. 13.

21   *Whitman was thrilled*: Ibid., pp. 15–16.

21   *A bill releasing $1.5 million*: William P. Randel, *Centennial: American Life in 1876* (Philadelphia: Chilton Book Company, 1969), p. 246.

22   *"was the author, knowingly"*: David Saville Muzzey, *James G. Blaine: A Political Idol of Other Days* (New York: Dodd, Mead, 1934), p. 78.

22   *"most auspicious inception"*: Randel, *Centennial*, p. 241.

22   *"Some of us had kinsmen there"*: Lloyd Robinson, *The Stolen Election: Hayes Versus Tilden—1876* (New York: Doubleday, 1968), pp. 53–54.

22   *"What Wirz would not say"*: Randel, *Centennial*, p. 244.

23   *mortality rate for prisoners*: James M. McPherson, *Battle Cry of Freedom: The Civil War Era* (New York: Oxford University Press, 1988), p. 797.

23   *"tear[ing] away the plasters"*: Randel, *Centennial*, p. 243.

23   *"the honorable hyena from Maine"*: Ibid., p. 244.

23   *"very discouraging"*: Ibid., p. 187.

23   *"I am ready to strike hands"*: Dee Brown, *The Year of the Century: 1876* (New York: Scribner's, 1966), p. 22.

24   *"He read sulkily"*: *New York Sun*, May 11, 1876.

24   *"There more more groans"*: Randel, *Centennial*, p. 291.

24   *"neuralgia of the brain"*: Brown, *Year of the Century*, pp. 110–11.

24   *"How old the president looks!"*: Ibid., p. 111.

25   *"unwise, unpatriotic, and fraught"*: Paul Leland Haworth, *The Hayes-Tilden Disputed Election of 1876* (Cleveland: Burrows Brothers Company, 1906), p. 11.

25   *"Let no guilty man escape"*: William S. McFeely, *Grant: A Biography* (New York: W.W. Norton, 1981), p. 410. For Bristow, see Ross A. Webb, *Benjamin Helm Bristow: Border State Politician* (Lexington: University Press of Kentucky, 1969).

25   *the real-life Sylph*: Brown, *Year of the Century*, pp. 86–87.

25   *"the essence of grace"*: Ibid., p. 87.

26   *Grant had enjoyed*: McFeely, *Grant*, pp. 409–10.

26   *Sherman's personal recommendation*: Randel, *Centennial*, p. 208.

27   *regularly receiving kickbacks*: Brown, *Year of the Century*, pp. 97–107. See also McFeely, *Grant*, pp. 427–35.

27   *he tearfully persuaded Grant:* McFeely, *Grant,* pp. 433–35.

28   *"Bottom rail on top":* McPherson, *Battle Cry of Freedom,* p. 862.

29   *Lincoln in December 1863:* David Herbert Donald, *Lincoln* (New York: Touchstone, 1995), p. 471.

29   *"freed the slave and ignored":* Eric Foner, *Reconstruction: America's Unfinished Revolution, 1863–1877* (New York: Harper & Row, 1988), p. 36.

29   *"there is too much":* Paul Johnson, *A History of the American People* (New York: HarperCollins, 1998), p. 499.

30   *"The pretended state government":* Donald, *Lincoln,* p. 564.

30   *"punish and impoverish":* Foner, *Reconstruction,* p. 177.

30   *"like the Bourbons":* Ibid., p. 192.

30   *"peace, order, tranquility":* Brooks D. Simpson, *Let Us Have Peace: Ulysses S. Grant and the Politics of War and Reconstruction, 1861–1868* (Chapel Hill: University of North Carolina Press, 1991), p. 145.

31   *"be kept as near":* Hodding Carter, *The Angry Scar: The Story of Reconstruction* (New York: Doubleday, 1959), p. 136.

31   *"Call your old Master":* Thomas Wagstaff, "Call Your Old Master—'Master': Southern Political Leaders and Negro Labor During Presidential Reconstruction," *Labor History* 10 (Summer 1969), p. 324.

31   *"the application of morals":* David Herbert Donald, *Charles Sumner and the Rights of Man* (New York: Alfred A. Knopf, 1970), p. 271.

32   *the "possum policy":* Morton Keller, *Affairs of State: Public Life in Late Nineteenth Century America* (Cambridge: Harvard University Press, 1977), pp. 225–26.

32   *"in a position of political impotence":* Charles H. Coleman, *The Election of 1868: The Democratic Effort to Regain Control* (New York: Columbia University Press, 1933), p. 46.

33   *A careful count:* Allen W. Trelease, *White Terror: The Ku Klux Klan Conspiracy and Southern Reconstruction* (Baton Rouge: Louisiana State University Press, 1971), p. 117.

33   *"to defy the reconstructed":* Foner, *Reconstruction,* p. 444.

33   *"I consider a government":* Ibid., p. 443.

34   *Schurz . . . considered the new act "insane":* Ibid., p. 456.

34   *"clasp hands across the bloody chasm":* Paul F. Boller, Jr., *Presidential Campaigns* (New York: Oxford University Press, 1984), p. 129.

35   *"going to the dogs":* Ibid., p. 127.

35   *"Go vote to burn":* Foner, *Reconstruction,* p. 509.

36   *"I have been assailed":* Boller, *Presidential Campaigns,* p. 129.

36   *had broken party ranks:* Donald, *Charles Sumner,* pp. 547–55.

36   *"A white man's government":* Kenneth M. Stampp and Leon F. Litwack,

eds., *Reconstruction: An Anthology of Revisionist Writings* (Baton Rouge: Louisiana State University Press, 1969), p. 477.

36   *"peaceably if we can":* Ibid., p. 481.

37   *"The truth is, our people":* Brooks D. Simpson, *The Reconstruction Presidents* (Lawrence: University Press of Kansas, 1998), p. 177.

37   *"a first-class cuss":* Ibid., p. 172.

38   *"The muddle down there":* William Gillette, *Retreat from Reconstruction, 1869–1879* (Baton Rouge: Louisiana State University, Press, 1979), p. 107.

39   *"to suspend the what-do-you-call-it":* Richard O'Connor, *Sheridan the Inevitable* (Indianapolis: Bobbs-Merrill, 1953), p. 330. For a full account of Sheridan's actions, see Roy Morris, Jr., *Sheridan: The Life and Wars of General Phil Sheridan* (New York: Crown, 1992), pp. 349–54.

39   *"riding rough-shod":* Paul Andrew Hutton, *Phil Sheridan and His Army* (Lincoln: University of Nebraska Press, 1985), p. 268.

39   *"so appalling that every American":* Simpson, *Reconstruction Presidents,* p. 177.

39   *"tear off his epaulets":* O'Connor, *Sheridan the Inevitable,* p. 330.

39   *"that a very able graduate":* Joseph G. Dawson III, *Army Generals and Reconstruction: Lousiana, 1862–1877* (Baton Rouge: Louisiana State University Press, 1982), p. 209.

40   *Democratic newspapers were less subdued:* Hutton, *Phil Sheridan,* pp. 267–68.

40   *"no desire to have United States troops":* McFeely, *Grant,* p. 418.

40   *"unjust, illegal, and arbitrary":* James T. Otten, "The Wheeler Adjustment in Louisiana: National Republicans Begin to Reappraise Their Reconstruction Policy," *Louisiana History* 13 (Fall 1972), pp. 349–67.

41   *"high-handed acts":* Gillette, *Retreat from Reconstruction,* p. 126.

41   *"were a close corporation":* Otto H. Olsen, ed., *Reconstruction and Redemption in the South* (Baton Rouge: Louisiana State University Press, 1980), p. 90.

41   *"The carpetbagger represents":* George C. Rable, *But There Was No Peace: The Role of Violence in the Politics of Reconstruction* (Athens: University of Georgia Press, 1984), p. 144.

42   *"somewhat perplexed to know":* Gillette, *Retreat from Reconstruction,* p. 157.

42   *"No matter if they":* Stampp and Litwack, *Reconstruction,* p. 490.

42   *"a revolution has taken place":* Richard Nelson Current, *Those Terrible Carpetbaggers* (New York: Oxford University Press, 1988), p. 323.

43   *"I am fighting for the Negro":* Gillette, *Retreat from Reconstruction,* p. 164.

43   *According to Lynch:* Ibid., p. 159.

43 *"I was sacrificed":* Ibid.

43 *"Nothing is charged":* Current, *Those Terrible Carpetbaggers,* p. 324.

44 *"My explanation may seem":* Ibid., p. 414.

Chapter Two: A Third-rate Nonentity

PAGE

46 *a self-described "meeting of notables":* Polakoff, *Politics of Inertia,* p. 40.

46 *the brainchild of Henry Adams:* Edward Chalfant, *Better in Darkness: A Biography of Henry Adams, His Second Life, 1862–1891* (New York: Archon Books, 1994), p. 314.

47 *"Nothing is more certain":* J. C. Levenson, ed., *The Letters of Henry Adams,* vol. 2 (Cambridge: Harvard University Press, 1982), p. 250.

47 *he changed the proposed time:* Chalfant, *Better in Darkness,* p. 319.

47 *"to consider what could be done":* Brown, *Year of the Century,* p. 203.

48 *"your name will not be trifled":* Polakoff, *Politics of Inertia,* pp. 41–42.

48 *"give us any sort":* Chalfant, *Better in Darkness,* p. 316.

48 *"distracted, disavowed and thwarted":* John A. Garraty, *Henry Cabot Lodge: A Biography* (New York: Alfred A. Knopf, 1953), p. 43.

48 *"the approach has been fairly made":* Ibid.

48 *the reformers might have to return:* Chalfant, *Better in Darkness,* p. 319.

48 *Adams did not see the wisdom:* Polakoff, *Politics of Inertia,* p. 40.

48 *"that lonely political Selkirk":* Brooks D. Simpson, *The Political Education of Henry Adams* (Columbia: University of South Carolina Press, 1996), p. 92.

49 *"annually returning periodical demand":* Martin B. Duberman, *Charles Francis Adams: 1807–1886* (Boston: Houghton Mifflin, 1961), p. 391.

49 *"too much a wire puller":* John G. Sproat, *"The Best Men": Liberal Reformers in the Gilded Age* (New York: Oxford University Press, 1968), p. 98.

49 *"however conspicuous his position":* Fuess, *Carl Schurz,* p. 222.

50 *"men whose names ring":* Boston Evening Transcript, May 16, 1876.

50 *"reestablish the moral character":* Sproat, *"The Best Men,"* p. 92.

50 *"cut his and our throats":* Levenson, ed., *Letters of Henry Adams,* 2:262.

50 *"soreheads and college professors":* New York World, May 16, 1876.

50 *"Oh, they have reenacted":* Garraty, *Henry Cabot Lodge,* p. 47.

50 *"ancient mariners on the sea":* New York Herald, May 17, 1876.

50 *"Business yesterday":* New York Commercial Advertiser, May 17, 1876.

51 *"the saving element":* New York Tribune, May 17, 1876.

51 *"Had he been a woman":* Mark Wahlgren Summers, *Rum, Romanism, and Rebellion: The Making of a President, 1884* (Chapel Hill: University of North Carolina Press, 2000), p. 5.

51   *"a thief by instinct"*: Brown, *Year of the Century,* p. 199.

52   *The only thing he feared:* Muzzey, *James G. Blaine,* p. 109.

52   *The story of Blaine's alleged misdoings:* Polakoff, *Politics of Inertia,* pp. 43–49.

52   *"various channels in which"*: Summers, *Rum, Romanism, and Rebellion,* p. 62.

53   *a $64,000 "loan"*: Ibid.

53   *"open as the day"*: Muzzey, *James G. Blaine,* p. 86.

53   *"who were from the South"*: Ibid., p. 93. For Hunton, see George R. Stewart, *Pickett's Charge* (Boston: Houghton Mifflin, 1959), pp. 169, 186. For Ashe, see Terry L. Seip, *The South Returns to Congress: Men, Economic Measures, and Intersectional Relationships, 1868–1879* (Baton Rouge: Louisiana State University Press, 1983), pp. 35, 46.

54   *His name was James Mulligan:* Muzzey, *James G. Blaine,* pp. 89–92.

54   *"Move an adjournment"*: Ibid., p. 90.

54   *"asked me if I would"*: Ibid., p. 91.

54   *"no more connection"*: Ibid., pp. 92–93.

54   *"I am not afraid to show"*: Ibid., p. 94.

55   *"one of the most extraordinary"*: Brown, *Year of the Century,* pp. 204–5.

55   *"I have never witnessed"*: Herbert Eaton, *Presidential Timber* (New York: Free Press, 1964), p. 49.

55   *"Your friend Blaine"*: Randel, *Centennial,* p. 219.

55   *"How splendidly Mr. Blaine"*: Muzzey, *James G. Blaine,* p. 98.

55   *"You have macerated these scamps"*: Ibid.

55   *Blaine attributed:* Polakoff, *Politics of Inertia,* p. 48.

55   *another round of histrionics:* Muzzey, *James G. Blaine,* pp. 99–100.

56   *"Blaine Feigns a Faint"*: *New York Sun,* June 12, 1876.

56   *"I have just read"*: Polakoff, *Politics of Inertia,* p. 53.

56   *Bristow went to call:* Webb, *Benjamin Helm Bristow,* pp. 239–41.

56   *"Mr. Bristow, you have got"*: Ibid., p. 241.

56   *"I am entirely convalescent"*: Muzzey, *James G. Blaine,* p. 100.

57   *Hayes entered the world:* Ari Hoogenboom, *Rutherford B. Hayes: Warrior and President* (Lawrence: University of Kansas Press, 1995), p. 7.

58   *He recovered quickly from his "prostrated" mind:* Ibid., pp. 60, 72.

58   *"a delightful little club"*: Ibid., p. 74.

58   *Hayes, still a neophyte:* Ibid., p. 105.

58   *"shrewd, able, and possess[ing]"*: R. B. Hayes to Sardis Birchard, Feb. 15, 1861, in Charles Richard Williams, ed., *The Diary and Letters of Rutherford Birchard Hayes: Nineteenth President of the United States,* 5 vols. (Columbus: Ohio State Archaeological and Historical Society, 1922–26), 2:5–6. Hereafter cited as *D&L.*

59 *"We are all for war"*: R. B. Hayes to S. Birchard, April 15, 1861, *D&L*, 2:9.

59 *"I would prefer to go"*: R. B. Hayes Diary, May 15, 1861, *D&L*, 2:14–15, 17.

59 *"What we don't know"*: R. B. Hayes to S. Birchard, June 14, 1861, *D&L*, 2:22, 24–25.

59 *Hayes enjoyed army life*: R. B. Hayes to Lucy Hayes, Aug. 30, 1861, *D&L*, 2:77.

60 *"Our men enjoyed it"*: R. B. Hayes to L. Hayes, July 27, 1861, *D&L*, 2:45–46.

60 *"Looking back upon it"*: Ambrose Bierce, *The Collected Works of Ambrose Bierce*, 12 vols. (New York: Neale Publishing Company, 1909–1912), 1:225–27.

60 *a fellow soldier named Abbott*: Ibid., 1:228–29.

60 *Hayes was seriously wounded*: Hoogenboom, *Rutherford B. Hayes*, pp. 146–49.

61 *nearly spent Rebel bullet*: R. B. Hayes to L. Hayes, Oct. 21, 1864, *D&L*, 2:527.

61 *"We'll whip 'em yet"*: Hoogenboom, *Rutherford B. Hayes*, p. 177.

61 *"utterly ruined Early"*: R. B. Hayes to S. Birchard, Oct. 21, 1864, *D&L*, 2:529.

61 *"An officer fit for duty"*: R. B. Hayes to William Henry Smith, Aug. 24, 1864, *D&L*, 2:493.

61 *"My real share of merit"*: R. B. Hayes to L. Hayes, Oct. 21, 1864, in Hayes Letters, Hayes Presidential Center.

61 *Hayes was promoted to brigadier general*: T. Harry Williams, *Hayes of the Twenty-third* (New York: Alfred A. Knopf, 1965), p. 315.

62 *"the best years of our lives"*: Ibid., pp. 5, 18.

62 *"The murderers must answer"*: David W. Blight, *Race and Reunion: The Civil War in American Memory* (Cambridge: Harvard University Press, 2001), p. 51.

62 *"perfect courage"*: R. B. Hayes Diary, Dec. 4, 1865, *D&L*, 3:7–8.

62 *"the Rebel states, having"*: R. B. Hayes to Manning F. Force, March 17, 1866, *D&L*, 3:20.

63 *"suffrage for all"*: R. B. Hayes Diary, May 15, 1866, *D&L*, 3:25.

63 *"We agree[d] to disregard"*: R. B. Hayes to Warner Bateman, Feb. 24, 1867, Hayes Papers, Hayes Presidential Center.

63 *"I went with the majority"*: R. B. Hayes to Warner Bateman, Feb. 9, 1867, Hayes Papers, Hayes Presidential Center.

63 *"The truth is"*: R. B. Hayes to L. Hayes, Jan. 10, 1866, *D&L*, 3:13.

64 *"beyond question"*: R. B. Hayes to S. Birchard, March 7, 1869, *D&L* 3:56.

64 *"If anybody could overthrow"*: R. B. Hayes to Unknown, Feb. 15, 1869, *D&L,* 3:59.

64 *"It strikes me as the pleasantest"*: R. B. Hayes to S. Birchard, Jan. 17, 1868, *D&L,* 3:51.

64 *"had both my respect"*: Hoogenboom, *Rutherford B. Hayes,* p. 220.

65 *"triumph of justice and humanity"*: R. B. Hayes to J. Irving Brooks, March 1, 1870, *D&L,* 3:90.

65 *"vote Republican almost solid"*: R. B. Hayes Diary, April 4, 1870, *D&L,* 3:94.

65 *"the final overthrow"*: R. B. Hayes to A. R. Keller, Jan. 25, 1870, Hayes Papers, Hayes Presidential Center.

65 *"a free man and jolly"*: R. B. Hayes to William Johnston, Jan. 9, 1872, *D&L,* 3:191.

65 *"After what I have been"*: R. B. Hayes Diary, March 26, 1873, *D&L,* 3:233.

66 *"now that I am in"*: R. B. Hayes to R. M. Stimson, June 6, 1875, Hayes Papers, Hayes Presidential Center.

66 *"The interesting point is"*: Diary, June 3, 1875, pp. 4–6.

66 *"We have here a large"*: William McKinley to R. B. Hayes, June 8, 1875, Hayes Papers, Hayes Presidential Center.

67 *"suggest[ed] that if elected"*: R. B. Hayes Diary, April 18, 1875, *D&L,* 3:269.

67 *"The election of a Democratic"*: John Sherman, *Recollections of Forty Years in the House, Senate and Cabinet: An Autobiography,* 2 vols. (Chicago: Werner Company 1895), 1:522–23.

67 *"He was a good soldier"*: Ibid., 1:523.

67 *"I would be glad"*: Diary, April 2, 1876, p. 18.

68 *"very few Republicans in Ohio"*: R. B. Hayes to Guy M. Bryan, April 23, 1876, Hayes Papers, Hayes Presidential Center.

68 *"I think I have a right"*: R. B. Hayes to Edwin Cowles, April 7, 1876, in *Diary,* pp. 19–20.

68 *"I don't meddle"*: Diary, April 11, 1876, p. 18.

68 *"It seems to me"*: Diary, March 21, 1876, p. 16.

69 *"an ambitious and disappointed"*: Eaton, *Presidential Timber,* p. 52.

69 *"There appears to be"*: Muzzey, *James G. Blaine,* p. 103.

69 *"a drunken Bristow man"*: Harry Barnard, *Rutherford B. Hayes and His America* (Indianapolis: Bobbs-Merrill, 1954), p. 292.

69 *"His one sole public act"*: Polakoff, *Politics of Inertia,* p. 23.

70 *"I will make the best fight"*: Webb, *Benjamin Helm Bristow,* p. 231.

70 *"Mr. Conkling is practically"*: *New York Times,* June 14, 1876.

70 *"an odious and intolerable"*: Muzzey, *James G. Blaine,* p. 104.

70   *"haughty disdain"*: Ibid., pp. 60–61.

70   *"No thank you"*: David M. Jordan, *Roscoe Conkling of New York: Voice in the Senate* (Ithaca: Cornell University Press, 1971), p. 421.

71   *"an unprincipled demagogue"*: Ibid., p. 230.

71   *"positively dreaded by the best"*: Ibid., p. 230n.

72   *a catchy campaign song*: Barnard, *Rutherford B. Hayes*, p. 289.

72   *"As to the candidate"*: Ibid., p. 127.

72   *"Do you mean to make"*: Gillette, *Retreat from Reconstruction*, p. 304.

73   *"plunge the dagger"*: Muzzey, *James G. Blaine*, p. 104.

73   *"in 1872"*: Brown, *Year of the Century*, pp. 148–49.

73   *"The women-folk are dabbling"*: *Chicago Tribune*, June 15, 1876.

73   *"Mrs. Spencer is a slightly"*: *New York Sun*, June 15, 1876.

74   *"Mrs. Spencer is a woman"*: *New York Herald*, June 15, 1876.

74   *"striped all over with treason"*: Muzzey, *James G. Blaine*, p. 104.

74   *"deprecate[d] all sectional feeling"*: Polakoff, *Politics of Inertia*, p. 60.

75   *"strike terror to the hearts"*: Muzzey, *James G. Blaine*, p. 106.

75   *"mode has been"*: Eaton, *Presidential Timber*, p. 59.

75   *"Let us understand"*: Muzzey, *James G. Blaine*, p. 107.

76   *"demand a man"*: Ibid., p. 110.

77   *"I am informed"*: Polakoff, *Politics of Inertia*, p. 62.

77   *reached out to Stanley Matthews*: Eaton, *Presidential Timber*, p. 55.

77   *"Governor Noyes instructs me"*: Barnard, *Rutherford B. Hayes*, p. 292.

78   *"the contingency of a union"*: *Diary*, May 19, 1876, p. 21.

78   *"There is a man"*: Charles Richard Williams, *The Life of Rutherford Birchard Hayes: Nineteenth President of the United States*. 2 vols. (Boston: Houghton Mifflin, 1914), 1:450n.

78   *"Anything like the scene"*: Ibid.

79   *Blaine's handlers made a crucial mistake*: Eaton, *Presidential Timber*, p. 57.

79   *"I must leave to the imagination"*: Williams, *Life of Hayes*, 1:451n.

80   *"Gen. Harlan rose"*: Loren P. Beth, *John Marshall Harlan: The Last Whig Justice* (Lexington: University Press of Kentucky, 1992), p. 104.

80   *"scene of wild and tumultuous applause"*: Ibid.

80   *"in the interests of amity"*: Muzzey, *James G. Blaine*, p. 112.

80   *"My hand [was] sore"*: R. B. Hayes to Birch A. Hayes, June 15, 1876, Hayes Papers, Hayes Presidential Center.

80   *"I am ashamed to say"*: R. B. Hayes to L. Hayes, Jan. 30, 1876, *D&L*, 3:300–301.

80   *"quite unmanned"*: *Diary*, June 18, 1876, pp. 26–27.

81   *"the cowardly good-will"*: Muzzey, *James G. Blaine*, p. 114.

81   *"To be candid"*: Ibid., p. 114n.

81 *"Men stood together"*: H. J. Eckenrode, *Rutherford B. Hayes, Statesman of Reunion* (New York: Dodd, Mead, 1930), p. 134.

81 *"the hounds pulled down"*: Eaton, *Presidential Timber*, p. 59.

82 *"It was of first importance"*: Williams, *Life of Hayes*, 1:453.

82 *"in no way conscious"*: R. B. Hayes to William Henry Smith, June 19, 1876, *D&L*, 3:326–27.

82 *"Be on your guard"*: R. B. Hayes to W. D. Bickham, May 23, 1876, Hayes Papers, Hayes Presidential Center.

82 *"The Republican Party"*: Brown, *Year of the Century*, p. 210.

82 *"I cannot help thinking"*: G. W. Curtis to R. B. Hayes, June 22, 1876, Hayes Papers, Hayes Presidential Center.

83 *"the ticket is an excellent one"*: Brown, *Year of the Century*, p. 210.

83 *"Governor Hayes"*: *New York Herald*, June 17, 1876.

83 *"Hayes has never stolen"*: Robinson, *Stolen Election*, p. 63.

83 *"a third-rate nonentity"*: Levenson, *Letters of Henry Adams*, 2:276.

83 *"Lincoln was nominated in 1860"*: Eaton, *Presidential Timber*, p. 51.

Chapter Three: Centennial Sam

PAGE

84 *Tilden was a congenital hypochondriac*: Flick, *Samuel Jones Tilden*, p. 6.

84 *"a weakened stomach"*: *New York Times*, April 17, 1927.

85 *"rowed to his object"*: Arthur M. Schlesinger, Jr., *The Age of Jackson* (Boston: Little, Brown, 1946), p. 49.

85 *"comical deference"*: John Bigelow, *The Life of Samuel J. Tilden*, 2 vols. (New York: Harper and Brothers, 1895), 1:19.

85 *"Day before yesterday morning"*: Ibid., 1:47.

86 *"in a spirited and eloquent manner"*: Ibid., 1:38.

86 *"his views [were] not substantially"*: Ibid., 1:308.

87 *"practically had no youth"*: Ibid., 1:18.

87 *Tilden sketched a strategy*: Flick, *Samuel Jones Tilden*, p. 36.

87 *"considering the game"*: S. J. Tilden to Elam Tilden, Dec. 12, 1836, Samuel J. Tilden Papers, New York Public Library.

88 *"wholly engrossed in practical politics"*: John Bigelow, *Retrospections of an Active Life*, 5 vols. (New York: Harper and Brothers, 1909), 1:55.

88 *"monarchy and a privileged nobility"*: *New York Evening Post*, Feb. 7, 1837.

88 *"Since Senator Tallmadge"*: Bigelow, *Life of Tilden*, 1:76.

88 *"rebuking a traitor"*: Ibid.

88 *"to appreciate the worth"*: Ibid., 1:93.

89 *"I never was more elated"*: R. B. Hayes to R. T. Russel, April 24, 1840, Hayes Papers, Hayes Presidential Center.

89 *No case was too small:* Flick, *Samuel Jones Tilden*, p. 53.

89 *"getting any business":* E. Tilden to S. J. Tilden, Feb. 7, 1842, Tilden Papers, New York Public Library.

89 *"I have nothing to do":* Flick, *Samuel Jones Tilden*, p. 54.

89 *"made a great sensation":* John Bigelow, ed., *Letters and Literary Memorials of Samuel J. Tilden*, 2 vols. (New York: Harper and Brothers, 1908), 1:9.

90 *In the official* Complaint Book: Flick, *Samuel Jones Tilden*, p. 58.

90 *"get[ting] away a day":* Ibid., p. 59.

90 *"a class of whom":* Ibid.

91 *"weak as dishwater":* Bigelow, *Letters*, 1:28.

91 *"a post of honor":* Bigelow, *Life of Tilden*, 1:110.

91 *"to help Mr. Wright":* Flick, *Samuel Jones Tilden*, p. 70.

91 *"It was an experiment":* N. J. Waterbury to Silas Wright, Aug. 30, 1846, Tilden Papers, New York Public Library.

92 *"sound political morals":* Flick, *Samuel Jones Tilden*, p. 76.

92 *"I have not been very fortunate":* Ibid., p. 110.

93 *basis for his growing personal fortune:* Ibid., p. 116.

93 *"My life has vibrated":* Bigelow, *Letters*, 1:72.

93 *"Miss Butler":* Flick, *Samuel Jones Tilden*, p. 107.

94 *"was happy to hear":* Martin Van Buren to S. J. Tilden, Aug. 3, 1855, Tilden Papers, New York Public Library.

94 *"I see that":* Martin Van Buren to S. J. Tilden, Dec. 19, 1856, Tilden Papers, New York Public Library.

94 *Tilden helped to write:* Bigelow, *Life of Tilden*, 1:118.

95 *"the greatest opprobrium of our age":* Flick, *Samuel Jones Tilden*, p. 85.

95 *"out of politics":* Ibid., p. 111.

95 *"by what process so clever":* Bigelow, *Letters*, 1:135.

95 *"Elect Lincoln, and we invite":* John Bigelow, ed., *The Writings and Speeches of Samuel J. Tilden*, 2 vols. (New York: Harper and Brothers, 1885), 1:289.

96 *"I would not have":* Bigelow, *Life of Tilden*, 1:153–54n.

96 *"a frank, genial":* Bigelow, *Letters*, 1:147.

96 *"I for one would resist":* Albany Argus, Feb. 2, 1861.

96 *twice he journeyed to Washington:* Flick, *Samuel Jones Tilden*, p. 133.

97 *"I beg you to remember":* Ibid.

97 *"arbitrary and unconstitutional":* Charles B. Murphy, "Samuel J. Tilden and the Civil War," *South Atlantic Quarterly* 33 (July 1934), pp. 266–67.

97 *In helping to defeat:* Flick, *Samuel Jones Tilden*, pp. 146–50.

98 *Tilden was closely involved:* Ibid., pp. 172–80.

98 *"I fear that when":* Ibid., p. 179.

98 *Tilden had been angling:* Ibid., p. 178.

98   *"Samuel Tilden wanted to be":* Howard K. Beale and Alan W. Brownsword, eds., *Diary of Gideon Welles,* 3 vols. (New York: W. W. Norton 1960), 3:446.

99   *William Marcy "Boss" Tweed:* For Tweed's remarkable career, see Alexander B. Callow, Jr., *The Tweed Ring* (New York: Oxford University Press, 1966).

99   *"What are you going":* Alexander B. Callow, Jr., "'What Are You Going to Do About It?': The Crusade Against the Tweed Ring," *New-York Historical Society Quarterly* 49 (April 1965), p. 118.

99   *Society of Saint Tammany:* "Tammany Hall: Inside the Corrupt 'Wigwam,'" www.mindspring.com, p. 1.

100 *the Tweed Ring stole:* Callow, "'What Are You Going to Do About It?'" p. 117.

100 *The scale of the frauds:* Mark Wahlgren Summers, *The Era of Good Stealings* (New York: Oxford University Press, 1993), p. 4.

100 *"If we get you":* Flick, *Samuel Jones Tilden,* p. 211.

101 *"I shall be busy":* John D. Bergamini, *The Hundredth Year: The United States in 1876* (New York: Putnam, 1976), p. 86.

101 *"I had no more knowledge":* Bigelow, *Writings,* 1:563.

101 *"We hope he has":* The Nation, Sept. 29, 1870.

102 *As early as December 1, 1869:* Flick, *Samuel Jones Tilden,* p. 202.

102 *"We must elect this ticket":* Ibid., p. 205.

102 *"Three years ago you started":* Roswell P. Flower to S. J. Tilden, June 17, 1870, Tilden Papers, New York Public Library.

102 *"What does old Sam Tilden want?":* Flick, *Samuel Jones Tilden,* p. 200.

102 *"Senator Tweed is in":* New York Times, Jan. 24, 1870.

103 *"would have more purity":* Bigelow, *Writings,* 1:568.

103 *"close his career in jail":* Flick, *Samuel Jones Tilden,* p. 207.

103 *"We have to face":* S. J. Tilden to Robert Minturn, Aug. 12, 1871, Tilden Papers, New York Public Library.

103 *Tilden allied himself:* Mark D. Hirsch, "Samuel J. Tilden: The Story of a Lost Opportunity," *American Historical Review* 56 (July 1951), pp. 795–99.

103 *"time to proclaim":* Bigelow, *Writings,* 1:484.

104 *But Tilden did more:* Ibid., 1:505.

104 *"The million of people":* Flick, *Samuel Jones Tilden,* p. 223.

104 *"I guess Tilden":* Ibid., p. 229.

105 *Tilden managed his own campaign:* Ibid., pp. 249–50.

105 *"a little in excess":* Allan Nevins, *Abram S. Hewitt* (New York: Harper and Brothers, 1935), pp. 297–98.

105 *"sinister, evil, and profligate":* Bigelow, *Letters,* 1:330. For a full account of Tilden's fight with the Canal Ring, see Thomas J. Archdeacon, "The Erie Canal Ring, Samuel J. Tilden, and the Democratic Party," *New York History* 59 (October 1978), pp. 408–29.

105 *"Would to God":* New York World, March 20, 1876.

105 *"illusion of a false prosperity":* Bigelow, *Life of Tilden,* 1:235.

106 *in his methodical way:* Flick, *Samuel Jones Tilden,* p. 281.

107 *"to the level of a White":* Cincinnati Enquirer, June 22, 1876.

107 *"Never a leading Southern man":* Henry Watterson, *"Marse Henry": An Autobiography,* 2 vols. (New York: George H. Doran Company, 1919), 1:288.

108 *hundreds of Democratic delegates:* Eaton, *Presidential Timber,* p. 60.

108 *the soft-money movement:* For the greenback movement, see Irwin Unger, *The Greenback Era: A Social and Political History of American Finance, 1865–1879* (Princeton: Princeton University Press, 1964).

110 *After Custer's death:* Robert M. Utley, *Cavalier in Buckskin: George Armstrong Custer and the Western Military Frontier* (Norman: University of Oklahoma Press, 1988), pp. 163–64.

110 *"A Dull Town Agog":* Chicago Tribune, June 23, 1876.

111 *"Honest John" Kelly:* Brown, *Year of the Century,* p. 220.

111 *"It is the issue":* Henry Watterson, "The Hayes-Tilden Contest for the Presidency," *Century Magazine* 86 (May 1913), pp. 10–20.

111 *Dorsheimer had the uncomfortable task:* Polakoff, *Politics of Inertia,* p. 88.

112 *"If I had had the triumph":* Eaton, *Presidential Timber,* p. 63.

112 *"In the good old days":* Brown, *Year of the Century,* pp. 149–51.

112 *"the substantial advances":* Ibid., p. 151.

113 *"cat calls, Indian yells":* Ibid., p. 222.

113 *"minatory language toward":* New York Herald, June 29, 1876.

113 *"Reform is necessary":* Kirk H. Porter and Donald Bruce Johnson, eds., *National Party Platforms, 1840–1960* (Urbana: University of Illinois Press, 1961), pp. 49–51.

113 *"the most elaborate paper":* James G. Blaine, *Twenty Years of Congress: From Lincoln to Garfield,* 2 vols. (Norwich, Conn.: Henry Bill Publishing Company, 1893), 2:578.

114 *"This announcement was like":* New York World, June 29, 1876.

114 *"The man of our party":* Thomas Bayard to Eppa Hunton, Thomas F. Bayard Papers, Library of Congress.

114 *"howling applause":* New York Herald, June 29, 1876.

115 *"The great issue upon":* Bigelow, *Writings,* 2:354.

115 *"Three cheers for Tilden!":* New York Herald, June 29, 1876.

116 *"was in constant fear"*: Bigelow, *Life of Tilden,* 1:310.

116 *"the wolf at the door"*: Ibid., 1:310–11.

117 *"with all its strength"*: Flick, *Samuel Jones Tilden,* pp. 91–92.

117 *"make my position"*: C. F. Adams to S. J. Tilden, July 10, 1876, Tilden Papers, New York Public Library.

117 *"A week ago"*: *New York Herald,* July 2, 1876.

Chapter Four: A Hot and Critical Contest

PAGE

119 *"must be part"*: Erik S. Lunde, "The Continued Search for National Unity: The United States Presidential Campaign of 1876," *Canadian Review of Studies in Nationalism* 15 (1980), p. 138.

120 *"The danger of giving"*: R. B. Hayes to James A. Garfield, Aug. 12, 1876, Hayes Papers, Hayes Presidential Center.

120 *"our strong ground is"*: R. B. Hayes to James G. Blaine, Sept. 14, 1876, Hayes Papers, Hayes Presidential Center.

120 *"If what [you advise]"*: R. B. Hayes to Carl Schurz, Sept. 6, 1876, Carl Schurz Papers, Library of Congress.

121 *"a plain departure from"*: R. B. Hayes to Richard C. McCormick, Sept. 8, 1876, Hayes Papers, Hayes Presidential Center.

121 *"That Zachariah Chandler is"*: Polakoff, *Politics of Inertia,* p. 99.

122 *"the enemy to be met"*: William Henry Smith to R. B. Hayes, July 1, 1876, Hayes Papers, Hayes Presidential Center.

122 *"We have a hard fight"*: Joseph Medill to R. B. Hayes, July 6, 1876, Hayes Papers, Hayes Presidential Center.

122 *"the most sagacious political"*: Whitelaw Reid to R. B. Hayes, July 21, 1876, Hayes Papers, Hayes Presidential Center.

122 *"a wonderful organizer"*: William Wheeler to R. B. Hayes, July 1, 1876, Hayes Papers, Hayes Presidential Center.

122 *"a hot and critical contest"*: R. B. Hayes to B. F. Potts, June 30, 1876, Hayes Papers, Hayes Presidential Center.

122 *As proof of Tilden's organizational skills:* Polakoff, *Politics of Inertia,* pp. 124–27.

123 *"To tell the truth"*: Abram Hewitt to Thomas Bayard, Sept. 20, 1876, Bayard Papers, Library of Congress.

124 *"to make a thorough"*: Polakoff, *Politics of Inertia,* pp. 129–30.

126 *"General Grant," complained:* McCabe, *Illustrated History,* p. 671.

126 *"The president's absence"*: *Atlantic Monthly* 38, July 1876, p. 91.

126 *the Fourth of July celebration:* Randel, *Centennial,* pp. 300–301.

127 *The biggest stir:* Brown, *Year of the Century,* pp. 165–66.

127 *Elsewhere across the nation:* Ibid., p. 169.

128 *in Hamburg, South Carolina:* Ibid., pp. 267–76.

129 *"a collision between the whites":* Ibid., p. 270.

130 *Butler . . . had already left the scene:* Ibid., p. 273.

130 *He appealed to Grant:* Richard Zuczek, "The Last Campaign of the Civil War: South Carolina and the Revolution of 1876," *Civil War History* 42 (March 1996), p. 20.

130 *"give every aid for which":* Ibid.

131 *pro-Hampton "rifle clubs":* Edmund L. Drago, *Hurrah for Hampton!: Black Red Shirts in South Carolina During Reconstruction* (Fayetteville: University of Arkansas Press, 1998), pp. 8–12.

131 *"All [the Republicans] want":* Gillette, *Retreat from Reconstruction,* p. 309.

131 *"I trust there will be":* Ibid.

131 *"It is not Tilden":* Brown, *Year of the Century,* p. 281.

132 *"extravagance and official incapacity":* Haworth, *The Hayes-Tilden Disputed Presidential Election,* p. 37.

132 *Within a week Grant dispatched:* Polakoff, *Politics of Inertia,* pp. 106–7.

132 *"would not be in their way":* R. B. Hayes to U.S. Grant, July 14, 1876, Hayes Papers, Hayes Presidential Center.

133 *"an intelligent and honest":* Polakoff, *Politics of Inertia,* p. 105.

133 *"The tone and grasp":* G. W. Curtis to R. B. Hayes, July 13, 1876, Hayes Papers, Hayes Presidential Center.

133 *"If it had been":* W. Reid to R. B. Hayes, July 21, 1876, Hayes Papers, Hayes Presidential Center.

133 *"a bold and honest letter":* R. B. Hayes to G. W. Curtis, July 10, 1876, Hayes Papers, Hayes Presidential Center.

134 *Tilden met privately:* Brown, *Year of the Century,* p. 230.

134 *"central reservoir":* Bigelow, *Writings,* 2:363–65.

134 *"Tilden writes like a schoolmaster":* New York *Herald,* Aug. 5, Aug. 19, 1876.

134 *"It was not intended":* Flick, *Samuel Jones Tilden,* p. 299.

134 *Tilden called for a systematic reform:* Bigelow, *Writings,* 2:359–73.

135 *"the systematic and insupportable":* Ibid., 2:361–62.

135 *"Niggers reformed at Hamburg, S.C.":* *Harper's Weekly,* Aug. 12, 1876.

135 *"If by trading him":* Gillette, *Retreat from Reconstruction,* p. 314.

136 *"Your letter gives general satisfaction":* Flick, *Samuel Jones Tilden,* pp. 298–99.

136 *"A flat and tame campaign":* New York *Herald,* Aug. 19, 1876.

136 *"No one remembered":* New York *Herald,* Aug. 26, 1876.

136 *"No ingenuity of interviewers":* *The Nation,* Feb. 1, 1977.

136 *"There was enough of Lincoln":* Roy Morris, Jr., *Ambrose Bierce: Alone in Bad Company* (New York: Crown, 1995), p. 161.

137 *"Be careful not to commit"*: R. B. Hayes to W. D. Howells, Aug. 24, 1876, Hayes Papers, Hayes Presidential Center.

137 *"Governor Hayes desires me"*: Alfred E. Lee to L. S. Tyler, July 10, 1876, Hayes Papers, Hayes Presidential Center.

137 *"Is Mr. Tilden a Perjurer?"* *New York Times*, Aug. 23, 1876.

137 *Tilden was furious*: Polakoff, *Politics of Inertia*, p. 116.

138 *B. E. Buckman*: Flick, *Samuel Jones Tilden*, pp. 312–13.

138 *"an ugly flaw"*: Ibid., p. 311.

138 *"I cannot express to you"*: Samuel Barlow to Abram Hewitt, Sept. 12, 1876, Samuel L. M. Barlow Papers, Library of Congress.

138 *"sacrifice personal feeling and delicacy"*: W. C. Whitney to S. J. Tilden, Sept. 5, 1876, Tilden Papers, New York Public Library.

138 *"worried the governor until"*: Polakoff, *Politics of Inertia*, pp. 117–18.

139 *"complete and satisfactory"*: *Chicago Daily News*, Sept. 23,1876.

139 *Bryant denounced the* Times: Flick, *Samuel Jones Tilden*, p. 311.

139 *"as full as men of his class"*: *The Nation*, Oct. 5, 1876.

139 *"What is there in the charge"*: R. B. Hayes to G. W. Curtis, Sept. 4, 1876, Hayes Papers, Hayes Presidential Center.

139 *"As an offset to what"*: *Diary*, Sept. 14, 1876, p. 35.

139 *Halstead and James M. Comly dissuaded*: Polakoff, *Politics of Inertia*, p. 119.

139 *J. S. Douglas, sent him*: Flick, *Samuel Jones Tilden*, p. 314.

140 *"every day and all day"*: Arthur M. Schlesinger, Jr., ed., *History of American Presidential Elections, 1789–1968*, 2 vols. (New York: Chelsea House, 1971), 2: 1402.

140 *"is weazened, and shrimpled"*: *Chicago Tribune*, Aug. 3, 1876.

140 *"All sorts of bad characters"*: *The Nation*, Feb. 1, 1877.

141 *"I am opposed"*: David A. Anderson, *Robert Ingersoll* (New York: Twayne, 1972), pp. 66–67.

142 *So many different women*: Bergamini, *Hundredth Year*, pp. 242–43.

142 *"the humblest member"*: Brown, *Year of the Century*, pp. 247–49.

143 *"somebody should have led him"*: Bergamini, *Hundredth Year*, p. 277.

143 *"civil service reform in a nutshell"*: Randel, *Centennial*, p. 225.

143 *"is as bound to go"*: Ibid.

143 *"raising the Tilden flag"*: Boller, *Presidential Campaigns*, 139.

144 *"Rally agin hard money"*: Ibid., p. 242.

144 *"The word 'reform'"*: Bigelow, *Letters*, 2:470.

144 *Smith warned him*: Hoogenboom, *Rutherford B. Hayes*, p. 268.

144 *"The K.N. [Know Nothing] charges"*: R. B. Hayes to W. H. Smith, Oct. 20, 1876, Hayes Papers, Hayes Presidential Center.

145 *James LeRoy claimed*: Polakoff, *Politics of Inertia*, pp. 119–20.

145 *"Unless I am very much mistaken"*: Sproat, *"The Best Men,"* p. 98.

145 *"faithful though uninfluential"*: Ibid., p. 102.

146 *"Are you for the Rebellion"*: *Diary*, Sept. 18, 1876, pp. 37–38.

146 *they relied on unsubtle economic suasion*: Jerrell H. Shofner, "Fraud and Intimidation in the Florida Election of 1876," *Florida Historical Quarterly* 42 (April 1964), p. 324.

147 *"to give the first preference"*: Ibid.

147 *Jacksonville, Pensacola and Mobile Railroad*: Ibid.

147 *an armed group of white men*: Ibid., p. 323.

147 *"We have come, sir"*: Ibid., p. 325.

147 *Florida Republicans relied*: Ibid., pp. 322–24.

148 *"as henceforth I shall be"*: Garnie W. McGinty, *Louisiana Redeemed* (New Orleans: Pelican Publishing Company, 1941), pp. 36–37.

148 *"General, all what's left"*: Ibid., p. 41.

148 *"the most dangerous politician"*: Ella Lonn, *Reconstruction in Louisiana After 1868* (New York: Russell and Russell, 1918), p. 408.

148 *"the most complete"*: New Orleans Democrat, July 6, 1876.

149 *"$100,000,000 in gold"*: McGinty, *Louisiana Redeemed*, p. 25.

149 *black Louisianans later cited*: T. B. Tunnell, Jr., "The Negro, the Republican Party, and the Election of 1876 in Louisiana," *Louisiana History* 7 (Spring 1966), pp. 109–10.

149 *"The reason"*: Ibid., p. 108.

149 *"One thing was quite apparent"*: Ibid.

150 *"It would be suicide"*: Ibid., p. 114.

150 *"be careful to say"*: Lonn, *Reconstruction in Louisiana*, p. 423.

150 *John H. Dinkgrave*: Ibid., p. 432.

150 *"The war has begun"*: Ibid., p. 433.

150 *Republican supervisor James E. Anderson*: McGinty, *Louisiana Redeemed*, p. 48.

150 *Henry Pinkston, was brutally murdered*: Lonn, *Reconstruction in Louisiana*, pp. 433–35. See also Tunnell, "The Negro, the Republican Party, and the Election of 1876 in Louisiana," pp. 104–5n.

151 *"a put-up job"*: Lonn, *Reconstruction in Louisiana*, p. 435n.

151 *Mrs. Pinkston reported*: Ibid., pp. 433–34.

151 *Mrs. Pinkston's testimony*: Ibid., pp. 434–35.

151 *29,000 advertising flyers*: Ibid., p. 429.

152 *"The only way to bring prosperity"*: Hampton J. Jarrell, *Wade Hampton and the Negro: The Road Not Taken* (Columbia: University of South Carolina Press, 1950), pp. 56–60.

152 *Hampton passed the word*: Francis Butler Simkins and Robert Hilliard

Woody, *South Carolina During Reconstruction* (Chapel Hill: University of North Carolina Press, 1932), pp. 509–12.

152 *eighteen separate black Democratic clubs:* Drago, *Hurrah for Hampton!,* p. 13.

153 *"by intimidation, purchase":* Zuczek, "The Last Campaign of the Civil War," p. 24.

153 *"never threaten a man":* Ibid.

153 *"were being put into execution":* Ibid.

154 *"force without violence":* Randel, *Centennial,* p. 254.

154 *in Charleston, a mob attacked:* Melinda Meek Hennessey, "Racial Violence During Reconstruction: The 1876 Riots in Charleston and Cainhoy," *South Carolina Historical Magazine* 86 (April 1985), pp. 104–5.

154 *Two weeks later, at Ellenton:* Rable, *But There Was No Peace,* pp. 173–74.

154 *The worst outbreak occurred:* Hennessey, "Racial Violence During Reconstruction," pp. 107–9.

155 *The newest state:* Polakoff, *Politics of Inertia,* pp. 149–50.

156 *James Butler Hickok:* For Hickok, see Richard O'Connor, *Wild Bill Hickok* (New York: Doubleday, 1959).

156 *Jesse James:* Dianne Stine Thomas, ed., *The Old West* (New York: Prentice Hall, 1990), p. 371.

156 *Buffalo Bill Cody:* Richard Slotkin, *Gunfighter Nation: The Myth of the Frontier in Twentieth-Century America* (New York: Atheneum, 1992), pp. 71–73.

157 *"my right arm is not wearied":* New York Tribune, Sept. 22, 1876.

158 *"Truth to say":* New York Times, Oct. 25, 1876.

158 *James D. "Blue Jeans" Williams:* Brown, *Year of the Century,* pp. 236–45.

159 *"October will not decide":* R. B. Hayes to W. H. Smith, Sept. 9, 1876, Hayes Papers, Hayes Presidential Center.

159 *Chandler advised Hayes:* W. E. Chandler to R. B. Hayes, Oct. 13, 1876, Hayes Papers, Hayes Presidential Center.

159 *"We should be prepared":* R. C. McCormick to R. B. Hayes, Oct. 16, 1876, Hayes Papers, Hayes Presidential Center.

159 *"The contest is now":* R. B. Hayes to R. C. McCormick, Oct. 14, 1876, Hayes Papers, Hayes Presidential Center.

160 *Grant dispatched hundreds:* Zuczek, "The Last Campaign of the Civil War," p. 26.

160 *"The soldiers who are now":* The Nation, Oct. 19, 1876.

160 *"the use of bayonets":* Robinson, *Stolen Election,* pp. 116–17.

160 *small army of federal marshals:* Hoogenboom, *Rutherford B. Hayes,* p. 272.

160 *John I. Davenport:* Polakoff, *Politics of Inertia,* pp. 168–71.

161 *"there will not be 100":* William K. Rogers to R. B. Hayes, Nov. 2, 1876, Hayes Papers, Hayes Presidential Center.

161   *Republicans revived old charges:* Polakoff, *Politics of Inertia,* p. 118.

161   *An enterprising Alabama newspaper: Auburn News and Democrat,* Nov. 2, 1876.

161   *"nothing in the world":* Nevins, *Abram S. Hewitt,* p. 314.

161   *"no rebel debt":* Bigelow, *Writings,* 1:382.

162   *"The calamities to individuals":* Ibid.

162   *Hayes . . . spent the day secluded: Diary,* Nov. 7, 1876, pp. 44–47.

162   *Tilden . . . went to the polls early:* Flick, *Samuel Jones Tilden,* p. 323.

Chapter Five: It Seemed As If the Dead Had Been Raised

PAGE

165   *"My election was due": New York World,* Nov. 9, 1876.

166   *"Troops and money":* Randel, *Centennial,* p. 227.

166   *"contented and cheerful": Diary,* Nov. 11, 1876, p. 48.

166   *"dispatches indicate New Jersey":* Polakoff, *Politics of Inertia,* pp. 204–5.

166   *"cheerful and philosophical":* R. B. Hayes to Rud Hayes, Nov. 8, 1876, Hayes Papers, Hayes Presidential Center.

167   *"The ordinary habitue": Ohio State Journal,* Nov. 9, 1876.

167   *"I don't care for myself": Cincinnati Times,* Nov. 9, 1876.

167   *"I think we are defeated": Diary,* Nov. 11, 1876, p. 47.

167   *"I seemed all day to walk":* Williams, *Life of Hayes,* 1:493n.

168   *"If you will keep order": Diary,* Nov. 11, 1876, pp. 48–49.

168   *"Dispatches received": New York Herald,* Nov. 9, 1876.

169   *Chandler followed up:* Brown, *Year of the Century,* p. 317.

169   *"When our people came around":* W. E. Chandler to R. B. Hayes, Nov. 9, 1876, Hayes Papers, Hayes Presidential Center.

170   *"The fiery zealots": New York Herald,* Nov. 11, 1876.

170   *"to protest against the frauds":* Nevins, *Abram S. Hewitt,* p. 324.

170   *"it would be safe to trust":* Ibid., p. 325.

170   *"the returns from Florida":* Watterson, "The Hayes-Tilden Contest," p. 13.

171   *"our friends in Louisiana":* Henry Watterson to S. J. Tilden, Nov. 9, 1876, Tilden Papers, New York Public Library.

171   *"Everything depends now upon": New York Herald,* Nov. 12, 1876.

171   *"expressed in the strongest":* Sherman, *Recollections,* 1:554.

171   *"The election has resulted": Diary,* Nov. 11, 1876, p. 47.

171   *"figures indicate that Florida": Diary,* Nov. 12, 1876, pp. 50–51.

172   *"whether he had been elected":* John Bigelow diary, Nov. 11, 1876, John Bigelow Papers, New York Public Library.

172   *"Another civil war may be":* Ibid.

172 *"You are the only man"*: Gideon J. Pillow to S. J. Tilden, Nov. 14, 1876, Tilden Papers, New York Public Library.

172 *"bloody revolution" and "liberties"*: Flick, *Samuel J. Tilden*, p. 331.

172 *"Only the most prompt"*: Polakoff, *Politics of Inertia*, p. 221.

172 *"Be satisfied with the reflection"*: *New York Herald*, Nov. 11, 1876.

172 *"He rides a waiting race"*: *New York Tribune*, Sep. 29, 1876.

172 *"wonderful self-control"*: *New York Herald*, Nov. 10, 1876.

173 *of war"*: Louis W. Koenig, "The Election That Got Away," *American Heritage* (October 1960), p. 107–8.

173 *Shadowy forces . . . organizing*: Flick, *Samuel Jones Tilden*, pp. 360–61.

173 *Union general George B. McClellan*: Polakoff, *Politics of Inertia*, pp. 206–7.

173 *Seven additional companies*: Brown, *Year of the Century*, p. 321.

174 *"We must protect"*: Ibid.

174 *"Instruct General [Christopher] Augur"*: Bigelow, *Life of Tilden*, 2:19.

174 *Hayes's sworn electors had carried the state*: Kenneth E. Davison, *The Presidency of Rutherford B. Hayes* (Westport, Conn.: Greenport Press, 1972), p. 28.

175 *Chamberlain was refusing*: Jarrell, *Wade Hampton and the Negro*, p. 89.

175 *The outcome of the election in Florida*: Flick, *Samuel Jones Tilden*, p. 344.

175 *Governor Marcellus Stearns charged*: Jerrell H. Shofner, *Nor Is It Over Yet: Florida in the Era of Reconstruction, 1863–1877* (Gainesville: University Presses of Florida, 1974), p. 316.

175 *the city was so quiet*: Jerrell H. Shofner, "Florida in the Balance: The Electoral Count of 1876," *Florida Historical Quarterly* 42 (April 1964), p. 124.

175 *squadrons of Republican and Democratic*: Shofner, *Nor Is It Over Yet*, p. 316.

176 *The canny Chandler also brought*: Richardson, *William E. Chandler*, p. 187.

176 *Tilden's electors had leads*: Lonn, *Reconstruction in Louisiana*, p. 460.

176 *Kellogg had set the stage*: Barnard, *Rutherford B. Hayes*, pp. 321–22.

176 *"the ablest politician"*: R. B. Hayes to Carl Schurz, Nov. 13, 1876, *D&L*, 3:378.

177 *"Within a week"*: Watterson, "The Hayes-Tilden Contest," p. 14.

177 *In South Carolina, the state board of canvassers*: Simkins and Woody, *South Carolina During Reconstruction*, p. 516.

177 *In Florida, the state canvassing board*: Richardson, *William E. Chandler*, p. 189.

177 *ensuring Cocke's unrelenting animosity*: Shofner, *Nor Is It Over Yet*, p. 319.

178 *Louisiana returning board*: McGinty, *Louisiana Redeemed*, pp. 55–56.

178 *the board chairman, Madison Wells*: Walter McG. Lowery, "The Political Career of James Madison Wells," *Louisiana Historical Quarterly* 31 (October 1948), pp. 995–1123.

178   *"a political trickster"*: Morris, *Sheridan*, p. 291.

178   *"All's well that ends Wells"*: Joe G. Taylor, *Louisiana Reconstructed, 1863–1877* (Baton Rouge: Louisiana State University Press, 1974), p. 140.

179   *Anderson . . . had used his legislative position*: Haworth, *The Hayes-Tilden Disputed Presidential Election*, p. 98.

179   *The two black members*: Ibid.

179   *"such indifference to the obligation"*: Cincinnati Enquirer, Nov. 18, 1876.

180   *One day earlier, in Charleston*: Henry T. Thompson, *Ousting the Carpetbagger from South Carolina* (Columbia: R. L. Bryan Company, 1927), pp. 133–34.

180   *The initial returns in South Carolina*: Simkins and Woody, *South Carolina During Reconstruction*, p. 514.

181   *"offering our people"*: Thompson, *Ousting the Carpetbagger from South Carolina*, p. 134.

181   *"visited this same precinct"*: Jarrell, *Wade Hampton and the Negro*, p. 94.

181   *"never witnessed a more"*: Ibid., p. 92.

181   *Captain James Stewart*: Ibid., p. 93.

181   *the canvassing board reconvened*: Simkins and Woody, *South Carolina During Reconstruction*, pp. 519–22.

182   *eight newly elected Democratic representatives*: Ibid., p. 523.

182   *the Democratic legislators returned*: Ibid., p. 524.

183   *John W. Watts*: Harold C. Dippre, "Corruption and the Disputed Election Vote of Oregon in the 1876 Election," *Oregon Historical Quarterly* 67 (September 1966), p. 259.

183   *"Upon careful investigation"*: Philip W. Kennedy, "Oregon and the Disputed Election of 1876," *Pacific Northwest Quarterly* 60 (July 1969), p. 137.

184   *"How any people could commit"*: James N. Tyner to James M. Comly, Nov. 14, 1876, Hayes Papers, Hayes Presidential Center.

184   *"If Tilden is president"*: Dippre, "Corruption and the Disputed Election Vote of Oregon," p. 269.

184   *Secret cipher telegrams*: Ibid., pp. 263–66.

184   *"decide every point . . . in favor"*: Flick, *Samuel Jones Tilden*, p. 349.

184   *Grover reasoned, any votes*: Kennedy, "Oregon and the Disputed Election of 1876," pp. 138–40.

185   *"without power or legal influence"*: Haworth, *The Hayes-Tilden Disputed Presidential Election*, p. 96.

185   *"I am convinced they will count"*: James McQuade to S. J. Tilden, Nov. 16, 1876, Tilden Papers, New York Public Library.

185   *"Well-organized plans supported"*: Flick, *Samuel Jones Tilden*, p. 339.

185 *"It is believed here"*: Polakoff, *Politics of Inertia*, p. 220.

186 *Wells explained the refusal*: Lonn, *Reconstruction in Louisiana*, p. 448.

186 *permitted the various registrars*: Bigelow, *Life of Tilden*, p. 38.

186 *"serve to inflame the public mind"*: Theodore Clarke Smith, *The Life and Letters of James Abram Garfield*, 2 vols. (New Haven: Yale University Press, 1925), 1:618.

186 *All the clerks were Republicans*: Lonn, *Reconstruction in Louisiana*, p. 446n.

187 *Under existing state law*: Haworth, *The Hayes-Tilden Disputed Presidential Election*, p. 102.

187 *"clerical errors"*: Bigelow, *Life of Tilden*, 2:41.

187 *a total of 157 subsequently testified*: Lonn, *Reconstruction in Louisiana*, p. 451.

187 *Mrs. Pinkston, borne*: Haworth, *The Hayes-Tilden Disputed Presidential Election*, p. 105.

187 *"embellish[ed] with details"*: Ibid., p. 108.

187 *reputed to have been a "good Negro"*: Ibid., p. 107.

188 *James E. Anderson testified*: Frank P. Vazzano, "The Louisiana Question Resurrected: The Potter Commission and the Election of 1876," *Louisiana History* 16 (Winter 1975), pp. 42–446.

188 *Sherman testified*: Ibid., p. 30.

188 *Anderson subsequently had managed to get*: Ibid., pp. 44–45.

188 *Hayes was sufficiently troubled*: Diary, June 2, 1878, pp. 143–44.

189 *"Two hundred and fifty thousand dollars"*: Watterson, "Marse Henry," 1:299.

189 *John T. Pickett*: Haworth, *The Hayes-Tilden Disputed Presidential Election*, pp. 111–12.

189 *"our right hand man"*: W. H. Smith to R. B. Hayes, Dec. 5, 1877, Hayes Papers, Hayes Presidential Center.

189 *"We are not to allow"*: Sherman, *Recollections*, 1:453.

189 *"Wells was a Union man"*: Polakoff, *Politics of Inertia*, pp. 212–13.

190 *"a graceless set of scamps"*: Smith, *Life and Letters*, 1:621.

190 *"My opinion of the Returning Board"*: Ibid., 1:622.

190 *"I will be able to draft"*: Ibid., 1:618.

190 *A careful comparison*: Bigelow, *Life of Tilden*, pp. 50–52.

190 *similar study of South Carolina's census figures*: Jarrell, *Wade Hampton and the Negro*, pp. 99–103.

190 *an earlier plan by the Republicans*: Bigelow, *Life of Tilden*, 2:49.

190 *One frequently cited example*: Tunnell, "The Negro, the Republican Party, and the Election of 1876 in Louisiana," p. 105n.

191 *The identities of many of the witnesses*: Lonn, *Reconstruction in Louisiana*, p. 452.

191 *prevent Tilden from claiming:* Haworth, *The Hayes-Tilden Disputed Presidential Election,* p. 113.

191 *"did not think it altogether wise":* Smith, *Life and Letters,* 1:622.

191 *"to resist the determined":* Ibid.

191 *"systematic intimidation":* New Orleans Republican, Dec. 4, 1876.

192 *In the allegedly bulldozed parishes:* Tunnell, "The Negro, the Republican Party, and the Election of 1876 in Louisiana," p. 115n.

192 *"arbitrary, unfair":* Chicago Times, Dec. 6, 1876.

192 *"be prepared":* W. E. Chandler to R. B. Hayes, Nov. 18, 1876, Hayes Papers, Hayes Presidential Center.

193 *The Democrats, by contrast:* Shofner, *Nor Is It Over Yet,* p. 318.

193 *a too-sweeping effort:* Shofner, "Florida in the Balance," p. 139.

193 *"irregular, false, or fraudulent":* Shofner, *Nor Is It Over Yet,* p. 316.

193 *sparsely populated Dade County:* Arva Moore Parks, "Miami in 1876," *Tequesta* 30 (1975), p. 4.

194 *A tactical mistake:* Shofner, *Nor Is It Over Yet,* pp. 320–21.

194 *A subsequent examination:* Shofner, "Florida in the Balance," p. 135.

194 *the ballot box in question:* Ibid., pp. 136–38.

194 *Noyes asked Dennis to testify:* Ibid., p. 137.

195 *Brooklyn-born General Francis Barlow:* Ibid., pp. 126–27.

195 *"not capable of a reasonable explanation":* Richardson, *William E. Chandler,* p. 192.

195 *"Cowgill . . . is an extraordinary":* S. B. Sherwin to W. E. Chandler, Dec. 14, 1876, Chandler Papers, Library of Congress.

195 *"I scarcely ever passed":* Lew Wallace, *An Autobiography,* 2 vols. (New York: Harper and Brothers, 1906), 2:901.

196 *"observance of legal forms":* Robert E. Morseberger and Katherine M. Morseberger, *Lew Wallace: Militant Romantic* (New York: McGraw-Hill, 1980), p. 249.

196 *Manton Marble and C. W. Woolley:* Shofner, "Florida in the Balance," pp. 138–39.

197 *"enormously wicked":* Richardson, *William E. Chandler,* p. 195.

197 *"The dark deed of infamy":* Atlanta Constitution, Dec. 6, 1876.

197 *Henry Grady:* Derrell Roberts, "Joseph E. Brown and the Florida Election of 1876," *Florida Historical Quarterly* 40 (June 1962), p. 220.

198 *a seriocomic charade:* Kennedy, "Oregon and the Disputed Election of 1876," pp. 138–39.

198 *"a lively happy little gathering":* Diary, Dec. 7–8, 1876, pp. 56–57.

198 *"I have no doubt":* R. B. Hayes to Carl Schurz, Dec. 6, 1876, *D&L,* 3:386.

199 *"Our presidential election":* Flick, *Samuel Jones Tilden,* p. 353.

Chapter Six: Eight Villains to Seven Patriots

PAGE

201   *Senate Republicans had taken steps:* Haworth, *The Hayes-Tilden Disputed Presidential Election,* pp. 178–87.

202   *"such a measure":* Polakoff, *Politics of Inertia,* pp. 269–70.

203   *Samuel Tilden devoted:* Bigelow, *Writings,* 2:384–452.

204   *"accomplished little of value":* Nevins, *Abram S. Hewitt,* p. 345.

204   *a Democratic congressman spent:* Ibid., p. 344.

205   *"Oh, Tilden won't do":* Ibid., p. 334.

205   *"I thought we were being robbed":* J. B. Gordon to Samuel Barlow, Jan. 2, 1877, Barlow Papers, Library of Congress.

205   *"intense quietude of our side":* Watterson, "The Hayes-Tilden Contest," p. 15.

206   *An increasingly exasperated Hewitt:* Nevins, *Abram S. Hewitt,* pp. 330–33.

206   *"When the time comes":* Polakoff, *Politics of Inertia,* p. 239.

206   *Not content to wait:* New York Herald, Dec. 14, 1876.

206   *"The Democrats are without":* Smith, *Life and Letters,* 1:624.

207   *"I fully expect to be inaugurated":* Randel, *Centennial,* p. 233.

207   *Hayes had met with one:* Polakoff, *Politics of Inertia,* p. 244.

207   *"If we felt that you":* Ibid.

207   *"carpetbag governments had not been":* C. Vann Woodward, *Reunion and Reaction: The Compromise of 1877 and the End of Reconstruction* (Boston: Little, Brown, 1951), p. 25.

207   *"meant all it said":* Diary, Dec. 1, 1876, pp. 52–53.

207   *The particulars of the meeting:* Cincinnati Enquirer, Dec. 2, 1876.

208   *"I am in intimate relations":* R. B. Bradford to S. J. Tilden, Dec. 18, 1876, Tilden Papers, New York Public Library.

208   *"the entire democracy of the South":* Flick, *Samuel Jones Tilden,* p. 339.

208   *A political gadfly:* Michael Les Benedict, "Southern Democrats in the Crisis of 1876–1877: A Reconsideration of *Reunion and Reaction,*" *Journal of Southern History* 46 (Nov. 1980), pp. 493–94.

209   *Kellar . . . hoped to checkmate:* For the inter-railroad infighting, see Woodward, *Reunion and Reaction,* pp. 68–100.

209   *"I am not a believer":* Diary, Jan. 3, 1877, D&L 3:399.

209   *"exceptionally liberal about":* R. B. Hayes to W. H. Smith, Dec. 24, 1876, D&L, 3:393.

209   *Conkling feared that Hayes:* Diary, Dec. 17, 1876, p. 58.

209   *"meant to act upon":* Bigelow, *Letters,* 2:491–92.

210   *"the friendship and support":* Diary, Dec. 17, 1876, p. 59.

210   *"I told him I was in no way"*: R. B. Hayes to John Sherman, Dec. 17, 1876, Hayes Papers, Hayes Presidential Center.

210   *"a political Hell Gate"*: Haworth, *The Hayes-Tilden Disputed Presidential Election*, p. 213.

210   *Ulysses S. Grant had also let it slip*: Nevins, *Abram S. Hewitt*, p. 339.

210   *"was in a very bad odor"*: Ibid.

211   *Comly met privately with Grant*: James M. Comly to R. B. Hayes, Jan. 8, 1877, Hayes Papers, Hayes Presidential Center.

211   *"They have no future"*: W. E. Chandler to R. B. Hayes, Jan. 13, 1877, Hayes Papers, Hayes Presidential Center.

211   *"to organize and unitize"*: J. M. Comly to R. B. Hayes, Jan. 8, 1877, Hayes Papers, Hayes Presidential Center.

212   *"I will do anything I can"*: Ibid.

212   *"had occasionally found"*: Ibid.

212   *"to confer with doubtful senators"*: Garfield diary, Jan. 17, 1877, James A. Garfield Papers, Library of Congress.

212   *"the anchor of our safety"*: George F. Edmunds to Carl Schurz, Dec. 23, 1876, Schurz Papers, Library of Congress.

212   *"We must look"*: Carl Schurz to R. B. Hayes, Dec. 4, 1876, Hayes Papers, Hayes Presidential Center.

212   *Hayes . . . ignored Schurz's recommendation*: Polakoff, *Politics of Inertia*, p. 267.

213   *Republicans on the committee wanted*: Ibid., pp. 270–72.

213   *Wild rumors persisted*: Brown, *Year of the Century*, pp. 328–30.

213   *Democratic Veteran Soldiers Association*: Haworth, *The Hayes-Tilden Disputed Presidential Election*, p. 188.

213   *"any demonstration"*: Ibid.

214   *"come fully armed"*: Watterson, "The Hayes-Tilden Contest," p. 17.

214   *"millions of men"*: *Indianapolis Journal*, Jan. 9, 1877.

214   *"It will not do to fight"*: Flick, *Samuel Jones Tilden*, p. 357.

214   *"invincible in peace"*: Woodward, *Reunion and Reaction*, p. 32.

215   *"we have got to see"*: Benedict, "Southern Democrats in the Crisis of 1876–1877," p. 503.

216   *"Is it not rather late"*: Nevins, *Abram S. Hewitt*, p. 352.

216   *"Why surrender now?"*: Ibid., p. 353.

216   *"I can't advise you to agree"*: Ibid., p. 354.

216   *"I am afraid"*: Ibid., p. 255.

217   *"The only effect"*: Ibid., pp. 358–59.

217   *"a surrender, at least"*: Diary, Jan. 21, 1877, pp. 69–70.

217   *"surrender of a certainty"*: Hoogenboom, *Rutherford B. Hayes*, p. 285.

217 *"the sentiment of the country"*: Carl Schurz to R. B. Hayes, Jan. 12, 1877, Hayes Papers, Hayes Presidential Center.

217 *"the appointment of the Commission"*: R. B. Hayes to Carl Schurz, Jan. 23, 1877, Schurz Papers, Library of Congress.

218 *The legislature. . . . chose Davis:* Polakoff, *Politics of Inertia*, pp. 280–83.

218 *Davis knew that he would inevitably alienate:* Ibid., p. 283.

218 *Joseph P. Bradley:* Woodward, *Reunion and Reaction*, p. 154. For *Cruikshank* decision, see Foner, *Reconstruction*, pp. 530–31.

219 *"entirely satisfactory"*: Nevins, *Abram S. Hewitt*, p. 368.

219 *While serving as a judge:* Woodward, *Reunion and Reaction*, pp. 157–58.

219 *"as safe as either of"*: W. E. Chandler to R. B. Hayes, Feb. 4, 1877, Hayes Papers, Hayes Presidential Center.

219 *"The bets are 5 to 1"*: Flick, *Samuel Jones Tilden*, p. 385.

219 *"the duties would be inconvenient"*: Polakoff, *Politics of Inertia*, p. 285.

220 *In front of the podium:* Haworth, *The Hayes-Tilden Disputed Presidential Election*, pp. 222–23.

220 *Associate Justice Nathan Clifford:* William A. DeGregorio, *The Complete Book of U.S. Presidents* (New York: Dembner Books, 1984), p. 169.

221 *"a sort of jugglery"*: Haworth, *The Hayes-Tilden Disputed Presidential Election*, p. 226.

221 *Piously decrying federal intrusion:* Ibid., pp. 227–31.

222 *"that the action of the Returning Boards"*: Nevins, *Abram S. Hewitt*, p. 370.

222 *"a screw loose somewhere"*: Haworth, *The Hayes-Tilden Disputed Presidential Election*, p. 259.

222 *"slight implication and vague conjecture"*: Jean Edward Smith, *John Marshall* (New York: Henry Holt, 1996), pp. 388–94.

222 *"The two houses of Congress"*: Jean Edward Smith, *Grant* (New York: Simon and Schuster, 2001), pp. 602–3.

223 *"eight villains to seven patriots"*: Bergamini, *The Hundredth Year*, p. 306.

223 *"in favor of counting"*: Nevins, *Abram S. Hewitt*, p. 371.

223 *"during the whole of that night"*: *New York Sun*, Aug. 4, 1877.

224 *in the judgment of English foreign minister:* McFeely, *Grant*, p. 347.

224 *"unexceptional"*: Ibid.

224 *he had somehow managed to deposit:* Ibid., p. 432.

224 *"a highly religious woman"*: Nevins, *Abram S. Hewitt*, p. 373.

224 *Bradley, for his part, stoutly denied:* Bigelow, *Letters*, 2:568–69.

224 *"as staunch a Republican"*: Perry Belmont, *An American Democrat: The Recollections of Perry Belmont* (New York: Columbia University Press, 1940), pp. 197–98.

225   *"the name of that man"*: Woodward, *Reunion and Reaction*, p. 162.

225   *Tilden told his friend John Bigelow*: Bigelow, *Retrospections*, 5:302.

225   *Hayes began drafting his inaugural address*: Hoogenboom, *Rutherford B. Hayes*, p. 287.

225   *Tilden began making plans*: Bigelow diary, Feb. 9, 1877, Bigelow Papers, Library of Congress.

226   *"there could be no doubt"*: Nevins, *Abram S. Hewitt*, p. 374.

226   *Conkling controlled enough votes*: Ibid., p. 377.

226   *Ferry improperly permitted Anderson*: Haworth, *The Hayes-Tilden Disputed Presidential Election*, pp. 115–17.

226   *"John Smith, bull-dozed governor"*: Ibid., pp. 238–39.

226   *"a day of the most nervous strain"*: Smith, *Life and Letters*, 1:640.

227   *furious cries of "Fraud!"*: Flick, *Samuel Jones Tilden*, p. 392.

227   *"in effect exalts fraud"*: Haworth, *The Hayes-Tilden Disputed Presidential Election*, p. 245.

227   *"Deep indeed is my sorrow"*: Ibid.

227   *Cox attempted to read a passage*: Ibid., p. 247.

227   *"It seems to me perfectly clear"*: Ibid., p. 248.

228   *"A good deal is said"*: Eckenrode, *Rutherford B. Hayes*, p. 215.

228   *"I would not consent"*: Flick, *Samuel Jones Tilden*, p. 392.

228   *"If you have anything to suggest"*: Ibid.

228   *"disposition to consult"*: Bigelow, *Retrospections*, 5:302.

229   *"After the electoral scheme"*: Flick, *Samuel Jones Tilden*, p. 379.

229   *Grover, they said, had acted improperly*: Haworth, *The Hayes-Tilden Disputed Presidential Election*, p. 256.

230   *House Speaker Samuel Randall suggested*: Polakoff, *Politics of Inertia*, pp. 304–5.

230   *"The Southern people who had agreed"*: Charles Foster to R. B. Hayes, Feb. 21, 1877, Hayes Papers, Hayes Presidential Center.

230   *"Representing as I do"*: Lonn, *Reconstruction in Louisiana*, pp. 506–7.

231   *an article appeared*: Barnard, *Rutherford B. Hayes*, p. 383.

231   *Garfield, for one, had heard rumors*: Smith, *Life and Letters*, 1:641.

232   *Burke . . . met privately with President Grant*: Woodward, *Reunion and Reaction*, pp. 194–95.

232   *"unequivocably that he is satisfied"*: Ibid., p. 195.

232   *Sherman wanted to know Burke's terms*: Ibid., 195–96.

233   *"Nobody has any authority"*: Polakoff, *Politics of Inertia*, p. 311.

234   *"added nothing to the agreements"*: Woodward, *Reunion and Reaction*, p. 196.

234   *Even Burke admitted later*: Ibid., p. 204.

235   *"If this thing stands accepted"*: Haworth, *The Hayes-Tilden Disputed Presidential Election*, pp. 265–66.

235   *"to obtain Tilden's explicit approval"*: Nevins, *Abram S. Hewitt*, pp. 382–83.

236   *"I don't care to reply to you, sir"*: Summers, *Era of Good Stealings*, p. 297.

236   *"Take him away,"*: Ibid.

236   *"that they are members"*: Haworth, *The Hayes-Tilden Disputed Presidential Election*, p. 277.

236   *"The people of Louisiana"*: Ibid., pp. 277–78.

236   *Mills introduced a motion*: Ibid., p. 280.

237   *"Mr. Speaker"*: Ibid.

237   *"I do not desire to retort"*: Ibid., pp. 280–81.

237   *a telegram from Tilden*: Nevins, *Abram S. Hewitt*, p. 385.

237   *"worthy of the respect of the world"*: Haworth, *The Hayes-Tilden Disputed Presidential Election*, p. 282.

238   *"It is about what I expected"*: Bigelow, *Life of Tilden*, 2:159.

238   *Abram Hewitt collapsed*: Nevins, *Abram S. Hewitt*, p. 385.

238   *"My fellow citizens"*: Williams, *Life of Rutherford Birchard Hayes*, 2:4.

238   *The party had been warned*: Eckenrode, *Rutherford B. Hayes*, p. 236.

239   *"Boys, boys, you'll waken"*: Barnard, *Rutherford B. Hayes*, p. 403.

239   *"seemed for a moment"*: McFeely, *Grant*, p. 448.

240   *Hayes was sworn into office secretly*: Eckenrode, *Rutherford B. Hayes*, p. 237.

Epilogue: I Still Trust the People

PAGE

241   *When Hayes visited New York*: Candace Stone, *Dana and the Sun* (New York: Dodd, Mead, 1938), p. 309.

242   *"duly elected President"*: Flick, *Tilden*, p. 396.

242   *"created no warrant of authority"*: Ibid., p. 406.

242   *"carried all before him"*: Watterson, "The Hayes-Tilden Contest," p. 20.

243   *"Hayes has passed"*: Brooks D. Simpson, *The Reconstruction Presidents* (Lawrence: University Press of Kansas, 1998), p. 214.

244   *"The inestimable blessing"*: Williams, *Life of Rutherford B. Hayes*, 2:7.

244   *"too crowded with business"*: *Diary*, March 16, 1877, p. 83.

245   *"It was understood"*: L. Q. C. Lamar to R. B. Hayes, March 22, 1877, Hayes Papers, Hayes Presidential Center.

245   *"by the order of the President"*: Current, *Those Terrible Carpetbaggers*, pp. 360–61.

245   *"wholly discouraged by the fact"*: Gillette, *Retreat from Reconstruction*, p. 345.

245   *Other principals*: Bigelow, *Life of Tilden*, 2:53–55.

246 *"The whole South"*: Foner, *Reconstruction*, p. 582.

247 *"To think that Hayes"*: Ibid.

247 *"I am a unprotected freedman"*: Unknown to R. B. Hayes, April 6, 1877, Hayes Papers, Hayes Presidential Center.

247 *"deceived, betrayed, and humiliated"*: Hoogenboom, *Rutherford B. Hayes*, p. 315.

247 *"Carpetbaggers to the rear"*: John A. Martin to Unknown, February 22, 1877, Hayes Papers, Hayes Presidential Center.

247 *"incorrigible enemies of equal rights"*: Hoogenboom, *Rutherford B. Hayes*, p. 315.

247 *"peculiar logic of curing"*: Gillette, *Retreat from Reconstruction*, pp. 346, 348.

247 *"extremely happy"*: Charles Foster to R. B. Hayes, April 27, 1877, Hayes Papers, Hayes Presidential Center.

247 *"the negro will disappear"*: The Nation, April 5, 1877.

247 *Even Grant allowed*: Foner, *Reconstruction*, p. 577.

248 *"What is called the President's policy"*: James M. McPherson, *Ordeal by Fire: The Civil War and Reconstruction* (New York: Alfred A. Knopf, 1982), p. 604.

248 *"may stand forever"*: Foner, *Reconstruction*, p. 590.

248 *"I am reluctantly forced to admit"*: Washington National Republican, Nov. 13, 1878.

249 *"The slave went free"*: W. E. B. Du Bois, *Black Reconstruction in America* (New York: Harcourt Brace, 1935), p. 30.

250 *"Why, what could Mr. Hayes do"*: Woodward, *Reunion and Reaction*, p. 9.

250 *so-called Cipher Telegrams*: Flick, *Samuel Jones Tilden*, pp. 429–42.

251 *great railroad strike of 1877*: For the strike of 1877, see Robert V. Bruce, *1877: Year of Violence* (Indianapolis: Bobbs-Merrill, 1959).

251 *"During my two terms of office"*: Gillette, *Retreat from Reconstruction*, p. 348.

252 *"he has done so well"*: Summers, *Rum, Romanism, and Rebellion*, p. 30.

253 *"I can retire to private life"*: Flick, *Samuel Jones Tilden*, p. 410.

255 *"came in by a majority"*: Ibid., p. 466.

256 *"Everybody knows that"*: New York Sun, June 14, 1877.

BIBLIOGRAPHY

Manuscripts

Samuel L. M. Barlow Papers, Library of Congress
Thomas F. Bayard Papers, Library of Congress
John Bigelow Papers, New York Public Library
William E. Chandler Papers, Library of Congress
James A. Garfield Papers, Library of Congress
Rutherford B. Hayes Papers, Rutherford B. Hayes Presidential Center, Fremont, Ohio
John C. Reid Military Service and Pension Records, National Archives
Carl Schurz Papers, Library of Congress
Samuel J. Tilden Papers, New York Public Library

Newspapers

Albany Argus
Atlanta Constitution
Auburn News and Democrat
Boston Evening Transcript
Chicago Daily News
Chicago Times
Chicago Tribune
Cincinnati Enquirer
Cincinnati Times
Harper's Weekly
Indianapolis Journal
The Nation

New Orleans Democrat
New Orleans Republican
New York Commercial Advertiser
New York Evening Post
New York Herald
New York Sun
New York Times
New York Tribune
New York World
Ohio State Journal
Savannah Morning News
Washington National Republican

Books and Articles

Alexander, Thomas B. "Persistent Whiggery in the Confederate South, 1860–1877." *Journal of Southern History* 27 (August 1961), pp. 305–29.

Anderson, David A. *Robert Ingersoll.* New York: Twayne, 1972.

Archdeacon, Thomas J. "The Erie Canal Ring, Samuel J. Tilden, and the Democratic Party." *New York History* 59 (October 1978), pp. 408–29.

Barnard, Harry. *Rutherford B. Hayes and His America.* Indianapolis: Bobbs-Merrill, 1954.

Beale, Howard K., and Alan W. Brownsword, eds. *Diary of Gideon Welles.* 3 vols. New York: W. W. Norton, 1960.

Belmont, Perry. *An American Democrat: The Recollections of Perry Belmont.* New York: Columbia University Press, 1940.

Benedict, Michael Les. "Southern Democrats in the Crisis of 1876–1877: A Reconsideration of *Reunion and Reaction.*" *Journal of Southern History* 46 (November 1980), pp. 489–521.

Bergamini, John D. *The Hundredth Year: The United States in 1876.* New York: Putnam, 1976.

Beth, Loren P. *John Marshall Harlan: The Last Whig Justice.* Lexington: University Press of Kentucky, 1992.

Bierce, Ambrose. *The Collected Works of Ambrose Bierce.* 12 vols. New York: Neale Publishing Company, 1909–1912.

Bigelow, John, ed. *Letters and Literary Memorials of Samuel J. Tilden.* 2 vols. New York: Harper and Brothers, 1908.

———. *The Life of Samuel J. Tilden.* 2 vols. New York: Harper and Brothers, 1895.

———. *Retrospections of an Active Life.* 5 vols. New York: Harper and Brothers, 1909.

———, ed. *The Writings and Speeches of Samuel J. Tilden.* 2 vols. New York: Harper and Brothers, 1885.

Blaine, James G. *Twenty Years of Congress: From Lincoln to Garfield.* 2 vols. Norwich, Conn.: Henry Bill Publishing Company, 1893.

Blight, David W. *Race and Reunion: The Civil War in American Memory.* Cambridge: Harvard University Press, 2001.

Boller, Paul F., Jr. *Presidential Campaigns.* New York: Oxford University Press, 1984.

Brandt, Nat. *The Congressman Who Got Away with Murder.* Syracuse: Syracuse University Press, 1991.

Brown, Dee. *The Year of the Century: 1876.* New York: Scribner's, 1966.

Bruce, Robert V. *1877: Year of Violence.* Indianapolis: Bobbs-Merrill, 1959.

Callow, Alexander B., Jr. *The Tweed Ring*. New York: Oxford University Press, 1966.

———. "'What Are You Going to Do About It?': The Crusade Against the Tweed Ring." *New-York Historical Society Quarterly* 49 (April 1965), pp. 117–42.

Carter, Hodding. *The Angry Scar: The Story of Reconstruction*. New York: Doubleday, 1959.

Cashman, Sean Dennis. *America in the Gilded Age: From the Death of Lincoln to the Rise of Theodore Roosevelt*. New York: New York University Press, 1984.

Chalfant, Edward. *Better in Darkness: A Biography of Henry Adams, His Second Life, 1862–1891*. New York: Archon Books, 1994.

Clark, James C. "The Fox Goes to France: Florida, Secret Codes, and the Election of 1876." *Florida Historical Quarterly* 69 (October 1991), pp. 430–39.

Clendenen, Clarence C. "President Hayes' 'Withdrawal' of the Troops—An Enduring Myth." *South Carolina Historical Magazine* 70 (October 1969), pp. 240–50.

Coker, William L. "The United States Senate Investigation of the Mississippi Election of 1875." *Journal of Mississippi History* 37 (May 1975), pp. 143–63.

Coleman, Charles H. *The Election of 1868: The Democratic Effort to Regain Control*. New York: Columbia University Press, 1933.

Cox, Lawanda, and John H. Cox. "Negro Suffrage and Republican Politics: The Problem of Motivation in Reconstruction Historiography." *Journal of Southern History* 33 (August 1967), pp. 301–30.

Current, Richard Nelson. *Those Terrible Carpetbaggers*. New York: Oxford University Press, 1988.

Davis, Elmer. *History of the New York Times, 1841–1951*. New York: J. Little & Ives, 1921.

Davison, Kenneth E. *The Presidency of Rutherford B. Hayes*. Westport, Conn.: Greenport Press, 1972.

Dawson, Joseph G., III. *Army Generals and Reconstruction: Louisiana, 1862–1877*. Baton Rouge: Louisiana State University Press, 1982.

DeGregorio, William A. *The Complete Book of U.S. Presidents*. New York: Dembner Books, 1984.

Dippre, Harold C. "Corruption and the Disputed Election Vote of Oregon in the 1876 Election." *Oregon Historical Quarterly* 67 (September 1966), pp. 257–72.

Donald, David Herbert. *Charles Sumner and the Rights of Man*. New York: Alfred A. Knopf, 1970.

————. *Lincoln*. New York: Touchstone, 1995.

Drago, Edmund L. *Hurrah for Hampton!: Black Red Shirts in South Carolina During Reconstruction*. Fayetteville: University of Arkansas Press, 1998.

Duberman, Martin B. *Charles Francis Adams: 1807–1886*. Boston: Houghton Mifflin, 1961.

Du Bois, W. E. B. *Black Reconstruction in America*. New York: Harcourt, Brace, 1935.

Eaton, Herbert. *Presidential Timber*. New York: Free Press, 1964.

Eckenrode, H. J. *Rutherford B. Hayes, Statesman of Reunion*. New York: Dodd, Mead, 1930.

Edmunds, George F. "Another View of 'The Hayes-Tilden Contest.'" *Century Magazine* 86 (June 1913), pp. 192–201.

Flick, Alexander Clarence. *Samuel Jones Tilden: A Study in Political Sagacity*. New York: Dodd, Mead, 1939.

Foner, Eric. *Reconstruction: America's Unfinished Revolution, 1863–1877*. New York: Harper & Row, 1988.

Foster, Gaines M. *Ghosts of the Confederacy: Defeat, the Lost Cause, and the Emergence of the New South*. New York: Oxford University Press, 1987.

Fuess, Claude Moore. *Carl Schurz, Reformer*. New York: Dodd, Mead, 1932.

Garraty, John A. *Henry Cabot Lodge: A Biography*. New York: Alfred A. Knopf, 1953.

Gillette, William. *Retreat from Reconstruction, 1869–1879*. Baton Rouge: Louisiana State University Press, 1979.

Grob, Gerald N., and George Athan Billias, eds. *Interpretations of American History*. Vol. 1. New York: Free Press, 1987.

Guenther, Karen. "Potter Committee Investigation of the Disputed Election of 1876." *Florida Historical Quarterly* 61 (January 1983), pp. 281–95.

Harmon, Mark D. "*The New York Times* and the Theft of the 1876 Presidential Election." *Journal of American Culture* 10 (1987), pp. 35–41.

Harris, Carl V. "Right Fork or Left Fork: The Section-Party Alignments of Southern Democrats in Congress, 1873–1897." *Journal of Southern History* 42 (November 1976), pp. 471–79.

Haworth, Paul Leland. *The Hayes-Tilden Disputed Presidential Election of 1876*. Cleveland: Burrows Brothers Company, 1906.

Hennessey, Melinda Meek. "Racial Violence During Reconstruction: The 1876 Riots in Charleston and Cainhoy." *South Carolina Historical Magazine* 86 (April 1985), pp. 100–112.

Hirsch, Mark D. "Samuel J. Tilden: The Story of a Lost Opportunity." *American Historical Review* 56 (July 1951), pp. 788–802.

Hirshson, Stanley P. *Farewell to the Bloody Shirt: Northern Republicans and the*

Southern Negro, 1877–1893. Bloomington: Indiana University Press, 1962.

Hoogenboom, Ari. *The Presidency of Rutherford B. Hayes.* Lawrence: University Press of Kansas, 1988.

———. *Rutherford B. Hayes: Warrior and President.* Lawrence: University Press of Kansas, 1995.

House, Albert V., Jr. "President Hayes's Selection of David M. Key for Postmaster General." *Journal of Southern History* 4 (February 1938), pp. 87–93.

Howells, William Dean. "A Sennight of the Centennial." *Atlantic Monthly* 38 (July 1876), pp. 93–107.

Hutton, Paul Andrew. *Phil Sheridan and His Army.* Lincoln: University of Nebraska Press, 1985.

Jarrell, Hampton J. *Wade Hampton and the Negro: The Road Not Taken.* Columbia: University of South Carolina Press, 1950.

Johnson, Paul. *A History of the American People.* New York: HarperCollins, 1998.

Jordan, David M. *Roscoe Conkling of New York: Voice in the Senate.* Ithaca: Cornell University Press, 1971.

Judis, John B. "Making Hayes: Why Election 2000 Is the Opposite of 1876." *New Republic,* Nov. 27, 2000.

Keller, Morton. *Affairs of State: Public Life in Late Nineteenth Century America.* Cambridge: Harvard University Press, 1977.

Kelley, Robert. "The Thought and Character of Samuel J. Tilden: The Democrat As Inheritor." *Historian* 26 (February 1964), pp. 176–205.

Kennedy, Philip W. "Oregon and the Disputed Election of 1876." *Pacific Northwest Quarterly* 60 (July 1969), pp. 135–44.

Koenig, Louis W. "The Election That Got Away." *American Heritage* 11 (October 1960), pp. 4–7, 99–204.

Kousser, J. Morgan, and James M. McPherson, eds. *Region, Race, and Reunion: Essays in Honor of C. Vann Woodward.* New York: Oxford University Press, 1982.

Larson, Orvin. *American Infidel: Robert G. Ingersoll.* New York: Citadel Press, 1962.

Leech, Margaret, and Harold J. Brown. *The Garfield Orbit.* New York: Harper and Row, 1978.

Levenson, J. C., ed. *The Letters of Henry Adams.* 2 vols. Cambridge: Harvard University Press, 1982.

Longacre, Edward. "Damnable Dan Sickles." *Civil War Times Illustrated* (May 1984), pp. 16–25.

Lonn, Ella. *Reconstruction in Louisiana After 1868*. New York: Russell and Russell, 1918.

Lowery, Walter McG. "The Political Career of James Madison Wells." *Louisiana Historical Quarterly* 31 (October 1948), pp. 995–1123.

Lunde, Erik S. "The Continued Search for National Unity: The United States Presidential Campaign of 1876." *Canadian Review of Studies in Nationalism* 15 (Fall 1980), pp. 131–49.

McCabe, John D. *The Illustrated History of the Centennial Exhibition*. Philadelphia: National Publishing Company, 1876.

McFeely, William S. *Grant: A Biography*. New York; W. W. Norton, 1981.

McGinty, Garnie W. *Louisiana Redeemed*. New Orleans: Pelican Publishing Company, 1941.

McPherson, James M. *Battle Cry of Freedom: The Civil War Era*. New York: Oxford University Press, 1988.

———. *Ordeal by Fire: The Civil War and Reconstruction*. New York: Alfred A. Knopf, 1982.

Miglian, Robert Murken. "California's Reaction to the Disputed Presidential Election of 1876." *Journal of the West* 15 (January 1976), pp. 9–28.

Moore, James Tice. "Redeemers Reconsidered: Change and Continuity in the Democratic South, 1870–1900." *Journal of Southern History* 44 (August 1978), pp. 357–78.

Morris, Roy, Jr. *Ambrose Bierce: Alone in Bad Company*. New York: Crown, 1995.

———. *The Better Angel: Walt Whitman in the Civil War*. New York: Oxford University Press, 2000.

———. *Sheridan: The Life and Wars of General Phil Sheridan*. New York: Crown, 1992.

Morseberger, Robert E., and Katherine M. Morseberger. *Lew Wallace: Militant Romantic*. New York: McGraw-Hill, 1980.

Murphy, Charles B. "Samuel J. Tilden and the Civil War." *South Atlantic Quarterly* 33 (July 1934), pp. 261–71.

Muzzey, David Saville. *James G. Blaine: A Political Idol of Other Days*. New York: Dodd, Mead, 1934.

Nevins, Allan. *Abram S. Hewitt*. New York: Harper and Brothers, 1935.

———, ed. *Selected Writings of Abram S. Hewitt*. New York: Columbia University Press, 1937.

O'Connor, Richard. *Sheridan the Inevitable*. Indianapolis: Bobbs-Merrill, 1953.

———. *Wild Bill Hickok*. New York: Doubleday, 1959.

Olmsted, Roger. "The Cigar-Box Papers: A Local View of the Centennial Electoral Scandals." *California Historical Quarterly* 55 (Fall 1976), pp. 256–69.

Olsen, Otto H., ed. *Reconstruction and Redemption in the South.* Baton Rouge: Louisiana State University Press, 1980.

Otten, James T. "The Wheeler Adjustment in Louisiana: National Republicans Begin to Reappraise Their Reconstruction Policy." *Louisiana History* 13 (Fall 1972), pp. 349–67.

Painter, Nell Irvin. *Standing at Armageddon: The United States, 1877–1919.* New York: W. W. Norton, 1987.

Parks, Arva Moore. "Miami in 1876." *Tequesta* 30 (1975), pp. 1–4.

Peskin, Allan. *Garfield.* Kent, Ohio: Kent State University Press, 1978.

———. "Was There a Compromise of 1877?" *Journal of American History* 60 (June 1973), pp. 63–75.

Polakoff, Keith Ian. *The Politics of Inertia: The Election of 1876 and the End of Reconstruction.* Baton Rouge: Louisiana State University Press, 1973.

Porter, Kirk H., and Donald Bruce Johnson, eds. *National Party Platforms, 1840–1960.* Urbana: University of Illinois Press, 1961.

Rabinowitz, Howard N., ed. *Southern Black Leaders of the Reconstruction Era.* Urbana: University of Illinois Press, 1982.

Rable, George C. *But There Was No Peace: The Role of Violence in the Politics of Reconstruction.* Athens: University of Georgia Press, 1984.

———. "Southern Interests and the Election of 1876: A Reappraisal." *Civil War History* 26 (December 1980), pp. 347–61.

Randel, William P. *Centennial: American Life in 1876.* Philadelphia: Chilton Book Company, 1969.

Richardson, Leon Burr. *William E. Chandler, Republican.* New York: Dodd, Mead, 1940.

Roberts, Derrell. "Joseph E. Brown and the Florida Election of 1876." *Florida Historical Quarterly* 40 (June 1962), pp. 217–25.

Robinson, Lloyd. *The Stolen Election: Hayes Versus Tilden—1876.* New York: Doubleday, 1968.

Rosebault, Charles J. *When Dana Was the Sun: A Story of Personal Journalism.* New York: R. M. McBride and Company, 1931.

Rosewater, Victor. "'The Oregon Muddle': A Curious Phase of the Hayes-Tilden Controversy." *Century Magazine* 64 (September 1913), pp. 764–66.

Roske, Ralph J. "'Visiting Statesmen' in Louisiana, 1876." *Mid-America* 33 (April 1951), pp. 89–102.

Rozwenc, Edwin C., ed. *Reconstruction in the South.* Boston: D. L. Heath and Company, 1952.

Rydell, Robert W. *All the World's a Fair: Visions of Empire at American International Expositions, 1876–1916.* Chicago: University of Chicago Press, 1984.

Sanson, Jerry Purvis. "Rapides Parish, Louisiana, During the End of Reconstruction." *Louisiana History* 27 (Spring 1986), pp. 167–82.

Schlereth, Thomas J. *Victorian America: Transformations in Everyday Life, 1876–1915*. New York: HarperCollins, 1991.

Schlesinger, Arthur M., Jr. *The Age of Jackson*. Boston: Little, Brown, 1946.

———, ed. *History of American Presidential Elections, 1789–1968*. 2 vols. New York: Chelsea House, 1971.

Seip, Terry L. *The South Returns to Congress: Men, Economic Measures, and Intersectional Relationships, 1868–1879*. Baton Rouge: Louisiana State University Press, 1983.

Shenkman, Richard. *Presidential Ambition: Gaining Power at Any Cost*. New York: HarperCollins, 1999.

Sherman, John. *Recollections of Forty Years in the House, Senate and Cabinet: An Autobiography*. 2 vols. Chicago: Werner Company, 1895.

Shofner, Jerrell H. "Florida Courts and the Disputed Election of 1876." *Florida Historical Quarterly* 48 (July 1969), pp. 26–46.

———. "Florida in the Balance: The Electoral Count of 1876." *Florida Historical Quarterly* 47 (October 1968), pp. 122–50.

———. "Fraud and Intimidation in the Florida Election of 1876." *Florida Historical Quarterly* 42 (April 1964), pp. 321–30.

———. *Nor Is It Over Yet: Florida in the Era of Reconstruction, 1863–1877*. Gainesville: University Presses of Florida, 1974.

Silber, Nina. *The Romance of Reunion: Northerners and the South, 1865–1900*. Chapel Hill: University of North Carolina Press, 1993.

Simkins, Francis Butler, and Robert Hilliard Woody. *South Carolina During Reconstruction*. Chapel Hill: University of North Carolina Press, 1932.

Simpson, Brooks D. *Let Us Have Peace: Ulysses S. Grant and the Politics of War and Reconstruction, 1861–1868*. Chapel Hill: University of North Carolina Press, 1991.

———. *The Political Education of Henry Adams*. Columbia: University of South Carolina Press, 1996.

———. *The Reconstruction Presidents*. Lawrence: University Press of Kansas, 1998.

Slotkin, Richard. *Gunfighter Nation: The Myth of the Frontier in Twentieth-Century America*. New York: Atheneum, 1992.

Smith, Jean. "Whispering Sammy." *American Heritage* 45 (May-June 1994), pp. 134–35.

Smith, Jean Edward. *Grant*. New York: Simon and Schuster, 2001.

———. *John Marshall*. New York: Henry Holt, 1996.

Smith, Page. *The Rise of Industrial America: A People's History of the Post-Reconstruction Era*. New York: McGraw-Hill, 1984.

Smith, Theodore Clarke. *The Life and Letters of James Abram Garfield.* 2 vols. New Haven: Yale University Press, 1925.

Sproat, John G. *"The Best Men": Liberal Reformers in the Gilded Age.* New York: Oxford University Press, 1968.

Stampp, Kenneth M., and Leon F. Litwack, eds. *Reconstruction: An Anthology of Revisionist Writings.* Baton Rouge: Lousiana State University Press, 1969.

Sternstein, Jerome L., ed. "The Sickles Memorandum: Another Look at the Hayes-Tilden Election-Night Conspiracy." *Journal of Southern History* 32 (August 1966), pp. 342–57.

Stewart, George R. *Pickett's Charge.* Boston: Houghton Mifflin, 1959.

Stone, Candace. *Dana and the Sun.* New York: Dodd, Mead, 1938.

Stukes, Joseph Taylor. "The American Nation in 1876." *Proceedings of the South Carolina Historical Association* (1976), pp. 39–52.

Summers, Mark Wahlgren. *The Era of Good Stealings.* New York: Oxford University Press, 1993.

———. *Rum, Romanism, and Rebellion: The Making of a President, 1884.* Chapel Hill: University of North Carolina Press, 2000.

Swinney, Everette. "Enforcing the Fifteenth Amendment, 1870–1877." *Journal of Southern History* 28 (May 1962), pp. 202–18.

Taylor, Joe G. *Louisiana Reconstructed, 1863–1877.* Baton Rouge: Louisiana State University Press, 1974.

Thomas, Dianne Stine, ed. *The Old West.* New York: Prentice Hall, 1990.

Thompson, Henry T. *Ousting the Carpetbagger from South Carolina.* Columbia: R. L. Bryan Company, 1927.

Trelease, Allen W. *White Terror: The Ku Klux Klan Conspiracy and Southern Reconstruction.* Baton Rouge: Louisiana State University Press, 1971.

Troy, Gil. *See How They Ran: The Changing Role of the Presidential Candidate.* New York: Free Press, 1991.

Tunnell, T. B., Jr. "The Negro, the Republican Party, and the Election of 1876 in Louisiana." *Louisiana History* 7 (Spring 1966), pp. 101–16.

Unger, Irwin. *The Greenback Era: A Social and Political History of American Finance, 1865–1879.* Princeton: Princeton University Press, 1964.

Utley, Robert M. *Cavalier in Buckskin: George Armstrong Custer and the Western Military Frontier.* Norman: University of Oklahoma Press, 1988.

Vazzano, Frank P. "The Louisiana Question Resurrected: The Potter Commission and the Election of 1876." *Louisiana History* 16 (Winter 1975), pp. 39–57.

Vidal, Gore. *1876: A Novel.* New York: Random House, 1976.

Wagstaff, Thomas. "Call Your Old Master—'Master': Southern Political Leaders and Negro Labor During Presidential Reconstruction." *Labor History* 10 (Summer 1969), pp. 323–45.

Wallace, D. D. "The Question of the Withdrawal of the Democratic Presidential Electors in South Carolina in 1876." *Journal of Southern History* 8 (August 1942), pp. 374–85.

Wallace, Lew. *An Autobiography.* 2 vols. New York: Harper and Brothers, 1906.

Watterson, Henry. "Colonel Watterson's Rejoinder to Ex-Senator Edmunds." *Century Magazine* 86 (June 1913), pp. 285–87.

———. "The Hayes-Tilden Contest for the Presidency." *Century Magazine* 86 (May 1913), pp. 10–20.

———. *"Marse Henry": An Autobiography.* 2 vols. New York: George H. Doran Company, 1919.

Waugh, John C. *Reelecting Lincoln: The Battle for the 1864 Presidency.* New York: Crown, 1997.

Webb, Ross A. *Benjamin Hélm Bristow: Border State Politician.* Lexington: University Press of Kentucky, 1969.

Weisberger, Bernard A. "The Stolen Election." *American Heritage* 41 (July-August 1990), pp. 18–20.

Wellman, Manly Wade. *Giant in Gray: A Biography of Wade Hampton of South Carolina.* New York: Charles Scribner's Sons, 1949.

Williams, Charles Richard, ed. *The Diary and Letters of Rutherford Birchard Hayes: Nineteenth President of the United States.* 5 vols. Columbus: Ohio State Archaeological and Historical Society, 1922–1926.

———. *The Life of Rutherford Birchard Hayes: Nineteenth President of the United States.* 2 vols. Boston: Houghton Mifflin, 1914.

Williams, T. Harry. *Hayes of the Twenty-third.* New York: Alfred A. Knopf, 1965.

———, ed. *Hayes: The Diary of a President, 1875–1881.* New York: David McKay, 1964.

Williamson, Edward C. "George F. Drew, Florida's Redemption Governor." Florida *Historical Quarterly* 38 (January 1950), pp. 206–15.

Woodward, C. Vann. *Reunion and Reaction: The Compromise of 1877 and the End of Reconstruction.* Boston: Little, Brown, 1951.

———. "Yes, There Was a Compromise of 1877." *Journal of American History* 60 (June 1973), pp. 215–23.

Zinn, Howard. "Disputed Elections, Concealed Facts." *The Progressive,* Feb. 16, 2001.

Zuczek, Richard. "The Last Campaign of the Civil War: South Carolina and the Revolution of 1876." *Civil War History* 42 (March 1996), pp. 18–31.

ACKNOWLEDGMENTS

More than most writers or, at any rate, most historians, I work alone—which really means that I balance myself uninvitedly on the shoulders of all those talented and dedicated historians who have come before. In the commission of this book, I have teetered most particularly atop the works of Keith Ian Polakoff, Ari Hoogenboom, C. Vann Woodward, Alexander C. Flick, and Eric Foner—none of whom I have met personally and all of whom I have disagreed with on certain particulars. Nevertheless, to each of these authors, and to the scores of other historians cited in the bibliography, I extend my heartfelt personal and professional thanks. I would also like to thank the staff of the Rutherford B. Hayes Presidential Center, the New York Public Library, the Library of Congress, the National Archives, and, last but not least, the interlibrary loan department of the Chattanooga Public Library, for their always courteous and professional help.

It is, of course, traditional for writers to thank publicly their editors, their agents, and their wives. I can only say that, for me, each of the people who have filled these roles—Roger Labrie of Simon and Schuster, Tom Wallace of T. C. Wallace, Ltd., and Leslie Morris of Chattanooga, Tennessee—have so far surpassed their typical roles that my own thanks here are far from traditional. In their different ways they have each been irreplaceable, and although I cannot thank them too much, I hope that I can thank them enough.

INDEX

CREDITS AND PERMISSIONS

The author and publisher gratefully acknowledge permission to reprint material from the following collections or works:

Excerpts from letters and diary entries credited to the Rutherford B. Hayes Papers: Reprinted courtesy of the Rutherford B. Hayes Presidential Center, Spiegel Grove, Fremont, Ohio.

Excerpts from letters credited to the Samuel J. Tilden Papers: Reprinted courtesy of Samuel J. Tilden Papers, Manuscripts and Archives Division, The New York Public Library, Astor, Lenox and Tilden Foundations.

Excerpts from the John Bigelow diary: Reprinted courtesy of John Bigelow Papers, Manuscripts and Archives Division, The New York Public Library, Astor, Lenox and Tilden Foundations.

Excerpts from *The Letters of Henry Adams*, edited by J. C. Levenson et al.: Reprinted by permission of the publisher from *The Letters of Henry Adams*, edited by J. C. Levenson, Ernest Samuels, Charles Vendersee and Viola Hopkins Winner, Cambridge, Mass.: The Belknap Press of Harvard University Press, copyright © 1982 by the Massachusetts Historical Society.

Sources for the images reproduced in the picture section:

Currier & Ives/Library of Congress: 1, 2

Harper's Weekly/Library of Congress: 3, 6, 23

Library of Congress: 4, 7, 9, 13, 16, 19, 21

National Archives: 5

Rutherford B. Hayes Presidential Center: 8, 10, 11, 12, 14, 15, 20, 22, 25, 27

Harper's Weekly/Rutherford B. Hayes Presidential Center: 17, 18, 26, 28

Frank Leslie's Illustrated Newspaper/Library of Congress: 24